The KARMIC BIRTHDAY BOOK

Discover the Meaning and Magic of the Day You Were Born

Amy Zerner & Monte Farber

FAIR WINDS

The Karmic Birthday Book

Brimming with creative inspiration, how-to projects, and useful information to enrich your everyday life, quarto.com is a favorite destination for those pursuing their interests and passions.

© 2023 Quarto Publishing Group USA Inc.
Text © 2022 Monte Farber
Art © 2022 Amy Zerner

First Published in 2022 by Fair Winds Press, an imprint of The Quarto Group, 100 Cummings Center, Suite 265-D, Beverly, MA 01915, USA.
T (978) 282-9590 F (978) 283-2742 Quarto.com

All rights reserved. No part of this book may be reproduced in any form without written permission of the copyright owners. All images in this book have been reproduced with the knowledge and prior consent of the artists concerned, and no responsibility is accepted by producer, publisher, or printer for any infringement of copyright or otherwise, arising from the contents of this publication. Every effort has been made to ensure that credits accurately comply with information supplied. We apologize for any inaccuracies that may have occurred and will resolve inaccurate or missing information in a subsequent reprinting of the book.

Fair Winds Press titles are also available at discount for retail, wholesale, promotional, and bulk purchase. For details, contact the Special Sales Manager by email at specialsales@quarto.com or by mail at The Quarto Group, Attn: Special Sales Manager, 100 Cummings Center, Suite 265-D, Beverly, MA 01915, USA.

25 24 23 22 21   1 2 3 4 5

ISBN: 978-0-7603-7723-9

This book was previously published in 2011 as *The Enchanted Birthday Book*, Sterling Publishing.

Digital edition published in 2022
eISBN: 978-0-7603-7724-6

Library of Congress Control Number available

Design and page layout: Ashley Prine, Tandem Books
Cover border and page trim illustrations: Amy Zerner
All art is by Amy Zerner with the following exceptions:
Interior: Stars on page 1 © Victoria Bat/Shutterstock; Sun line art on page 6 © Pixejoo/Shutterstock; Personality icon, Life path icon, Destiny icon, Karmic Lesson icon, and Secret icon used throughout © Arelix/Shutterstock
Cover: Stars back cover frame © Victoria Bat/Shutterstock; Symbols © Arelix/Shutterstock; Gold texture © seksan wangkeeree/Shutterstock

Printed in Singapore

CONTENTS

INTRODUCTION
Personality, Life Path, Secret, Destiny, and Karma
7

JANUARY 15	**JULY** 203
FEBRUARY 47	**AUGUST** 235
MARCH 77	**SEPTEMBER** 267
APRIL 109	**OCTOBER** 298
MAY 140	**NOVEMBER** 330
JUNE 172	**DECEMBER** 361

About the Authors
392

INTRODUCTION
Personality, Life Path, Secret, Destiny, and Karma

> *"There are two great days in a person's life—the day we are born and the day we discover why."* —William Barclay

I must be one of the luckiest people on Earth because I've actually had not two but three great days in my life: the day I was born, the day I discovered why, and the day in 1974 that I met my wife, Amy Zerner, cocreator of this book and of our wonderful life together. Back then, Amy was studying astrology and I was studying Amy, so I learned astrology, tarot, and many more secret ancient practices.

The first of the many secrets we will be sharing with you in this book is that in relationships, either you grow together or you grow apart. Amy and I have grown together, and those secret ancient practices have proven themselves useful. So useful, in fact, that the information you will soon be enjoying in *The Karmic Birthday Book* represents the culmination of our decades of study and practice of all of them. They have profoundly changed and enriched our lives, and we have mastered them to the point where we can now share their powerful wisdom and guidance with you by using the best they have to offer as we focused on each of the three hundred and sixty-six days of the year, one karmic birthday at a time.

The day I discovered why I was born was the day in 1988 that my first book, *Karma Cards: Amazing Fun-to-Use Astrology Cards to Read Your Future*, was published internationally. It has sold hundreds of thousands of copies and is still going strong, published in eighteen languages.

Back then, relatively few people knew what the word "karma" meant! I had to convince its publisher that *Karma Cards* was a title that was going to sell a lot of copies, even though so few American book buyers knew what karma was and those who did thought it was the Hindu equivalent of Christianity's Golden Rule: Do unto others as you would have them do unto you, or "What goes around comes around."

Today, most people know those two meanings, and a surprisingly large number know that "Karma" is the ancient Sanskrit word for the consequences that result from the actions a person takes in this life—and that those actions may even influence the circumstances of a future life. As someone whose decades of expanding my mind through the invention and use of intuition-building oracle systems has enabled me to become so psychically attuned that I am able to hear the voices of those who've passed over, I know that the law of karma, that what you do comes back to you, always holds true.

Secret number two I would like to share with you is that the reason we have called the book you are reading *The Karmic Birthday Book* is the same reason I called my first book *Karma Cards*—Edgar Cayce's definition of karma.

Edgar Cayce, who was the most famous and influential psychic channeler of the twentieth century, defined karma as "meeting yourself." I believe he meant that quite literally, that when we encounter positive and negative consequences of our past actions, we are meeting our Higher Self, the part of us that knows what we need to learn for our highest good and greatest joy. Sometimes what we need to learn is painful. But forewarned is forearmed, and that is where *The Karmic Birthday Book* comes in.

The Karmic Birthday Book is the culmination of our entire life's work as respected metaphysical authors and teachers of more than a dozen subjects using the medium of oracle systems that develop the reader's intuition and decision-making skills. Since 1988, my beloved wife and I have produced a best-selling series of more than fifty books, kits, and games that we call our family of "spiritual power tools," each one of them based on an ancient system of personal guidance, such as astrology, the tarot, alchemy, psychic phenomena, automatic writing, numerology, radionics, pendulum dowsing, and several other metaphysical subjects.

We have thought long and hard about what makes us all unique and what binds us together as human beings. And, from the reader feedback we get, it seems that we have developed the ability to help people help themselves through supporting their self-knowledge and self-development.

A few years ago, Amy and I felt it was time to combine everything we knew about human behavior and personality into one book that would offer useful information to every person based on the day they were born. We did not want to limit it to astrology, however. *The Karmic Birthday Book* is designed to help you discover your own enchanted world—a world just on the other side of your resistance to knowing who you are.

These "revealed" and revealing messages are divided into five sections: PERSONALITY, LIFE PATH, DESTINY, KARMIC LESSON, and SECRET. These comprise what we are dubbing your "Birthscope." For each birthday, we have also included an insightful quote that has a special meaning.

The Karmic Birthday Book incorporates everything we have learned and taught about individual character analysis and cosmic guidance in our more than forty-year study of things metaphysical (beyond the physical). In its pages, we have put only our most perceptive insights into the distinctive nature and vibration of each birth date. Each day of the year has a full page devoted to it, so the reader can easily look up his or her birthday and the birthdays of others to learn and compare.

Your birthday PERSONALITY identifies, evaluates, and helps you understand your true nature through the patterns revealed in your birth date.

Your DESTINY is like a castle you are building, stone by stone—it is where you are heading in this life.

Your LIFE PATH gets you there. Throughout your life, you have lessons to learn so you can then help and teach others.

The KARMIC LESSONS are what you will encounter on your journey along your life path.

The SECRET offers insights designed to help you discover your very own hidden talents and character traits.

If you read the description of your birthscope or that of someone else and it sounds too positive, and beyond your reach, then you are being challenged to develop your innate potential to be this person who presently sounds too good to be true. Conversely, if what you read sounds too negative, then you have probably overcome this negative tendency and should feel good about yourself for having done so.

Our books and teaching systems have succeeded because Amy and I recognize that being human is not easy for anyone. We want to share with you what has enabled us to live in what we call The Enchanted World of Amy Zerner and Monte Farber. It's our "brand," but it also happens to be true, though we are realists and know that nothing lasts forever.

That realistic attitude and meeting your Higher Self here in *The Karmic Birthday Book* is actually the place where the enchantment becomes very important. The word "enchanted" is derived from the Latin word *incantare*, *in* meaning "into" and *cantare* meaning "to sing." We become enchanted when something is "sung into" us, the most obvious time being when we are captivated by a singer's voice.

Enchantment reminds us of fairy tales and myths, especially the Greek mythology's epic poem, "The Odyssey." The hero, Odysseus, has his ship's crew plug their ears and himself tied to the mast so that he can hear the captivating song of the Sirens without going mad, as all others before him had done, and avoid crashing his ship on the rocks of the Sirens' Island.

Somewhere out there, whether it's in this or some other dimension, exists the sum total of everything that is, everything that ever was, and, yes, everything that ever will be. So a description of and useful information for all 366 possible birthdays—don't forget leap year!—is really not too much to ask from this ultimate library, which Edgar Cayce called the Akashic Records and quantum physicists call the Quantum Field.

Yes, even quantum mechanics contributes to the information you will read about your birthday and that of those you are interested in. I wrote a book called *Quantum Affirmations: The New Energy Science of Conscious Manifestation* in which I postulated that consciousness can be viewed as the smallest wave/particle, smaller even than light, and that the laws of quantum mechanics could be applied to my five-step process for navigating to the probable future in which you desire to be living. Anyone who knows anything about quantum mechanics knows that its theorists sound more and more like metaphysical practitioners have sounded for centuries.

The information in our *Karmic Birthday Book* has been channeled from the same source as the guidance I received for inventing my *Quantum Affirmations* techniques, as well as for both *Karma Cards* and *Instant Tarot*, two unique approaches to astrology and tarot that did not exist until I channeled them. I don't blame anyone for thinking that this is odd, but for me this enchanted way of living is my daily experience. I would be lying if I said I wasn't psychic, since I've proved it beyond doubt to my own skeptical inner critic (yes, psychics have them, too!).

But calling yourself enchanted is not enough. After writing more than fifty books on developing self-knowledge, intuition, and the ability to accurately predict a person's future by understanding his or her character and the aforementioned metaphysical studies, I cannot deny that I have actually become "enchanted," a much prettier word than "psychic," though the meaning in this case is practically the same.

As an intuitive counselor, I am able to listen to the Siren songs of my personal intuition, to a small degree, and also, more importantly, to the guidance available to every sensitive person from . . . what shall we call it? The beyond? Our guardian angels? Our spirit guides? The universe? The great mystery?

Whatever you want to call the underlying intelligence I've found to exist beyond the physical, I have spent my life learning how to internally call out to it and to keep my internal dialogue out of the picture when my call for guidance is answered. I let the metaphysical forces sing into me their amazing guidance for my clients and for my friends and family alike.

I have mentioned that we did not want to create this book using astrology only. Our spirit guides, however, were not under the same constraints! Sometimes I channeled information from them about "Neptune rays" or "Mars rays" or other planetary references. The meaning of such information is spelled out in the text, but it can't hurt to give you a quick understanding of the astrological meaning of the planets mentioned, Mercury through Neptune.

Astrology is not what you read in your daily horoscope (from the Greek *horo*, meaning "hour," and *skopos*, meaning "to look at"). A real astrology chart examines the hour of your birth; your astrology chart is based on how the planets lined up around you at the very moment of your birth, as viewed from the exact place you were born.

The planet Mercury and its "rays" are associated with communication and mental activity. Venus is concerned with attractiveness and love. Mars is all about the physical drive to accomplish your goals. Jupiter is about growth and good fortune. Saturn concerns itself with caution, structure, and timing. The planet Uranus promises freedom, inventiveness, and eccentricity or genius. Finally, Neptune brings inspiration, compassion, and connection to the unseen worlds around us and their inhabitants, our very special "coauthors."

Some of the words and concepts contained in these sentences may be crucial to your birthscope—tendencies that may have been acknowledged as personal traits but are articulated and interpreted here in a far more engaging way. Not every single description will apply, but usually a sentence or important fragment will jump out at you as "the truth." Our friends and family often see the spot-on accuracy of the characteristics described more easily than we do! It's entertaining to see the reactions to the descriptions when we share them with each other. Note that we have provided a space on each page in the book for you to keep the names of friends and family who are born on that date so you can remember their birthdays.

We also include a short list of celebrities who share your birthday. In some cases, the cosmic connections will be immediately apparent while others may make you shake your head or have a good laugh. We all have the opportunity to live up to the highest frequency of ideals portrayed in our birthscope; some of us may choose to develop the more negative expressions of our personalities. It is up to each of us to use our strengths to compensate for our weaknesses and to choose to grow spiritually, given the opportunities and challenges that life offers.

The Karmic Birthday Book is packed with ideas that are thought-provoking, fun, friendly, and personalized. We are confident that you will find it an unusual, accurate, and interesting guide to exploring birth-date traits. This book will make you appreciate what your birthday really means. It is a book that can add life to any party or gathering of friends and family.

It is our most sincere wish that you find it useful enough to keep on your desk or coffee table to be consulted again and again. The words won't change, but I think you'll be surprised at how, over the years, your understanding of what they're saying will change and deepen as your life progresses. Amy and I have created *The Karmic Birthday Book* to help you find enchantment always and in all ways.

The Karmic Birthday Book

JANUARY 1

All truth is an achievement. If you would have truth at its value, go with it.
—Thornton T. Munger

BORN ON THIS DAY
- **Lorenzo de' Medici**
  Italian statesman
- **Paul Revere**
  patriot
- **J.D. Salinger**
  author
- **J. Edgar Hoover**
  FBI director
- **Alfred Stieglitz**
  photographer

PERSONALITY
You who were born on this date have a rare distinction, indeed, in having ushered in the New Year. Much of your character may be understood from this unusual event, because you like to be the herald of new experiences and novel ways of doing things. You have a great deal of initiative, and you enjoy beginning movements and sponsoring causes. For your courage and hearty enthusiasm, you are dearly loved by many friends. Even though you prefer to be the leader in your social group, you know when to take a back seat graciously. In business, you show that you have tact. When dealing with people in business, your polite ways win you favors and bargains. Your birthday is the anniversary of many great historical events and is also the birthday of Betsy Ross, who made the first American flag.

LIFE PATH
You are studious and original and possess considerable executive ability. You have self-respect and the ability to draw people to you. You have great affection for your family and would make any sacrifice for your loved ones.

DESTINY
You will work to reduce the number of your responsibilities, or your attitude toward duties and obligations will make you notice them less. Cheerfulness predominates, giving you a positive outlook. At times, your optimism may easily exceed justified bounds. Be cautious: Do not take unwise chances or give way to gullibility. You can place yourself well ahead of the crowd because the rays of Uranus, the planet of advancement, dominates your birthday.

KARMIC LESSON
Born with great determination and strength of character, you are a natural leader in most things and have strength of personality, which inclines you to a disciplined life. You would, in fact, make a good life coach. You are fond of family life and have a great love for those around you—brothers, sisters, and so on. Compared with the ties of blood relationships, all others seem small to you. You are naturally something of a fighter, though only when you feel you have right on your side. You do not care much for the opinions of others but are admired by a large circle of friends for all that—perhaps for this independence of character.

SECRET
You long to follow a literary bent, even though the path seems difficult in the beginning. By working with women, you are more likely to succeed in a big way.

FRIENDS & FAMILY

JANUARY 2

The less people speak of their greatness, the more we think of it.
—Francis Bacon

BORN ON THIS DAY

★ **Cuba Gooding, Jr.**
actor

★ **Christy Turlington**
model

★ **Roger Miller**
singer

★ **Taye Diggs**
actor

★ **Jack Hanna**
zookeeper, biologist

FRIENDS & FAMILY

PERSONALITY
You have the success type of personality. Personal magnetism is so strongly accented in your makeup that you can make anyone in any walk of life your friend. Many people criticize you for one fault in your nature—that you don't concentrate your abilities in one direction. It seems you have so many talents that you spread them thin instead of concentrating them in the one place they will do the most good. In some respects, you are unpredictable. For example, you will go along cooperatively and smoothly, and then, suddenly, when you think someone is taking advantage of you, you will become aggressively domineering. For the most part, you are unselfish and generous, but you dislike people who never give, and you loathe people who break appointments.

LIFE PATH
Your love of family is so great that it may be regarded as the keystone of your character. For the ones you love, you would attempt anything, and the very intensity of your love and determination to succeed for them will carry you far on the road to success. Your wholeheartedness will win for you an unusual degree of loyalty, fidelity, and devotion.

DESTINY
Success in business depends on your solving each problem as it comes up, rather than postponing decisions. Study carefully every situation involving money. Important facts requiring cautious scrutiny lie hidden from others but are obvious to you. In considering old plans, you sometimes find worthwhile possibilities for new endeavors. Analyze your goals in life, and keep your attention steadfastly fixed on them.

KARMIC LESSON
You are extremely tactful and resourceful, born on this day, and you love intrigue and puzzles. You have a great eye for detail and are a good judge of human nature. You are a hard worker and do not take many holidays. You are not naturally affectionate, though you often do acts of kindness, which you know will be appreciated. You are intensely interested in practical and material things, and you have probably so developed this side of your nature that it dwarfs your spiritual side. You are inclined to be melancholy at times, and this you should aim to overcome partly by mental methods and partly by making yourself go outdoors more into the air and sunshine, even if you don't care to.

SECRET
You may instinctively be a good interior designer and good with color. You may be capricious in relationships.

JANUARY 3

To live long it is necessary to live slowly.
—Cicero

BORN ON THIS DAY

★ **J.R.R. Tolkien**
author

★ **Mel Gibson**
actor

★ **Eli Manning**
football player

★ **Victoria Principal**
actor

★ **Robert Loggia**
actor

FRIENDS & FAMILY

PERSONALITY

Your intellect is as incisive as a surgeon's knife, for you can get to the core of any situation with the least effort. When you have a problem, you face it, diagnose it, prescribe for yourself, and take the cure. In many ways, you are a user of tools, for you like to build things, not only physical ones but also the more stately mansions of the soul. While your initiative may sometimes be swamped in the slough of social activity and pleasures, which you enjoy, you do possess the quality of leadership. Few people would ever deny you a favor, because you are generous and helpful yourself, and others like you. You hate injustice and inequality, but even more you despise seeing the strong take advantage of the weak. On the stage of life, you are no mere player but a real artistic director and producer.

LIFE PATH

You should cultivate application, diligence, and perseverance, as you can be too prone to tire of an undertaking before it is completed, and the results then are not as good as you are capable of. You like to form new friendships and make new acquaintances. Your personality is strong enough to make your friendships and loves constant, true, and based on high ideals.

DESTINY

It is beneficial to take periods of preparation for future accomplishment—this keeps you from getting distracted. Do not let impulsive enthusiasm force you into activities that do not have a part in your long-range hopes and aspirations. However, be alert for opportunities. Through a sometimes lazy or indifferent attitude, you can miss some excellent chances. Reestablish past friendships for both pleasure and profit.

KARMIC LESSON

You are probably of a mostly happy-go-lucky, jovial nature; your good vibes are infectious. You love everybody, and everybody loves you in return. You are the life and the fun of a party, and people naturally look to you for leadership, which you usurp simply by force of your great vitality and good nature. Fond of children and animals, you are loving but not sentimental. You make friends easily and are at home wherever you go. You are earnest and sincere. If you live alone to any great extent, however, a great change may come over you, and you may become quite ascetic and spiritual in your life. It all depends! You are wholesome and sweet, however, and of a straightforward, honest disposition.

SECRET

You may have a despondent nature when you feel overwhelmed or affairs are not running smoothly. Don't be afraid to change fields of activity and cultivate more determination.

JANUARY 4

Heaven on Earth is a choice you must make, not a place you must find.
—Wayne Dyer

BORN ON THIS DAY

- **Michael Stipe**
  singer
- **Doris Kearns Goodwin**
  historian
- **Dave Foley**
  comedian, actor
- **James Milner**
  soccer player
- **Tina Knowles**
  fashion designer

FRIENDS & FAMILY

PERSONALITY

Yours is a quickly changing nature. Because you are a bit eccentric, volatile, and love variety, you have a reputation for being temperamental. Everything you do is done with speed and impatience. You hate waste, and you find shortcuts to all your duties. Your vocabulary is extensive, and you are a good talker. Knowing your own qualifications along these lines, you are tempted to hold the floor. However, your mind is alert, and you also know the correct time to yield. As a result of your mercurial wit and keen analytical ability, you are quite a critic. If the stage attracts you, it is a natural attraction, because you have talent in that direction. You can do well in any field of endeavor where you have to deal with the public. Although you are inclined to be eclectic in your tastes, you are a good mixer socially, and you know how to combine business with pleasure.

LIFE PATH

You are always busy. Many people born on this date accumulate a reasonable degree of wealth. You are shrewd in your estimate of people, and your intuition will tell you who you may trust. Anyone to whom you disclose your inner self and accept as worthy of your confidence will prove faithful to you.

DESTINY

Stimulating solar vibrations dominate your birthday, emphasizing the possibility of satisfying progress both in business and in the receipt of affection. For all romantic matters, concentrate on big things and forget petty ones. Success depends on your ability to ignore trifles and meet responsibilities energetically and with enthusiasm. Make adequate preparations for everything well in advance.

KARMIC LESSON

You are fond of travel and will probably have a good deal of it in your life. You are interested in other nations and their ways and would like to study them if you traveled abroad. You like comfort, but you can also do without it if it is not forthcoming and make the best of things. You are, in many ways, a mixture of opposite tendencies and desires. Born on this day, you really have exceptional talents, and you can become one of the great persons of your time if you make up your mind to concentrate, study, and work.

SECRET

You will climb to the top of the ladder, but not without many setbacks. Those who were born on this date have tenacious wills and place career above domestic affairs.

JANUARY 5

Short absence quickens love; long absence kills it.
—Marquis de Mirabeau

BORN ON THIS DAY

- **Bradley Cooper**
  actor
- **Umberto Eco**
  historian, critic
- **Alvin Ailey**
  choreographer
- **Paramahansa Yogananda**
  yogi
- **Charlie Rose**
  talk show host

PERSONALITY
You are interested in artistic pursuits and creative forms of expression. Natural curiosity makes you a good student, and besides academic subjects, you find life itself a fascinating study. All the decorative arts have a strong appeal for you, thus making you happy when you are decorating your home, choosing clothing, or making something attractive with your hands. You get a thrill out of seeing your friends and family happy, finding it no trouble to entertain them and think up surprises to delight them. Sometimes your generosity in this respect leads to people's taking advantage of you, but you have broad shoulders and do not mind the burdens that come to you. Life does not always let you have your way. You probably desire more freedom of action than you have, but you are compensated by your independence of thought and spirit.

LIFE PATH
You are truthful to an extraordinary degree, kindhearted, lovable, and fond of children. Adaptability should be one of your chief characteristics, but you must take considerable care not to allow a tendency to criticize others to overcome it. Your home ties will play a very important part in your life.

DESTINY
Changing your environment may be the necessary impetus to put some of your wishes or ideas into effect. Opportunities and advantages can come from this change, so be ready for them. Stir up your own initiative rather than wait for the pressure of outside forces. Forget the disappointments and delays of the past. Develop the roots of happiness by striving for worthwhile realities.

KARMIC LESSON
A natural leader, you are active and dislike being idle: You always want to be doing something. You would make a fine writer or a good teacher and could fill well any position offered to you, no matter what it might be or how great its responsibilities. You are fond of travel and have many friends all over, so wherever you go you are sure of a hearty welcome. Persistent and persevering, you have good taste and a pleasant personality, and you have the power to please, if you choose to do so. Do not allow yourself to be spoiled by flattery or manipulation, to which you are partial. You demand much of those you love but are willing to give much in return.

SECRET
You enjoy dominance, and you demand too much from your employees or coworkers. You can spare yourself much discomfort by giving in occasionally.

FRIENDS & FAMILY

JANUARY 6

Not everything that is faced can be changed, but nothing can be changed until it is faced.
—James Baldwin

BORN ON THIS DAY

- **Eddie Redmayne**
  actor
- **Ree Drummond**
  chef, TV personality
- **Alan Wilson**
  philosopher
- **Charles Sumner**
  abolitionist statesman
- **Joan of Arc**
  French heroine and saint

FRIENDS & FAMILY

PERSONALITY

You have a nature that is deeply mystical, and your intuition is very good. In many respects, you are a kind of wonder to your friends because your guesses have such a high percentage of accuracy. It is as though you have the sixth sense, the traditional name for psychic intuition. You are inclined to be quiet and to enjoy the less raucous forms of entertainment offered by the modern world. Books, music, and art delight you. Sometimes you feel as though you are carrying all of the world's burdens and troubles. The reason is that you are sensitive to such vibrations, and you take on other people's responsibilities. But you have a tender heart and a generous nature. You can hardly say no, when giving in means depriving yourself. You can have a very happy life simply by living up to your own ideals.

LIFE PATH

You are inclined to be impulsive. Your actions are liable to be misunderstood, and your motives questioned. You think and act quickly but not always with logical or rational judgment. You should cultivate more self-restraint, or your passions will lead you into serious difficulty, even though your thoughts and intentions are the best.

DESTINY

Swift action is usually your keynote. The adage "He who hesitates is lost" is especially true for you. Make practical use of inspirational ideas and motivational teachers and classes. Exhilarating influences can fill you with a sense of accomplishment if you have planned well. Communications by social media, telephone, or e-mail can always play an important part in your life.

KARMIC LESSON

The men and women born on this day often differ greatly. The women are inclined to be intuitive, spiritually minded, and interested in occult and philosophical subjects. They have a good deal of poise and earnestness in all they do and are above all original and ingenious. The men, on the contrary, are very practical and businesslike. Esoteric subjects do not always interest them. They are just and fair, but their own interests always come first. Male or female, you are a stickler for doing the right thing, and you won't bargain with anyone over your code of right and wrong. Obstacles you encounter will be minor ones for the most part and can be overcome by persistence, as you are very lucky.

SECRET

You could be a fine teacher, inspiring the affection and admiration of serious students. You may be a seeker who is restless and demands more than the ordinary.

JANUARY 7

Pleasure is the flower that fades; remembrance is the lasting perfume.
—Stanislas-Jean de Boufflers

BORN ON THIS DAY

- **Millard Fillmore**
  U.S. president
- **Zora Neale Hurston**
  author, filmmaker, civil rights advocate
- **Nicolas Cage**
  actor
- **Katie Couric**
  TV journalist
- **Jeremy Renner**
  actor

PERSONALITY

Because you have a fine financial sense, you can achieve success in almost any line of business. For instance, even if you bake at home and sell your products, you are likely to wind up having a big baking business. Your best procedure is to work by yourself, for you are much more efficient when you do not have to take orders from anyone else. As you are good at getting people together, you are also able to make a go of work in a corporate body or any large institution. One of your best bets would be to work in a philanthropic or educational institution where you could eventually take on an executive job. You are affectionate by nature, and you wish those to whom you give your love to return it in a demonstrative and ardent way.

LIFE PATH

Restrain your inclination to be overly exacting and domineering, and do not give way to anger. You think a great deal of the opinion of others and always try to make a good impression. Unless the partner you choose is one of sufficient character to stimulate your ambition and keep you always at your best, or works together with you, your domestic life will be unfulfilling.

DESTINY

The power of reason and philosophy is apparent in your actions and can be significant in your relationships. This is because of the influence of the planet Saturn. A great range of interest and deep understanding characterize your attitude, giving you a positive point of view when you reflect on your future. Satisfying progress will be made in matters that concern personal property, business, and organizations.

KARMIC LESSON

Born on this day, you are probably very sociable in nature and have a large number of friends of all genders. You are kind and generous. You have distinct dramatic ability, which is shown most in your power of imitation and in your ability to tell stories as they should be told. You have great personal magnetism and are ambitious, and there is no end to the things you want to do and accomplish. You are diplomatic and have plenty of tact. You are self-confident and do not rely on others to any great extent. You may not be the kind of person who achieves success under others; you should be the boss.

SECRET

You are one who is lucky with legal matters, particularly in the understanding of briefs and other meticulous, detailed material. You make a patient parent or partner.

FRIENDS & FAMILY

JANUARY 8

Only those who will risk going too far can possibly find out how far one can go.
—T.S. Eliot

BORN ON THIS DAY
- **Elvis Presley**
  singer
- **David Bowie**
  singer
- **Stephen Hawking**
  physicist
- **R. Kelly**
  singer
- **Kim Jong-un**
  leader of North Korea

FRIENDS & FAMILY

PERSONALITY
The beautiful quality of imagination has been endowed upon you as the finest gift in the cornucopia of destiny. Because you possess this charming trait, you are able to live in two worlds at once, the real one and the one of fantasy. However, you also may combine these two worlds, making of the combination a brilliant career for yourself. All the great writers, artists, actors, musicians, and directors do exactly this, and with the same endowment, you should be able to do it, too. Plays, movies, music, and art are, after all, the products of the imagination of the artist and creator; they are the real expression of the life of the mind. Since you have the power within you, it is your duty to produce.

LIFE PATH
You are self-reliant, careful, and shrewd. Your ability to interpret the actions of others makes it comparatively easy for you to detect deception. Any task entrusted to you will be done satisfactorily. You love detective stories and psychoanalysis. Your health should be rugged, and you should have a lot of vitality.

DESTINY
Direct your imagination into practical avenues. Control a tendency to go off on flights of fancy. Search for a grounding for your ideas. A systematic schedule can help you avoid repeating your efforts. Complete each job you start. Joining an organization could be fortunate because of help you may receive in solving pressing problems. Try to find passion and mental stimulation in whatever you attempt.

KARMIC LESSON
You have large projects in mind that you find difficult to accomplish, simply because you lack some essential ingredient. Try to figure out just what is missing and resolve to obtain it by persistent work and study. Once you have done so, undoubtedly brilliant success will be yours. You do not believe in living your life haphazardly; instead, you plan ahead a good deal and often think out exactly what you will do tomorrow before going to sleep. Originality marks everything you do. You should be a true example of success. You are a stickler for doing the right thing, and you won't bargain with anyone over your code of right and wrong. You are careful, sincere, and honest.

SECRET
Born on this day, you might gravitate naturally to the stage or screen and work that concerns itself with appearing before large audiences. You like admiration.

JANUARY 9

So long as we love, we serve.
—Robert Louis Stevenson

BORN ON THIS DAY

★ **Richard Nixon**
U.S. president

★ **Simone de Beauvoir**
writer, intellectual

★ **Joan Baez**
singer

★ **Chad "Ochocinco" Johnson**
football player

★ **J.K. Simmons**
actor

PERSONALITY
You are inclined to be an independent person, taking no orders from anyone except those who have official positions. Of course, the reason for your attitude is that you want to give the orders yourself, if they are to be given. As you have the ability to lead, this is not a bad habit. However, you must see to it that your orders are given courteously and tactfully to avoid the friction you would create by being commandeering. You will have every type of experience in life. What you learn from your various adventures will depend on the attitude that you alone create. Use your abilities to organize in order to get ahead in the world. You may be given to doing too much for others and neglecting yourself. It is necessary to overcome that habit before you can attain your individual goals in life.

LIFE PATH
Born on this day, you possess frank, energetic, and progressive natures and are blessed with faith in the good performed by others. You achieve your highest success in life by keeping your thoughts steadily fixed on that sterling maxim, "Be the master of your own success."

DESTINY
The popularity that can come your way should bring happiness. However, see that affection is not scared away by conceit or excessive ego or exuberance.

KARMIC LESSON
You are sometimes a little too sure of your own judgment. It is usually good and correct, but, like all things, it needs revision and overhauling every now and then! The ruby is a lucky stone for you to wear; also the moonstone. People born on this day are full of courage and grit; they follow up on any task or important venture undertaken. You are generous with advice and openhanded with charity. Continue to help business associates when a task is difficult. You should endeavor to strike out in business for yourself, though you would probably also succeed in a small partnership.

SECRET
You can be discreet and prudent in financial matters, rarely taking another into your confidence. You are one in whom great trust can be placed.

FRIENDS & FAMILY

JANUARY 10

Life often seems like a shipwreck of which the debris are friendship, glory, and love.
—Anonymous

BORN ON THIS DAY

★ **George Foreman**
boxer

★ **Rod Stewart**
singer

★ **Pat Benatar**
singer

★ **Max Roach**
jazz drummer

★ **Aleksey Tolstoy**
author

FRIENDS & FAMILY

✹ PERSONALITY

Because of the vibrancy in your birthday, you are able to take the position comparable to that of the top rank in the work you do. In other words, you are able to assume command when the chief is away or to take their orders and see that they are carried out to the letter. However, you are not satisfied with merely executing processes thought up by others; you have a large amount of originality in your makeup, and you will either do the job in a unique way or make suggestions of such ingenuity that it will be tantamount to the original work. This is all to the good and should help you get promotions.

✹ LIFE PATH

You are a natural leader and a clear thinker. Success in commercial enterprises invariably will be yours. Do not be overly self-conscious, and do not lack in self-esteem. You are greatly attracted to romantic situations and unusually popular among your friends.

✹ DESTINY

New friends and new interests always come into your life when you need them. These may come as the result of a complete change in environment or as the result of a change in your own viewpoints. Keep an open mind and avoid disputes when you participate in events or enter discussions.

✹ KARMIC LESSON

You are rather optimistic and inclined to look on the bright side of things. You are of a sociable nature and naturally crave company. You are always at your best under these conditions. You are fond of intellectual pursuits and studies but remember that passion and devotion are higher human attributes than intellect and that these are the most important in the long run. You have great determination. Plan your recreations but make playtime secondary to work that you love. You are fond of nature and see in it much beauty and symbolism that may escape the average beholder.

✹ SECRET

You have a sympathetic nature, with a marked sense of loyalty to friends, particularly those made in childhood. The hospitality business is recommended.

JANUARY 11

Then the effort that I have made is what people are pleased to call the fruit of genius. It is the fruit of labor and thought.
—Alexander Hamilton

BORN ON THIS DAY

- **Alexander Hamilton**
  U.S. statesman
- **Alice Paul**
  feminist, suffragist
- **Mary J. Blige**
  singer
- **Leroy Sané**
  soccer player
- **Aldo Leopold**
  environmentalist

PERSONALITY
The number eleven is always said to be a "master number," so it is no wonder that you share your birthday with some of the most renowned persons in the creative arts. Thus, you can see that today is a date of distinction, which gives to its children talent, fame, and genius. You share these traits and rewards to the extent that you seek to deserve them. You can make almost anyone like you, and thus you have a tremendous advantage in getting ahead in the world. You can work to make good fortune flow to and through you, especially if you take the time to develop your gifts and talents. You are fond of puzzles, games, and sports of all kinds, and you are a great lover of nature.

LIFE PATH
You are kindhearted, constant, and winsome, but secretive. Once you become a friend, you are a friend for all time. But be careful in some friendships, as you are inclined to overlook serious faults in others. You will be successful as a creative entrepreneur and will make a wonderful partner.

DESTINY
When you feel inspired, it obliterates the memory of the past's troubles and disillusionments. Rather than wait for events to happen, let your own zeal help you achieve the results you want. Do not be impatient. Meet each problem separately as it arises.

KARMIC LESSON
You are steadfast and not easily swayed by flattery. You are original, inventive, and farseeing, have an open and well-balanced mind, and are receptive to new truths. You are careful in your dealings and rarely come out with "the short end of the deal." You make the most of your natural gifts and talents. You have good taste and judgment, and much more goes on beneath that calm exterior of yours than people think! As a matter of fact, you would do well teaching or in a profession where you have an audience.

SECRET
A builder and a maker, you aspire to make big dreams come true. You have a romantic nature but are not always amenable to the demands of a traditional marriage.

FRIENDS & FAMILY

JANUARY 12

Nothing is so good as it seems beforehand.
—George Eliot

BORN ON THIS DAY

- **Jeff Bezos**
  entrepreneur
- **Howard Stern**
  radio personality
- **Rush Limbaugh**
  political commentator
- **Rob Zombie**
  singer, filmmaker
- **Kirstie Alley**
  actor

FRIENDS & FAMILY

PERSONALITY

Although you may at times feel that severe restrictions are keeping you from succeeding in your goals, you may find, through self-examination, that those restrictions are ones you are imposing on yourself. If you will do this honestly, you will find that it is only you who is holding you back! Within you is the power to break the chains that make you unhappy. You're a hard worker; you have many gifts; your limitations are only those of the imagination. If you would be free, you must break the bonds of illusory fear and free yourself. Once you realize this, you become truly empowered, confident, responsible, and successful and are able to coach, inspire, and guide others to overcome their own blocks and difficulties.

LIFE PATH

You are original in almost everything you do. Cultivate this power, as it will bring you good results in abundance. If you have children, they will have a bent for mechanics or art. If you nurture and protect your naturally strong and robust physique, you can stay well.

DESTINY

Even the small steps you take to utilize your opportunities should prove advantageous. The events that occur from each move forward can enrich your life from both a financial and an emotional standpoint. Aim for accomplishments of permanent value.

KARMIC LESSON

You have a very deeply emotional nature, which is hard to comprehend. You are cautious and secretive and are always in an intrigue of some kind. When spiritually inclined, you are rather traditional in your views and values. You are loyal, sincere, true, honest, and always polite. In business affairs, you can be more than usually successful, and travel will come to you later in life. You can adapt yourself readily to almost any situation when you think positively. You have a great deal of originality and might be an inventor.

SECRET

You possess unusual energy and discipline. You can excel in a career in the commercial world in addition to finding soul-mate love.

JANUARY 13

The reward of a thing well done is having done it.
—Ralph Waldo Emerson

BORN ON THIS DAY
- **Julia Louis-Dreyfus**
  comedian
- **Gal Gadot**
  actor
- **Horatio Alger, Jr.**
  author
- **Michael Peña**
  actor
- **Sophie Tucker**
  radio personality

PERSONALITY
Poverty and riches, obscurity and fame—all the extremes of life are within the scope of your experience. And that includes ecstatic happiness and gnawing misery. You are so volatile that you respond emotionally to every stimulus. No one could have more ups and downs in life than you have. However, to tell the truth, you enjoy it. To you, all such emotional experiences that stir you deeply are like the catharsis the Greeks felt at the theater; they became washed of their feelings through overplay. You enjoy participating in the events or landmarks in the lives of your friends. Birthdays, anniversaries, and holidays mean a round of activity to you, and you love being busy helping with planning parties, celebrations, and feasts.

LIFE PATH
You are unusually active, independent, and persevering. Get to work for yourself as much as you can. Persons of your nature wear themselves out without fulfillment when too tied to others. Gain self-poise. If you learn how to nurture and protect your naturally strong mind, body, and spirit, you will be rewarded.

DESTINY
An end to many of your worries can come automatically, as you will always show unusual dedication and initiative. Permanent serenity is not necessarily satisfying to you as a goal, however. Speed and variety also are requirements, because you like to respond to problems and find inspiration to meet them. Let your personal feelings and intuition rather than the suggestions or pressure of other people be the source of your decisions. Develop harmonious, friendly relationships, and there will be longtime loyalty.

KARMIC LESSON
You have a peculiar temperament. It is a very deep nature, one hard to comprehend. You can be cautious and secretive, often involved in intrigue of some kind. You love power and want a lot of money—for the power it will give you. You are something of a fatalist and are determined to get the most you can out of life. You are rather orthodox in your spiritual and religious views. You must watch an aspect of yourself that may become obsessed with seeing to it that justice is satisfied. There is a little too much of this about you; you are inclined to be hard on others and need a little more of the milk of human kindness.

SECRET
You are inclined to vanity because you overestimate your abilities. Women born this day, while somewhat detached, demand constant attention. The men need respect for standing up for their beliefs.

FRIENDS & FAMILY

JANUARY 14

The man who trusts men will make fewer mistakes than he who distrusts them.
—Camillo di Cavour

BORN ON THIS DAY

* **Mark Antony**
  Roman general
* **Albert Schweitzer**
  theologian, philosopher
* **LL Cool J**
  rapper
* **Jason Bateman**
  actor
* **Faye Dunaway**
  actor

FRIENDS & FAMILY

PERSONALITY
No matter what kind of work you do in the world, or what your status is in life, you have the soul of a poet. You think of all things from the point of view of their beauty, and you, too, create beauty when it is in your power to do so. The functional element has little significance for you, as your standards do not apply to the usefulness. As someone once said, "Love, light and laughter are the holy trinity"; so might it be said of you that these three form the pattern of your ideals. You have a deep regard for the conventions, for family life, and for the arts. Yet, even in conformity, you never lose sight of your originality and ideals. A vivid imagination makes you capable of artistic creation, but it is more likely that you will express yourself on the plane of criticism, which is also, in its way, a creative function.

LIFE PATH
You have the ability to accomplish big things and should never be satisfied with results that will barely fill the requirements. You are not easily discouraged. You have a large, sympathetic heart, and the ills of your fellows weigh heavily upon you. You will be a loving friend and probably will have an art-filled home.

DESTINY
Make steady progress toward the goals you have set. Do not be afraid to express yourself creatively. Take an interest in the efforts of others and emulate their achievements. Let genuine affection prevail to bring happiness. The present and future need more of your attention than the past.

KARMIC LESSON
You are very original. You also have good business abilities and are inventive, very curious, sociable, and rather optimistic. You should never lose confidence in yourself but always keep up a brave front, no matter how adverse the circumstances may appear. Born on this day, you have a large share of ambition and the desire to get ahead in the world. Do not undervalue the things of the mind and the soul. You want and need true love, but it is sometimes hard for you to learn how to give it.

SECRET
There may be a tendency to magnify worries and to inflict them on other people, without regard for their own problems. You have a talent for appraising, inspecting, and correcting.

JANUARY 15

The greater the obstacle, the more glory in overcoming it.
—Molière

⊛ PERSONALITY
Cultural pursuits form a large part of the pattern of your life. It is your pleasure to introduce new ideas, to cultivate groups for the study of esoteric subjects, and to promulgate the finest products of the minds of the greatest thinkers and creators. Because you are intuitional in many matters, you can see ahead, forecast events, and prepare yourself for the shape of things to come. You are interested in "the man on the street," that fictional character that symbolizes the ordinary person, and you work with a will for his betterment in economic, social, and mental ways. To you, life is an adventure of the mind. You like to explore the hidden places of personality and are a good psychologist whether you practice as a professional or an amateur.

⊛ LIFE PATH
You have original ideas, a keen mind, and shrewd perception, and if you are engaged in business, it should be your own. You are also an excellent manager and a careful buyer. For the most part, you are diplomatic. You should curb a tendency to speak sharply and sarcastically to subordinates, and encourage friendships, which you can easily secure.

⊛ DESTINY
Destiny has chosen an important role in the drama of life for you. Beneficent Jupiter rays on your birthday work to enhance your chances for peace of mind. Satisfying associations with people around you can yield contentment, as well as opportunities for self-expression.

⊛ KARMIC LESSON
You are a good judge of human nature. There is a strain of humor in your makeup that enables you to see the funny side of a situation. You have a certain amount of self-assurance, but this is right in your case and is not overdone. You are well poised and seldom lose your temper. You are naturally affectionate and desire the same from others. You are a hard worker; you have a universal interest, in fact, in nearly everything. Always be on the alert for new ideas, and use them. Respect the opinions and suggestions of others.

⊛ SECRET
You should avoid employment by others, as you are best cut out to succeed in enterprises founded by yourself. You may find the greatest happiness in another's family.

BORN ON THIS DAY
★ **Martin Luther King, Jr.**
civil rights leader
★ **Molière**
playwright
★ **Drew Brees**
football player
★ **Regina King**
actor
★ **Pitbull**
rapper

FRIENDS & FAMILY

JANUARY 16

A bird doesn't sing because it has an answer, it sings because it has a song.
—Joan Walsh Anglund

BORN ON THIS DAY

- ★ **Lin-Manuel Miranda**
  actor, playwright
- ★ **Kate Moss**
  model
- ★ **Joe Flacco**
  football player
- ★ **Susan Sontag**
  philosopher, activist
- ★ **Sade**
  singer

FRIENDS & FAMILY

PERSONALITY
You are probably more typical of your sign group, Capricorn, than most people born under your sign. Politics and the government and its various functions are matters of deep interest to you, and you are very likely to take your place at the head of some branch of your community or national affairs. You have the ability to organize people, groups, and important matters, and you are efficient as an executive. When you give an order, you do so with authority, and your work constitutes the law. In addition to these traits, you are well versed in artistic matters and enjoy success in fields of scholarship where you wish to devote your attention.

LIFE PATH
You have courage, ambition, and a singleness of purpose, which should carry you far. You are not impulsive, you are sincere and just, and your head rules your heart. You may marry young, and you do not mar your love with a too-critical analysis of motives and emotions. You work hard to make your partner happy.

DESTINY
Give full attention to matters that can have a significant effect on you. Plan and adhere to an effective schedule to accomplish your objectives. Try to fulfill your wishes. Look to the future with optimism and confidence in yourself.

KARMIC LESSON
You have great powers of concentration, born on this day, and should be a splendid reader of character. You can size up a situation quickly and see its good and its bad points. You have talent in several directions, which should certainly be cultivated. This is particularly noted in artistic lines, and in these you should do some really creative work. You are sincere and earnest in all that you do. Overall a very good character is yours, if you live up to your capabilities. You doubtless love romantic stories, and there is a distinctly romantic streak in your makeup.

SECRET
You hold a dread of public opinion, which hampers any bold step. You may be uncomplaining, sharing problems without a whimper.

JANUARY 17

Never leave that till tomorrow which you can do today.
—Benjamin Franklin

◉ PERSONALITY

You possess an intellectual curiosity that drives you to investigate strange and mysterious subjects. One of these may well be esoteric philosophy or psychic phenomena. You would probably become an adept in the field of occultism if you took up this study seriously. By nature, you are inclined to be spiritual, or at least to have epiphanies frequently, even though in your case it may only be your feeling of awe or devotion, which is a reaction to the wonders of the world. You are kindly, sympathetic, devoted, and loyal. You could entertain careers in charity work or nonprofit organizations or as a writer, statesman, or philanthropist.

◉ LIFE PATH

You are sure to rise in life, through perseverance and application. You are fair-minded, just, and loving, and true happiness will be found only in true love—the love of perfect trust, respect, and confidence.

◉ DESTINY

Your skill in such a field as writing or acting or as a maker can help to bring you honor as well as great personal satisfaction. Make use of inspirations that occur to you. Keep your mind and hands busy. The planet Mercury is emphasized in your birthday. It encourages associations with progressive people who will appreciate your innovations and help you to put them into effect.

◉ KARMIC LESSON

You are ambitious and anxious to have and utilize power. You like the "real thing" of life and not the gaudy make-believes. You have a great respect for the unseen and unknown, though, in certain circumstances, you have to pretend not to believe in it. You have distinct scientific abilities should you choose to cultivate them. You are loyal, sincere, true, and honest, but always political. In business affairs, you will be more than usually successful, and travel will come to you later in life.

◉ SECRET

You can live without intense excitement, as you are more likely given to studies or a methodical process. You derive quiet happiness from a balanced way of living. You can achieve true contentment.

BORN ON THIS DAY

★ **Benjamin Franklin**
statesman, inventor

★ **Betty White**
actor

★ **Muhammad Ali**
boxer

★ **Michelle Obama**
former First Wife

★ **James Earl Jones**
actor

FRIENDS & FAMILY

JANUARY 18

There is no exercise better for the heart than reaching down and lifting people up.
—John Andrew Holmes, Jr.

BORN ON THIS DAY

- **Cary Grant**
  actor
- **Kevin Costner**
  actor
- **Dave Bautista**
  wrestler
- **Daniel Webster**
  jurist, statesman
- **Oliver Hardy**
  comic actor

FRIENDS & FAMILY

PERSONALITY

Oratorical powers and a truly convincing manner can take you to the heights of success. You can be so persuasive that you are able to override every obstacle in the path of your success. You prefer outside activity to the duties and joys of homelife. In fact, you like all forms of activity that keep you on the go, as you soon become bored with the various projects that attract your attention. Then you seek the new, the adventurous, and the stimulating. As soon as you have used up your interest, you become very restless. Because you have the ability to talk and present arguments so well, you could be a good salesperson, marketer, and communicator. You should use your energy to get to the high places you aim for and, by concentration, conquer the heights.

LIFE PATH

You have great reserves of power, but it is to be regretted that you do not utilize your special gift to the best advantage. You are cautious and somewhat inclined toward suspicion, yet generous to a fault. Your desire is to love and be loved, yet you unconsciously repel advances and sometimes seem incapable of fully opening your heart to your friends or family.

DESTINY

Beneficent Venus rays influence and favor a flair for good taste. Take an interest in beautifying your home and making it the scene of pleasant entertainment for your friends. Thank the well-meaning people who offer you sincere advice, but do not allow anyone to dictate your actions or opinions.

KARMIC LESSON

You possess courage and power and the ability to put into operation anything that strikes you as particularly good. You have good business ability but also talent in other directions. Thus, you should design, as you have distinct ability in that direction. You can shoulder any responsibility that comes along, partly because you do not feel its weight as much as many others would in your position.

SECRET

Your deep spiritual nature can be developed if excessive material considerations are renounced. This will produce an inner struggle, as, born on this day, you want power and respect.

JANUARY 19

⊛ PERSONALITY
You are the embodiment of the loyalty of Capricorn and the personification of the selflessness of Aquarius. You are quick to make up your mind and have powerful intellectual qualities and a commanding manner. As you go through life, you become mellower. Yet, you will not tolerate any hurt to yourself, because you have a sensitivity that you do your best to conceal. Under the surface, however, you really want the finest love and devotion that an admirable person can offer. You respond with all your heart to the love that is offered you, and you suffer to the extreme when anyone wounds your feelings. You are capable of revenge and also of being subtle and cruel in administering it. Wit and talent make you a truly fascinating personality.

⊛ LIFE PATH
Born on this day, you are likely to write and teach and are fond of learning new skills. As a rule, you are of a kindly disposition, considerate of others, and always ready to lend a helping hand to those who fall by the wayside. You are imaginative, poetic, artistic, kind, and affectionate.

⊛ DESTINY
An opportunity to participate in a community enterprise may give you the chance to express your own ideas and methods. Beneficial Uranus influences indicate freedom in working out your own solutions to problems. Take an interest in everything and everyone around you.

⊛ KARMIC LESSON
You are inclined to be reserved, quiet, and calm under all circumstances and are considered to have a very level head by all who know you. You inspire a good deal of confidence, and if there were any trouble brewing, you would be the person all would turn to naturally as the one having the most practical ideas as to how to get out of the difficulty. You are fit for an emergency and are always cool and calm at such times. This is one of your strongest points.

⊛ SECRET
You enjoy sharing and being listened to and are inclined to be depressed when not getting enough attention. A hard worker, you always insist upon more than adequate rewards.

You never change things by fighting the existing reality. To change something, build a new model that makes the existing model obsolete.
—*Buckminster Fuller*

BORN ON THIS DAY
★ **Dolly Parton**
singer
★ **Edgar Allan Poe**
poet
★ **Robert E. Lee**
U.S. general
★ **Janis Joplin**
singer
★ **Paula Deen**
chef, TV personality

FRIENDS & FAMILY

JANUARY 20

He that goes a-borrowing goes a-sorrowing.
—Benjamin Franklin

BORN ON THIS DAY

- ★ **Buzz Aldrin**
  astronaut
- ★ **Federico Fellini**
  filmmaker
- ★ **David Lynch**
  filmmaker
- ★ **George Burns**
  comedian
- ★ **Fareed Zakaria**
  journalist

FRIENDS & FAMILY

😀 PERSONALITY

Because you have a variety of talents, a strong social instinct, and an optimistic outlook, you are a popular person. It may be that you will not learn self-reliance until you have attained your maturity, but when you do, success is sure to follow. In your early years, you are too much like the chameleon, which changes its color to match its background as a protective device. Thus, you take on the attitudes of the people you are with instead of just being yourself. Once your own nature has developed into a definite personality, you will be much more self-assertive and successful.

🌀 LIFE PATH

Be self-reliant, and your success is assured. Be diligent in your avocation and truthful beyond all question. Work will then become a pleasure with but few burdens. Begin all important business in March and November. These are the months that indicate your greatest success, and Tuesdays and Saturdays are the days most favorable to you.

👁 DESTINY

Your courage and determination are strengthened by Mars influences. Express yourself with confidence. Take pride in your creative efforts, and do not be discouraged by preliminary results. Take the time to make sure that what you do is correct; then surge ahead successfully.

☯ KARMIC LESSON

You can do a variety of things and do them all more or less well. You have marked technical ability, especially in the line of computer work. You would make a good linguist, and if you travel abroad, as you doubtless will later on in life, you will be able to pick up the language of the country in which you are residing easily. You have distinct and peculiar leanings and talents, and you had best stick to them and go without at first, so that you may ultimately triumph over your difficulties and do the work for which you are best suited.

🧘 SECRET

Born on this day, you are a lover of quiet surroundings and a serene homelife. Meditation and yoga would be good practices.

JANUARY 21

Peace is the happy natural state of man; war is corruption and disgrace.
—James Thomson

PERSONALITY
You are a pathfinder in the forest of experience that constitutes life. Because you have courage, tenacity, and intuition, you will find your way through mazes that might well confuse others who lack your perceptiveness. No amount of work holds any fears for you. Because you are realistic in your attitude, you tackle the chores of daily life with a will, and you stick to your last until your job is done. This gives you a reputation for tenacity that brings you splendid rewards. The negative side of your personality is stubbornness, and you should fight this trait, because it brings enmity and opposition when you express it.

LIFE PATH
You are fond of pleasure and somewhat apt to take things for granted. You may travel a great deal even if it is short distances. Unless you correct your general tendencies toward being judgmental and stubborn, your love life will not be satisfactory. Be sure to be straightforward and frank in everything.

DESTINY
Reawakened interest in many activities from the past should make your life more colorful and stimulate optimism about the future. Include other persons in your plans rather than try to do things alone. Give praise and sympathetic understanding when deserved; it can have a valuable influence.

KARMIC LESSON
Born this day, you have great strength of character and an innate force that makes you a naturally good manager. You are quiet, reserved, and dignified and generally looked up to by those in immediate association with you. You are cool and a good person in times of emergency. You usually see the realistic side of everything. You never get into any difficulty that you cannot manage to get out of in some way. You balance love of travel with love of home and its domesticated comforts.

SECRET
You have a progressive nature with an excellent memory for faces and places rather than figures. You are also good with important detail work.

BORN ON THIS DAY
- **Grigori Rasputin** — mystic
- **Placido Domingo** — singer
- **Geena Davis** — actor
- **Christian Dior** — fashion designer
- **Jack Nicklaus** — golfer

FRIENDS & FAMILY

JANUARY 22

*Sleep hath its own world,
a boundary between the things
misnamed death and existence.*
—Lord Byron

BORN ON THIS DAY
- **Sir Francis Bacon**
  philosopher and statesman
- **Lord Byron**
  poet
- **Beatrice Webb**
  social reformer
- **Diane Lane**
  actor
- **Monte Farber**
  author, astrologer

FRIENDS & FAMILY

PERSONALITY
A wonderfully creative imagination has been endowed upon you, which should enable you to introduce new forms and ways of thought, new concepts, and novel procedures. As your date of birth is attuned to communication vibrations, you have the power to use words to great advantage. Whether in conversation, public speaking, acting, electronic media, or writing, you can master your audience and make them think as you wish or react as you wish through your persuasive manner. You have highly romantic ideas about life, and you do not hesitate to put them into practice. You find that convention hampers your style, so you courageously disregard it. This may give you the reputation of being a radical, in the true sense of the word, but you will carry your head high all your life.

LIFE PATH
You are independent, tactful, diplomatic, and self-reliant, fond of dressing well, and generally careful of appearances in your home, as well. You are secretive in your dealings but never to the extent of trickery. You are loving and lovable and generously share your original philosophies and opinions with your friends and acquaintances.

DESTINY
Even though minor obstacles dampen the ardor of some days, you maintain steady adherence to the worth of your ideals and ambitions. You learn from the hard lessons of past experiences, even though you optimistically hope for the best. Instead of discussing what you want, let actual achievements be the result. You know how to turn new beginnings into successful accomplishments. In the midst of it all, however, find time for hobbies and relaxation.

KARMIC LESSON
You are usually bighearted and good-natured, but a good deal of a "bluff" all the same. You often make great promises with the best faith in the world, yet you know it will be impossible for you to make good when the time comes. Your happy-go-lucky disposition does not let you worry over things such as this, however. You are rather dogged, even pigheaded at times. You have a strong character, with a calm and sensible demeanor and a naturally fine intellect, which you are sometimes too inclined to neglect. You have good literary ability and should write if ever you become sufficiently inspired.

SECRET
You may be moody unless you find your perfect career and perfect partner. You have a highly romantic and idealistic nature and will stick to your beliefs.

JANUARY 23

It is better to suffer wrong than to do it, and happier to be sometimes cheated than not to trust.
—Samuel Johnson

BORN ON THIS DAY

★ **Édouard Manet**
painter

★ **John Hancock**
patriot, statesman

★ **Rutger Hauer**
actor

★ **Mariska Hargitay**
actor

★ **Tiffani Thiessen**
actor

PERSONALITY
You may begin your life in absolute obscurity and, like Lord Byron, wake up one morning to find yourself famous. The reason behind this possibility is that you are a conscientious worker, ever building upon the foundations of your career, until one day the structure of success and acclaim is suddenly complete. People like your dependability, and they are willing to give you every assistance within their power. You, in turn, are free with your help, guidance, advice, and material aid. You are especially fond of your family, doing all you can to make them comfortable and happy. Because of your sympathetic manner, you could do well in one of the healing arts or education.

LIFE PATH
You are inclined to be somewhat introverted, difficult to reach or late at times. It is hard to drive you to do anything, but, by those who know your weaknesses, you are easily ruled. You are generally well-liked, and you have the respect of those who really know you. Your intimate relationships, once committed to, will be long lasting.

DESTINY
Put your inspirations to practical use. Employ your hands as well as your head. Speed of action can make you rebel and dig in your heels. Be willing to adjust yourself to changing conditions. You'll be rewarded when you take time for introspection, writing, talking, drawing, or creating.

KARMIC LESSON
You are practical and businesslike and especially interested in how things work or are made. To you, inventiveness might be recreation and a hobby. You probably like puzzles of all kinds—anagrams, cryptograms, conundrums—anything that makes you exercise your mind in this direction and presents a problem calling for a solution. At the same time, you can be bright and witty. You are not of an overly emotional temperament, and you like to get an insight into life by studying the people around you.

SECRET
A love of handmade artistry dominates this life, and a career too far away from it will not bring the highest satisfaction.

FRIENDS & FAMILY

JANUARY 24

At the center of your being, you have the answer; you know who you are and you know what you want.
—M.J. Ryan

BORN ON THIS DAY
- **Frederick the Great**
  Prussian king
- **Hadrian**
  Roman emperor
- **Michio Kaku**
  physicist
- **Neil Diamond**
  singer
- **Edith Wharton**
  author

FRIENDS & FAMILY

PERSONALITY
A combination of spirituality and practicality make you an unusual and interesting person. You could be an aggressive businessperson in the world of competition yet retain your innate and ardent faith. Your creative powers are great, being enhanced by natural intelligence. You can adapt yourself to whatever circumstances you find yourself in, and it is likely that over your life you will move many times to various places to live and work. Because you have vision and imagination, you should succeed in the arts, particularly those connected with writing, movies, or some form of drama. You regard life as a play, and it is your intention to take a leading part in it.

LIFE PATH
Preferably your partner should be born in May, July, or November and should be spiritually inclined. You sometimes regress into self-centeredness, but for the most part you are good-natured, fair-minded, and truthful.

DESTINY
Good fortune is dependent on your alertness to responsibilities that present themselves. You work to create favorable progress as well as initiate new beginnings. Find pleasure and companionship in associations with other creative people. Look for possessions you can afford that will give you long-anticipated satisfaction.

KARMIC LESSON
You have strong spiritual tendencies, though the practical affairs of life can make them recede into the background of your mind and thoughts. You may have a great many difficulties to encounter in your life, but you rise triumphant above them all. You like excitement and dislike more than anything else to just sit down and fold your hands and do nothing. You have great possibilities; make use of them. You have a very ardent, amorous nature, which it is difficult to control at times. You can learn to have a little more faith in divine timing.

SECRET
You will be drawn into positions of great responsibility because you can direct others.

JANUARY 25

Man's inhumanity to man makes countless thousands mourn.
—Robert Burns

⬢ PERSONALITY

In modern psychological terminology, you are an extrovert. That is, your interests and attention are focused on the outside world; you are not pathologically concerned with the "inner life" of the workings of your mind or the state of your soul. Your keen judgment can be overcome only at such times as you allow anger instead of your intelligence to rule you. You need little stimulus to spur you on because you are strongly imbued with ambition, and you intend to make your mark in the world. Even in your homelife, you express your talent for management, for you take charge of the budget, arrange for the education of the younger members of the family, and in general act the part of the executive. You assume leadership because it is your natural role.

⬢ LIFE PATH

Strive to be a leader, for nature has fitted you for such a position. Surrounded by congenial friends, you will be extremely happy, and your homelife will furnish you with constant ambition to improve. Do not let anger or jealousy get the better of your good judgment.

⬢ DESTINY

Saturn rays emphasize your attention to responsibilities to get what you want. An accelerated rate of speed to success is possible if you follow the path of duty without complaint. Adventure, romance, pleasure, and an opportunity for travel are within the range of your probabilities in this life, so welcome each new day optimistically.

⬢ KARMIC LESSON

You have distinct talent for communications, as well as ability in the line of lecturing or public speaking. You can be rather poetic and romantic. You have a roving, restless disposition, but one adaptable to circumstances. You must develop more foresight. You have ability as a performer, as those talents are prominent in your life. Make a study of your own character and learn to understand yourself. If you gain mastery over yourself, you can gain mastery over your surroundings.

⬢ SECRET

You have a gift for speaking that can be used to good advantage either in the workplace or on the lecture platform.

BORN ON THIS DAY

- **Virginia Woolf**
  author
- **Alicia Keys**
  singer
- **Marcus Samuelsson**
  celebrity chef, TV personality
- **Etta James**
  singer
- **Robert Burns**
  Scottish poet

FRIENDS & FAMILY

JANUARY 26

Love in marriage should be the accomplishment of a beautiful dream, and not, as it too often is, the end.
—Alphonse Karr

BORN ON THIS DAY

★ **Douglas MacArthur**
U.S. general

★ **Ellen DeGeneres**
comedian, talk show host

★ **Paul Newman**
actor

★ **Wayne Gretzky**
ice hockey player

★ **Jules Feiffer**
cartoonist

FRIENDS & FAMILY

PERSONALITY

In some persons the ability to be devoted to an individual or a small family group is restricted by a love of all humanity. You are such a person, for you have a truly open heart that embraces the world rather than the individuals of which it is composed. You would be a splendid social service worker or spiritual counselor because of your deep well of sympathy and kindness.

Your understanding embraces all the foibles of weak humanity, and you make a wonderful helper to those in need. The material requirements of life play a minor role in your scheme of existence. You believe in living as you wish, and not according to the dictates of society or convention.

LIFE PATH

You are endowed with a personal magnetism that will bring people under your influence. Use them to stimulate your life and enjoy them to the best of your ability. Your affections are not always deep-seated, although you will be loyal and true to the one upon whom you bestow your hand.

DESTINY

Keep abreast of new responsibilities and conquer the challenges and difficulties they entail. The influence of this date encourages the use of speed and ingenuity in whatever you do. Try to be ahead of everyone else. A show of aggressiveness should propel you along the path of success and happiness with great strides. Added satisfaction is inherent in your harmonious associations with friends and family.

KARMIC LESSON

You have a natural psychic power if you were born on this day, and you are strongly intuitive and responsive. When you enter a house, you at once know whether you like it or not, as you somehow sense its atmosphere—a "something" about it that either attracts or repels you. You are positive and energetic and put all your vim and vigor into anything you are doing. You also have determination and the ability to push things through to a successful conclusion.

SECRET

You have a tendency to radicalism and a disdain for convention. People born on this date should guard against too free an expression of their feelings; some will always misunderstand you.

JANUARY 27

Music hath charms to soothe the savage breast, to soften rocks, and bend the knotted oak.
—*William Congreve*

BORN ON THIS DAY

★ **Wolfgang Amadeus Mozart**
composer

★ **Lewis Carroll**
author

★ **Mikhail Baryshnikov**
dancer

★ **Bridget Fonda**
actor

★ **G. E. Smith**
musician

PERSONALITY
If you focus your mind on doing creative work, concentrate on your aim, and work with diligence, success is bound to be yours. You have executive ability and the qualifications needed to be a good director. However, you could easily express the negative value of your abilities in the form of being dictatorial. Therefore, you must direct your energies into the proper channels. Learn to get your way and to reach your goal by work, diplomacy, and optimism. Early in life, you display the mental adroitness with which you have been endowed. Many musicians of fame have been born on this day, among them Mozart in 1756.

LIFE PATH
Be all things to all people, but remember that the higher nature governs us. Your ambition and desires will take you far if you accept the help your fellow men and women can give, instead of trying to climb to the summit by trampling others underfoot. Accept love when it comes to you, even if at times it seems to slow you down in your upward struggle.

DESTINY
Be careful not to ignore details. Do each job that comes up with efficiency and dispatch. Personal ambition should not mean the weakening of harmonious relationships with relatives and friends but rather the strengthening of ties of affection and tenderness. Seek cooperation to help get the things you want.

KARMIC LESSON
You have a great deal of ambition if you were born on this day. You have a natural force of character and are independent in your thoughts. You are dignified and have a good appreciation of your own worth. This does not mean that you are vain but that you know your own powers and capabilities and determine that you will get what they are worth. You have a distinct ability for music and should be able to do some really good creative work if you settle down for serious study. You will surely accomplish great things in this life, and you will be duly rewarded for it.

SECRET
You have a fine sense of rhythm and perfect control over your body. Dancing and working out would be suitable commitments.

FRIENDS & FAMILY

JANUARY 28

Many know how to flatter; few know how to praise.
—Wendell Phillips

BORN ON THIS DAY
- **Jackson Pollock**
  painter
- **Elijah Wood**
  actor
- **J. Cole**
  fashion designer
- **Alan Alda**
  actor
- **Sarah McLachlan**
  singer

FRIENDS & FAMILY

◉ PERSONALITY
You have a loving nature but sometimes can have a jealous disposition. When you are fond of a person, you are willing to give him or her all your affection and devotion, but you expect the same exclusive love in return and are disappointed and bitter if you do not get it. In your relationship in daily life with people other than your family and loved ones, you are very fair and much admired for your admirable traits. Generosity abounds in your makeup. You love to show your affection by giving lavish gifts, and you could never cheat anyone out of a penny. You could learn to be a little more impersonal in your dealings with people. In that way, you will spare yourself possible hurts, and you will also allow others liberty in pursuing their own happiness.

◉ LIFE PATH
Make the most of your talents. Do not hesitate to attempt what seems beyond your reach. Be ever cautious and prudent, for such virtues invariably produce success. Put your trust in those who are worthy, and never let jealousy come between you and your happiness.

◉ DESTINY
Originality and initiative create the cosmic stimulation you need. It would be advantageous for you to keep your thoughts and plans to yourself until they have had the chance to become realities. Avoid the possibility of being misunderstood or having other obstacles placed in your way by working on your own. In that way, you will not invite trouble.

◉ KARMIC LESSON
You are naturally of a creative nature, but you are also practical in the affairs of life. You have an inveterate love of adventure, which makes you keenly interested in foreign countries and their people's habits and customs. At one time in your life, you were probably profoundly interested in exploring exotic territories or cultures. This is very predominant in your nature. You are naturally restless and nervous and need to learn to relax more than you do.

◉ SECRET
Guard against nervousness and apprehension when under a great mental strain, as you have a tendency to fret over trifles.

JANUARY 29

All the great things are simple, and many can be expressed in a single word: freedom, justice, honor, duty, mercy, hope.
—Winston Churchill

BORN ON THIS DAY
- **Thomas Paine**
  patriot
- **Oprah Winfrey**
  talk show host
- **Adam Lambert**
  singer
- **Katharine Ross**
  actor
- **Tom Selleck**
  actor

PERSONALITY
Regardless of your abode, you could never be truly happy if you were limited to knowing only a few people or to leading a life that did not include a program of associating with large groups. As a matter of fact, you visualize yourself as an efficient executive, managing large affairs and directing the course of the lives of many people. Some people with ambitions similar to yours seek their outlet in politics, others in activism, but whatever their form of expression, they are not happy unless they are very busy. You think in terms of the happiness of the whole human family, and you are a real visionary in that respect.

LIFE PATH
You are naturally of an ambitious turn of mind. Be careful in directing it. Choose one profession or calling and adhere to it strictly. No matter what you undertake, do it carefully and thoroughly. You are capable of deep love and will have an ideal homelife.

DESTINY
A certain amount of impetuosity will help you break the bonds of the past and make the present cycle an active one. Avoid risking money. Constructive effort and achievement on your part will prove superior to get-rich-quick schemes. Your popularity can increase through use of your special skills and display of good sportsmanship.

KARMIC LESSON
Born on this day, you have a naturally fine mind; you are scientific and technical to a remarkable degree, if not in detailed knowledge, then at least in your manner of thinking. You would be a good all-round technology person. At the same time, you have remarkable psychic power. You are probably strongly intuitive. Yet you are practical and do not let these things overtake your good common sense.

SECRET
Once convinced that their course is the right one, those born on this day cannot be swerved. With a little luck, they can succeed admirably in a cutting-edge business.

FRIENDS & FAMILY

January 30

Life is to be fortified by many friendships. To love and to be loved is the greatest happiness of existence.
—Sydney Smith

BORN ON THIS DAY

- **Franklin D. Roosevelt**
  U.S. president
- **Saul Alinsky**
  activist, political theorist
- **Vanessa Redgrave**
  actor
- **Phil Collins**
  singer
- **Junior dos Santos**
  MMX fighter and wrestler

FRIENDS & FAMILY

PERSONALITY

In your efforts to help yourself and others, your imagination may make you overreach yourself. You must make up your mind very early in life just what you want to do or to be. The reason this statement is made so emphatically is that you have the ability to become whatever you want, so know what you want before you ever do anything. Decide whether you are still going to want it after you have attained your wish. You have vision, a strong sense of your own willpower, and a gracious manner. As no chains will ever bind you, you are perfectly willing to give up associations or projects at the drop of a hat to go on to something more amusing, better, or even merely novel. There is likely but one true love in your life, and to that person you will give all your loyalty.

LIFE PATH

You have the power to influence all with whom you come in contact, either for good or for bad. This will be a danger to you if it is used in the wrong direction. Follow your inclination to investigate things and develop your mind to the extent of its capabilities. You will never be too physically demonstrative, but you will nevertheless love with a true, strong passion.

DESTINY

Harness your inspiration and put it into channels that can be beneficial to you. Try to achieve the results you expect of yourself and fulfill the hopes that are dear to your heart. Be grateful for benefits already available now rather than yearning for more.

KARMIC LESSON

You have, if you were born on this day, one very striking and distinguishing characteristic: It is your insatiable curiosity on all subjects. For this reason, you are interested in psychic and occult phenomena, but only in a curious and not an emotional way. You are plucky and determined and can undergo a great deal of hardship, if necessary, to achieve your goals. You are very interested in the human mind for its workings and have great sympathy for those who have mental health issues.

SECRET

You are responsive to sympathy and never forget a favor. It is advisable to have the guidance and inspiration of a close partner in life.

JANUARY 31

There's nothing half so sweet in life as love's young dream.
—Thomas Moore

BORN ON THIS DAY
- ★ **Jackie Robinson**
  baseball player
- ★ **Justin Timberlake**
  singer
- ★ **Carol Channing**
  actor
- ★ **Philip Glass**
  composer
- ★ **Tallulah Bankhead**
  actor

PERSONALITY
Because you know what the public likes, you can succeed in any line of work where you come in contact with the masses. Whether as a writer, entertainer, or salesperson, online, or in any capacity in which you sell your services to the world at large, you are bound to put yourself over. Success is likely to come to you at an early age, if you apply yourself. However, you must specialize in a single line of endeavor to get the most out of life. You are faithful and demonstrative with your affections. Honesty is one of your most outstanding traits, and you have built up a wonderful reputation because of it.

LIFE PATH
You have a keen sense of justice and an artistic temperament and are a lover of nature and outdoor life. You are ambitious but are sometimes too easily discouraged. You might accomplish many things that you give up in despair. What you need most is perseverance and a greater degree of confidence in your own ability.

DESTINY
Your success destiny is highlighted by the Sun's powerful rays of leadership and progress. Even activities that some might consider commonplace and routine can take on great meaning for you. Always be sure to aim toward the future with resolution and faith in your own capabilities.

KARMIC LESSON
You have a great deal of personal charisma, which draws to you all with whom you associate closely. You have a powerful personality and a commanding eye, which seems to master all those who dare look you squarely in the face. You would make a very successful healer for this reason and also because you have understanding and a good deal of compassion. You may not be aware of this power, but you have it.

SECRET
You are an interesting conversationalist with the power to explain things to others. You would make a good teacher and an encouraging coach.

FRIENDS & FAMILY

FEBRUARY 1

Temptation rarely comes in working hours. It is in their leisure time that men are made or marred.
—W.N. Taylor

BORN ON THIS DAY
- **Boris Yeltsin**
  politician
- **Cary Grant**
  actor
- **Langston Hughes**
  poet
- **Vivian Maier**
  photographer
- **Pauly Shore**
  comedian

PERSONALITY
Because of your wit and charm, you are a popular person. Somehow, you know just what to say to people when you are introduced to them to make them want to become your friends. As you enjoy the accompaniments of social life, you never find it a bore to entertain people in your own home or to go out visiting and attending parties. You can inject the spirit of fun into any gathering and take the lead in games, sports, and amusements. It gets on your nerves to be too long in one place, and you become impatient when your duties confine you to a single locale, desk, or even the kitchen. When the urge comes over you, you must pick up your belongings and obey the wanderlust.

LIFE PATH
You are a good and loyal friend but an exceedingly bitter enemy. Curb your lust for revenge, or it may wreck your whole life's happiness. You are a lover of home and home ties, but you should be aware and careful of a tendency to be a perfectionist.

DESTINY
Courage and daring can further your ambitions. Taking time to review past accomplishments will help you take action that will better them. Assistance will usually come from unexpected sources, so that's why it's a good idea to offer friendliness, courtesy, and sympathy to everyone with whom you are associated. Take time to enjoy what you have accomplished rather than rush around for excitement.

KARMIC LESSON
You are naturally fond of intrigue, and you always wait to see which way public opinion will go before you announce your own attitude. You are clever, intellectual, and interested in a large number of creative pursuits. Being a natural manager, you like to run things in your own home and to direct them in your business dealings. You have a natural taste for good design and a head for business, which especially fits you to be an organizer. People born on this day are loving until pushed too far.

SECRET
While you are loyal to your friends, you have a tendency to be unpunctual due to a meditative mind. You make a rather indulgent parent and friend.

FRIENDS & FAMILY

FEBRUARY 2

Sadness is but a wall between two gardens.
—Kahlil Gibran

BORN ON THIS DAY

- **Ayn Rand**
  author
- **James Joyce**
  author
- **Shakira**
  singer
- **Ina Garten**
  cook, TV personality
- **Brent Spiner**
  actor

FRIENDS & FAMILY

PERSONALITY

You don't believe in letting everybody know your business or in revealing your hidden traits to the world at large. There is a sense of secrecy about you, almost like a superstition, that makes you keep your own counsel. You can work in solitude, plan without collaborators, and suddenly emerge from your deep study with some surprising and rather startling accomplishments. You love this sensation of surprising others because it gives you a sense of attainment; you know that what you wrought, you have wrought alone—and you are willing to take the blame or accept the praise on merit alone. Being happily endowed with a creative imagination, you should succeed in whatever field of action you choose for your work, play, and productivity.

LIFE PATH

You have a powerful personality and are capable of great good or bad. Do not let your powers for good be squandered by wasteful habits. Constant and active employment should be your method of life. You are an excellent conversationalist and lean toward culture and refinement.

DESTINY

Your inspirations and philosophic understanding can be of significance, so do not subdue them. In addition to thinking about the meaning of the universe, establish a detailed and practical plan to get what you want out of life. Take a few others into your confidence. Listen appreciatively to their advice even if you intend a different approach. Solitude has a lot to offer in happiness for you, but also seek encouragement from those who surround you.

KARMIC LESSON

You are very versatile if you were born on this day and capable of many things. You are distinctly interested in good books and inspired writing and should keep a journal, do a podcast, or write a blog. You can at times be cold and unemotional, yet passionate at the same time! You have a great natural ability but are inclined to overestimate it. With those you trust, you are a good talker, but you also like to hear yourself a little too much. You are shrewd and can always get your money's worth.

SECRET

If your higher, spiritual nature is aroused and your philosophical urges are properly developed, you will become a great promoter and communicator of high ideals.

FEBRUARY 3

Be loved, be admired, be necessary; be somebody.
—Simone de Beauvoir

⊛ PERSONALITY
No matter what your status in life may be, you possess the spirit of the trailblazer. You find it exciting to try new methods, to institute novel systems, and to make experiments. It is your idea that nothing succeeds like variety, and so you try to fill your life with a series of experiences that give you a taste of each facet of living. You have an adventurous nature, and your courage allows you to visit places that are strange and to make unusual friends who may or may not be the type to conform to convention. You like to change things around, and even when you visit friends, you always have suggestions as to how they should rearrange their furniture. Carried to the extremes, this desire leads you to try to change their whole lives. Be careful that your advice is constructive, lest you lose your friends.

⊛ LIFE PATH
You should choose a creative partner, especially one who is born in January, June, or October. You have excellent self-control, know how to keep your own counsel, and are affectionate and kindhearted. You are also very fond of pets and animals.

⊛ DESTINY
In addition to working on the beautification of the things around you and adding harmony to your environment, always extend hospitality to your friends, as you attract goodwill by showing generosity and willingness to help others. You can make much headway by using your skills to do the things you may have postponed but that are dear to your heart.

⊛ KARMIC LESSON
You have a natural talent for multitasking, and you take in many wide interests at once. You think in terms of big things—nations and humanity—and cannot bring yourself to put yourself in a box. You have a good aesthetic sense and would make a good designer—of either your own home or those of others. You are a natural promoter and are suited for a successful professional life, even if you work from home. You need at least more than one intellectual interest, since you need many outlets for your abilities and energies.

⊛ SECRET
Your business acumen and salesmanship are strong, and you have a great interest in personal adornment. You take extreme pride in your home surroundings.

BORN ON THIS DAY
★ **Gertrude Stein**
author
★ **Norman Rockwell**
painter
★ **James Michener**
author
★ **Nathan Lane**
actor
★ **Christie Brinkley**
model

FRIENDS & FAMILY

FEBRUARY 4

Great souls have wills; feeble ones have only wishes.
—Chinese proverb

BORN ON THIS DAY
- ★ **Charles Lindbergh**
  pilot
- ★ **Rosa Parks**
  civil rights icon
- ★ **Clint Black**
  singer
- ★ **Betty Friedan**
  feminist author
- ★ **Alice Cooper**
  singer

FRIENDS & FAMILY

_____
_____
_____
_____
_____
_____
_____
_____
_____
_____

PERSONALITY
You are fond of your family, to the extent of being willing to sacrifice everything for them. Be sure that you do not lose sight of your own needs in caring for those of others. Your own kindness and unselfishness may, strange as it seems, sometimes lead you to a position where you will be misunderstood. Your mind operates in such a way that you see better than others where events and traits of character are leading, and your desire is to help others by offering your advice. However, you will find that most people resent being told what to do, even when it is for their own good. The result is that you can lose your friends as well as your good name. Therefore, tell the truth but be sure that what you say is carefully considered in advance.

LIFE PATH
Be truthful and you will be successful. You have an inborn honesty and frankness that will not permit doubtful business methods or anything but straightforwardness in love. You are shrewd and compelling, gaining the confidence and respect of many with whom you come in contact. You are also fond of children.

DESTINY
Your friendliness and personal appearance can be unusually attractive and make an effective impression on others. Seek for, and grasp, opportunities for leadership and popularity. Perseverance will always help you see the successful initiation of new projects or the happy conclusions of endeavors you began long ago. Loyalty to friends of long standing can pay dividends.

KARMIC LESSON
You are quiet, self-reliant, and reserved. Try not to come to definite decisions until you have gone over the situation carefully in your mind, and don't be hurried by anyone in making your deliberate choice. You have a great interest in all things pertaining to the occult and mysterious, though you keep this to yourself and few suspect it. You are nervously energetic and apt to wear yourself out. Learn to rest more, as you need it, with your disposition and temperament. You are not naturally affectionate, but you are kind and intense at times in your love life.

SECRET
You possess strong instincts, at times illogical, which may offend some insecure people. You should enter independent ventures.

FEBRUARY 5

Life is what we make it, always has been, always will be.
—*Grandma Moses*

⊙ PERSONALITY

The fascination that you have for people is due to the subtlety of your nature. There is nothing on the surface of your personality that reveals the real you; those facets of your character that are deep and sincere you keep well hidden from prying eyes because you are very eclectic about to whom you choose to reveal your true self. You are more or less casual with people ordinarily, but once you have decided on making friends with a person, you are open, honest, loyal, and sincere. Then you are a friend for life, for you will keep up the relationship even after you have discovered the faults or weaknesses of the other person. You are courteous and thoughtful and always good company.

⊙ LIFE PATH

Do not build castles in the air. You are inclined to be visionary rather than practical and should try to correct this fault with a balance between the two. Let each creation of your mind be of merit. Do not choose your friends on account of their family connections, as this will cause you only unhappiness and trouble. Be prudent rather than generous in your giving.

⊙ DESTINY

Honors and benefits are attracted by the favorable Jupiter influences of your day. Prepare for good things by attending to the details that can help make them become realities. You can find lasting value in developing friendships with business associates. Do not cling too much to the past, but neither should you lose respect for the lessons it has taught and the benefits it has granted.

⊙ KARMIC LESSON

You have good natural common sense if you were born on this day, yet you are also a dreamer and an enthusiast and have wild notions at times that you want to carry out. You have distinct musical talent and should be able to compose. You are agile on your feet and should do a workout that involves dancing, as you could do this well. You might even make a profession of this and utilize your talent in this direction. You can be very charming when you want to be.

⊙ SECRET

Subjects born on this day are ambitious to become prominent socially. They make excellent hosts and companions and have much natural charm and grace.

BORN ON THIS DAY

★ **William S. Burroughs**
author

★ **Cristiano Ronaldo**
soccer player

★ **Hank Aaron**
baseball player

★ **Bobby Brown**
singer

★ **Laura Linney**
actor

FRIENDS & FAMILY

FEBRUARY 6

I would rather be able to appreciate things I cannot have than to have things I am not able to appreciate.
—Elbert Hubbard

BORN ON THIS DAY
- **Ronald Reagan**
  U.S. president
- **George Herman "Babe" Ruth**
  baseball player
- **Tom Brokaw**
  news anchor
- **Bob Marley**
  singer
- **Natalie Cole**
  singer

FRIENDS & FAMILY

PERSONALITY
Formality and convention play a large role in your life, for you believe in living according to a code. This policy has won you a fine reputation for sincerity and has brought to you the opportunity to exercise your capabilities as an executive. By being the leader, even in family life, you can wring success from the most adverse circumstances. Given a lucky break, you can really ring the bell. You are a good manager of money, and you should take charge of the family and your own budget. By being compassionate to others, you will build up a great store of goodwill.

LIFE PATH
Your sense of honor is exceedingly high, but you combine with it a sensitiveness that causes you both worry and annoyance. Be in all cases self-reliant. You are also witty and fond of fun, economical, and prudent. You are loving and demonstrative and will reap what you sow.

DESTINY
The Saturn influence emphasizes the need for conscientious attention to whatever you do. At the same time, however, free yourself from unnecessary restraints. Life can be pleasurable in the midst of responsibilities if you maintain a cheerful outlook toward duties. Plan a well-rounded schedule that allows for recreation and relaxation as well as work. Let your viewpoints be broad and comprehensive rather than restricted to narrow channels.

KARMIC LESSON
Born this day, you have a good deal of natural ability in certain directions. Distinctly, you have the talent for photography, and this you should cultivate. You are also poetic and a daydreamer at times. You might make a good architect or designer. You are naturally feisty and have the courage of your convictions. Above all else, it is important that you be empathetic and nonjudgmental in your friendships—this is very important.

SECRET
You possess an ability to be a convincing salesperson and distributor of investments in unusual business ventures. You are perhaps inclined to be a bit unsteady in marital affairs.

FEBRUARY 7

*I can never close my lips where
I have opened my heart.*
—Charles Dickens

BORN ON THIS DAY
- **Sir Thomas More**
  social philosopher, author
- **Charles Dickens**
  author
- **Chris Rock**
  comedian
- **Ashton Kutcher**
  actor
- **Garth Brooks**
  singer

PERSONALITY
You have a deep concern for the welfare of humanity. Your intuition is well developed, and your understanding is as deep as your sympathy. You know how to put yourself in someone else's position. You comprehend the workings of the mind, and you might well be a superb psychologist. You might like to study astrology, another language for psychology. You like the idea of psychodrama to help work out trauma and painful past experiences. You give great advice to your friends, and they look to you for recommendations about wellness and food and the latest health innovations. Your affection for your personal friends and family is as strong as your love for humankind.

LIFE PATH
Be sanguine. Your mentality leans that way. It will also induce you to love your home and all its comforts, although you never get too attached to one place. You possess good taste, excellent judgment, and a thorough knowledge of character. See that you do not abuse them.

DESTINY
If you have difficulty controlling your changing moods, associate the mental effect of the planet Mercury, which affects your birthday, with the trends and cycles in your life marked by sudden events requiring speedy decisions. If making business changes or a move becomes necessary, you can usually take the changes in stride. Strange surroundings and new acquaintances can give you as much satisfaction as old surroundings and friendships.

KARMIC LESSON
You have a rather roving spirit and are not much of a person to stay at home in the evenings. You like going out a great deal, to social gatherings and to dine at restaurants whenever possible. Yet you do not altogether like the conversation you get there, and you wish, in your heart of hearts, that it would be more interesting and more intellectual and solid. You have a good conscience, but it is in need of repair! Get it out, look it over, oil it, and set it to work, and you will make a fine person with the innate abilities you possess.

SECRET
You possess the fault of sometimes talking too freely about your private affairs. This should be curbed. You are devoted to having certain spiritual rituals in your daily routine.

FRIENDS & FAMILY

FEBRUARY 8

Thinking is the hardest work there is, which is probably the reason why so few engage in it.
—Henry Ford

BORN ON THIS DAY

- **James Dean**
  actor
- **John Williams**
  composer
- **Jules Verne**
  author
- **Cecily Strong**
  actor
- **Evangeline Adams**
  astrologer

FRIENDS & FAMILY

_____
_____
_____
_____
_____
_____
_____
_____
_____
_____

PERSONALITY
Because you possess a pronounced degree of showmanship, you can sell your unique ideas. Through the use of your dramatic powers, you can make others visualize what you have in mind and creatively convert them to your way of thinking. You have the type of imagination that takes a practical form of expression, and thus you can make a garden or conduct a marketing campaign with equal ardor and success. Your managerial qualifications are well-known, and you are therefore trusted with a position of responsibility in every undertaking with which you are associated.

LIFE PATH
Your memory is one of your strongest characteristics. Without apparent effort, you seem to imbibe universal knowledge. Use it well. You can be very practical and not in the least inclined to take anything for granted, even in love. You are capable of deep affection but are backward in the acceptance of others at their seeming worth.

DESTINY
Congenial relationships with neighbors and relatives make close bonds especially enjoyable for you. Some unusual happenings between the ages of thirty and forty may change the pattern of your life, but the general trend will be one of harmony. Make use of every opportunity to develop your inherent talents and interests. Take time to enjoy beauty wherever you find it. Find satisfaction in the things you do.

KARMIC LESSON
You are interested in serious things, but in rather a superficial way, as you dislike systemic, sustained work. You love argument and often talk a great deal just for the sake of having your say. You are interested in psychic phenomena and all that pertains to the novel and mysterious in all branches of science and metaphysics. You probably have a great desire to try odd things. You are fun to be around, clever, and a trifle sarcastic.

SECRET
You have a nature given to pioneering and exploring, with little concern for the glory in it. You chafe under the strain of humdrum responsibilities.

FEBRUARY 9

If you want work well done, select a busy man—the other man has no time.
—Elbert Hubbard

BORN ON THIS DAY
- **William Henry Harrison**
  U.S. president
- **Carole King**
  singer/songwriter
- **Alice Walker**
  author
- **Mia Farrow**
  actor
- **Tom Hiddleston**
  actor

PERSONALITY
Whatever you decide to do with your life, you are going to do it with a strong will. There is little on this earth that can deter you from reaching your goal or the height of your ambition. Fortunately, you are possessed of sufficient talent to get where you want to go without being overly aggressive or dictatorial and without having to push others out of your way. Once you decide on a career, you set out to discover all you can about it. If parenthood were your part in the drama of life, you would, with the utmost efficiency, go about learning all about it. In other words, you do a good job no matter what.

LIFE PATH
The strongest and weakest physically are reputed to be born in this month, and all are credited with possessing some great possibility, which in some reaches a very high spiritual order. Study your ability and inclination carefully, and then apply yourself diligently. You are sympathetic and kind, faithful to friends, and constant in your love.

DESTINY
Obstacles that have blocked your progress in the past can gradually disappear over time, leaving you imbued with new enthusiasm that will always keep you young. Once you attain freedom from restraint, you initiate your ideas and strive for the fulfillment of big ambitions. Participate in interesting activities. See sights and join groups that can give pleasure to you. Make mental pictures of the future and shape your plans for the development of constructive projects.

KARMIC LESSON
You have a good sense of humor and are naturally witty in public. At the same time, you have a deeper and more serious nature than many give you credit for possessing. You have good musical talent and should also dance; you have dramatic ability, as well. In fact, you have varied gifts, and because of this you hardly know which one to select. You must choose one and then follow it, no matter where it may lead or how hard the road. In this way, you will ultimately achieve great success.

SECRET
You have a love of the outdoors and of unusual wellness practices. You would excel in unfamiliar environments or working with people who do not share your background.

FRIENDS & FAMILY

FEBRUARY 10

The greatest pleasure I know is to do a good action by stealth and to have it found out by accident.
—Charles Lamb

BORN ON THIS DAY

- **Emma Roberts**
  actor
- **Laura Dern**
  actor
- **Roberta Flack**
  singer
- **George Stephanopoulos**
  TV host
- **Glenn Beck**
  TV commentator

FRIENDS & FAMILY

_____
_____
_____
_____
_____
_____
_____
_____
_____
_____

PERSONALITY

There is a touch of cuteness about you that is very appealing. You like to have fun, and if it is mildly impish at someone else's expense, that doesn't stop you. However, you don't go to such extremes as to become offensive or to hurt anyone else's feelings beyond repair. Because you have such a delightful sense of humor, you are popular with your set. You have a good business sense, and you know how to make a social introduction lead to business connections that work out to your advantage. Watch your tendency to be careless about where you put your valuables, your important papers, and other obligations. You seem to have such a plethora of things on your mind that you are quite capable of forgetting something important.

LIFE PATH

Be self-reliant and concentrated. Those who make a study of these virtues will lead rich and successful lives. You are apt to make engagements hastily and break them when they interfere with your convenience. You are affectionate, pure-minded, energetic, and kindly. When you win love, you will hold it.

DESTINY

You are not the type to take a back seat. Assert yourself. Benefits earned through aggressive action will be well worth the effort you make. Seek new means of expression. Do not be frightened by the novelty or unusual nature of events—make the most of them. Barge ahead with confidence that you can get what you want if you try hard enough. Adhere to the well-known maxim that "those who seek will find."

KARMIC LESSON

You are very fond of children and will take infinite pains to entertain them. You have good judgment, wry wit, and a sympathetic and kindly nature, and you like to see those about you well and happy. You are fond of home and its comforts and do not care so much for traveling. You are optimistic and always look on the bright side of things. You have a deep sense of honor; you are affectionate and should make a devoted partner. You are probably a very lovable character.

SECRET

You have a strange hypnotic power that, when developed, can be used to influence others. You go naturally to unique adventures and ventures. You can be rather spontaneously silly.

FEBRUARY 11

I never did anything worth doing by accident, nor did any of my inventions come by accident.
—Thomas A. Edison

BORN ON THIS DAY
- **Thomas Edison**
  inventor
- **Burt Reynolds**
  actor
- **Jennifer Aniston**
  actor
- **Sarah Palin**
  former Alaska governor
- **Brandy**
  singer

PERSONALITY
Because you have an inventive turn of mind, you can work out ideas and concepts that eventually prove their value in cash. Not only are you fortunate in possessing this creative ability, but you have that infinite capacity for taking pains that has been given as the definition of genius. In other words, if you're a hard worker, then failure will not discourage you. Once you decide that an idea is worth your working on, you refuse to give up until you have succeeded in carrying it out or proved to your own satisfaction that it just won't work. Such tenacity deserves the rich rewards that you must eventually receive from life and destiny.

LIFE PATH
The vices of envy or arrogance you should fight with all your might. You are usually very positive although somewhat cynical, and you possess considerable visionary talent, which should be developed. You can be passionate and excitable but are generally cool and composed. You are not indifferent in love.

DESTINY
Have confidence in your beliefs and find encouragement as well as inspiration in the events going on around you. While others are expressing pessimism, it is just the time for you to emphasize optimism. Improve the new by adding a touch of the old. Take the initiative when necessary, but be equally interested in stimulating others into action. This can mean a gain for you, as well as fame in the development of your hopes, wishes, and thoughts.

KARMIC LESSON
You are, as a rule, a very kindly, likable person, though you like your own way in things and are apt to be upset if you don't get it. You have distinct trendsetting abilities and might make a success as an innovator if you made up your mind to do so and worked sufficiently hard at your chosen occupation. You have good judgment but are inclined to overestimate it. You are rather affectionate, but only to those who are of use or benefit to you. You have great power for work and a naturally powerful mind. You are very ingenious and original.

SECRET
Too many castles in the air impede your mind. You are sometimes inclined to daydream rather than work. You should think twice before any big commitments, as you dislike responsibility.

FRIENDS & FAMILY

FEBRUARY 12

Government of the people, by the people, and for the people shall not perish from the earth.
—Abraham Lincoln

BORN ON THIS DAY

★ **Abraham Lincoln**
U.S. president

★ **Charles Darwin**
scientist

★ **Christina Ricci**
actor

★ **Arsenio Hall**
talk show host

★ **Bill Russell**
basketball player

FRIENDS & FAMILY

_____

_____

_____

_____

_____

_____

_____

_____

_____

_____

PERSONALITY

It need hardly be explained to you that the principles of democracy are so dear to your heart that you would sacrifice anything for them. You have very high standards. You might well take a chance for one of your high ideals, but it would be foolish for you to risk money or valuables in private ventures of a gambling nature. Because you are a convincing debater, you can win adherents to your way of thinking. Be self-reliant, and you are sure to achieve your dearest wishes. You may reject practical concerns in favor of the pursuit of justice or a worthy cause.

LIFE PATH

Speculation is dangerous for you, for although you are a very good reasoner, you are at critical times quite impractical. You are fond of art and music and prefer to be in the company of creative thinkers, with whom you enjoy sharing tips and techniques.

DESTINY

It is good for you to look forward. Do not be content with mediocre goals or achievements. Use your ability and show your leadership, as the cosmic influences for you favor initiative and prestige. Be proud but not overbearing. Win respect and popularity by showing you can accomplish more than others are able to.

KARMIC LESSON

Born this day, you have your own life in your hands, more than almost any other individual. You have the power of making yourself what you will and molding your own destiny. But it depends on you. You must have your eye open to every opportunity that presents itself, and you must be quick to grasp it. Be not a dreamer but a worker! Regard everything that occurs in your life as a stepping-stone to something greater. If you follow your own instincts and make the best use of your splendid gifts, all your worthy desires will ultimately be gratified.

SECRET

You have rare traits with strongly developed willpower and mind. You are a natural leader, and you are a lover of literature and the arts.

FEBRUARY 13

The best preparation for good work tomorrow is to do good work today.
—Elbert Hubbard

BORN ON THIS DAY
- **Stockard Channing**
  actor
- **Peter Gabriel**
  singer
- **Randy Moss**
  football player
- **Chuck Yeager**
  test pilot
- **Robbie Williams**
  singer

PERSONALITY
Although you are quiet in the way you approach things, you get them done. Perhaps it is the stealth-like approach itself that produces efficiency of a sort, or perhaps it is the undaunted courage that promotes your progress without fanfare. In either case, you like to investigate new ways of doing things and you usually find or discover novel methods of procedure, which might apply to baking, manufacturing, or finance—whatever the field may be. You have such good taste that you are the trendsetter of fashions and fads among your friends. Because you have cultivated your taste for the finer things in life, you can enjoy sharing them with others. You may flit from flower to flower in the garden of romance in early life but will eventually settle down with one bloom that has the strongest appeal.

LIFE PATH
You are changeable as a lover, but after finding "the one," you will be very happy. You are naturally joyous and exuberant and are considerate of the rights of others. You are refined and cultivated in your tastes, fond of good journalism and books, and ambitious to learn.

DESTINY
Pleasure and satisfaction can have a direct association with entertainment schedules and hospitality. Attract popularity and friendship through genuine cordiality. Think up ideas for parties and other recreational activities. Watch out, however, not to neglect responsibilities, for it would be easy for them to become troublesome. Success depends on how well you can manage the things that you have to handle personally or how you supervise and direct the work of others.

KARMIC LESSON
You are fond of ease and comfort, and you dislike intensely having to get out and hustle for a living. This is a habit of mind you must learn to outgrow. You have good natural talents, but these must be cultivated to be effective. If you once learn to overcome inertia in yourself, which is a natural and innate characteristic and no fault of your own, you should become a commendable person and a great success.

SECRET
You are rather fond of the physical and inclined to enjoy risks. You should cultivate balance and a steadying, grounding force.

FRIENDS & FAMILY

FEBRUARY 14

The cure for all the ill and wrongs, the cares, the sorrows, and the crimes of humanity, all lie in the one word "love."
—Lydia M. Child

BORN ON THIS DAY
- **Michael Bloomberg**
  businessman
- **Rob Thomas**
  singer
- **Jimmy Hoffa**
  mob boss
- **Jack Benny**
  entertainer
- **Florence Henderson**
  actor

FRIENDS & FAMILY

_____
_____
_____
_____
_____
_____
_____
_____
_____

PERSONALITY
If romance surges through your soul and you are filled with the urges of love, remember that you were born on St. Valentine's Day! You do take love seriously, regardless of how much people may tease you or joke about your date of birth. On the serious side, you are an excellent critic because you have keen powers of observation and good judgment. You are a good student of economics even if your dealings are limited to purchases made for the home. When it comes to performing your daily chores, you find the most economical way to do them, too, thus saving time and energy. You are a good balance, as you enjoy the little pleasures of life, and that fact makes you a true romantic.

LIFE PATH
Independence is a great virtue and one of your chief characteristics, but you must be careful that it does not merge into selfishness. You are inclined to claim the glory when results are praiseworthy and blame when disaster comes. You are masterful and very positive with those you respect and rather indifferent toward those you do not.

DESTINY
A formula for successful living can include consideration of friends, hobbies, recreation, and work, as well as the effective handling of responsibilities. The influence of Jupiter vibrations on your birthday is not limited to matters of abundance and money. If you take time to review your hopes and ambitions, you will plan a program that can help create realities of these wishes. Utilize your talents, especially during times that would otherwise be frittered away.

KARMIC LESSON
You are bright, hopeful, and cheerful if born on this day. You are fond of animals, and they are fond of you. You also have rather a legal turn of mind and might make a good lawyer or analyst. Your heart will never run away with your head, and it is always pretty well under control. It is probable in your life that you will get a great deal of help from others, but you should not depend on this in any way, because one day, when you think you can count on this, it may not be forthcoming.

SECRET
Music means a great deal to you and serves as a balance to soothe your soul. Life should be good to you because you are wise and considerate.

FEBRUARY 15

What matters most is that we learn from living.
—Doris Lessing

PERSONALITY
You like to feel that the human race is not at a standstill, and if it is within your power to add to its progress, you are certainly going to do it. Most likely, your capabilities consist of being able to handle financial affairs, contribute your executive and consulting services to institutions devoted to research, or ameliorate human relations and understanding. You share the traits with those like Galileo, the astronomer whose great discovery was the working of the solar system.

LIFE PATH
You can be overly attentive to satisfying your own whims and fancies. You have great ability, but it will lie dormant until a serious crisis in your life awakens you to a realization of your own capabilities. You care a great deal for what you have to eat and what supplements you take. You like to take care of yourself and are devoted to looking the best you can. You are focused on well-being and have few outside interests.

DESTINY
You can triumph over hindrances and disappointments by maintaining your courage. You can reach your goals by exercising self-discipline. Have respect for others, but do not let yourself be unduly influenced by them. Show sufficient confidence in your own ideas and know-how. Attention to organizational matters and the details of business is your cosmic domain. Associate only with those in whom you have confidence and on whom you can depend for trustworthy advice and genuine encouragement.

KARMIC LESSON
You have distinct creative talents, especially in the direction of voice culture, and would make a good singer. You would also make a good teacher, as you have the necessary talent, perseverance, and other qualifications. You are interested in all things pertaining to the occult and mysterious, and at times you are a little psychic yourself. You tend to be a little anxious over your mental and physical health, but try to overcome this tendency.

SECRET
You have a high degree of honor but are inclined to be oversensitive. You can be successful when unhampered by self-criticism.

BORN ON THIS DAY
- **Galileo Galilei** — scientific luminary
- **Susan B. Anthony** — women's rights activist
- **Chris Farley** — comedian
- **Ernest Shackleton** — explorer
- **Jeremy Bentham** — social reformer

FRIENDS & FAMILY

FEBRUARY 16

Every man's life lies within the present; for the past is spent and done with, and the future is uncertain.
—Marcus Aurelius Antoninus

BORN ON THIS DAY

★ **Ice-T**
rapper, actor

★ **Mahershala Ali**
actor

★ **LeVar Burton**
actor

★ **The Weekend**
singer

★ **Carl Icahn**
activist shareholder

FRIENDS & FAMILY

PERSONALITY

If you are a mystery even to your most intimate friends and associates, it is no wonder, for you believe that your integrity as a human being and an individual can be preserved only by keeping your thoughts and character to yourself. The surface that you show the world has charm, a certain mystical appeal, and an evasiveness that is magnetic. For that reason, you would be a fine actor. You have the quality that allures while it does not part with your inherent integrity. You seem to give and withhold at the same time. Should you become interested in mysticism, occultism, or philosophy, you would soon master all that one person can in a single lifetime because you have a natural affinity for such subjects.

LIFE PATH

Be ever ready for leadership. It is yours by right of birth. You cherish above all else your integrity and honor and are careful and conscientious in all you do. You are fond of learning about and acquiring the finer things of life, and your love is wholehearted and enduring.

DESTINY

You can accomplish a great deal once you make up your mind. Take advantage of beneficial Mercury influences by thinking and planning ahead of time. You will gain worthwhile rewards. If your present schedule seems humdrum, change it. Adaptability can be one of the outstanding traits of your birthday. For you, it is best to concentrate on the present and forget the past. There is ample opportunity for lucrative employment in addition to admiration and contentment.

KARMIC LESSON

You are tenderhearted and friendly, and you are very interested in psychology. You can listen to the woes and troubles of others for hours together and help them out of difficulties. You are fond of reading and might be a bookworm or computer addict if you gave full sway to your passions, and you long for affection and love from others. You are sympathetic, kind, and appreciative.

SECRET

You are best suited to rural or suburban life, delighting in simple honors and natural surroundings, hopefully with a garden.

FEBRUARY 17

When love and skill work together, expect a masterpiece.
—John Ruskin

⭐ PERSONALITY
Your aim in life is to lead the richest and fullest existence that your intellect can think up and your abilities provide. There is no barrier in your mind to having a fine homelife, a career, and rich, friendly associations. Energy abounding combined with intellectual qualifications make it possible for you to fulfill your every wish as you generously share your good fortune with friends, family, and those who are less richly endowed than you are. Look within for the innate talents that are lurking undiscovered in your makeup. Try forms of expression in all of the arts; you are liable to discover that you can put your personality into writing, painting, and music with equal success.

⭐ LIFE PATH
You should study yourself. People born on this day have exceptional opportunities offered them, in both love and business, and you can reach the summit in your career. Your homelife could also be ideal. You love with vigor and are very considerate and thoughtful where those most dear to you are concerned.

⭐ DESTINY
Pleasant scenes and events that touch your emotions are in your destiny. Rather than race from day to day without enjoying the things around you, take time to be observant. Appreciate the marvels of nature, and find pleasure in art, music, writing, and other mental pursuits. Develop sincere friendships to increase happiness. Find satisfaction in the things you already have. Useful facts can be acquired during conversation and leisurely travel.

⭐ KARMIC LESSON
Born on this day, you possess a combination of two very different temperaments and dispositions. Half of you is strong, determined, and aggressive, with fierce willpower and the ability to carry out any project to its bitter end. The other half is naturally charming, intuitive, and loving. You are fond of the homelife and family, and your circle of friends are like family to you. You are naturally domestic and can be very handy at fixing things.

⭐ SECRET
You have mental quickness but a changeable temperament, which renders you slightly unreliable, except in great emergencies.

BORN ON THIS DAY
- **Michael Jordan** basketball player
- **Ed Sheeran** singer
- **Joseph Gordon-Levitt** actor
- **Paris Hilton** DJ, actor
- **Billie Joe Armstrong** musician, singer

FRIENDS & FAMILY

_____

_____

_____

_____

_____

_____

_____

_____

_____

_____

_____

FEBRUARY 18

I do not think much of a man who is not wiser today than he was yesterday.
—Abraham Lincoln

BORN ON THIS DAY
★ **Toni Morrison**
author
★ **Audre Lorde**
poet
★ **Yoko Ono**
artist, singer
★ **Molly Ringwald**
actor
★ **Matt Dillon**
actor

FRIENDS & FAMILY

PERSONALITY
You share the characteristics of people born under Aquarius and Pisces. You are quite smart and sensitive and believe in living a full life, sometimes going to extremes to do so. Be careful to avoid extremes in what you do, because it is a great temptation for you to overindulge yourself in many ways, emotionally as well as physically and sensationally. There are times when you burn yourself out. You are stubborn and determined to get your way, and you will fly in the face of convention to get it. Of course, there is usually a price to be paid for such conduct, so decide before you act whether it is worth it.

LIFE PATH
Determination is one of your best gifts, and through your methodical, painstaking methods you can surmount great difficulties. You can be careful and thrifty, you are a good planner, and you have excellent executive ability. You are a general favorite among your friends and acquaintances.

DESTINY
Give yourself the opportunity to enjoy life. Express yourself when possible, letting your imagination, humor, and originality contribute to the sparkle of your personality. Make worthwhile use of opportunities for advancement that are available to you. As restraints, which have held you back, ease up, you may be able to do most of the things you want. Keep your eyes on and investigate commercial and business trends and currents. Also, develop your skill in one of the manual arts for your own pleasure.

KARMIC LESSON
If you are born this day, you sometimes have a temperament of a rather matter-of-fact order: straightforward, frank, and easy to understand. You know just what you want and move toward your goal with slow but unerring steps. However, you can't be hurried or scared into doing anything you don't want to. You have distinct intuitive ability, which stands out in rather sharp contrast to the rest of your nature. You are fond of building and planning and take an interest in all the "solid" things in life.

SECRET
You are an excellent judge of human nature and a lover of nostalgia. You should rise high in an unusual profession.

FEBRUARY 19

Every man has his secret sorrows which the world knows not; and often times we call a man cold when he is only sad.
—Henry Wadsworth Longfellow

BORN ON THIS DAY
- **Nicolaus Copernicus**
  scientist
- **Andrew Ross Sorkin**
  author
- **Cynthia Bailey**
  model
- **Benicio del Toro**
  actor
- **Smokey Robinson**
  singer

PERSONALITY
You have a flair for gathering people around you in a warm and congenial circle. They like your stories, your manners, and your charming way of making everyone feel at ease. Thus, you are popular with many folks from all walks of life. You enjoy wandering around in strange and unusual places, getting the thrill of having new experiences that eventually are added to the repertory of stories that you tell. All that is original has such an appeal for you that you are inclined to take chances, but you generally come out safe and sound because a lucky star is guiding you. The cinema has a very strong appeal for your imagination, and its colorfulness and storytelling thrill you.

LIFE PATH
Your inclination is toward mechanics or handicrafts. You are adventurous, curious, and reliable, as well as conscientious in all you do for others. You are fond of travel and a change of scene. You love with a wholeheartedness that will bring peace and comfort to many around you.

DESTINY
If you develop the talents you may have neglected, you will be rewarded. If you study subjects that have always interested you but have never received your thoughtful attention, the planet Mars will encourage and inspire your moving ahead. Set your sights high and achieve the outstanding results that can be satisfying to you and persons who love you. Whenever you are planning to take a long journey, arrange for travel reservations well in advance.

KARMIC LESSON
You are interested in many subjects and are very active mentally. You are fond of theater, music, and all that is beautiful and sublime in nature. You have many friends who admire your undoubted talents. You are keen to divine the motives of others, and this takes the form, in you, of almost telepathic power. You are sensitive and feel keenly the "atmosphere" of places you enter. You like a constant change of circumstances and environment. You should try to cultivate evenness of mind and temper, steadiness, firmness of will, reserve, and determination.

SECRET
You have graceful instincts with a pleasing personality, which should carry you far in an enterprise catering to the public's taste for color, style, and design.

FRIENDS & FAMILY

FEBRUARY 20

Snobbery is the pride of those who are not sure of their position.
—Berton Braley

BORN ON THIS DAY
★ **Rihanna Fenty**
singer

★ **Amy Tan**
author

★ **Sidney Poitier**
actor

★ **Cindy Crawford**
model

★ **Kurt Cobain**
singer

FRIENDS & FAMILY

PERSONALITY
There is an old saying in the Bible that "pride goeth before a fall." You should take this to heart, for you have a deeply moving sense of pride, will not give in to anyone whom you do not respect profoundly, and will endure no offensive remarks or insults from anyone. Such sensitivity is all right in a general way, but if you allow it to grow, it will master you instead of you mastering it and, in that way, become foolishness. Not everyone can be an executive; your best role is that of the clever collaborator or worker who translates the orders into action. That position is as necessary to winning the battle as that of the general; never forget it. You are capable of very hard work, thoughtful concentration, and brilliant strategy.

LIFE PATH
You lose control of your emotions quickly and easily and act hastily when excited, but your better judgment soon asserts itself, and you hasten to make such amends as the occasion calls for. Your passions are deep, and you love or hate with intensity. You have a great deal of dignity, and you love to let people know how you feel.

DESTINY
Praise and applause, which spur your ambition, may be plentiful. Accept favors, yet be ready to return them. Because Neptune rays predominate, there is a strong emphasis on your feelings and inspirations. Offer understanding, help, and guidance without waiting to be asked. Your philosophic outlook can play an important part in the pleasure and contentment available to you. Read about philosophy, browse the Internet, and study teachers who inspire you to increase your knowledge.

KARMIC LESSON
You are scrupulously careful in all your duties and in their fulfillment. If you take up anything, you are sure to carry it through to a successful conclusion. You have rather an optimistic nature, making light of trials and troubles that come to you, and in this way you earn the admiration of many who encounter you. You are very much drawn to flirtation and will probably have many romantic episodes in your younger life, but most of them will not prove serious.

SECRET
You have rather a dreamy nature given to speculative whims. If it is combined with industry and a practical turn, you will succeed in a big way.

FEBRUARY 21

He alone has lost the art to live who cannot win new friends.
—S. Weir Mitchell

✦ PERSONALITY
You love speed, admire active people, and want to be busily occupied at all times. It seems that there is a dynamo of energy or strength within you that drives you on to do things, go places, and command performances wherever you are. Nor do you find this life of activity tiring, for you like action so much that you can go on forever. Even if you are somewhat restricted by physical limitations, you will find a way to bring such motion and activity around you that it seems as though you are part and parcel thereof. You have a very nimble mind that impresses others, and you can express yourself with both acerbity and wit. Let the person who crosses your path be careful, because you can give a tongue lashing that is the height of sarcasm.

✦ LIFE PATH
You are studious, serious, and self-contained, a lover of good entertainment and of the finer things in life. You have excellent reasoning powers and are somewhat critical in your opinions. You care for people only when they are authentic and vigorous.

✦ DESTINY
Being able to rid yourself of some irritating influences that have bothered you will give you a new lease on life. Others who share your enthusiasm will be glad to have you lead them to fuller participation in worthwhile activities. Perhaps you will use some of your original ideas to inaugurate a new project in a club or other organization of which you are a member.

✦ KARMIC LESSON
Born this day, you are an odd mixture and difficult to describe. You are flighty at times, yet you have a firm foundation, and the light and frivolous do not attract you for any length of time. You are quick to see things and take in their good and bad qualities, and this makes you a good critic. If you fall in love, you are inclined to love to distraction and can express your emotions with a ardor that few others possess. You also demand intense love in return from the other person—no half-hearted affection will suit you.

✦ SECRET
You have administrative gifts. Also, you have a love of music, cooking, and the gentler arts, combined with a delight in distinctive home surroundings.

BORN ON THIS DAY
- **Elliot Page**
  actor
- **Nina Simone**
  singer
- **Scott and Mark Kelly**
  U.S. astronauts
- **Alan Rickman**
  actor
- **W.H. Auden**
  British-American poet

FRIENDS & FAMILY

FEBRUARY 22

We must learn to live together as brothers or perish together as fools.
—Martin Luther King, Jr.

BORN ON THIS DAY

- **George Washington**
  U.S. president
- **Julius Erving**
  basketball player
- **Frédéric Chopin**
  composer
- **Drew Barrymore**
  actor
- **Kyle MacLachlan**
  actor

FRIENDS & FAMILY

_____

_____

_____

_____

_____

_____

_____

_____

PERSONALITY
Those born on this date are good executives, wise planners, and clever managers. It is therefore your role in life to assume the power that is your cosmic heritage. You are deeply concerned with the welfare of other people, particularly the members of your own family, as well as animals. You may be involved in service work. While romantic love or obsessions may have a magnetic attraction for you in early youth, you might eventually settle down and surrender to a more contemplative life. You can express yourself well, and for this reason you have an advantage over others in participating in community life—you may be chosen to articulate plans and strategies.

LIFE PATH
Try to not look on the dark side of life and try to stop worrying about what may happen. You need to work on your anxieties, instill in your life more sunshine and cheeriness, and hold yourself in higher esteem. You are capable of greater deeds than you realize, if you will be surer of yourself.

DESTINY
Friction in family matters will be lessened if you work on your confidence. In your career, be willing to shift your direction on tasks that are not putting you ahead fast enough. Reexamine your ultimate goals. You will find yourself willing to work hard for success, but you also will discover joy in the increased activities and opportunities that are available.

KARMIC LESSON
You have a naturally self-sacrificing and generous nature, and you must take care that this is not abused and trampled upon by others, who are inclined to take advantage of your kindness, not understanding your motives. You have a firm, even, determined will, but this is not usually exhibited to outsiders, and they do not suspect how determined you are. You must learn to be more earnest in your talk, to emphasize what you say more, to think of what you say more, and to remember that the more feeling and emotion you place into your words, the more weight they will carry.

SECRET
Even though you are sometimes shy, you have the trait of leadership and the power to rise from any circumstances to a position of power and honor.

FEBRUARY 23

Nothing is impossible unless you think it is.
—Paramahansa Yogananda

⊛ PERSONALITY
You who were born on this date are endowed with innate artistic talent. Of course, in some cases this is evident from childhood; in others, it seems to remain latent until some self-study or analysis brings it out. In the last case, you have a deep appreciation of the arts even though you may not express your own talent in a productive or creative way. This suggests a way of life that should be very interesting, for, regardless of your status in life, you can lead a life of the mind that brings rich rewards. You are considerate of the feelings of others, and you have a knack for knowing what they like and dislike. Your feelings are easily hurt, a trait—or weakness—that you could discipline yourself to overcome.

⊛ LIFE PATH
You are lucky and could well be blessed with a good portion of wealth. You are farsighted, determined, and well balanced, and you are accepted by all who know you at your true worth. You have a keen sense of justice, and you love sharing good conversation with close friends above all else.

⊛ DESTINY
The true meaning of the word "luck" will become apparent to you if you show persistence. Take your good fortune in your stride. You can profitably invest in sound securities. Take time to plan and concentrate on financial protection for the future. Make use of any chances for travel or trying new social pastimes in order to learn, as well as to have fun. Through acquaintances, you may get the most worthwhile business leads.

⊛ KARMIC LESSON
You should be popular, as you have a temperament that would naturally make you so. You have a great deal of natural wit and ability and can entertain at a party well—if you make up your mind to do so. You will probably find that a person born in January, June, or October is best for you to have a relationship with. Learn to speak not only the truth but also the exact and whole truth; be frank and sincere, even if the truth hurts at times. You will find it pays in the long run.

⊛ SECRET
The subjects of this day are flirtatious, demanding the admiration of many, rather than the devotion of one.

BORN ON THIS DAY
- ★ **George Frideric Handel**
  composer
- ★ **W.E.B. Du Bois**
  historian, civil rights activist
- ★ **Howard Jones**
  singer
- ★ **Aziz Ansari**
  actor, comedian
- ★ **Andre Ward**
  boxer

FRIENDS & FAMILY

_____
_____
_____
_____
_____
_____
_____
_____
_____
_____
_____

FEBRUARY 24

He is happiest, be he king or peasant, who finds peace in his home.
—Johann Wolfgang von Goethe

BORN ON THIS DAY
- **Steve Jobs**
  business magnate
- **Judith Butler**
  gender theorist
- **Edward James Olmos**
  actor
- **Floyd Mayweather**
  boxer
- **Kristin Davis**
  actor

FRIENDS & FAMILY

PERSONALITY
Life beckons you with a welcoming finger to come and enjoy the finest things. You have a deep sense of appreciation of nature and her beautiful creations, which give you great inspiration. You can enjoy the quiet rural scenes, flowers, and country lanes. The other side of your nature, the realistic, practical side, makes it possible for you to take care of life's material requirements. However, you do not need a palace to be happy or status labels and fancy cars to assume your proper place in the world. You have an inner life that is far superior to the hustle and bustle of this noisy world. You understand life as it really is, and your understanding of the afterlife makes you a true philosopher.

LIFE PATH
Unite yourself with a person of a strong, self-assertive nature. You are mostly sweet-tempered, kindly, and acquiescent; you need the more robust and go-getter type to round out your life. You enjoy being surrounded with beauty and quiet.

DESTINY
Your past kindnesses will always be rewarded. Your problems will never seem overwhelming, and you will approach them cheerfully, with determination. Your sincerity not only attracts but also keeps friends. By carefully budgeting your expenses, you can usually improve your economic standing. Beware of large expenditures for amusements. You can enjoy simple, inexpensive pleasures just as much as you like those that require that you spend large sums of money.

KARMIC LESSON
You have remarkable creative ability and could make a name for yourself as a writer or in publishing. You are naturally humorous, and this is the form your writing might take, if you look to it as a living. You have dramatic ability also and might make a success performing. Your popularity is great and easily assumed by you. You are loyal and sincere in your friendships and never suspect duplicity in others until too late.

SECRET
You have an interest in collecting books, coins, or curiosities and can become absorbed in historical affairs. You have little care for worldly success but more for artistic expression.

FEBRUARY 25

The farther backward you can look, the farther forward you are likely to see.
—*Winston Churchill*

BORN ON THIS DAY
- **George Harrison**
  singer
- **Pierre-Auguste Renoir**
  painter
- **Rashida Jones**
  actor
- **Chelsea Handler**
  comedian, TV host
- **Carrot Top**
  comedian

PERSONALITY
Because you are a very impressionable person, you immediately become aware of the subtlest events taking place and of the motives that make people act the way they do. Natural sympathy for your fellow human beings moves you to do whatever you can to alleviate suffering. This trait is rather exaggerated in your makeup, and you should guard yourself against being too self-sacrificing. Your sensitivity makes you an excellent judge of people, and thus your reactions and opinions are very keen. You are an amateur psychologist with the latent ability to become a superb professional. Since you have a strong imagination, you could be successful in one of the arts.

LIFE PATH
Quickness of perception is a gift possessed by you in no ordinary degree. You should use it intelligently and to the fullest extent. Coupled with this gift is vividness of memory. Your first impressions of people are best, and you might commit to a partner after a very brief courtship.

DESTINY
Let calmness be your watchword. As attractive as your joviality and exuberance sometimes are for cheering up other people, they must be curbed on certain occasions. Also, when your associates are faced with serious problems, they may be offended if you give the impression that you feel sorry for them. Continue to be optimistic and caring. Success will mark your efforts if you are willing to devote extra time to it.

KARMIC LESSON
Born on this day, you are probably fond of society and delight in going out a great deal. You are a good guest and participant and can feel at home in nearly any kind of social gathering. You are good-tempered and like to have a good time. You are also naturally of a romantic temperament, and you love the ideal and the aesthetic. Nothing else satisfies you. You want the best or nothing at all! You could learn to cultivate a little more practicality.

SECRET
There is a daring, fearless pioneer spirit in you; you may shun domestic careers for unusual, atypical exploits.

FRIENDS & FAMILY

FEBRUARY 26

Every day the world shows you your state of mind.
—Robert Holden

BORN ON THIS DAY
- **Victor Hugo**
  author
- **Johnny Cash**
  singer
- **Jackie Gleason**
  actor
- **Erykah Badu**
  singer
- **Buffalo Bill**
  showman

FRIENDS & FAMILY

_____
_____
_____
_____
_____
_____
_____
_____

PERSONALITY
You are very selective about the people you care to have as friends or associates. Most likely you see the faults in others, and they must reveal their good qualities to you before you will accept them socially or in business. You like to have things your own way, and even when you make purchases, you insist on being waited on by someone who shows you proper courtesy and understanding. Although you possess a certain amount of savoir faire, you are also inclined to be naturally sensitive. That is, your nature is to be quiet and retiring, but you have learned to put on a surface appearance or protective shell in order to get along in a world that is occupied by so many extroverts. The real you that you reveal to your true friends is an enchanting person, indeed.

LIFE PATH
Timidity and oversensitivity are your two quirks. These you should try to overcome, for you are intellectual, and when you forget yourself, you are most entertaining and attractive. You are slow in drawing conclusions but more accurate in those conclusions than most. You care a great deal for attentions shown you.

DESTINY
Congeniality and social life are important to you. If you develop better self-esteem, you will be able to make many friends in your life that can be of assistance to you in your work. There are many bursts of advancement in your career or in a business of your own. If you have set ideas about certain subjects, do not be afraid to change them in order to keep up with the times. Take an open-minded view on any controversial issue.

KARMIC LESSON
You take a deep interest in all that happens around you. You are intuitive and quick to grasp a situation. You know how to make a point but talk little and can keep a quiet reserve on your own affairs and on those of others, too. You have an empathetic character. You are a lover of the outdoors; the grand and the sublime in nature haunt you. You are naturally loving, and you are strong in your affections. You are most happy in a quiet place, and you should try not to change this side of your nature too much.

SECRET
You have a mediumistic power with a feeling for the occult. You should guard against obsessive absorption in these affairs—protect yourself, as you feel others' pain deeply.

FEBRUARY 27

There is nothing holier in this life of ours than the first consciousness of love.
—Henry Wadsworth Longfellow

BORN ON THIS DAY

★ **Henry Wadsworth Longfellow**
author

★ **Elizabeth Taylor**
actor

★ **John Steinbeck**
author

★ **Josh Groban**
singer

★ **Chelsea Clinton**
global health advocate

PERSONALITY
You have the power within you to sculpt success out of the molding clay of life. Like an artist or sculptor who is planning a statue, you look at the raw material of existence, plan what you intend to make of it, and then go ahead with willpower and determination to fashion a work of art for yourself. In your life, you will have a large variety of experiences, each of which will teach you something that will prove valuable to you. When you have mastered your own philosophy of life, you will be a truly mature and intelligent person, one who is well worth knowing. Your ability to look ahead and your stamina for sticking to your own program are very admirable qualities.

LIFE PATH
Notwithstanding your restlessness, you are methodical in your habits and acquisitive in no small degree. Cultivate this habit and you will never need help from the outside. You are fond of responsibility and like to be a leader. You are devoted to your family and receive a large measure of love in return.

DESTINY
You will have many chances to assert your will and be the master of difficult situations. Have no qualms about giving orders or suggestions to people who may have previously told you what to do. Happiness will come from an entertaining social life. Do not forget your responsibilities, however, when you are searching for the fun to which you are entitled.

KARMIC LESSON
Born on this day, a strong imagination is one of your most characteristic features. You are fond of the artistic and exalted, and the commonplace cannot be made attractive to you. You have the distinct ability to diversify and should achieve success using that skill. You also have technical ability. You do not like monotony of any kind and are consequently inclined to speculate and make your living in a manner more to your taste, even if that living is more uncertain and on a smaller scale than it otherwise would be.

SECRET
You take keen pleasure in water and so may like to live near a seaport or derive a livelihood from such a place.

FRIENDS & FAMILY

FEBRUARY 28

I never found the companion that was so companionable as solitude.
—Henry David Thoreau

BORN ON THIS DAY
- **Frank Gehry**
  architect
- **Bernadette Peters**
  actor, singer
- **Paul Krugman**
  economist
- **Gilbert Gottfried**
  comedian
- **Tasha Smith**
  actor

FRIENDS & FAMILY

PERSONALITY
Your enjoyment of music, art, and explorations of the virtual universe gives you a great deal of pleasure, many hours of happy amusement, and a well-rounded outlook on life. You are a socially minded person, with a mature, adult outlook, respect for your fellow human beings, and a joyous attitude toward your loved ones. Because you are rational and generous, you are never a burden to anyone, and you never ask for much or interfere in the lives of other people. This makes you admired and a great asset at all social gatherings. People know they can depend on you to be interesting, stimulating, and uncritical.

LIFE PATH
Your interest in spirituality and philosophy is very remarkable, not only for the good you may do but also as abstract questions and answers. You like to follow the advanced thought of others, although your analytical mind will not allow you to accept any doctrine without a thorough understanding of it. You are fond of travel and discovering treasures.

DESTINY
No dullness is in store for you in this life. You will be kept busy both while you are working and while you are playing. It would be to your advantage if you could combine your occupational duties with your amusements and hobbies. Find hobbies that are lively but at the same time do not require unending patience. A few good friends will be more useful than countless acquaintances.

KARMIC LESSON
You are very fond of reading and like nothing better than to get a good book and be left alone until you have had a chance to finish it. You are mostly quiet and reserved and not at all the kind of person, when you are out, who insists on "holding the floor" and taking up the attention of everybody. At the same time, you have very strong and decided opinions, and you are not easily moved from these. On the whole, you are a desirable companion, lover, and friend.

SECRET
You may show a tendency toward melancholy and an underestimation of yourself. You should cultivate more courage and confidence.

FEBRUARY 29

The world is blessed most by men who do things, and not by those who merely talk about them.
—James Oliver

BORN ON THIS DAY
- **Tony Robbins** — motivational speaker
- **Dinah Shore** — actor
- **Jimmy Dorsey** — big band leader
- **Ja Rule** — rapper
- **Antonio Sabàto, Jr.** — model, actor

PERSONALITY
Whenever there is an emergency in which the people you know require help, they are sure to call upon you. Of course, you always respond willingly because you are a generous person, and you can be depended upon for assistance. You like to regulate your life according to a rational schedule, and because you generally have the willpower to stick to it, you are always up to date on your work. From day to day, you like to prepare the routine of your tasks, finish each in turn, and then feel free to do whatever takes your fancy. You are very sensible in your outlook on life, and if you have been criticized for lacking spontaneity, you have other qualities that more than compensate for it.

LIFE PATH
You are very considerate of others, gentle, and sympathetic. You can be easily influenced and like a change of environment, readily adapting yourself to circumstances. You like to read and are a fluent talker about subjects with which you are familiar. You like personal attention, and you love with strength and constancy.

DESTINY
You do not depend on luck, and therefore you will usually take the steps necessary to bring you closer to your goals. It is good to keep close tabs on your budget; do not overspend. Establish close friendships with kindred spirits. One of them may be of great assistance to you in your work or in the acquisition of valuable property, and all of them will add to your happiness and pleasure in a social way.

KARMIC LESSON
You have a friendly personality, being possessed of great charm and personal magnetism. You should make a career in communications and could be a fine mimic. You have a good deal of self-confidence and self-assurance and would make a natural leader in any movement you might undertake. You have a strong character, though there are weak spots in the armor, such as seeing the weak points in other people's characters. Make up your mind to see the best in everything, and only the best, and you should develop lasting relationships.

SECRET
You are curiously marked by conflicting tendencies to be controlling and adaptable at the same time. You should be guided early in life toward a specific goal.

FRIENDS & FAMILY

MARCH 1

The victory of success is half won when one gains the habit of work.
—Sarah Knowles Bolton

BORN ON THIS DAY
- **Javier Bardem**
  actor
- **Justin Bieber**
  singer
- **Ron Howard**
  actor, director
- **Kesha**
  singer
- **Harry Belafonte**
  singer

PERSONALITY
A passion for creativity seems to be part of your soul. You respond to rhythm with instantaneous and lilting joy, while your senses seem to sway in happiness with unusual works of art or a song to which you are listening. You can express yourself well and make quite a convincing argument. Whether in public or private, you know how to get your way by being persuasive at the right time. There is a knack to the use of words, and you have it. You should certainly try to express yourself in some artistic way, because this birth date inevitably endows you with talent.

LIFE PATH
Your artistic instincts are strong and worthy of development. You believe in yourself and in your ability and have sufficient perseverance to bring you success. You are honest, frank, good-natured, constant in your affections, and capable of great love.

DESTINY
Improved financial conditions over time bring a change in your environment and the opportunity to meet new and interesting people. Let the adventurous side of your nature assert itself. Inhibitions make not only you but also those around you feel uncomfortable. Relax and enjoy life. Then you will be able to take full advantage of the exciting chapters and shifts of fortune that are in store for you.

KARMIC LESSON
You are firm, determined, and practical and have a dogged, rugged nature that fits you for opposition and the bitter battles of life. You may be afraid, but you can weather anything, no matter how strong the opposition is. You are artistic but at the same time well suited to business life and should make a great success in this direction. You could manage a large corporation with skill and competence. At the same time, you are not so obstinate as to be blind to the impossible. You are strong, loyal, and true in your affections but not always demonstrative. One can always depend on you as a true friend.

SECRET
You have an inventive mind that is particularly suited to working out mechanical problems that baffle others.

FRIENDS & FAMILY

MARCH 2

A man's wisdom is his best friend; folly his worst enemy.
—William Temple

BORN ON THIS DAY
- **Desi Arnaz**
  actor
- **Jon Bon Jovi**
  singer
- **Dr. Seuss**
  author
- **Ben Roethlisberger**
  football player
- **Karen Carpenter**
  singer

FRIENDS & FAMILY

PERSONALITY
You have remarkable control over your emotions as far as showing them is concerned. However, what you think in the silent recesses of your mind is quite another story. When you are alone and being honest with yourself, you can be inclined to be more or less filled with self-pity and to dramatize yourself and whatever romantic or emotional situation you are in. It would be much better for you to devote your energy to getting what you want in life and putting up a strong front than to feel sorry for yourself. When you are with other people, you put on a pretty good show, for then you are really more at ease and generally manage to have a good time.

LIFE PATH
Be neither restless nor skeptical. Those who are sincere, earnest, and patient in whatever they undertake invariably succeed. You have strong psychic powers and great self-control and are a quick learner. You prefer the company of those who agree with you politically, but you are tolerant and understanding of those who do not.

DESTINY
An executive position either in your work or in an organization in which you have membership will give you the opportunity to display your managerial ability. This responsibility may at some point come to you as a complete surprise, but have no fear. You will be able to handle the office admirably and win esteem and public applause. Conquer any anticipatory nervousness and assume new duties with confidence.

KARMIC LESSON
Born on this day, you are extremely adaptable to circumstances and can fit yourself into any position that offers itself. You are a natural diplomat: fond of intrigue, rather fond of finery and show, but not taken in by an imitation said to be the real thing. You are sometimes careful, even cheap, in money matters, but you might be a little more liberal and openhanded at times. You can be a strong friend or a bitter enemy. You are rather sarcastic, but you are kind when everything looks favorable to you. You have a strong personality and might become a leader in your field.

SECRET
You have a fondness for learning new skills, paying more attention to cultivation of mind and personality than to material success.

MARCH 3

Before anything else, preparation is the key to success. Concentrate all your thoughts upon the work at hand.
—Alexander Graham Bell

BORN ON THIS DAY
- **Alexander Graham Bell**
  inventor
- **Ronan Keating**
  singer
- **Perry Ellis**
  fashion designer
- **Jessica Biel**
  actor
- **Hershel Walker**
  football player

PERSONALITY
You have a lot of latent inventive genius in your makeup and could be quite a success at any kind of work requiring mechanical aptitude. Perhaps you express this in the way you do your work, or run your home, but it must come out in some way that brings just compensation for the exercise of your ability. Your tastes are very individual, and you make no effort to hide your likes and dislikes. Whenever you are pleased, the world knows it, and when you dislike anything, you let everyone hear about it. You can acquire the success you wish for by combining your initiative with your social sense.

LIFE PATH
You are magnetic in your bearing. Be careful of this great gift, as it may lead you into paths that are better left untrodden. Your passions are deep-seated and overpowering, and your love is fervent and constant. You love music and love to share your favorite tunes and musicians.

DESTINY
At some point, a rejuvenated interest in an old subject may make success possible in a project that you thought was a failure. Although this may seem to be a life of ups and downs, your later years will yield satisfaction and accomplishment. Be patient and understanding even when annoyed by minor inconveniences. Pleasant relationships with new friends will always grow and prosper.

KARMIC LESSON
You have an ingenious, inventive turn of mind, which should stand you in good stead and, if applied in a practical manner, should bring you lasting financial results. You have a good, clear mind and great natural abilities. You are fond of mechanical devices and have always delighted in studying and experimenting with tech. You have a naturally good memory and an eye for detail. For this reason, you should become invaluable in certain areas. Your love nature is strong, and you demand much from others in your relationships; at the same time, you are intense and demonstrative. You have a strong will, ambition, and purpose.

SECRET
You have an inquisitive nature but are pleased to share worldly goods with loyal friends and your partner.

FRIENDS & FAMILY

MARCH 4

The cynic is the one who knows the price of everything and the value of nothing.
—Oscar Wilde

BORN ON THIS DAY
- **Antonio Vivaldi**
  composer
- **Catherine O'Hara**
  actor
- **Bobbi Kristina Brown**
  reality TV actor
- **Emilio Estefan Gómez**
  music producer
- **Patricia Heaton**
  actor

FRIENDS & FAMILY

PERSONALITY
You are quick on your feet, quick with your answers, and what might be called a speedy person in most respects. Because you abound in energy, you find life rather a strong stimulant, which gives you a big thrill. Even in adversity, you do not become disheartened. You examine the position you are in, and you think out what you should do to make the best of things. This rational way of thinking certainly saves you many unnecessary aches and pains and also makes you a very congenial person to be with. People like you for your good common sense and your optimistic point of view. By following the dictates of your mind and the wisdom from your experience, you can hardly make a mistake in life.

LIFE PATH
Be bold, diligent, and faithful. Wavering and vacillating conduct will never inspire the world or make a conqueror of you. You are a shrewd judge of people and seldom make mistakes in your estimates. You have a winning personality but are also somewhat given to taking on too many commitments.

DESTINY
The opinion others have of your ability will be increased the better they know you. This is due to your consistent reliability and trustworthiness. Growing appreciation will always meet your efforts. Be true to your ideals, and you will be ready to receive the blessings of prosperity that will come your way. Trust your friends but retain your natural skepticism of insincere people.

KARMIC LESSON
You are an idealist, fond of all the good things of life, as well as of good food, music, and museums. You are inclined to lack the aggressive quality that makes for super financial success, and you lack a certain amount of self-esteem, which you should have, since you have good qualities, and others should be made to appreciate them. You would probably be more successful if you associated in business with someone of an opposite nature to yourself—one with a dogged and determined character. Your own nature is to act rather than to talk, to say little, and then suddenly to jump, like a cat upon a mouse. Learn to cultivate your will and self-reliance, and there is no limit to what you can accomplish.

SECRET
You are affable and kindhearted but stand firm in demands of duty. You would make an excellent assistant or manager in charge of workers and details.

MARCH 5

Sail away from the safe harbor. Catch the trade winds in your sails. Explore. Dream. Discover.
—Mark Twain

PERSONALITY
The aura of success seems to surround you, and you enjoy it very much. Your motto is that nothing succeeds like success, so you try to earn money, live well, and make a wonderful impression on people. Your efforts are rewarded in time because you are sincere, hardworking, and clever. You like to plan your life, not to live it haphazardly. In this way, you are able to advance, save money, and rise in your station in life from year to year. However, you are not so foolish as to devote every minute of your time to running your home or business with the maximum efficiency. You also like to go out and have some fun occasionally, and you are known for being a good sport.

LIFE PATH
The most important months of the year for you are May and June, and it would be well to begin all great undertakings during that period. You care a great deal for show and fine effects. Farsighted, you can be a good planner, an ardent lover, and a faithful friend.

DESTINY
Your work must receive your earnest and attentive effort, as your birthday is under the influence of the Saturn rays. Never slight details. The castles you build in the air can become actualities if you are determined in your work. The benefits of a club or organization that you support can be more extensive than the social pleasures that are provided by membership.

KARMIC LESSON
You are one of those happy-go-lucky mortals who take life as they find it and do not think about it and its problems and mysteries any more than you have to. You are self-confident, and this is legitimate in your case, as it comes from experience. Owing to your disposition, you are a little too inclined to make friends without discernment. Learn to be more self-contained and reserved in your friendships. You will probably find that the person most suited to you is born in July, September, or October.

SECRET
You can be slightly obsessed by metaphysics and supernatural subjects. You should cultivate tolerance for nonbelievers. When you apply yourself to practical problems, you have a sharp mind.

BORN ON THIS DAY
- ★ **Kevin Connolly** — actor
- ★ **Michael Irvin** — football player
- ★ **Lynn Margulis** — scientist
- ★ **Eva Mendes** — actor
- ★ **Penn Jillette** — magician

FRIENDS & FAMILY

MARCH 6

The true work of art is but a shadow of the divine perfection.
—Michelangelo

BORN ON THIS DAY

- **Michelangelo**
  artist
- **Shaquille O'Neal**
  basketball player
- **Elizabeth Barrett Browning**
  poet
- **Alan Greenspan**
  economist
- **Gabriel García Márquez**
  author

FRIENDS & FAMILY

PERSONALITY

Very deep understanding and tenderness make you a rather remarkable personality. You might go on for many years about your affairs, large or small, in a limited group. But the effect of your sympathetic charm will spread until it includes a large circle of admirers, although they may admire you only from afar. There is nothing shallow about you. Your feelings are deep, and you are considerate to the extreme. To you every human being is an individual worthy of your best thought and feeling. Those born on your birthday often have a psychic sense that acts as a guide throughout life. This fine instinct for prediction will probably see you through many trying circumstances. There is an artistic side to your nature that makes you appreciate the finer things of life and gives you much pleasure and refinement.

LIFE PATH

Your will is strong but should be kept under better control. You have a fair amount of self-reliance and an analytical mind. You are fond of parties and excitement and like to make new acquaintances. You should not marry hastily, for your disposition is such that if you do not secure a partner who is perfectly compatible, you will be very restless.

DESTINY

Vivacious activity will be your path, for your birthday is under the influence of beneficent Mercury. Pursuits for you will include musical festivities, sports, travel, and interesting debates. Business matters will usually be transacted in a congenial atmosphere and with profit to you. Always attend to personal correspondence quickly and clearly.

KARMIC LESSON

You should have exceptional judgment, born on this day, and clear vision, enabling you to see things as they are and in their true perspective. You have ability as a storyteller. You are probably self-reliant and have a pretty good reason for everything you do. You have no use for intuition alone. You also demand logical reasons for all that you endeavor to do. Learn to understand the human mind and its operations and put what you learn into words for others to follow.

SECRET

You gravitate naturally to working out and to yoga and would do well in such pursuits. You may be easily distracted.

MARCH 7

The secret of happiness is not in doing what one likes, but in liking what one does.
—James M. Barrie

PERSONALITY
You are distinguished by a fine sense of proportion that makes you see things in their true light. Because you have an inventive turn of mind, you can discover new ways of doing things that prove to be efficient and worthwhile. You like to use the so-called scientific way of living; that is, you observe, try, and then repeat experiments in living until you determine the best course for you to follow. Your flair for learning through analogies makes you a careful observer of life and nature, and through your observations, you eventually develop a deep philosophy of life.

LIFE PATH
You are a careful, methodical person but tend to be a perfectionist. You plan things that you do not even attempt because of your extreme caution. Sometimes you procrastinate. You are very tenderhearted and will often allow others to impose upon you rather than hurt their feelings.

DESTINY
There may be many occasions when you will be undecided. In such cases, do not act impulsively, but take time to study the situation from every angle. Seek the counsel of those who have had more experience than you. Search for worthwhile as well as pleasant recreational activities. Express freely the affection you feel for those with whom you are on friendly terms.

KARMIC LESSON
You have a distinct talent for music and may be able to sing or play one or more musical instruments. At the same time, you have good scientific attainments, if cultivated, but these run to the practical and commercial side of the sciences. You will apply what you know to turn it to financial success. You are ambitious and you desire to rise above the ordinary. Nothing is more repellant to you than the thought of a mediocre life. If you are to attain this objective, you must learn how to use and concentrate your mind—since only in this way is success attained.

SECRET
You have a nature given to anxiety through a fear of not being able to fulfill the expectations of others. Swifter actions and decisions are needed for success.

BORN ON THIS DAY
- **Amanda Gorman** — poet
- **Rachel Weisz** — actor
- **Piet Mondrian** — painter
- **Bryan Cranston** — actor
- **Wanda Sykes** — comedian, actor

FRIENDS & FAMILY

MARCH 8

To be seventy years young is sometimes far more cheerful and hopeful than to be forty years old.
—Oliver Wendell Holmes

BORN ON THIS DAY

★ **Lynn Redgrave**
actor

★ **Hines Ward**
football player

★ **Randy Meisner**
singer

★ **Freddie Prinze, Jr.**
actor

★ **James van der Beek**
actor

FRIENDS & FAMILY

PERSONALITY
You have a flair for politics that you may express either by actual engagement in it or by the clever way that you handle your relations with other people. No slight is meant by this description of your character; in fact, it takes real intelligence to conduct one's affairs the way you do. You plan campaigns, develop friendships, and direct your energies in such a way that you make everything you do significant. Each step you take is deliberately planned to be a step ahead. If you see no significance or importance in a relationship or an act, you simply disregard it. This is conversation in the best sense of the word, and you are a master of it. Life will be a series of successes to you because you will mold it to be so.

LIFE PATH
You are fond of social media and popular culture and have considerable ability as a critic in both of these fields. You are scrupulously honest, frank, and straightforward and care a great deal for popularity. Your love is expressive, true, and steadfast.

DESTINY
Your poise will carry you through situations that could prove difficult for a less confident person. Depend on your reasoning power in solving the problems that will be manifest during the year. Do not be afraid of the new ways of doing things that will occur to you under the Uranus rays of your birthday. Your judgment is usually good, and you should act on it.

KARMIC LESSON
Strong in your beliefs, you are yet able to change them if sufficiently strong facts are presented to shake you in your present convictions. You are interested in a wide range of topics. You have strong convictions and the courage and consistency to stand by them. You are interested in all people alike—no matter what their religious, political, or social creed may be. Live up to your ideals. Live up to the best in yourself, and all good things will come to you. You will succeed if you keep at it.

SECRET
You have a concern for money matters and a strong desire to provide for old age. You are an economical house and business manager.

MARCH 9

Short absence quickens love; long absence kills it.
—Honoré Gabriel Riqueti, comte de Mirabeau

BORN ON THIS DAY

★ **Yuri Gagarin**
cosmonaut

★ **Bobby Fischer**
world chess champion

★ **Brian Bosworth**
football player

★ **Walter Mercado**
astrologer

★ **Kato Kaelin**
actor

PERSONALITY
You can put on a remarkable show as though you were a professional actor. To get your way, or to make an impression you want to make, you can act clever, naive, sophisticated, or coy. You know what people like at first sight, and if you want to please them for purposes of your own, you know just exactly how to behave. Natural magnetism makes you draw others to you, and you are generally surrounded by many friends. As a matter of fact, the facility with which you attract others may become a drawback, because you like the company of other people, and you are inclined to waste time in congenial social life, time that could be spent in more creative activities than having a good time. By gathering your forces and focusing them on a single pursuit, you will gain many advantages.

LIFE PATH
You are spiritual in your nature, and refinement and culture mean much to you. While you dearly love your homelife, you have many outside interests of the higher type. You plan carefully, execute intelligently, and can always interest others in any project in which you are interested.

DESTINY
Keep your hands busy, transforming illusive ideas into interesting and useful results. This purposeful activity will bring financial gain as well as social pleasures. The influence of Mars rays on your birthday will give you the encouragement to continue your quest for success.

KARMIC LESSON
Fond of romance, travel, and adventure, you have an active, lively disposition. You are of a practical, skeptical turn of mind, quick to see an opportunity and quick to seize it. You are apt to work too long, until exhausted, and then drop from overwork. Learn to cultivate and conserve your forces. You have a large stock of vitality, but there is no reason why you should abuse this "gift of the Goddess" and wear yourself out prematurely.

SECRET
You have a love of food, cooking, wellness, and the cultivation of natural plants. Also, you have a romantic nature and are devoted, with a fervent gratitude for life.

FRIENDS & FAMILY

MARCH 10

Affection can withstand very severe storms of vigor, but not a long polar frost of indifference.
—Sir Walter Scott

BORN ON THIS DAY

★ **Jon Hamm**
actor

★ **Chuck Norris**
actor

★ **Carrie Underwood**
singer

★ **Robin Thicke**
singer

★ **Biz Markie**
rapper

★ **Nobu Matsuhisa**
celebrity chef

FRIENDS & FAMILY

PERSONALITY
You are the kind of person who has a strong value system. In your dealings with other people, you are always respectful of their feelings. As a result, you are known for your own sincerity, and people treat you with the consideration that is your due. You never allow the glitter of passing fancies to lead you too far astray, for you believe only in permanent principles. You want your friendships as well as material possessions to have a lasting quality. Suitors find you attractive because of your serious outlook on life, which gives the impression of intelligence and sincerity rather than frivolity or flirtatiousness. As your mental qualities are outstanding, you are sure to get ahead in life. Your knowledge that glamour is only fleeting will always help you to maintain a very sensible balance in the way you live.

LIFE PATH
You have quick perception and a keen understanding of human nature and are led by suggestion rather than positive force. People like you and trust you, and the friendship and love you inspire are lasting. You have no real enemies. You will probably travel a great deal, and it will be with an intelligent understanding of what you see and hear.

DESTINY
Researching your ancestry will be important and enjoyable to you. You may be torn between desires to save and to spend money. Make compromises by investing in worthwhile purchases and by eliminating expensive frivolities from your budget. You may also be able to give friends advice about money matters. Read books on personal growth and inspiration.

KARMIC LESSON
Born on this day, you have a strong, magnetic, forceful character, inclined to be dogmatic at times and determined that others shall see things from your viewpoint. For you, there is only one right way of doing anything—yours. In this you are right, to a certain extent, as you have good judgment and clear vision. Learn to be a little more charitable in your opinions and views of others. You are inventive and ingenious and have a taste for mechanical things of all kinds.

SECRET
You are sometimes inclined to be a bit careless in talk and habits. You should learn to control this.

MARCH 11

One can never consent to creep when one feels an impulse to soar.
—Helen Keller

BORN ON THIS DAY
- **Antonin Scalia**
  U.S. Supreme Court justice
- **Douglas Adams**
  author
- **Johnny Knoxville**
  actor
- **John Barrowman**
  actor
- **Bobby McFerrin**
  singer

PERSONALITY
Few people enjoy living as much as you do, because you are imbued with the spirit of fun and adventure. You like to think of life as a glorious game, which you play fair and square. Because you have a talent for putting your imaginative thoughts into expressive language, you speak well and make a good impression. By extending this ability in public performances, you might succeed as a professional entertainer or public speaker. Do not neglect this latent ability, as it might well prove a means of livelihood for you. In any group, you are capable of attracting attention by your powers of magnetism. However, you are inclined to mercurial changes or attitude, against which you should take precautions. Ever changeful is a worthwhile policy only if the change means improvement; if it refers merely to temperament, learn to control it.

LIFE PATH
You are an ardent lover and a bitter enemy. No one will be indifferent toward you, for you will be either well-liked or thoroughly disliked. Adversity stimulates you to further and more earnest endeavor instead of crushing and disheartening you.

DESTINY
There are so many opportunities for impressive self-expression for you during this life that you are going to have a difficult time deciding which activity to emphasize first. Do not get restless. You will have ample time for many thrilling experiences. You can develop a balanced attitude that will ensure consistent progress.

KARMIC LESSON
You are industrious, and not many hours find you idle or unemployed. You love to study humanity, and to outline, in your own mind, the characters of others—guessing at the motives that prompt certain actions. You have great research ability and should be able to tell engaging stories and also write them, if you try. You have a good sense of humor and are keen in your appreciation of all that pertains to wit and satire. You can be studious and fond of forensic and philosophical studies and pastimes. You are happy at home and do not like being disturbed. A fine future should be yours, as you have great natural abilities.

SECRET
You have a boundless ambition with a rare ability to hold eagerness in check. You may consider marriage a restraint and prefer career pursuits.

FRIENDS & FAMILY

MARCH 12

There is no better compass than compassion.
—Amanda Gorman

BORN ON THIS DAY
- **Jack Kerouac**
  author, poet
- **James Taylor**
  singer
- **Edward Albee**
  playwright
- **Liza Minnelli**
  singer
- **Dont'a Hightower**
  football player

FRIENDS & FAMILY

PERSONALITY
You should feel an innate call to one of the arts as the expression of your highest talent. If you have had no yearning toward self-expression in painting, writing, drama, or dance, you have not yet discovered yourself. By probing your reactions to the various types of artistic expression, you will most likely find some hidden desire to excel in one of them. Once you have found such a desire, do all you can to fulfill it, for your birthday signifies the free expression of latent ability. You are very fond of the people you have chosen as your friends and are very loyal to the members of your family. Probably your most used phrase is "let me do it," because you are so helpful by nature. People like you for the way you cooperate and for your gentle understanding.

LIFE PATH
Your intuitive judgment is remarkably accurate and is a much better guide than your carefully drawn conclusions and studied decisions. In love, you are impulsive, wholehearted, and constant. You have the ability to form friendships with a wide variety of people.

DESTINY
You are justified in taking a conservative attitude toward money. Never listen to smooth-talking promoters. Be content with sound conservative investments and association with friends who are tried and true. You can protect your family, too, by this attitude of caution. Do not be afraid of being rejected as a skeptic. Rather, people will look up to you for your wisdom and judgment.

KARMIC LESSON
Clever and ingenious, you have a naturally kind nature, a well-stocked mind, and a sly sense of humor. You are always ready to see the quirky side of everything. You are popular with most people you meet, and you know how to find the good in them. For this reason, you have a great many friends. You are cheery and whole-souled. You are inclined to look lightly on things and never dwell too long on the serious side. Cultivate this in yourself, and you will be the better for it.

SECRET
You are a stickler for your own rights, to the point of being relentless. You can be a hard creditor but a faithful friend.

MARCH 13

The worst sorrows in life are not in its losses and misfortunes, but its fears.
—A.C. Benson

BORN ON THIS DAY

- **Common**
  actor and rapper
- **Neil Sedaka**
  singer
- **L. Ron Hubbard**
  author
- **William H. Macy**
  actor
- **Charo**
  guitarist, performer

PERSONALITY
When you face your daily tasks and chores, you do so with the idea that this is a job that must be done, and you know the only way to finish is by doing one thing at a time until the routine is mastered. Although you have a generally placid disposition, you are given to occasional moods of melancholy. This is accounted for by the fact that you are a very sensitive person, and you take slights too much to heart. By training yourself not to pay so much attention to what other people say, and developing your own self-reliance, you can master this sensitivity and become a more extroverted personality. Despite these moods, however, you have a lot of determination, which shows itself in the way you work. You have an infinite capacity for getting things done, and in the right way.

LIFE PATH
You are too much inclined toward fretting over past failures or misfortunes. Let your ambition carry you forward to such a degree of success that you will forget all that was unpleasant in the past. You are capable of great things if your ability is properly applied. You are rather secretive and do not form friendships quickly, but your friends are staunch and true and will make great sacrifices on your behalf.

DESTINY
Do not be reluctant to spend money on the things you want. Excessive thrift is as foolish as extravagance and often just as unwise. Expect help from people who are close to you, but the suggestions of comparative strangers may bear looking into on occasion. Do not trust just anyone with your valuable papers or possessions. You have reason to be proud of your business acumen.

KARMIC LESSON
You are interested in science and politics, and have a good grasp of such subjects, but also a love of the romantic, which is, at times, inclined to tinge your speculations and ideas. A steady worker, you are naturally quiet and reserved. You are also gifted and talented in the art of entertaining and make a charming host but do not have much interest in large gatherings. You need a lot of love and sympathy to be really happy.

SECRET
You have an uncompromising streak and are sometimes more interested in creative pursuits than in commerce. You have spot-on perceptions and a capacity for endless work.

FRIENDS & FAMILY

MARCH 14

To love and win is the best thing. To love and lose, the next best.
—William Makepeace Thackeray

BORN ON THIS DAY
- **Albert Einstein**
  physicist
- **Quincy Jones**
  music producer
- **Billy Crystal**
  actor, comedian
- **Simone Biles**
  gymnast
- **Jamie Bell**
  actor

FRIENDS & FAMILY

PERSONALITY
Because you have an excellent business sense, you can make a success of anything you try along commercial lines. Even if you confine your business dealings to working from home, you know how to do so efficiently and cleverly. It seems as though you have a wonderful gift for finding bargains, and you could easily make a go of buying and selling if you were interested in starting a business. You have a great capacity for work, and you never complain as long as you feel that you are accomplishing something worthwhile. Like most people born on this day, you feel the need for love. You can't be truly happy unless you feel that your romance is growing from day to day. Although you would probably never go out of your way to look for it, a mild flirtation will always amuse you.

LIFE PATH
Energetic and ambitious, you are a quick thinker and should achieve more than a moderate degree of success in anything you undertake. You are fond of social media, a good conversationalist, and quick at repartee. You care a great deal for your home but also derive a great deal of enjoyment from the evenings spent in pursuit of pleasure outside.

DESTINY
You will have more than your share of enthusiasm and ambition during your life. However, guard against momentary periods of stalled energy and lack of self-confidence. Do not try to conceal the sympathy you feel for friends or relatives who are unhappy. You will enjoy the close companionship of a few intimates, and you will find that a harmonious domestic life can be a real blessing.

KARMIC LESSON
You have distinct talent for performing and should be able to document with video and still photos. You might also be able to compose—when the mood is on you. You are subject to dreams of all kinds and like to experiment in this direction. You do not pursue metaphysical things as keenly as many others do and are not the woo-woo sort—the kind of person who needs to consult psychics for major decisions. You can be inclined to be skeptical and domineering in your views. Try to place yourself in other people's shoes and see through their eyes. If you did this, you would have more appreciation for the cares of others.

SECRET
You have times when you really need to be lazy, with an interest in luxurious surroundings. You enjoy idleness and silly movies.

MARCH 15

Let us endeavor so to live that when we come to die even the undertaker will be sorry.
—Mark Twain

BORN ON THIS DAY
- **Andrew Jackson**
  U.S. president
- **Ruth Bader Ginsburg**
  U.S. Supreme Court justice
- **Lynda La Plante**
  author
- **Mike Tomlin**
  football coach
- **will.i.am**
  singer

PERSONALITY
As long as you live, you will enjoy a reputation for being astute, clever, perceptive, and intuitive. You really have remarkable powers of observation, and anyone who follows your advice can hardly go wrong. You seem to understand human nature so well that you can predict what people are going to do even before they have thought how they are going to act. This ability gives you power. Although you have a somewhat jealous disposition, you try not to show it. However, once you have chosen your love, you really are very possessive, and you want no one to share it with you. Your interests and hobbies increase from year to year, so that it might be said that you grow as you grow older.

LIFE PATH
You are modest and unassuming but possess a dynamic force that brings you success and enables you to assume a leading role. You enjoy the utmost confidence of all who know you, and you will love with a strength and sincerity that will never falter.

DESTINY
Always be prepared for swift turns of events under the quicksilver influence of the Mercury rays of your birthday. You will at some point have the chance to direct or carry out an important plan that has already been formulated. You may receive recognition for some work done in the past or have the opportunity to make an outstanding success of a new endeavor. Incidents that occur at social functions may have important bearing on your life.

KARMIC LESSON
You are not, in all probability, an over-thinker, but you have a mind that takes an interest in a wide range of subjects. You have a restless, active disposition and are ever on the move. You have good intuitions and a fine, active imagination—one that is inclined to run away with you at times. You should be able to excel in being a maker of crafts—particularly mixed media—and have marked imitative ability. Learn to relax and cultivate a more studious, patient nature.

SECRET
You have a tendency to cross a bridge long before you reach it. Save your energies, and don't give in to useless worry and anxiety.

FRIENDS & FAMILY

MARCH 16

A real friend is one who walks in when the rest of the world walks out.
—Walter Winchell

BORN ON THIS DAY

★ **James Madison**
U.S. president

★ **Jerry Lewis**
actor

★ **Chuck Woolery**
game show host

★ **Victor Garber**
actor

★ **Flavor Flav**
rapper

FRIENDS & FAMILY

PERSONALITY
Although you are capable of very deep emotions, you rarely show how much your feelings are moved. Under almost any circumstances, you make every effort to appear calm and unperturbed. This is a wise policy to follow, for the complexity of modern life does not allow other people much time to sympathize, no matter what one's feelings are. However, you are a very sympathetic person in regard to your own conduct, and you find it almost impossible to refuse to help a friend and often a stranger. You are ever ready with cash or time, to lend assistance, give advice, and do real hard work if necessary. You really should think a little more of yourself and less of others.

LIFE PATH
You have a blithe, cheerful manner that masks a seriousness of purpose of which few suspect you and only your most intimate friends know about. Whatever trouble you may have will never appear upon the surface. You do not care for show; you do many kind and charitable deeds that are never known.

DESTINY
You will probe problems deeply and work out happy solutions to difficult situations. Have faith in your abilities. Carry out sound ideas and carefully laid plans that can prove profitable. Heed your generous impulses, which direct you to the expression of affection and tenderness. You will inspire devotion as well as respect and esteem.

KARMIC LESSON
You have good business ability and can stand any amount of work placed upon your shoulders, which are always found broad enough to bear it. You are methodical and accurate and should make an expert accountant or a mathematician. You might also make a good engineer. You are inclined to take things as you find them and not bother thinking about tomorrow—thinking that it can take care of itself. Cultivate forethought, and you will find that life is far more profitable and pleasurable than you imagined it could be.

SECRET
You are trustworthy and competent in positions of office managing and bookkeeping. You should, however, also develop the art of relaxation.

MARCH 17

Who controls the past controls the future: who controls the present controls the past.
—George Orwell

BORN ON THIS DAY
- **Nat King Cole**
  singer
- **Rob Lowe**
  actor
- **Mia Hamm**
  soccer player
- **Alexander McQueen**
  fashion designer
- **John Boyega**
  actor

PERSONALITY
You are a person of great strength of character. Once you make up your mind how you are going to act in a situation, you stick to your plan, and you let nothing change your course of action. You are interested in the law, and you might well succeed as a lawyer, or a person in some way officially connected with carrying out the laws. You make friends easily but are inclined to be a little choosy. However, you are very tolerant of the faults of the people that you have chosen as your friends. After you have given your affection, you will not take it away. Your loyalty knows no bounds and no barriers. Your ideals are high; you really want to accomplish worthwhile things in life, and you should be able to do so with your abilities.

LIFE PATH
You are thoughtful, rather philosophical, and very positive in your opinions. You are not in the least inclined to make advances, and you receive the advances of others with indifference. If, however, anyone succeeds in gaining access to your innermost self, you are constant, true, and devoted and can hold their love and friendship through any vicissitudes.

DESTINY
Follow the path of free will. Uranus rays will guide you to impressive expressions of your original ideas. New surroundings can revitalize your interest in endeavors that, for a time, had lost their glamour. Give careful thought to the choice of new companions and enjoy the enduring friendship of those you already know.

KARMIC LESSON
Born on this day, you have a very good eye for details and are conscientious and accurate in all you do or undertake. Nothing escapes you; you see and hear everything that goes on around you—though you may not appear to do so. In money matters, you are extremely accurate and careful, and this should qualify you for the position of bookkeeper or expert accountant. You have a fairly artistic taste, and this will probably enable you to become a good designer. If your tastes run to scientific and mechanical occupations, you should be good at very detailed work.

SECRET
You sometimes are inclined to be overcautious, particularly about having faith even in deserving people. You are easily irritated in household affairs.

FRIENDS & FAMILY

MARCH 18

A man who stands for nothing will fall for anything.
—Malcolm X

BORN ON THIS DAY
- **Grover Cleveland**
  U.S. president
- **Queen Latifah**
  singer
- **Luc Besson**
  filmmaker
- **Adam Levine**
  singer
- **Vanessa Williams**
  actor, singer

FRIENDS & FAMILY

PERSONALITY
Ideas flow through your mind with amazing speed and infinite variety. You can see ahead, getting a clear picture of the results of what you plan, and as a result you manage to succeed in most things. You are fond of being social, and you like people in general. Others like you, as well, for your pleasant ways, good humor, and natural manner. You are interested in government affairs, and you like to follow the news of the day. You might succeed in some branch of politics or local government because of your innate executive ability. Never allow sentiment to keep you from fulfilling the adventurous notions that inspire you. You like travel, new faces, and new experiences. There is no reason for you to deny yourself the fun that life holds in store for you.

LIFE PATH
Restlessness and anxiety are your worst enemies. You have ability and need only a greater degree of drive to compete. You love your home and home ties, although you are inclined to be irritable if things do not run as smoothly as you think they should. You are sometimes not terribly appreciative and fail to give kudos, and so there can be miscommunications.

DESTINY
Subtlety and secrecy will play a part in your activities. There will be action, too, due to a beneficent Mars rays influence. Upon many occasions, impetuous behavior will be superior to exaggerated caution. Self-confidence is essential to success in the business world and the continued respect of your associates in every field. Allow ample time for relaxation and social pleasures.

KARMIC LESSON
Born on this day, you have strong political tendencies and should make a good politician. You would also make a good orator and are probably a good presenter, entertainer, and host. You are the hearty, jovial type that it does everyone good to meet. You brace up, invigorate, and enthuse everyone in your immediate environment. You cannot stand much opposition, however, and are inclined to be domineering at times. You have a great deal of animal magnetism and are equally attractive to men and women.

SECRET
You have an idealism that will suffer much from contact with mundane affairs. If it is properly attuned, you should achieve great success and high influence upon others.

MARCH 19

Little minds are tamed and subdued by misfortune; but great minds rise above them.
—Washington Irving

BORN ON THIS DAY

- **Earl Warren**
  U.S. Supreme Court justice
- **Bruce Willis**
  actor
- **Edgar Cayce**
  clairvoyant
- **Wyatt Earp**
  lawman and gambler
- **Richard Boles**
  clergyman, author

PERSONALITY

You will have just about every kind of experience that a person can have in life. Your destiny is to know happiness, sadness, love, and loneliness. The effect of this variety of experiences will be to make you a very mellow personality, very understanding, and very tolerant. Some of your experiences will be the direct result of your curiosity. You like to discover the new, investigate the untried, and experiment with the novel. As a result, you know much more than education teaches, and you can summarize your philosophy most succinctly. You like to give advice, and many people ask you for your opinion. You are distinguished by your know-how, and you can direct affairs with great éclat and efficiency. By living up to your own ideals, you will always find the success you seek.

LIFE PATH

You are diplomatic, kindhearted, and constant but chafe in inharmonious surroundings. Your happiness demands an unusual amount of devoted attention, and your winning personality will probably secure this for you.

DESTINY

When you have an inclination to follow a hunch, yield to it. You can be proud of your original ideas and decisive actions. Spend your time in those activities that most delight you. Do not let others dictate your lifestyle. Give as much consideration to future security as you do to present comfort and pleasures in undertaking any kind of business or legal transaction.

KARMIC LESSON

You have a firm, strong nature, which masters fate rather than submits to it. You are, however, kindly and sympathetic. You are naturally very affectionate—and this applies to family, friends, and lovers. Your passionate nature is very strong. It is kept in control, however, by the force of your character, as a rule. You are a hard worker by nature and rarely inactive. You do not get much rest and are doing something at all times. You are rather matter-of-fact and not flighty. Learn to hold fast to your one ambition or ideal until it comes true, and it will always be realized.

SECRET

Your birthday denotes a love of colorful surroundings and a desire to revel in recreation, sometimes to the neglect of practical matters.

FRIENDS & FAMILY

MARCH 20

The best things in life are not things.
—Anonymous

BORN ON THIS DAY
- **Spike Lee**
  director
- **Fred Rogers**
  TV personality
- **Chester Bennington**
  singer
- **B.F. Skinner**
  psychologist
- **Kathy Ireland**
  model

FRIENDS & FAMILY

PERSONALITY
Because you possess a sense of social reform, you try to make your own life and that of other people better. When you see a fault in the social structure or in your own way of living, you make an effort to correct it. This does not make you a crabby person or a carping critic, because you have a sense of the right way to do things, and you get around people, making them think in more ethical, moral ways. You should bear in mind that you were born on the cusp between two signs and therefore have traits belonging to the Pisces and Aries groups. You have both the innocent initiative of Aries and the intuitive, kind understanding of Pisces; this combination makes a balance in your nature, which must prove of great advantage to you.

LIFE PATH
You are studious, intellectual, sensitive, and fond of helping those in need. You will love with ardor, work with vigor, and play with a childlike abandon. Your retrospective tendency makes your pleasures lifelong, and what you have learned or seen you do not forget.

DESTINY
Your future holds the promise of interesting travels and happy friendships with new and interesting people. Your personal magnetism is powerful, drawing others to you with incredible force. Respond to the affection and consideration bestowed upon you by reciprocating with generous favors and personal attention. Give sympathy and understanding when your confidence and counsel are sought.

KARMIC LESSON
You could have a great deal of executive ability, coupled with learning and a love for nature. You are fond of the occult and mysterious, though you do not like this fact always to be known or discussed in public. You may be rather shy in the presence of a large group of strangers, but this will gradually wear off as you grow older into years of greater maturity. You may be lacking in self-assurance, but you remember that you are just as good as anyone else and that self-deprecation is self-imposed or self-permitted. For that reason, you can rid yourself of the idea if you make up your mind to do so.

SECRET
You have a practical, progressive mind with a financial wizardry best employed in stock and banking manipulations. You would make an extremely generous partner and parent.

MARCH 21

Self-confidence is the first requisite to great undertakings.
—Samuel Johnson

✦ PERSONALITY
You combine two rather opposing traits: an extreme aggressiveness, coming from your being the first birthday in the prime sign of the zodiac, and an extreme empathy for those you love. Whereas strangers or business acquaintances may consider you bossy or difficult to deal with, your family can get anything they want from you. Your tastes run all along intellectual lines, and you prefer reading, plays, and conversation to outdoor sports. It is easy for you to lose your temper, because you are impatient. This goes for your dealings with others and for your self-appraisal. A slow waiter in a restaurant can irritate you to distraction, but you criticize yourself just as severely if you are doing something creative and it seems to be coming along too slowly. You like to hang out with the "big shots" and thus often give the impression of being a snob. Only a few intimates know you really well.

✦ LIFE PATH
You are impetuous and persistent, loath to yield a point, and quick to score a point against an opponent. In your conjugal relationships, you are understanding and loving, and when your impatience manifests itself, you are quick to make amends. You rule in your home mostly by kindness.

✦ DESTINY
Thoughtful work will be adequately rewarded. You will realize the joy of domestic life and take interest in beautifying your home and entertaining your friends. Animal rights, activism, and philanthropic organizations will give you the opportunity to express the humanitarian side of your nature in a truly effective way.

✦ KARMIC LESSON
Born on this day, you have marked organizational ability and should turn your talent toward this line of work, as this is where you could excel. You also have intellectual ability and could write well. You have a philosophical turn of mind and take a delight in studying humanity. You have rather spiritual instincts, and the ideal and the sublime appeal to you. You lack, perhaps, a certain sense of humor and are inclined to sometimes take yourself too seriously. When you are disappointed or despondent, try to find something to laugh about.

✦ SECRET
You show unusual originality and aggressiveness, with an outstanding desire to be first. You are very jealous of rivals and not the most agreeable when in that mood.

BORN ON THIS DAY
- **Johann Sebastian Bach**, composer
- **Matthew Broderick**, actor
- **Gary Oldman**, actor
- **Rosie O'Donnell**, TV personality
- **Kevin Federline**, singer

FRIENDS & FAMILY

MARCH 22

Life is made up of sobs, sniffles, and smiles, with sniffles predominating.
—O. Henry

BORN ON THIS DAY

- **Reese Witherspoon**
  actor
- **Andrew Lloyd Webber**
  musical theater composer
- **Stephen Sondheim**
  musical theater composer
- **William Shatner**
  actor
- **James Patterson**
  author

FRIENDS & FAMILY

PERSONALITY
A highly developed intuition makes you keenly aware of events taking place around you and gives you the incisive perception you have into people's motives. You know how to use this wisdom to your advantage. However, you are rather easygoing, not believing that there is much to be gained in rushing. Although you always know your own goal, you believe that the best progress is made slowly. For this reason, you have a reputation for poise, which you well deserve. Symbolically, your birth date represents the master builder. You conceive brilliant plans, and you know well how to execute them efficiently. Natural leadership is one of your outstanding traits. You are an ardent lover, and you desire to have mutual love in return. However, tasteless people never attract you, as all your aspirations are on the highest plane.

LIFE PATH
You are hearty and joyous, fond of pleasure, and an indefatigable worker when you turn your attention to the serious side of life. You have many friends who like to be in your company and who show you many favors, if only you would ask.

DESTINY
When you feel restless, seek constructive outlets. Improve your home, your mind, or the lot of others. From discussions of current topics with friends you also can find profit and pleasure. Have faith in your own convictions, but learn to listen.

KARMIC LESSON
The artistic sense is prominent in those born on this day and will probably run along the lines of painting, music, or literature. You might also make a good sculptor. You have a very balanced nature, being able to do a variety of things well. You are practical and businesslike, as well as artistic, popular, and fond of socializing. You are loving, kindly, and sympathetic. But you need some ambition, concentration, and power. Determine to get them. If you make up your mind on that, you will.

SECRET
You have generous powers of concentration, with a sharp mind for facts and figures. This trait shows up when you are industrious and regular in habits of work and life.

MARCH 23

Genius is the gold in the mine; talent is the miner who works and brings it out.
—Marguerite Blessington

BORN ON THIS DAY

★ **Amy Zerner**
author and artist

★ **Joan Crawford**
actor

★ **Chaka Khan**
singer

★ **Brandon Marshall**
football player

★ **Keri Russell**
actor

★ **Perez Hilton**
media personality

PERSONALITY
You have a splendid knack for business transactions. Whether you are just running errands or are a business tycoon, you always know how to get a bargain and exit with a great deal. The gift of words belongs to you, and you can talk your way into or out of any situation that you desire. This ability, combined with your natural bent for domineering persons and events, makes you potentially successful at anything you try. You could be a fine teacher, as you understand the workings of the mind and would be able to relay knowledge and skills very cleverly. In your sympathetic moods, you can organize benefits, parties, and charity affairs with great efficiency. Because you can analyze people so well, you are likely to be very choosy in picking a partner, but you are popular and socially successful. Greater happiness is in store for you after middle life.

LIFE PATH
You are a cheerleader, both in your social life and in your business. You have good executive ability and are excellent at working out details. Your married life will be very happy, and you will be blessed to have many adorable children in your life and talented, helpful friends.

DESTINY
Always tie your ideas together into an integrated plan. Avoid inconsistency or undue attention to trifles. Even though there are fluctuating currents, you can operate with permanent benefits if you take a positive stand and go with the flow. Determination and ingenuity will help you through tight spots. Do not hesitate to ask advice of expert healers or professionals if personal problems become too involved.

KARMIC LESSON
Born on this day, you have a distinct leaning toward systems and methods, and you have a fine memory and grasp of things in this realm. You could spend a good part of your life in research or studies, without bothering about the necessities of life. This will doubtless come to you later on—though you must give up much for many years before you will be placed in this enviable position. On the whole, you are a distinctly kind and unusual person.

SECRET
You are a lover of ease and luxury, slow to temper and inclined to compromise. When driven beyond a certain point, you can be rash.

FRIENDS & FAMILY

MARCH 24

To thine own self be true.
—William Shakespeare

BORN ON THIS DAY
- **Harry Houdini**
  magician
- **Tommy Hilfiger**
  fashion designer
- **Jim Parsons**
  actor
- **Peyton Manning**
  football player
- **Steve McQueen**
  actor

FRIENDS & FAMILY

😊 PERSONALITY
You combine very compatible traits that make you a natural, or "born," leader. You can plan well, carry out your plans, and also lead others in executing the blueprint of the destiny you choose to carve out of life. There is a surprising core of hardness within you, which you do not often show to the world, but when you are offended or hurt, you can freeze up and become very severe. Only the one you love really knows the very fine and caring nature that you possess, for you do not believe in wearing your heart on your sleeve or showing your emotions to the world at large. Nature and art are sources of constant delight to you, and you seem to be able to understand the hidden meaning in their outward appearance. Your loyalty has never been questioned, and those who are your true friends will remain so throughout your life.

🌀 LIFE PATH
You are very affectionate. You will do anything within your power for those you love, but you will not be told what to do. You are intuitive, while using common sense, but can be somewhat headstrong at times.

👁 DESTINY
You will arrive at balanced decisions without bias and emotional prejudices. You will be appreciated as a lively, amiable companion. Do not be afraid to assert yourself and stand up for your rights when you feel your good nature is being imposed on. Be precise in your statements and arrive at them through careful deliberation.

☯ KARMIC LESSON
Born on this day, your character should be emotionally stable and well adjusted. You have a keen sense of justice and right and cannot bear to see anyone trampled in the dust. You are generous and openhanded but not lavish. You have great natural determination and willpower and generally manage to get what you want. You are naturally adaptable and can fit yourself into any position in which you happen to find yourself. You should succeed in your goals, whatever they are.

🧿 SECRET
You have a nature somewhat fond of display and in need of gratification tending to overindulgence. In an emergency, however, you are reliable and restrained.

MARCH 25

When the power of love overcomes the love of power, the world will know peace.
—Jimi Hendrix

BORN ON THIS DAY
- **Elton John**
  singer
- **Aretha Franklin**
  singer
- **Norman Borlaug**
  biologist
- **Gloria Steinem**
  feminist
- **Sarah Jessica Parker**
  actor

PERSONALITY
When your friends, family, or business associates want good ideas, they come to you. The reason for this is that you have a high degree of originality and intellectual gifts. You have great creative ideas, and you know how to get people to do things efficiently. You rarely seek advice yourself, because you have the feeling that the answer to your problems lies within yourself, and you are right in depending upon your inner dictates. Persuasive in your conversation and convincing in your logic, you open the door to opportunity as few people know how to do. You can work alone or in a group equally successfully. People like you for your honesty and loyalty. There is no malice in your makeup, and you feel that the world would be a better place if everyone were more understanding. Because leadership is one of your outstanding traits, you could do well in politics, education, and counseling.

LIFE PATH
You are capable of planning for your future and of carrying out your plans. You are warmhearted, generous, careful, and thrifty. You will be very fortunate in your love and choice of partner and will have many warm, supportive friends.

DESTINY
This will be an active life for you in both business and social endeavors. Always try to avoid the temporary delays that anxious impatience can cause. Show your appreciation of friendly gestures by sincere expressions of affection. Be appreciative of favors extended to you, for you should highly value true friendship.

KARMIC LESSON
You are doubtless shrewd and practical, born on this day, and not, as a rule, interested in the superficial things of life. You are interested in useful things. Your mind is very discriminating and knows how to perceive the truth in a matter. You are naturally a good cook and suited to homelife and all the solid comfort it brings. Your life can be fulfilling and crowned with an above-average amount of success and the goodness of the world.

SECRET
You show a great deal of primitive courage, with a love of adventure for its own sake, regardless of the goal. You would be well suited to pioneering work.

FRIENDS & FAMILY

MARCH 26

Don't swap horses in the middle of the stream.
—Abraham Lincoln

BORN ON THIS DAY

★ **Diana Ross**
singer, actor

★ **Steven Tyler**
singer

★ **Leonard Nimoy**
actor

★ **Robert Frost**
poet

★ **Larry Page**
computer scientist

★ **Nancy Pelosi**
congresswoman, Speaker of the U.S. House of Representatives

FRIENDS & FAMILY

PERSONALITY
There is a duality in your nature that sometimes makes it difficult for you to decide just what you want in life. For the most part, you are aggressive and masterful, but you are liable to change your mind at a moment's notice. However, you usually get what you want—provided you decide seriously to affirm what your real aim is. You are often imposed on by your loved ones and family, for you have a good nature that rarely lets you say no to any request. You should not allow people to throw you off because of their selfishness. Romantic interests do not play too great a role in your life because you are so picky and discriminating. Luxurious surroundings delight you, and you want the finest of everything in your home. You are often quite content to be alone, for you have within yourself the ability to find hobbies and pastimes to keep you occupied.

LIFE PATH
You are fair-minded, rather positive, and somewhat inclined to become bitter under opposition. You will never allow anyone to get away with lying to you. You will not fall in love at first sight and will be inclined to deny or downplay the passion when it seems to be coming your way. But when you do yield, your love will be overpowering.

DESTINY
Resist the impulse to reveal your original ideas until you have worked out the details of your operation. Be considerate of other people's feelings as well as their rights. Let those things you most desire come first in your attention if you want to see their speedy accomplishment. Other matters will fall into their natural place in your schedule, and in this way, you will avoid confusion and resentment.

KARMIC LESSON
Born on this day, you should have a naturally fine memory, which will stand you in good stead in all the affairs of life and particularly fit you for callings where a mind for detail is needed. You have a deep nature, yet none can be more lively, not to say goofy, than you, when you want to be. You would make a good historian, as you have a love of delving into the obscure records of the past. You have distinct talent for communications, and if you took to journalism, you would doubtless have a clear, unique, and forceful style.

SECRET
You are a definite executive type, most successful when in control of people under you. You have a tendency to be impatient if someone's work is not up to your standards.

MARCH 27

✦ PERSONALITY
Although you have a strong sense of responsibility, your sense of humor doesn't let you take life too seriously. You know how to separate your business life and your duties from your social life, so that you create a balance between work and play. There is a natural magnetism to your makeup that brings you many friends, with whom you are very popular. As a host, you give joy to those you entertain. As a guest, you are welcome everywhere. You would be happiest in an occupation where you could be your own boss, or at least where you were not restricted by a schedule or program that had to be adhered to rigidly. You should make a comfortable place for yourself, perhaps working from home, for that way you would attain both your highest achievement and greatest happiness. People sometimes say that you are "in love with love," and this may well be true, for you have a warm and nurturing nature.

✦ LIFE PATH
You care a great deal for pleasure and enjoyment but always endeavor to have someone to share it with you. You are original, courageous, not very verbal or communicative, and quite polite. You have a quirky sense of humor, are popular among your friends and acquaintances, and generally know how to make lemonade out of lemons.

✦ DESTINY
"Look before you leap" will be a good motto for you to follow. Check information before you take any steps that will alter your business or social life. Give the same careful thought to domestic problems. Avoid extremes. To be known for having radical ideas can hurt an endeavor in which you have been interested for a long time. Take a conservative attitude regarding investments, as well.

✦ KARMIC LESSON
You are naturally broad-minded and strong, born on this day. You might be a good organizer and run things on a large scale. You are generous and sympathetic and have the ability to see things from another person's standpoint. You have good knowledge of art and music, though these tastes may be neglected in yourself. You enjoy all the good things of this life and are never happier than when entertaining others. You are a person of very strong affections and crave a certain amount of reciprocal affection or love.

✦ SECRET
You are a wily, prudent person, often defeating your own ends by too much cleverness. You also suffer sometimes from too many indulgences.

To believe in immortality is one thing, but it is first needful to believe in life.
—Robert Louis Stevenson

BORN ON THIS DAY
- **Vivien Duffield** philanthropist
- **Mariah Carey** singer
- **Quentin Tarantino** filmmaker
- **Fergie** singer
- **Manuel Neuer** soccer player

FRIENDS & FAMILY

MARCH 28

The ladder of life is full of splinters, but they always prick the hardest when we're sliding down.
—William L. Brownell

BORN ON THIS DAY

- **Raphael**
  painter, sculptor
- **Maxim Gorky**
  author
- **Lady Gaga**
  singer
- **Reba McEntire**
  singer
- **Vince Vaughn**
  actor

FRIENDS & FAMILY

✦ PERSONALITY

When you make up your mind to achieve a certain goal, nothing is allowed to stand in your way. You go ahead like a tank, sweeping before you any obstacle that comes into your path. This is a splendid way to get ahead in a world of competition, but it is a tiring and wearing process. You should develop your sense of diplomacy so that you get more with less effort. No one can deny that you are a hard worker, and you hate to see a task that is on today's list left for tomorrow. You would rather work all night to get a thing done than let it go over until the next day. This conscientious behavior has won you a fine reputation. People know that you are responsible, professional, dependable, and trustworthy. You make no snap judgments but weigh the evidence very carefully before you come to a conclusion. You win acclaim because you are firm and fair.

✦ LIFE PATH

Born on this day, you are fortunate in business and are generally a money getter. You are talented as far as management goes, but the actual dirty work is distasteful to you. You are positive and aggressive and like to associate with people of culture and refinement.

✦ DESTINY

A public incident will have a great significance in your life. To appreciate all the aspects of it, take an interest in current affairs. Consult many newspapers, blogs, websites, and social media accounts, and listen to different new commentators on the radio or podcasts in order to have an unbiased opinion. You will be aware of favorable influences if you keep alert mentally. Share and compare opinions with friends.

✦ KARMIC LESSON

Love of travel is probably one of the best distinguishing characteristics of your nature. You want to see the world and all there is in it for yourself, and no amount of description by others will satisfy you. You are interested in psychics, magic, and all such curious and out-of-the-ordinary pursuits and interests. At the same time, you do not let these interests interfere with your life; you are very sane and matter-of-fact. You have a natural interest in technology, particularly those fields that involve inventions and discoveries whose impact is still cutting-edge.

✦ SECRET

You are a rather groping and wandering type, until catastrophe points the way in life. Successful after maturity, you would be a good teacher or coach.

MARCH 29

Every moment of resistance to temptation is a victory.
—Frederick W. Faber

◉ PERSONALITY

You are rather changeable in nature, for you have many likes and dislikes and can switch your feelings and opinions without notice. Voluble and expressive, you make your feelings known, sometimes to the consternation of those to whom you express yourself. Because you are so fond of variety, you are often unpredictable. However, this mercurial temperament has its advantages, because it enables you to fit into almost any situation. You are at ease wherever you go and in whatever kind of company you find yourself. Because you have a flair for words, you would be successful in the fields of essay writing or as a critic or blogger. Being quick-witted, you are rather impatient with people who are not snappy in grasping situations or understanding a joke. You can be a severe critic when you want to, and you have the knack of hitting the weak spot almost psychically. If you are as severe in criticizing your own faults as you are in criticizing those of others, you're bound to be a success.

◉ LIFE PATH

You are not always so easy to get along with because you are an excellent critic. Strive to overcome this drawback to what otherwise would be a nicer disposition and develop a keener sense of justice and fair play. Your affections are deep-seated but should not be allowed to influence your judgment unduly.

◉ DESTINY

Be sure that your information is adequate before making definite statements or taking steps on business matters. You will usually be able to avert crises by quick and decisive action. You have an uncanny knack for anticipating how plans can be successfully completed. Keep your life rich with varied activities. Rely on your intuition when choosing between two equally attractive alternatives.

◉ KARMIC LESSON

Born on this day, you have, in all probability, a good deal of bodily energy and staying power, which often stands you in good stead through life. You should be very competent both in large projects and in detailed work and so might be suited for such work as that of a contractor, supervisor, and the like. You also have artistic sense, which gives you a flair for good taste. You should be successful in business and are counted on for your input, on account of your frank and knowledgeable nature. Never hesitate to learn your faults from another and profit from this advice.

◉ SECRET

You are more easygoing than it appears and have an exuberant sense of humor. You must be stirred by a profound passion to rise to unexpected heights of achievement.

BORN ON THIS DAY

★ **John Tyler**
U.S. president

★ **Vangelis**
musician

★ **Cy Young**
baseball player

★ **Chris D'Elia**
comedian

★ **Amy Sedaris**
actor

FRIENDS & FAMILY

MARCH 30

Life will give you what you ask of her, if only you ask long enough and plainly enough.
—Edith Nesbit

BORN ON THIS DAY
- **Vincent van Gogh**
  artist
- **Celine Dion**
  singer
- **Paul Reiser**
  actor
- **Tracy Chapman**
  singer
- **Eric Clapton**
  musician

FRIENDS & FAMILY

PERSONALITY
You regard life from the intellectual heights. Because you are clever, incisive, and analytical, you see the faults in people and situations and thus know how to gauge your own conduct. Fortunately, you do not care much about the opinions of other people and therefore generally keep your thoughts to yourself. Life has taught you that a lot of patience is needed to get along well, and you have developed this trait with remarkable perspicacity. Little delays do not discourage you, nor do disappointments swerve you from your path. Your greatest success lies in fields where logic and the scientific approach are required. Beauty is necessary to your happiness, and it is good to be surrounded by choice colors, tasteful furnishings, and meaningful works of art.

LIFE PATH
Your mind is analytical, your tendency is toward thoughtful consideration of any important step, and your judgment is, on the whole, sound. You are too much inclined to search for motives underlying other people's acts, and there is danger of disappointment coming into your life through it. You do not trust easily. You should excel in an unconventional, professional career.

DESTINY
Avoid making promises that are difficult to keep, and do not expect them of others. Make a rule to be on time for appointments. Otherwise, you may miss out on a golden opportunity, which is likely to come your way more than once. Good fortune will accompany a systematic method of operation and steadfast devotion to your ideals and ambitions.

KARMIC LESSON
You are a strong, original character, living your own life, thinking your own thoughts. If you are not, you ought at once to begin to do so, as you will never make a complete success of anything until you do so, breaking away from the cramping and restraining influences that hamper and bind you. You have great natural capabilities and resources, which need only cultivation. Live up to your ideals, and things will come out for the best. Yours is the personality that can win success in the long run, with patience.

SECRET
You desire to be just and scrupulously honest in all dealings. You befriend many and generally enjoy a good attitude of gratitude.

MARCH 31

Judge a man by his questions rather than by his answers.
—Voltaire

PERSONALITY
You are rather placid in temperament and know how to adjust your life to the complications of modern existence. Although you want material success, you know full well that it doesn't always spell happiness. Because you have discovered this important secret, you seek the development of your material and spiritual potentialities rather than the increase of your bank balance. It may truthfully be said of you that you are the friend in need, for when anyone needs advice or consolation, you are the first one they seek out. From the well of your wisdom, experience, and inner peace, you are able to provide just the right words to change a glum mood to an optimistic one. Good taste characterizes everything about you. Your home has charm, your conversation has sympathy, and your personality expresses inward beauty.

LIFE PATH
Your temperament is artistic, and you are particularly fond of stories and films about real relationships. You are deep, intellectual, kindhearted, and loving and could have a very happy homelife. The people born on this date are excellent parents and retain an unusual hold upon their children as they grow up.

DESTINY
You will be rewarded for your conscientiousness and high idealism. Tie up your abilities with available opportunities to establish a constructive plan. Realization of some of your fondest dreams within a short time is possible. Try to take a practical rather than an imaginative point of view when contemplating big changes. Do not be hurt by unintentional slights and discourtesies. Friends will always trust you and take you into their confidence, and their advice will be helpful.

KARMIC LESSON
Born on this day, you have great natural talents and infinite ability to take pains to do things correctly. You are good at detail work, though also capable of undertaking complex tasks. You have remarkable talent in creative directions; you also have a philosophic and reflective mind. You do not have an earthy nature and are probably of the sensitive, refined order rather than the heavy and aggressive. You sometimes do not think of yourself and your own life seriously enough; you can think of abstract problems all night—but when it comes to applying it yourself, you do not always do it. Learn to do this, and you should make a greater success of your life.

SECRET
You can be a little eccentric. You will achieve your greatest accomplishments by yielding to the guidance of wiser and more proficient experts.

BORN ON THIS DAY
- **Joseph Haydn** composer
- **Al Gore** U.S. vice president
- **Ewan McGregor** actor
- **Cesar Chavez** civil rights activist
- **Christopher Walken** actor

FRIENDS & FAMILY

APRIL 1

Your task is not to seek for love, but merely to seek and find all the barriers within yourself that you have built against it.
—Jalāl ad-Dīn Rumi

BORN ON THIS DAY
- **Otto von Bismarck**
  statesman
- **Sergei Rachmaninoff**
  composer
- **Samuel Alito**
  U.S. Supreme Court justice
- **Debbie Reynolds**
  actor
- **Rachel Maddow**
  TV host

FRIENDS & FAMILY

PERSONALITY
In the great drama of life, your role is that of a designer. You are able to imagine plans for improvement and blueprints for living that ameliorate your own life and the lives of people who are associated with you. Fortunately, you are also endowed with the ability to supervise the carrying out of these noble products of your mind, for a design without the follow-up of construction is useless. You are known to be very versatile, and you wisely choose each of your talents to suit the task before you. Although this sounds very serious, it is not meant to imply that you lack a fun-loving spirit. You can join in the gaiety of any party and have a grand time, but you know how to choose the time for fun just as you know how to choose the time for work. Never try to be a lone wolf, for you are most successful in any project when you work with a lively and stimulating group.

LIFE PATH
Your reasoning powers are fine, and you are a good planner, but you are not always so efficient in execution yourself. As a manager you can get other people to do things for you better than you can do them yourself. Your aims are high, and you are capable of much self-sacrifice to attain your goals. Your love will be the most important and helpful influence in your life.

DESTINY
You are able to shine as a boss. Do not take a back seat for anyone. Your destiny is to show off your executive ability. Success vibrations will grow particularly strong as the years progress, so use earlier years to prepare for coming triumphs. Always keep your wardrobe up to the minute. Watch the popular trends, too, in other matters.

KARMIC LESSON
Born on this day, you have great practical ability and a stern determination to carry through anything you undertake. You have naturally great staying powers and a good memory, and you never seem to get exhausted or even tired. You should make a good critic, as you generally know just where to put your finger on a weak spot. You have a purposeful and strong character, one that many people envy. You are destined to accomplish great things before you pass, if only you live up to your highest aims and ambitions.

SECRET
You will have a life of considerable adventure, both physically and spiritually, depending on the nature of the environment.

APRIL 2

Every man's life is a fairy tale written by God's fingers.
—Hans Christian Andersen

BORN ON THIS DAY
- **Marvin Gaye**
  singer
- **Hans Christian Andersen**
  author
- **Camille Paglia**
  feminist
- **Sergei Kovalev**
  boxer
- **Michael Fassbender**
  actor

FRIENDS & FAMILY

PERSONALITY
There seems to be a subtle tie between you and the people you love, a kind of unspoken understanding that makes you the most vital member of your family and the most important person in your group of friends. Of course, much of this is due to the profound sense of responsibility you have. It seems as though you would never let anyone suffer want, deprivation, or disappointment if you could help it. You are generous almost to a fault, but you love giving. Educational work is your forte, and this applies to you whether your aim is to teach in a classroom or to instruct others by the precepts of your life or the example that you set by living according to the Golden Rule. Your heart is as big as you are, and you should be happy with the one you love because you are able to spread a positive aura wherever you go.

LIFE PATH
You are kind, loving, sweet-tempered, and patient to a degree that can often bring you mental anguish because of others' thoughtless imposition. Your home and your immediate family fill your heart, although you love hosting friends. You like to be outdoors and are passionately fond of flowers and gardening.

DESTINY
Your tolerance and kindness will always stand you in good stead. Do not be careless about money—what you put into the bank may be greatly appreciated in the future. An opportunity may arise at crucial points, which you can take advantage of if you have a cash reserve. Get all the fun you can out of browsing the Internet and social media. Develop your own talents as a means of recreation and share them. Control a tendency to "go overboard" for ideas that sound good but have not been tested.

KARMIC LESSON
You probably have considerable ability in communications and a discerning perception of all that goes on around you. You don't miss a trick. You are a good judge and a good analyzer of character and can "see through" a person about as quickly as anyone you know. You also have great intuitive ability. You are fond of research and study and grasp every opportunity that is presented to read; you simply devour information. You are fond of the psychic, and you like trying experiments and attending sittings or readings where such things are presented.

SECRET
You are a lover of horticulture and are happiest when engaged in such activities as landscape design, gardening, natural cooking, and eating.

APRIL 3

Friendship is the highest degree of perfection in society.
—Michel Eyquem de Montaigne

✸ PERSONALITY
You can make your life just about anything you desire because you have imagination plus practicality in your makeup. You see ahead with great clarity of vision, and you can tell people what the outcome of events will be long before they are definitely decided. Once in a while, you go off on a tangent because it seems that the events in your life are either boring or repetitious. Since you understand that you are doing this for the purpose of breaking up the monotony of daily routine, no harm is likely to come of it. But do not inflict any bursts of temper on your loved ones if you can help it, because this would not be fair. An important facet of your true nature is your psychic intuition. This is really highly developed in you, and you may well depend upon it to guide you through moments of indecision or doubt.

✸ LIFE PATH
You will secure the greatest degree of happiness if you know how to value your long-standing relationships. Your temperament is such that early in life you will have to develop positive habits and later in life you will not have as much adaptability. Your perseverance and steadiness will bring you much success where impulsive action would bring more failure.

✸ DESTINY
Your quiet and unassuming appearance will belie your aggressive and tenacious actions. Your sense of humor will always carry you over a few bad moments. You will generally prefer to see the funny side of a situation even though you understand its serious implications. A philosophical attitude combined with your own capability will enable you to combat disappointments and temporary setbacks successfully.

✸ KARMIC LESSON
You have a naturally kind and sympathetic disposition, but you give yourself rather too freely to others, who often impose upon you in return and do not fully appreciate what you do or the sacrifices you make for them. You are a good and true friend. You have many talents; you are naturally enthusiastic and eager to learn; and you are independent, choosing not to follow rules and regulations simply because they are accepted and universal. You are extremely critical but have a fair and open mind.

✸ SECRET
You secretly have a tendency toward moodiness and over-reflection, which frequently arrests action. Try to cultivate the implementation of your ideas.

BORN ON THIS DAY
★ **Marlon Brando**
actor
★ **Eddie Murphy**
actor, comedian
★ **Alec Baldwin**
actor
★ **Jane Goodall**
biologist
★ **Doris Day**
actor

FRIENDS & FAMILY

APRIL 4

When you define liberty you limit it, and when you limit it you destroy it.
—Brand Whitlock

BORN ON THIS DAY

- **Dorothea Dix**
  mental health advocate
- **Robert Downey, Jr.**
  actor
- **Maya Angelou**
  poet
- **Graham Norton**
  TV host
- **David Blaine**
  magician

FRIENDS & FAMILY

PERSONALITY
You possess exceptional qualities because a kind of destiny has endowed you with rather remarkable traits, particularly along the lines of organization. In other words, you can take a rough idea, visualize it, and bring about a working organization that will produce something worthwhile. This ability takes you to the forefront of any project with which you become associated. You are fired by ambition and desire to see results, so you usually work hard. Some people may consider you overly conscientious, but you will follow the dictates of your inner voice regardless of the opinion of anyone else. Because you are inclined to be demanding in your relationships with other people, you may have to wait to meet the type of partner who would make you truly happy. However, it would be foolish for you to compromise for anything less than your ideal. Try to accumulate happiness as you do material things, and you should lead a rewarding life.

LIFE PATH
Without the well-being of your mind/body/spirit, you cannot enjoy wealth or life's pleasures. That is why you try to develop habits to take care of yourself. You must curb a natural ambitiousness so that overdoing may not impair your health. Do not brood over misfortune, for you are resourceful and capable of the successful accomplishment of your desires. You will be ultimately fortunate in affairs of the heart—don't give up.

DESTINY
As you mature, there will be little time for or benefit to brooding or mulling over the past. Events in your life will proceed with such force that you need to bear in mind the importance of self-discipline or you can be swept away by the current of opportunities and relationships. Keep your feet on the ground. You will have some emotional and intellectual problems to solve, but you can meet them with confidence in your ability to master any situation in which you are involved.

KARMIC LESSON
You are exacting and methodical and have a good head for figures and details. This would naturally fit you for such occupations as expert accountant or bookkeeper. You are not as fond of staying home as you might be. You like to spend your evenings in some really interesting and entertaining manner, if possible, and not fritter them away with details and small talk. You are fond of going out and will probably find interests such as clubs to engage you. Once in your life a great opportunity will be offered you—do not hesitate or let it slip away!

SECRET
Your dominant trait is a love for the arts, notably photography and video. You would take good portraits.

APRIL 5

Wisdom is to the mind what health is to the body.
—François de La Rochefoucauld

BORN ON THIS DAY
- **Colin Powell**
  U.S. general, statesman
- **Bette Davis**
  actor
- **Booker T. Washington**
  African American community leader
- **Pharrell Williams**
  singer
- **Gregory Peck**
  actor

PERSONALITY
You have a deeply sympathetic nature, but you also require a lot of affection and understanding. It is easy for you to comprehend the inner workings of the minds and the emotions of others, but you must realize that they may not have the same facility to understand you. You are disheartened by delays and disappointments, and sometimes you just feel that life consists of nothing else. At such times, however, you should count your blessings rather than complain. You must be careful not to waste the talents that have been endowed upon you. Your conviviality, power of expression, and love of entertainment will get you many friends. See to it that these qualities also get you a good reputation, material rewards, and the station in life to which you aspire. Life does not lie within one's grasp, but by working for the things you want, you will have the joy of working plus the sweetness of attainment.

LIFE PATH
Don't be too whimsical or fickle. You are endowed with strength and fortitude, and these attributes should be cultivated. You have the ability and magnetic qualities of a person in charge, especially to attract your goals. While you love your life, you tend to chafe under petty, irritating annoyances.

DESTINY
There will be many chances for successful endeavors, and you may have difficulty deciding what to focus on. Being an advocate for a worthy cause is a great activity in which you can make remarkable strides toward your goals. You need not limit yourself to one activity, but be careful that you do not take on more than you can stand, physically and emotionally. Do your best to add to the pleasant surroundings in your home.

KARMIC LESSON
Born on this day, you have a determined will, and if you conceive that you are in the right, you will fight to maintain your position to the very end. You can at times be very impulsive and quick to act. You see everything that goes on around you, though you often pretend that you don't. You have strong intuitions, which are usually right, and you should learn to depend upon and follow these more. You should be interested in technology, for it will give you the power you need. You have good practical ability and good judgment.

SECRET
Although you are blessed with versatility, this talent for doing many things fairly well may mislead you. You should try to concentrate on an uplifting line of work.

FRIENDS & FAMILY

APRIL 6

Make yourself an honest man, and then you may be sure there is one less rascal in the world.
—Thomas Carlyle

BORN ON THIS DAY
- **Paul Rudd**
  actor
- **Billy Dee Williams**
  singer, actor
- **Gregory Peck**
  actor
- **Leonora Carrington**
  artist
- **Ram Dass**
  yogi

FRIENDS & FAMILY

PERSONALITY
A neat balance between aggressive powers and intellectual interests makes you a person full of promise and accomplishment. If you use your mental qualifications to plan your life and your powers of domination to put the plan through, nothing can stop you from reaching the top rung of the ladder of achievement. You would make an excellent teacher or coach, for you are interested in letting others have the benefit of your own acquisition of knowledge. However, you can succeed in other fields where the activity of the mind is dominant or required. You are very discriminating in your choice of companions and can criticize the faults of members of your family. That is because your own standards are very high. While you are active when necessary, you prefer sedentary occupations. For this reason, you generally stay close to home, enjoying the pleasures of a comfortable chair and a computer rather than seeking adventure away from home.

LIFE PATH
You care much for constantly stimulating ideas and for intellectual friends. The light chaff of small talk does not appeal to you, but you are an excellent conversationalist when you can converse with people who are interested along the lines your reading takes. Your pastimes involve the studying of human nature, but you live very much within yourself.

DESTINY
You will use your foresight and concentration to better yourself economically. Always strive not to be vague and not to make unwise changes socially or in business. Resist the temptation to experiment with impractical ideas. However, if you are dissatisfied or disagree with methods in your work, try some other way of operation. Concentrate on being friendly and showing goodwill in all your endeavors. An optimistic attitude will favorably impress associates, and you can go far.

KARMIC LESSON
You have distinctly artistic ability and could make a name for yourself with a pencil, pen, or computer brush—if you gave serious thought to this direction. You also have strong investigative abilities, and some form of psychology draws you intensely at times. You are impulsive and a hard worker; you have an artistic temperament par excellence. Quick and active, you have a very ardent nature. You are a great talker, full of interesting and entertaining stories, but you must learn that the intellect is to be controlled and cultivated. Hard work is necessary for those who wish to succeed—even the artist.

SECRET
You are a person with fine instincts and great powers of acquisition. You could be a leader in your field.

APRIL 7

Soft is the music that would charm forever.
—William Wordsworth

⊛ PERSONALITY
Somewhat of a mystic by nature, you sometimes baffle your friends and family who cannot understand your urge to be alone at times. However, these periods of quiet solitude are very enjoyable to you; they fill the needs of the spirit, and they refresh you mentally. You are prone to being agreeable, even when it is against your wishes, and you should assert yourself more so that you have those pleasures, which you enjoy, rather than those activities forced upon you by others whose feelings you do not want to hurt. Ingenuity marks everything you do, unless you let things slide due to a pessimistic attitude. You are liable to moods, so you should make one of your major aims the conquest of despondency. It should not be difficult for you to do this, as you are clever, and you can figure out that there is no return or profit in brooding. Get out as much as possible when you feel that you are slumping mentally, and you will soon be your clever, cheerful self again.

⊛ LIFE PATH
You are enthusiastic in planning but not always as persevering as you could be in executing your plans, being inclined to let "good enough" suffice. You are fond of your many caring friends, and your intuitive judgment is very good. Your pride sometimes circumvents your happiness. Your love is strong, authentic, and enduring.

⊛ DESTINY
Keep your thinking clear and direct and be candid in your opinions. Accept unavoidable situations gracefully rather than waste time or effort in useless faultfinding. Handle each problem as it comes up as well as you can, and then forget about it. Relax with pleasant companions, discuss your plans for the future, and engage in recreational activities when opportunities are available. This will keep you balanced in mind, body, and spirit.

⊛ KARMIC LESSON
You have a great deal of compassion in your character and a determination to succeed and get on in life. You desire money and what money brings. You are interested in public affairs, yet you are retiring and exclusive at times. You have literary tastes, and when you are alone, in the country, you may be carried away by the still loneliness and beauty of the scene and become quite poetical. As soon as the spell is removed, however, and you return to civilization, you at once become practical and businesslike again. Born on this day, you are very emotional and sensitive and are attracted to others who can articulate their feelings.

⊛ SECRET
You are a lover of theater, although not necessarily as an actor. You may lean toward stage sets or costume design.

BORN ON THIS DAY
- **Francis Ford Coppola**
  filmmaker
- **Billie Holiday**
  singer
- **Jackie Chan**
  actor
- **Tony Dorsett**
  football player
- **Russell Crowe**
  actor

FRIENDS & FAMILY

APRIL 8

Industry, economy, honesty, and kindness form a quartet of virtues that will never be improved upon.
—James Oliver

BORN ON THIS DAY

- **Vivienne Westwood**
  fashion designer
- **Félix Hernández**
  baseball player
- **Robin Wright**
  actor
- **Patricia Arquette**
  actor
- **Julian Lennon**
  singer/songwriter

FRIENDS & FAMILY

PERSONALITY
You are inclined to demand your own way with others, for you have good ideas and feel that they, rather than the less brilliant ones conceived by other people, should be put to use. However, this does not detract from your popularity, because you have appealing ways, and you are wise enough to try to get your way with a winning smile instead of a veiled threat. Great enthusiasm stimulates your greatest efforts. You can inspire others to be just as interested as you are in the latest fad, fashion trend, or whatever strikes your fancy. Although this makes life very interesting for you, you don't maintain your interest in any particular project or favorite for long. Soon you grow tired of the fun or bored with the idea, and you go on to the next interest, seeking what amusement you can get out of it. Ability and self-confidence will see you through any situation in which you are a part.

LIFE PATH
You are impatient, impulsive, and sometimes argumentative. You like to see things started on time and then moved rapidly to completion. You are energetic and self-confident and will form many close friendships. Your love is irresistible and impetuous.

DESTINY
A certain amount of force and focus are necessary if you want to see your plans materialize. This does not mean that you have to be belligerent. In fact, you must avoid unpleasant encounters with others if you would see the successful accomplishment of your fondest wishes. Listen to the counsel of friends, but do not think that you are bound to follow it if it does not coincide with your own thoughtful conclusions.

KARMIC LESSON
Born on this day, you have good judgment and strong intuitions. In these you are almost invariably right. You have an instinctively practical nature, but it is undeveloped, and in all probability most people would not believe that you possessed it. You are full of fun and animated by nature, constant in your spiritual beliefs, and could become jealous to a degree. Learn to be more fair, wholesome, and democratic.

SECRET
Although you may argue a great deal, you do so not from a quarrelsome nature but from a desire to put across your point of view.

APRIL 9

The present moment is the only moment available to us, and it is the door to all moments.
—Thich Nhat Hanh

★ PERSONALITY
Quite a homebody, you get the most fun and pleasure out of those activities and tasks associated with your habitat. Excitement and adventure that draw others away from the domestic scene hold little if any attraction for you. You would rather putter around in your own garden than get dressed up to attend a social function. However, when you are required to go out socially or with business associates, you make a good impression mainly because of your deep sincerity, which everyone recognizes immediately for its true worth. It seems that when your friends need advice, they turn to you. That is because they also see in you the well of conscientiousness that is so deeply a part of your nature. You are innately gentle and could never hurt anyone. It offends you to see people acting bawdy and rude. Because you give so much to life, you should have big returns in enjoyment of close relationships.

★ LIFE PATH
Honesty, integrity, and ambition are your chief characteristics. You are well-rounded and dependable, and your advice and counsel are often sought and usually followed, much to the advantage of the recipient. You stick to your friends with your heart and soul, and you love your home ties above all else.

★ DESTINY
The resignation or retirement of someone who holds a superior position may mean an opportunity for you or your life partner to obtain desired advancement. The obligations required for this opportunity can seem pressing at first, but they are not overwhelming. Neptune favors the effective application of inspirations, but the responsibility still remains with you to apply them at the proper time. Guard your honesty in certain social activities.

★ KARMIC LESSON
You have a natural interest in philosophy, but you desire to excel in whatever engages your attention. You always set your sites on the next challenge. You are quite fearless and ambitious and not easily discouraged. You are naturally kind, not the type of person who would hold a grudge against another for any length of time. You have a strong will and are not easily led by others. You also have a big heart; you are always exceptionally attractive to people who, like you, love to ponder the mysteries of the universe.

★ SECRET
There is a streak of restlessness in your makeup. You could be an extensive traveler but are satisfied to sightsee in your mind.

BORN ON THIS DAY
★ **Lil Nas X**
rapper

★ **Hugh Hefner**
publisher

★ **Marc Jacobs**
fashion designer

★ **Sam Harris**
philosopher, neuroscientist

★ **Linda Goodman**
astrologer

FRIENDS & FAMILY

APRIL 10

Perfect love reposes on the object of its choice, like the halcyon on the wave.
—William Hazlitt

BORN ON THIS DAY

★ **Joseph Pulitzer**
publisher

★ **Omar Sharif**
actor

★ **John Madden**
football coach

★ **Daisy Ridley**
actor

★ **Mandy Moore**
singer, actor

FRIENDS & FAMILY

PERSONALITY

No doubt you are known as one of the most affable people in your group, and the reason for this reputation is that you know instinctively how to adjust yourself to any circumstance. In addition, you have an innate sense of diplomacy that makes it possible for you to feel at home with any and all kinds of people. You can put others at ease, and you know that all people are human so that there is no need for you to ever put on airs. It might be said of you, whether you are male or female, that you are a "regular guy." You have a gift for words, and you know how to impress people when it is necessary for business or social reasons. Because you have a sort of stubborn streak in your makeup, you get what you desire from life. You are not easily discouraged, and circumstances that would defeat others seem more like a challenge to you. For this reason, you are bound to succeed.

LIFE PATH

You are faithful to duty, adaptable to environment, loyal to friends, and enthusiastic in your work. You are strong and forceful; you surmount difficulties by sheer determination. The love you compel will withstand any vicissitude.

DESTINY

Your destiny picture favors your use of authority to accomplish measures that will prove to be of general as well as personal benefit. Friendliness will benefit you in the role of either buyer or seller. If too stubborn or reactionary, some members of your family might offer opposition to innovations you think are wise; be courteous but adamant in resisting their efforts to keep you from traveling the road of progress.

KARMIC LESSON

You have great natural powers; you have deep sympathy and interest in the affairs and troubles of others. You are a born debater and would make a very good public speaker. Your spiritual interests are profound, but you do not give them free play. At the same time, you are very practical. You are tenacious in your beliefs and wide in your interests. You have a great independence of thought—also action, but this is not so developed as your independence of thought.

SECRET

You have a physically aggressive nature and may possibly become a workout enthusiast. In domestic relations, however, you are tender and understanding.

APRIL 11

Men do not break down from overwork, but from worry and dissipation.
—Charles E. Hughes

BORN ON THIS DAY
- **Jennifer Esposito**
  actor
- **David Banner**
  rapper
- **Meshach Taylor**
  actor
- **Dean Acheson**
  statesman
- **Daryl Simmons**
  musician

PERSONALITY
You have a magnetic personality. This attraction is absolutely natural to you; you do not plan to charm others, nor do you set out to make any conquests; nevertheless, you have a host of admirers and friends. This innate quality of drawing others to you makes you very popular socially and guarantees your success in the world of business. You like to dress well, to make a good impression, and to have elegant furnishings in your home. The luxurious attracts you to a high degree, and you prefer the best to the mediocre. No one can blame you for this, although you must restrain a certain extravagance you possess just to get hold of the lovely things of life—on the material plane. By controlling your taste for lavish elegance, you should make out better financially and at the same time put away money for future security.

LIFE PATH
You possess a considerable amount of vanity, like to live well, and are always careful of appearances. You are artistic and idealistic, think quickly, act slowly, and love deeply. You are tender, kind, and thoughtful and are quite respected by your kin and immediate circle.

DESTINY
You should tackle each job with vim and vigor. You may have the opportunity to take some constructive action along educational lines. Do not ignore the chance to increase your store of information through travel or discussion. When matters concerning family affairs arise, do not become involved in petty squabbles. Pay no attention to pessimistic remarks, and do not judge the acts of others. Stay on your own path as much as is practical.

KARMIC LESSON
You are popular and make friends easily. Loyal and true in your friendships, you stick to a friend, once made, through all his or her adversities and trials. You are intuitive and quickly ascertain the thoughts and motives of others. You are very sure of your own judgment and are inclined to defend it at all costs. Very exacting in love affairs, you tend to make much of slights that are in themselves very small. You must learn to "find yourself" early in life, for if you do not, you will go through life frittering away your talents.

SECRET
You have a distinct fondness for style and a genuine creative inclination. You could succeed as a designer of jewelry or accessories.

FRIENDS & FAMILY

APRIL 12

It is the picayune compliments which are the most appreciated; far more than the double ones we sometimes pay.
—Henry Clay

BORN ON THIS DAY

★ **Henry Clay**
statesman

★ **Herbie Hancock**
jazz musician

★ **Tom Clancy**
author

★ **David Letterman**
talk show host

★ **Brendon Urie**
singer

FRIENDS & FAMILY

☀ PERSONALITY

The extent of your intentional thinking is boundless. You know what you want, and you can discern the best course to pursue so as to succeed in almost any situation. You can rarely be charged with indecision. Financial security means a lot to you, so you are especially desirous of having a guaranteed income, sound investments, or an estate from which you can derive revenue when you grow older. Since you are also sensitive to the needs of others, you have the ability to succeed in work that requires service to others. Medicine, social work, and the law are excellent professions for you, because you have the temperament to be kind and sympathetic to those who are in trouble. You also should do well in work that requires precision. You depend on the delicacy of your impressions regarding the mechanics, the exact timing, and the details of each task.

☯ LIFE PATH

You are careful and cautious, never taking an important step without thoroughly considering it from every angle. When once a decision is reached, however, you will not shirk any responsibility your decision may entail. You love your personal environment and devote a great deal of energy to making it pleasant.

☉ DESTINY

Business affairs can prosper under your direction. Do a little investigating, however, before you make any irrevocable decisions. Avoid unnecessary worry, and do not indulge in wishful thinking. Favorable trends can occur in endeavors connected with the home. Games or competitions offer enjoyable means of recreation in which you may find pleasurable participation.

☯ KARMIC LESSON

You are fond of your home and all the comforts that word embodies. At the same time, you are fond of going out a great deal—or would like to. You should marry only after a very long acquaintance since it would be unwise for you to trust your impressions in matters of this kind. You have not a great deal of patience, which is a virtue you should cultivate. Learn to cultivate the cheerful side of yourself, as sometimes the blues overtake you; develop your positive attitude.

☸ SECRET

You have a tendency to place pride above all other considerations, causing much personal disappointment. You are particularly sensitive and get hurt easily.

APRIL 13

When angry, count to ten before you speak; when very angry, count to one hundred.
—Thomas Jefferson

BORN ON THIS DAY

- **Catherine de Medici**
  noblewoman
- **Thomas Jefferson**
  U.S. president
- **Gary Kasparov**
  world chess champion
- **Samuel Beckett**
  playwright
- **Christopher Hitchens**
  author

PERSONALITY

Appearances are deceiving in your case, and while you give the impression of being a very easygoing person, you have a will of iron that drives you on to the achievement of your personal ambition no matter what other people may think. Because you are generally unobtrusive, you give certain people a terrific shock when you suddenly put your foot down and say no. This sort of tactic never fails to get results, however, and you should know pretty well what you are doing and what results you have gotten from your plan of action up to the present time. You prefer a small and select group of friends to a large group of acquaintances. This is wise, for it permits you to enjoy associating with those you really like all the more. There are times you get into a funk over some financial slight. You should rout out this sensitiveness. Don't let natural or innate economical tendencies ever earn you a reputation for being a spoilsport or a cheapskate. Generosity always pays big returns.

LIFE PATH

You are persevering, energetic, authoritative, and versatile. You move along the line of least resistance, and if balked in your purpose one way, you will accomplish it in another. You are quiet and uncommunicative and do not make friends readily, but those you make you hold. The one you love best holds a place in your heart that nothing can assail.

DESTINY

Heavy obligations and responsibilities will be important, because the Saturn rays rule your birth date. Matters of insurance, assessments, and economy will merit your attention. Do not let unfinished business matters ride but always seek to clear them up as soon as possible. This will keep your mind clear and calm.

KARMIC LESSON

You have distinct creative talents that should be given more attention. The probability is that you possess considerable gifts in this line that are not recognized, and you suffer in consequence. There are currents of success and nonsuccess that run in your life, up and down, and you must learn to strike the current and swim with it. Occasionally you are inclined to become melancholy, at which times you should read a little inspiring and motivational wisdom and cheer yourself up again.

SECRET

A love of escape or procrastination may defeat your chances for some accomplishments you desire. Learn early to cultivate focus and concentration, and you will achieve your ambition.

FRIENDS & FAMILY

APRIL 14

Live as with God; and whatever be your calling, pray for the gift that will perfectly qualify you in it.
—Horace Bushnell

BORN ON THIS DAY

★ **Pete Rose**
baseball player

★ **Loretta Lynn**
singer

★ **Julie Christie**
actor

★ **Adrien Brody**
actor

★ **Sarah Michelle Gellar**
actor

FRIENDS & FAMILY

✨ PERSONALITY
Play is one of the main objectives of your life. No one can have a better time than you, for you see humor where others don't even realize it exists. This gives you an edge on some people who don't quite understand how life seems such a grand adventure to you while to them it is just torture to go from day to day. There is another side to your nature, too, but that side you do not put on display for the world to see. That is your serious side, the sensitive, spiritual aspect of your nature. You can be deeply wounded by neglect, disappointments, and delays. Such slights hurt you more than you will ever admit, but the pain is there just the same. An active interest in things of a theatrical nature takes you to TV, websites, radio, YouTube, and movies whenever the opportunity arises. These would make perfect occupational areas for you, too. You have a romantic nature that requires unconditional love and understanding.

🌀 LIFE PATH
You have a strong, open mind, a sweet temper, a kindly spirit, and intuitive judgment. Most of your ideas are realistic and original, and you are able to think and act quickly. Your love is inflexible and might be called excessive in its manifestations.

👁 DESTINY
You should be conservative in your business dealings. Cater to those in authority, and do not insist on having your own way. A worthy idea will receive the attention it deserves if you do not force it upon others. Do not let unexpected happenings or rejection cause confusion. Increased concentration on your own inventions could prove to be financially and socially rewarding.

☯ KARMIC LESSON
Born on this day, you have a certain perseverance and determination that carry you successfully through most of the jobs you undertake. Your humor helps you survive; this very quality often makes you successful where you would otherwise fail. You are straightforward, sincere, and very earnest in all that you do. You must never forget that all success depends upon the use you make of the forces within yourself, which you should aim to understand and cultivate. Exert your own winning, fun charm, and you should attain anything you desire.

🧘 SECRET
You are a very fortunate combination of the artistic type with a practical sensibility. You will do particularly well in some fashion-related industry.

APRIL 15

Habit is a cable; we weave a thread of it each day, and at last we cannot break it.
—Horace Mann

BORN ON THIS DAY
- **Leonardo da Vinci**
  inventor
- **Henry James**
  author
- **Bessie Smith**
  singer
- **Emma Watson**
  actor
- **Émile Durkheim**
  sociologist

PERSONALITY
You might be called the extroverted type. In other words, you are interested in outside things, and you are not too deeply or seriously concerned with the problems of the soul or the fulfillment of spiritual needs. You prefer getting away from the domestic scene and those activities connected with the home. Adventure seems to call you with a most compelling voice, and most likely you are only too willing to answer that call. In your dealings with others, you are known as a good sport, a person who is understanding of faults and tolerant of them, too. People like you for your hail-fellow-well-met attitude toward life. All in all, you are likable, sensible, and bound to succeed. Diplomacy is essential in all associations with strangers or new acquaintances.

LIFE PATH
Your perception is keen, your mind analytical, and your heart courageous. You are fond of networking, enjoy traveling, court popularity, and let your ambition lead you. You seldom allow unpleasant surroundings to disturb the tranquility of your mind. You are a strong lover.

DESTINY
You need to more fully utilize your unique understanding of human nature. You will enjoy working with an expert to make a few innovations in your dress and home decor. Toward business transactions, take a more conservative point of view. Venus rays on your birthday favor romance and happy friendships rather than excursions into economic or political fields.

KARMIC LESSON
Your character is a very mixed one and is hard to delineate for that reason. You are eminently practical and material in many things, yet you have a distinct interest in creative people. You are a good judge of human nature and a reader of character. You are a "people person" and have a natural gift for speaking in public. You are clever and outgoing but also take a serious interest in many things. You are practical and have excellent executive powers. You demand a good deal of love from others but are willing to give a great deal in return.

SECRET
You have decidedly colorful tastes. You may make material sacrifices, but you will never regret them.

FRIENDS & FAMILY

APRIL 16

One must follow circumstances, use the forces about us, do in a word what we find to do.
—Anatole France

BORN ON THIS DAY

★ **Kareem Abdul-Jabbar**
basketball player

★ **Charlie Chaplin**
comic actor

★ **Dusty Springfield**
singer

★ **Martin Lawrence**
actor

★ **Selena**
singer/songwriter

FRIENDS & FAMILY

● PERSONALITY

Your character is marked by intelligence, originality, executive ability, and constructive mental powers. Because you combine these traits with a spirit of cooperation, you should be able to attain almost any goal you set for yourself in life. In the game of life, you are capable of being the coach, the player, or the spectator. That is because you are very versatile. You look around first to see what's what; then you decide just what you are going to do: watch, play, or judge! This is indeed an intelligent attitude to adopt, and you should make the most of the game for knowing the secret of philosophy. You need not be warned not to bet on the game, for you are clever enough to know that the odds are in favor only of the person who doesn't gamble.

● LIFE PATH

No undertaking is too great to discourage you, and you are usually able to carry your projects to completion. You are not overly exuberant or enthusiastic. You will listen carefully to the advice of others and just as carefully pursue your own course. Your homelife can probably be very satisfying.

● DESTINY

Spontaneity will be your keynote. When a decision is needed, you will have the answer ready. Do not give too much time to problems that have not materialized. Keep secret ambitions to yourself until you see practical steps you can take toward their realization. Do not go in for drastic changes. Use gentle, subtle, persuasive methods to bring others around to your point of view.

● KARMIC LESSON

You have a naturally strong character, which is not at all dependent but sufficient unto itself. You are a great believer in karmic justice, and your actions are guided by respect for the Golden Rule. You are especially fond of the sea and may need to be near water. You have a strong sense of humor and a retentive memory. You are sympathetic, yet at the same time a little stoic. You are generous and openhanded. You have good taste and would excel in artful hobbies or in making a garden beautiful.

● SECRET

Guard your times of rest very carefully, as you show a tendency to not get enough sleep. This is an annoyance rather than a real danger.

APRIL 17

And the day came when the risk to remain tight in a bud was more painful than the risk it took to blossom.
—Anaïs Nin

BORN ON THIS DAY

- **J.P. Morgan**
  financier
- **Boomer Esiason**
  football player
- **Jennifer Garner**
  actor
- **Victoria Beckham**
  singer, fashion designer
- **Redman**
  rapper

PERSONALITY
Your mental capacities enable you to form a sane and wise balance between the externals of life and the inner emotions and spiritual satisfactions. In business dealings, you are fair, but you allow no one to take advantage of you. In social dealings, you are tolerant and amicable. In spiritual leanings, you are all-embracing of the larger principles of philosophy rather than bound to the conventions of any organized sect. You see the interconnections of nature and of humankind as part of a harmonious whole. This combination makes you a well-rounded individual who faces life as it is and makes the best of it. You do your best work with large groups of people and achieve your greatest success with organizations rather than individuals. Affectionate and generous by nature, you require mutual love for your true happiness.

LIFE PATH
Your nature is affectionate, and you require much love and give much in return. If you are happy, you are very happy, and if you are unhappy, you are very unhappy. You are an omnivorous reader, assimilate what you read, and are ambitious to elevate and improve yourself.

DESTINY
You must work to concentrate on matters at hand rather than visionary ideas. Do not permit small domestic and business details to remain unattended. Also avoid extravagant purchases. Shop around, and do not take the first bargain you see. Be loyal to old friends and assure them of your willingness to stand by them in times of trouble. This karma will come back to you.

KARMIC LESSON
You have a very busy mind that demands something to interest it at all times. You have a keen interest in current affairs and a constant desire for more knowledge. You are a delver into whatever comes your way, and you also have a great interest in all psychic and mysterious things. You are fond of music and would make a good performer if you studied faithfully. You should have a naturally good singing voice, which stimulates your throat chakra. You have good judgment and a good mind and are, on the whole, a very resourceful person.

SECRET
You are a born supervisor. If given educational advantages and proper inspiration, you could become the head of a cultural or social movement.

FRIENDS & FAMILY

APRIL 18

Character is built out of circumstance.
—G.H. Lewes

BORN ON THIS DAY

★ **Conan O'Brien**
TV host

★ **James Woods**
actor

★ **Jeff Dunham**
comedian

★ **Kourtney Kardashian**
reality TV actor

★ **Eli Roth**
film director

FRIENDS & FAMILY

⊕ PERSONALITY
You are attracted by the more soothing and subtle manifestations of life. Poetry, music, art, and romance entertain you more than violent movies or competitive sports. You like home and garden and are very considerate of your friends and family. On the negative side, you may be inclined to occasional dark moods when things don't go as you would like them to. You have a genius for business affairs, but you are not as intrigued by them as some people are. You would prefer to have a steady income without the headaches of having a large income with large responsibilities. Because you have a deep understanding of human foibles, you would do well in areas of activity such as philanthropy, social service, and social reform. Comfort and peace of mind are your ideals of existence, and you sometimes remove yourself from the hubbub of life to enjoy a full and compatible life with a person whom you truly care for.

◉ LIFE PATH
Your great desire and ambition are to accomplish something out of the ordinary. Persevere, and do not let the magnitude of any undertaking deter you from the effort. You are intellectually capable and strong. You have a mostly well-balanced disposition and are moderately patient and very loving.

◉ DESTINY
Your ideas will be practical, and you will have opportunities to use them effectively. Overcome any tendency to be hasty or negligent when you feel burdened by small details. Speak your mind with freedom as long as you have considered your statements carefully beforehand. Games of chance may prove pleasurable, but do not lose your perspective. Set aside part of your income in your bank account each month. Make it a habit.

☯ KARMIC LESSON
You are artistic and handy, born on this day, and exceedingly drawn to exhibits, concerts, and all that pertains to the performing arts. You have a natural gift for communications, and you are probably good at telling stories. You should prove successful in business and should trust your instincts in your relationships and dealings with people. You could be attracted to exercise like yoga and tai chi. You are fond of animals. Cultivate your mind more, and learn to grasp opportunities when they come.

☻ SECRET
You have a fascination with those to whom you are attracted that can border on obsession. You might be drawn to create light plays, such as musical comedies.

APRIL 19

Action may not always bring happiness, but there is no happiness without action.
—Benjamin Disraeli

PERSONALITY
You combine the best qualities possessed by the introverted and extroverted types. Because you can get the best out of the life of competition in the busy world and the best out of intellectual pursuits, you reach an acme of achievement. To you, the doors of the worlds of business, art, and romance seem always to be open. This is no fluke of destiny, but the result of your studies, observations, and judgment. Where aggression is needed, you put on your armor and do battle for any cause that you believe worthy of your espousal. Where understanding and tolerance are more appropriate, you are gentle and kind. This is a winning combination of facets to your nature, and they should bring to you the kind of calm and reflective existence that you admire and seek. Never share your love with anyone who is not worthy of it.

LIFE PATH
You are of an academic temperament, intellectual and shrewd, and fond of music and travel. You are a great lover of nature and spend as much time as possible outdoors. You are careful of your possessions and know how to make the best of them. You have many close friendships.

DESTINY
You will see chances for promotion or advancement in your present work. A favor from an especially helpful person of prestige may take you several steps up the ladder of success. Always avoid jumping to hasty conclusions, and be careful about anything you put in writing. Correspondence by a third person may be worthwhile, but it can be unfortunate, too, if it is carried on in a thoughtless manner. Be considerate of your family's feelings when making social plans.

KARMIC LESSON
Born on this day, you are naturally tasteful and refined and would make a very good designer. You are fond of good clothes and would spend everything you had on an extravagant outfit. In other ways, you are careful in money matters and would make a good financial planner. Public life fascinates you, and you are eminently suited to it. You have vigorous willpower, and logic is your strong suit. You are contemplative and fond of philosophical and metaphysical considerations. You have a distinct talent for creative work, at which you could excel.

SECRET
You have the gift of creative powers balanced by a practical turn of mind. You are a lover of repose and of the serenity that comes with a time-out.

BORN ON THIS DAY
- **Jayne Mansfield** — actor
- **James Franco** — actor
- **Jim Curry** — actor
- **Maria Sharapova** — tennis player
- **Troy Polamalu** — football player

FRIENDS & FAMILY

APRIL 20

Thinking is the talking of the soul with itself.
—Plato

BORN ON THIS DAY

- **Tan France**
  fashion designer
- **John Paul Stephens**
  U.S. Supreme Court justice
- **George Takei**
  actor
- **Jessica Lange**
  actor
- **Ryan O'Neal**
  actor

FRIENDS & FAMILY

◉ PERSONALITY

You have a deeply affectionate nature, a sense of responsibility, and a strong conscience. Yet, if this gives the impression that you have no fun in life, it is erroneous. You simply enjoy doing the things that others consider it their duty to do. Family affairs give you pleasure, and you are never happier than when you are planning some delightful surprise for your loved ones. By nature, you are quite imaginative, and your interests are along the lines of cultural pursuits. You enjoy attending lectures, going to museums, and keeping up on the current trends on all artistic levels. You are great at cooperating in any cause or project that attracts your interest. Others may make the plans, but you know how to execute them no matter what a handful of detailed work this entails. In this life, you may give more love than you receive, but you also know it is more blessed to give than to receive.

◉ LIFE PATH

You are rather positive and headstrong and bound to succeed despite obstacles. Your tendency is to make others stand aside or be trampled upon. Praise and flattery influence you more than an attempt to drive you. You have the devoted love and understanding of the members of your household.

◉ DESTINY

Your willingness to do a little more than is required will be rewarded. A favor you grant to another can be the stepping-stone to success, but do not sacrifice dignity by trying to make good impressions. Do not let baseless fears delay your plans. There are times when taking a chance is better than holding back and being too conservative. Refuse to take part in malicious gossip, for its harmful effects may return to haunt you.

◉ KARMIC LESSON

You have great tact and patience, and you have a kind, quiet disposition. You possess psychic powers and are probably a trifle mediumistic. You need a wise, guiding hand over your life, in which case you could make it a great success, as you have great ability and native talents. You are easily excitable, emotional, and amorous. At the same time, you have a naturally aesthetic side, which leads you to the life of a recluse; you like independence above all else and cannot bear to have anyone prying into your affairs. Cultivate cheer, and a sense of the humorous aspect of many situations, and a life of happiness and profit will be yours.

◉ SECRET

You have an intense personality possessed of profound emotions. Get enough sleep or you will tend to become morose.

APRIL 21

Life appears to me too short to be spent in nursing animosity or registering wrong.
—Charlotte Brontë

PERSONALITY
There is significance in the fact that you were born on the anniversary of the day when Rome was founded. First seat of culture in its own hemisphere, first home of civilization, and first city for almost three thousand years, this historic spot has the same birthday that you have. The qualities of persistence, interest in the arts, and dominance of the surrounding world are also qualities possessed by you who share this important date of birth. The brooding that poets speak of is also a part of your makeup, for you may be subject to dark moods. However, you have an intelligent perspective, and so you realize that these moods are as swift to go as they are to come, and you therefore do not allow them to dominate you. You look at things from the long-range point of view, and you are willing to undergo present sacrifices for the sake of future safety and security.

LIFE PATH
You care a great deal for culture and refinement and should succeed in any of the humanities. You are kindhearted, tractable, generous, and ambitious. Your inclination will be to marry your first love, but much care should be exercised that you do not select an uncongenial partner and cause unhappiness for you both.

DESTINY
Good fortunes will attend social and business endeavors. Take your responsibilities, but not yourself, seriously. Enjoy every minute of your vacations, including the opportunity to meet interesting people. Do not work for too long of a period. Though you should not feel that you must get everything done at once, do avoid going to the opposite extreme and letting too many details wait for tomorrow.

KARMIC LESSON
Born on this day, you have a straightforward, honest nature, with great clarity of judgment and a keen perception of the truth. You have a great love of justice and cannot bear to see wrong done to anyone, at any time. You are fond of animals, and they are usually fond of you. Naturally serious-minded, you are a great reader and student. Clear vision and insight characterize you. You are very sociable, generous, and sympathetic. You are fond of social activities and good food and like the best of everything. You have a strong spirit and a strong will.

SECRET
You are a person of notable patience, with a tendency to make education in some field your lifework. You also have gourmet tastes.

BORN ON THIS DAY
- **Queen Elizabeth II** — British monarch
- **Max Weber** — sociologist, historian
- **Charlotte Brontë** — author
- **James McAvoy** — actor
- **Tony Romo** — football player

FRIENDS & FAMILY

APRIL 22

Indifference is the invincible giant of the world.
—Ouida

BORN ON THIS DAY

- ★ **J. Robert Oppenheimer**
  physicist
- ★ **John Waters**
  filmmaker
- ★ **Jack Nicholson**
  actor
- ★ **Spencer Haywood**
  basketball player
- ★ **Sherri Shepherd**
  TV personality

FRIENDS & FAMILY

✦ PERSONALITY
You have an unusual amount of executive ability, which you express in directing the affairs of your personal life and those of your family, friends, and business associates. Your taking the lead is appreciated rather than resented. As you have an especially keen sense for business, you succeed in all matters where buying, selling, hiring, and producing are involved. Even if your actual business deals are restricted to household purchases, you know how to get value for your money. Cooperation is the important keyword to understanding you, for you have a grand spirit of amiability that you put into everything you do. You are quick to show your appreciation for a favor granted you, and you're very big about doing favors for others. You don't want rewards or publicity for the kindness you perform; you just like to do nice things.

◉ LIFE PATH
You are creatively inclined and should develop your talents, which mean a great deal to you. You like to read, but what you like even more is to have a library full of books that date back from the earliest years of your childhood. You are positive about your opinions and argumentative, but you will yield a point with good grace when thoroughly convinced. You have a high degree of intelligence and uncanny foresight.

◉ DESTINY
You should bear in mind that all work and no play is not only boring but also dangerous physically and emotionally. You should overcome the tendency to become so engrossed in your tasks that you forget to take time out to relax. Do not feel that you must carry your business over into your pleasures. Do some of the things that you have been postponing.

☯ KARMIC LESSON
You could make a great success of your life and will probably travel a lot. You are not extravagant in your tastes, but at the same time, you never throw any money away—you shop for the best buy. You have many ups and downs in life but can adapt yourself to any circumstances. You blend fixed attributes with changing qualities. You are fearless in all that you do and say, and, so long as you feel you are in the right, it does not matter to you what others may think of your actions or manner of life. You are witty, lively, and popular; you are strong in showing your affections.

◉ SECRET
You have an entertaining personality and are a lover of adventure. You are also an epicure, devoted to fine food and drink.

APRIL 23

Love looks not with the eyes, but with the mind.
—William Shakespeare

BORN ON THIS DAY

- **James Buchanan**
  U.S. president
- **Halston**
  fashion designer
- **Shirley Temple**
  actor
- **John Oliver**
  TV commentator
- **Roy Orbison**
  singer/songwriter

PERSONALITY
When anyone in your family or circle of friends needs sympathy or a helping hand, you are the one they come to. This is because you have an understanding heart and a tolerant mind, two things of which you may be duly proud. You are not given to loud lamenting when things go wrong, even though you are, to a certain degree, impatient. However, you have learned to adjust yourself to the ups and downs of life so that you no longer bemoan situations that you feel are beyond your control. This is true in general of your attitude to life. You know that there are certain situations that arise despite your best efforts, that they are hard to take, but that the only adult and sensible thing to do is to accept what is inevitable. From year to year, your mind grows, and with it your character. You have good taste in material and intellectual pursuits, and you enjoy the best of these that life has to offer.

LIFE PATH
You express a strong will and a fearless, dominating manner. You care a great deal for fine surroundings and are inclined to fret if you do not have them. You like to lead and take the initiative, demanding explicit obedience from those over whom you have any control. Your love is masterful and commanding.

DESTINY
You should keep your ultimate goals firmly fixed in mind and not stray from the paths that lead to them. Carefully select those pursuits that warrant the greatest expenditure of time and effort, as these will be the most rewarding. Consider the security that comes from being loved and respected as equally important as that of money. You will always learn the lesson of valuing dear friends.

KARMIC LESSON
You have remarkable latent abilities, which need only to be cultivated to make you famous—if you so desire. You have literary, communication, and oratorical abilities as well as a keen sense of humor. You are a great student of human nature and like mingling with and studying people of all kinds and stations. You have strong socialistic tendencies and interests. You are drawn to the good things of this life; you should travel much and see a great deal of the world, if only virtually at times. You have great natural power of intention and need only to cultivate diligence to make your dreams manifest.

SECRET
You have a rather submerged nature, inclined to underestimating your own abilities. A culmination at one point in life will bring out your talents to full and deserved success.

FRIENDS & FAMILY

APRIL 24

He is not only idle who does nothing, but he is idle who might be better employed.
—Socrates

BORN ON THIS DAY

★ **Barbra Streisand**
singer, actor

★ **Shirley MacLaine**
actor

★ **Jean Paul Gaultier**
fashion designer

★ **Kelly Clarkson**
singer

★ **Cedric the Entertainer**
actor, comedian

FRIENDS & FAMILY

● PERSONALITY
A lively sense of humor makes you generally see things in their true light. You cannot take too seriously the minor mishaps of daily life, because you see how insignificant they are in comparison to the large blueprint of life. This ability makes you a wonderful companion. You put others at their ease, and you are at home in any type of group or social situation. There is a remarkable quality of something luminous about you; you seem to light up a room when you enter; people smile when they are introduced to you. This is, of course, the inner light of spiritual illumination, which you radiate to other people. You cooperate with others willingly, and you can also assume charge of anything that has to be done. You are a good planner and can see ahead. Hard work does not frighten you, as you are capable of whatever tasks you are called upon to perform. It might be said that you mean well, and it surely would be the truth.

● LIFE PATH
You probably read a great deal and have considerable aptitude in assimilating what you read and embodying the results in your conversation. You are not content with superficial study and like to associate with intellectual and cultured people. You like personal attention if it does not assume the form of false flattery.

● DESTINY
You will develop a lot of independence in your life and have learned not to depend on others too much. However, you should curb impetuous actions and hold back decisions until you analyze the situations that arise. Keep alert so that you will be able to recognize opportunity when it knocks at your door. Try your hand at renovating possessions, the beauty and usability of which have been diminished by time.

● KARMIC LESSON
You are inquisitive and fond of trying everything new as it comes out and experimenting in all sorts of ways with innovative inventions. You are original and have high ideals. You have a magnetic personality and can hold a crowd of people anywhere. As soon as a great idea strikes you, you must learn to write it down, in case you forget it. You are capable and like detail work. You like to do things your own way and do not like taking advice from others. Use your will more, and success will be yours.

● SECRET
You are a good organizer and would make an excellent businessperson in foreign enterprises.

APRIL 25

Subtlety may deceive you; integrity never will.
—Oliver Cromwell

BORN ON THIS DAY

★ **Pyotr Ilyich Tchaikovsky**
composer

★ **Ella Fitzgerald**
singer

★ **Al Pacino**
actor

★ **Tim Duncan**
basketball player

PERSONALITY

You are generally placid and agreeable, but there is a side to your nature that can be quite volatile. You may flare up at a moment's notice and give quite a martial performance—if your anger is aroused by unfairness, or if you think that someone is taking advantage of that good side of your nature. Since you do not often give way to such expressions of passion, few people know that you have such a side to your makeup. This fiery quality is the shadow side of your aggressive, domineering sense of things, the potential fighter, leader, and builder qualities that you need today in a world of competition. You have strong persuasive powers and can talk people into practically anything you want. With your family and loved ones, you are usually gentle, affectionate, and demonstrative. You should be successful in fields of endeavor where personal service is important.

LIFE PATH

You are a clever and skillful worker with your hands. You are frank and outspoken but not in the least malicious. You love with a passion that is irresistible. You might be prone to have a jealous nature and demand undivided affection and constant attention.

DESTINY

You will have no trouble convincing others that your intentions are honest. Consequently, you will find friends cooperating with you and your ideas. Avoid a tendency to become unduly upset over temporary setbacks. Relatives or close friends can be helpful during a period of adjustment by offering you moral support. However, do not let them become too dependent on you or vice versa. Do not take on more work than you can complete. You should not let your enthusiasm run away with you.

KARMIC LESSON

You are naturally quite cautious in temperament and rather inclined to be a hoarder in money matters. Learn to open your hand a little more fully and be more natural and spontaneous in your dealings with others. You are not as simple as you look, and underneath your calm and serene exterior slumber fires that few surmise—even yourself. You are very conscientious and should have savvy business ability. Yours is a life that can run smoothly if its way has no catastrophes or other ripples to ruffle the surface of the water. Learn to be a little more tolerant of the views of others, for as a rule you are not.

SECRET

Born on this day, you are blessed with a fine speaking and singing voice and should, where the talent warrants, make sure to use your voice in special ways.

FRIENDS & FAMILY

April 26

It is good to be content with anything that is available.
—Buddha

BORN ON THIS DAY

- ★ **William Shakespeare**
  playwright, poet
- ★ **Giorgio Moroder**
  music producer
- ★ **Carol Burnett**
  actor, comedian
- ★ **Jet Li**
  actor
- ★ **Frederick Law Olmsted**
  landscape architect

FRIENDS & FAMILY

◉ PERSONALITY

You have an affable nature, a love of friends and family, and an affectionately demonstrative disposition. Nothing pleases you more than to be surrounded by a group of congenial people, having a pleasant time. Because you are kind and considerate, most people like you, and you enjoy a large social acquaintanceship. At times, you go a little overboard on the fun side of life, but when duty calls, you are able to snap back and attend to your duties conscientiously. This even combination of the serious and the amusing interests in your life makes for a fairly well-organized existence. In addition to this way of life, you have a sensible balance of pursuits along intellectual and business lines. You are creative and productive, and although you enjoy gatherings and parties, you are also happy reading a book, seeing a show, and attending lectures. You have a lot of pride, and it is not false pride by any means.

◉ LIFE PATH

You are ambitious, shrewd, and farsighted and have the confidence of your associates. Your friends are your most valuable possessions and will be the means of helping you over many rough spots. You love decorating your home, and within your family, relations are mostly kind, patient, and considerate.

◉ DESTINY

You are one who should initiate action. Friends who are more speculative in their outlook will aid you in your business affairs. When new interests demand attention, combine them with previously enjoyed activities. Do not suddenly replace old diversions with new. Watch the chance to explain your opinions. Read all correspondence carefully, with an eye to hidden meanings. Do not be taken in by false propaganda. Be sincere and daring in all your dealings.

◉ KARMIC LESSON

You have a strong will and active intelligence, as well as a great deal of tact and diplomacy. You are very fond of healing modalities that are cutting-edge. Works of art fascinate you; you should be able to paint or draw. You have a strong inclination for politics and should participate in them as you understand their importance. You also have strong technology interests that attract you especially. You are more or less intellectual, but this side of you gets pushed into the background by the practical interests of your life, which occupy the foreground. If you determine to live up to the best that is in you, yours should be a very fulfilled life.

◉ SECRET

You are nimble and patient with your fingers. You could do well as a surgeon or a craftsperson.

APRIL 27

Poverty is no disgrace to a man, but it is confoundedly inconvenient.
—Sydney Smith

✦ PERSONALITY
You approach life with a resolve, trying your best to mold circumstances to your desires. This is an excellent philosophy, for it suits your temperament, and it succeeds in bringing to you those rewards that you think a human being should win for personal growth. In your associations with other people, you may meet individuals who disagree with your way of thinking and who may consider you overly aggressive. In dealing with such people, do not try to impose your will upon them, for that might lead to an unpleasant argument. Use the tactics of a diplomat, avoid being domineering, and get your way through your cleverness instead of through strength of will. While it is true that your interests may be centered on material things, you should not neglect those aspects of life that bring spiritual peace and calm. Meditation, yoga, occasional solitude, and prayer should be enlightening aids to your development of character.

✦ LIFE PATH
You can be inclined to be aggressive, but not to the extent of quarrelsomeness. You always insist upon getting your just dues and will always give others a "square deal." You have a strong, passionate spirit, which exerts its influence in affairs of the heart.

✦ DESTINY
You will always profitably alter some of your working methods in business or at home to improve your circumstances. Give consideration to the inspirational ideas of others as well as to your own intuitions. Guard against errors when outlining plans that will be submitted to one in authority. Your originality and initiative should attract much favorable notice in your life.

✦ KARMIC LESSON
You are naturally very neat and tidy; you are careful about money matters and apt to save something for a rainy day. You are fond of travel and have a bucket list to see a good deal of the world. You are apparently not attracted to just one person, as underneath you have very strong desires, which are at times hard to keep under control. You are probably fertile in imagination, fond of reading, and a true romantic. The beautiful in nature appeals to you. You have salable ideas and should be able to share ideas well if you try to do so systematically for some time.

✦ SECRET
You can be somewhat of a recluse, driven to isolation by reason of an unusually single-track view.

BORN ON THIS DAY
- **Ulysses S. Grant** — U.S. president, Civil War hero
- **Mary Wollstonecraft** — author
- **Coretta Scott King** — civil rights activist
- **Sheena Easton** — singer
- **Casey Kasem** — radio personality

FRIENDS & FAMILY

APRIL 28

Nothing liberates our greatness like the desire to help, the desire to serve.
—Marianne Williamson

BORN ON THIS DAY

★ **James Monroe**
U.S. president

★ **Jay Leno**
talk show host

★ **Harper Lee**
author

★ **Elena Kagan**
U.S. Supreme Court justice

★ **Ann-Margret**
actor, singer

FRIENDS & FAMILY

PERSONALITY
You have a very expressive personality and can convince others to think your way. This gives you a great advantage in carrying out your plans and in getting your way when you decide upon a course of conduct. Your generosity does not permit you to take advantage of your powers but rather to establish fair play as your philosophy of life. All things that have an aura or flavor of the dramatic appeal to you. You therefore enjoy situations that are exotic or colorful, and you respond with deep appreciation to the artistic creations of talented people. In financial affairs, you have a certain flair, particularly in being able to help others in their plans for promotion. You give excellent advice—it comes to you naturally because of your experience, which you combine with an innate aptitude. Your cleverness and unselfishness bring you many friends and much popularity.

LIFE PATH
You are sympathetic, kind, loving, and generous to a fault. You are not always communicative about your own problems and will struggle alone with trouble or worry rather than take those you love into your confidence. When you make up your mind to do a thing, you do it.

DESTINY
You are advised to associate with people in a position to help you in your career. Accept assistance without a mistaken feeling of inferiority. Your own talents and accomplishments merit the rewards you will gain. When the spotlight is turned on, you keep it there by your attitude of poise and self-confidence. Pride, which is justified, is a real asset to continued progress. You will have the opportunity to aid a close friend in life and will be never forgotten for it.

KARMIC LESSON
You have a strong character, are rather dogmatic and set in your ways, and are usually right. You like to be well thought of and will sacrifice much to attain this end. You are very interested in things psychic yet inclined to be down-to-earth and often skeptical at the same time. You should learn to trust your intuitions and judgment and not be so swayed by the opinions of others. You have varied talents and gifts and are in many ways a natural bohemian. You like lots of fun and excitement and are inclined to indulge in it, with no thought of tomorrow. You must experience several hard knocks in life for you to arrive at your true goal and in order to bring out the best that is in you.

SECRET
Born on this day, you can rise from humble origins to great heights through fierce determination.

APRIL 29

Let us have faith that right makes might.
—Abraham Lincoln

⊛ PERSONALITY
It sometimes seems as though the wisdom of the ages is at your command, for you have such a strong intuition that you surprise your friends and the members of your family with the accuracy of your hunches. A study of occult philosophy would be interesting and profitable to you because it would help to develop your innate psychic powers and would reveal to you the thoughts of the wise people of all times. This sensitivity to things around you occasionally makes you feel slighted when no slight is intended. Do not probe too deeply into the motives of others but accept their kind offers of friendship and geniality. By creating a balance between the inner or spiritual life and the world of externals or outside things, you can attain lasting happiness and peace of mind. You are an ideal partner, and you could have a long reign of partnership bliss.

⊛ LIFE PATH
You are shrewd, intuitive, decisive, and positive, yet also very cautious. Your intuition and decision-making ability are continually at war with your caution. Sometimes people take advantage of you despite your insight. You have a sympathetic and sensitive nature and so are easily offended. You trust only a special few.

⊛ DESTINY
Your willingness to accept the advice of others will serve you well in your career path. You will experience the feeling of satisfaction that comes when you know you are a master at doing a good job. There will be many who will appreciate the quality of your service and give you devotion in addition to respect. Your intuition will enable you to estimate shrewdly the worth of people, and it will be of assistance in obtaining financial and social success.

⊛ KARMIC LESSON
You have a good memory, are observant, and can handle many difficult situations. You appreciate the beautiful in life and have thought on various occasions of trying your hand as an artist. You have an avid interest in the occult and are probably more or less deeply involved in psychic studies and investigations. You are rather romantic in temperament and would rather talk to one person, off in a corner, than have a crowd around you and talk to half a dozen at once. At the same time, public life attracts you, but from a distance, as from a podcast or website, for example, where you can reach a large audience. You have a great eye for beauty, and very little in this direction escapes you.

⊛ SECRET
You show a strategic trend of mind. You could develop into an inventor, a wizard with figures, or even a stock expert.

BORN ON THIS DAY
- **William Randolph Hearst** — publisher, politician
- **Daniel Day Lewis** — actor
- **Jerry Seinfeld** — comedian
- **Willie Nelson** — singer
- **Michelle Pfeiffer** — actor

FRIENDS & FAMILY

APRIL 30

Initiative is doing the right thing without being told.
—Elbert Hubbard

BORN ON THIS DAY
- **Jane Campion**
  film director
- **Isiah Thomas**
  basketball player
- **Gal Gadot**
  actor
- **Cloris Leachman**
  actor
- **Travis Scott**
  rapper

FRIENDS & FAMILY

● PERSONALITY
A lovely combination of traits makes you quite a well-balanced individual. You enjoy company, good times, and social gatherings. But you also like your work, get satisfaction from the successful completion of your duties, and understand that there is an alternation of work and play in the way life's cycles work out. You enjoy the finer things, like books, plays, and music. However, you do not neglect the types of sports or activities appropriate to your age, health, and circumstances. It may be that at times you are tempted to overdo social events and pleasure-seeking, but that is more likely your easy acquiescing to the suggestions of friends than to your natural inclinations. You should definitely try to regulate your life according to a sensible program, making up a schedule for long periods of time as well as for daily use. In this way, you will develop your efficiency and accomplish more.

● LIFE PATH
You are outspoken, often to the point of bluntness, sometimes unintentionally hurting other people's feelings. But still you are mostly faithful, steady, dependable, and conscientious. The devoted love you show to those dearest to you is returned in ample measure.

● DESTINY
There will be more than one occasion when you will be proud of your financial acumen. Helping others with money problems will be part of your karmic activities. Do not hesitate to assert yourself when you feel you should. Business matters will grow over time and be consummated successfully. Participation in charities and philanthropic organizations can bring personal satisfaction. Do not underestimate your social assets.

● KARMIC LESSON
You are generally serious-minded, contemplative, and critical. You have a great love of nature, which typifies a wonderful spirituality to you. You have great staying power and can stand a good deal of knocking about. You are excitable, but you do not lose your head under trying circumstances. Then you are more wideawake and alert in mind than at any other time. You are good at figures and ought to make a good investor. You will be comfortably off in later life and will always have an abundance of friends around you who are exceedingly fond of you.

● SECRET
You possess a strange combination of a roving mind and a methodical mind. You would make a good salesperson of what you believe in strongly.

MAY 1

Every great mistake has a halfway moment, a split second when it can be recalled and perhaps remedied.
—Pearl S. Buck

BORN ON THIS DAY

- **Joseph Heller**
  author
- **Wes Anderson**
  filmmaker
- **Joanna Lumley**
  actor
- **Tim McGraw**
  singer
- **Judy Collins**
  singer/songwriter

FRIENDS & FAMILY

PERSONALITY

Education would be a profession well suited to you, as you have a natural bent for teaching others. Of course, this means that you can do your teaching in real-life situations as well as in a school or classroom. You are fond of your family, so much so that you often assume tasks and responsibilities that should rightfully belong to others. Bear in mind that everyone has chores in life; don't leap to perform duties that are not yours. Because you are inclined to be somewhat overemotional, you are subject to feeling the blues. When such moods come, you should intensify your interest in outside things. According to your age and capabilities, you should work off some of the doldrums in exercise, sports, and helping others. However, you need not be too concerned about such things, for you are usually alert, optimistic, and considerate of others. You crave affection, and you make a wonderful partner.

LIFE PATH

You have a strong will, a commanding personality, and the ability to plan and execute. You are intense in love or hatred, impulsive, and full of energy. In love, your path takes twists and turns and has ups and downs, but you will gain ultimate happiness.

DESTINY

You will make the force of your personality felt in both business and social circles. You can get a lot of pleasure in making your homelife comfortable and interesting, especially for one close member of the family. This does not mean, however, that you should assume more than your share of work, taxing your capacities to the point of mental or emotional tenseness. Your life will be a constructive one, for you have enough varied activities to ward off boredom.

KARMIC LESSON

Steadfast in your friendships, you rarely forsake a friend who appeals to you for aid. Penetrating in your analysis of people, you appreciate all the subtleties of character. You are rather tenacious; once you have set your mind to do a certain thing, nothing can stop you. You have many talents and are interested in a wide range of general information. You have no use for the liars and con artists of life but stand by truth and honesty. When people let you down, you take it to heart. You have a sharp wit and can be sarcastic at times, even when you don't intend to be. On the whole, you are serious-minded, though you can enter into goofiness when you are in the right mood.

SECRET

You are a person of strong will and extreme good nature but are saddled with a sensitive soul. You become particularly hurt by gossip against you or someone you care about.

MAY 2

I'm not afraid of storms, for I'm learning how to sail my ship.
—Louisa May Alcott

BORN ON THIS DAY
- **Dwayne Johnson**
  actor
- **David Beckham**
  soccer player
- **Donatella Versace**
  fashion designer
- **Christine Baranski**
  actor
- **Hedda Hopper**
  gossip columnist

PERSONALITY
Persistence and patience mark the manner in which you conduct your life. It is infrequent indeed that you take up arms to battle your troubles, for you know how to arrange your life in a sensible and comfortable manner, so that there will be a minimum of hassles and intrusions. When the unexpected occurs, you know how to handle the situation, and if it is beyond your control, you can wait until the disturbing element has passed. This seems to give you wisdom beyond your years or experience, because it reaches out in evanescent space and transcends the limitations of time. Whenever others need help, you are ready, willing, and most generous. Your private life is sacred and important to you, and you like your periods of solitude to think and meditate. Nevertheless, when the practical duties of daily life must be performed, you are ever there, fulfilling your obligations. You are calm and have a rather remarkable—almost healing—influence upon those who come to you for help, solace, and advice.

LIFE PATH
You are patient, loving, and kind and very fond of young children. You are not a big talker and don't ask for help, sometimes suffering in uncomplaining silence. You are loved by most who know you well and will seldom have an enemy.

DESTINY
You have reason to expect good fortune, but you should cultivate and embrace the necessary patience and persistence that is an important part of your character. There is no need for you to become excited or confused when an unfamiliar situation arises. You are at your best when you are living up to your innate tendency toward calm and sensible planning. Events in life will give you an opportunity to show just how strong this side of your nature is. You will always value and nurture your self-reliance.

KARMIC LESSON
You are original and inventive. You have great natural resources and are careful about the friends you make. You are born to work on your own and cannot serve well under the rule of others. You are a great lover of order and cannot bear to see anything disarranged. You are fond of music, fashion, and the fine arts and take a great interest in such things. You are naturally a good diplomat and can live a double life very easily, if you make up your mind to do so. Above all, you should be independent, for you will never be happy otherwise.

SECRET
You are inclined to be showy in dress and in your worldly goods. You derive pleasure from being conspicuous.

FRIENDS & FAMILY

MAY 3

Ambition is so powerful a passion in the human breast, that however high we reach we are never satisfied.
—Machiavelli

BORN ON THIS DAY

★ **Golda Meir**
Israeli politician

★ **James Brown**
singer

★ **Frankie Vallie**
singer

★ **Sugar Ray Robinson**
boxer

★ **Nina García**
editor-in-chief of *Elle*

FRIENDS & FAMILY

PERSONALITY

You feel quite at home in the hustle and bustle of the busy world. You are a true executive, and you enjoy being busy, having many appointments, running around, checking your e-mail and cell phone, solving the problems that others bring you, and managing the affairs of your own life with efficiency and ingenuity. In business, you can conceive clever ways of doing things quickly and profitably. In home affairs, you can take charge, straighten problems out, and keep things running smoothly. Your interests are large, and your mental horizons are wide. You like to look ahead, plan intelligently, and carry out your plans with a minimum of fuss. Because you possess this ability for organization, you have a reputation for smart ideas, and friends and relatives like to consult you for advice. Your outlook is optimistic because you feel strength in your ability to handle the problems that arise in living the best possible life.

LIFE PATH

You are shrewd and calculating and will not enter into any project blindly. Upright and meticulous yourself, you are prone to be harsh in your judgment of others. You sometimes do not allow yourself to gather the full enjoyment of your homelife because you are so picky, although your family understands this about you.

DESTINY

Because your finest qualities are best illustrated in the midst of hard work and a heavy schedule, you always will welcome the busy life. Imagination will help you solve many problems without the necessity for great effort. Because of the way you work out the details of your many responsibilities, your reputation for being so capable will increase over time the more people hear about you.

KARMIC LESSON

You have a great love of humanity and do all that you can for suffering people on many occasions. You also love animals, and they in turn love you. You have a good head for business and good judgment. You are unselfish and constantly making sacrifices for others, which are not always sufficiently appreciated. You have an avid interest in foreign countries, and the dream of your life is to travel more. You have a naturally strong willpower, but you do not make quite as much use of this as you could. You might like outdoor activities of all kinds, particularly with dogs and horses.

SECRET

You have an active, sharp intellect, with a secretive nature. You would make a good detective or investigator.

MAY 4

Let us be thankful for the fools. But for them the rest of us could not succeed.
—Mark Twain

BORN ON THIS DAY
- **Audrey Hepburn**
  actor
- **Keith Haring**
  artist
- **Will Arnett**
  actor
- **Kimora Lee Simmons**
  model, reality TV personality
- **James Harrison**
  football player

PERSONALITY
An unusual amount of intuition makes you very sympathetic. In almost any situation, you can put yourself in the other person's place and clearly understand the emotions and motives they are experiencing. Although this gives you deep insight into human nature, it can work negatively if you allow it to upset your own way of life. While it is noble and generous to be helpful to others, you must realize that each person must solve his or her own problems and carry out their own duties. Do not, therefore, assume the burdens of another; be helpful, as is your inclination, but do not shoulder another's responsibilities. One facet of your nature is extreme practicability. You should allow this trait to come to the fore in your dealings with the world. Your inner life you should guard from public view, for you have a deep understanding of spiritual values. A vivid imagination spurs you on to creative and artistic endeavors.

LIFE PATH
You are bright, witty, and original and may be counted upon to do the unexpected thing. You are generally popular and have many close friends. You are adaptable, generous, and kindhearted and fond of children and pets.

DESTINY
You should remember that you can hurt, rather than help, someone you love by assuming duties that are not yours. Limit your assistance on such occasions to advice and sympathetic listening, rather than the actual shouldering of responsibilities. You can expect an active social life, but you will not lose the practical side of your nature. Do not neglect the development of your unique creative talents.

KARMIC LESSON
You are straightforward, sincere, and direct while being kind and respectful. Self-help is the great interest of your life. You should be placed so that you can devote your time to study of psychology. If you do not, the world will be deprived of the results of your labors, which could be influential. You are very savvy in money matters and can make a dollar go as far as anyone you have ever met. You should be very successful in speculation of all kinds and probably are fortunate at games of chance. If you come across a friend in need, you will share every cent you have. You are bright and cheerful and should live a fulfilling life.

SECRET
You are an all-rounder. You could make a moderate success in all undertakings, as you are possessed of an orderly mind and great powers of application.

FRIENDS & FAMILY

MAY 5

It is much easier to be critical than to be correct.
—Benjamin Disraeli

BORN ON THIS DAY

★ **Karl Marx**
philosopher, sociologist

★ **Adele**
singer

★ **Tammy Wynette**
singer

★ **Søren Kierkegaard**
philosopher

★ **Henry Cavill**
actor

★ **Craig David**
rapper

FRIENDS & FAMILY

_____
_____
_____
_____
_____
_____
_____
_____

✦ PERSONALITY

You are loquacious, talented, versatile, and magnetic. There is always an aura of excitement around you, because you love activity and are bored with anything that is slow, mundane, or lackluster. Because you have so much vitality, you are very popular, especially with young-thinking and fun-loving folks. Always the center of attention at parties and gatherings, you are an excellent organizer of games, sports, meetings, and entertainments. This ability to get people together stands you in good stead in business and in your family relationships. There is an irresistible quality about you that makes it possible for you to get your way, and this may tend to spoil you. You should not allow praise and flattery to go to your head, for then you would impair the rather remarkable talent that you possess. Your greatest success is in dealing with large groups of people or being in the public eye.

✦ LIFE PATH

You are imaginative, almost visionary. You care a lot about good clothes, enjoy flattery and attention, and like to be noticed. Responsibility does not weigh heavily upon you. However, you are a most agreeable person to live with and are very happy when your partner is happy.

✦ DESTINY

Your ability to get along with other people, so valuable in your business dealings, can be put to good use in organizing a new group or taking part in a community or charitable enterprise. If you have occasion to speak in public, have no fears. You can handle this assignment beautifully. Others will be attracted instinctively to you, and you will keep their affection and respect.

✦ KARMIC LESSON

You have a remarkably retentive memory and should be good at facts and figures. You never forget a face. You are probably fond of video games, ones that involve a certain amount of brain work. You should have a good speaking voice and probably would make a good public speaker. With money, you learn to think of the future and save up for a rainy day. At the same time, you should be able to accumulate quite a small fortune. Remember, though, that all you will ever get will be the result of your own energies and exertions, and no one will help you to any great extent in your efforts. Cultivate self-reliance.

✦ SECRET

You have a nature given to accepting life without complaint. Though you are outgoing, your greatest happiness will be derived from homelife, children, and honest work.

MAY 6

Silence is a true friend who never betrays.
—Confucius

BORD ON THIS DAY

- **Sigmund Freud**
  founder of psychoanalysis
- **Orson Wells**
  actor
- **George Clooney**
  actor
- **Willie Mays**
  baseball player
- **Gabourey Sidibe**
  actor

PERSONALITY

Because you have unusual qualities, you have a reputation that is one to be proud of. Intellectual traits make you admired for the accomplishments within your power, while personal courage and fearlessness also characterize you. You regulate your relationships with other people according to a standard of ethics and decency that makes it a pleasure to be associated with you. If all this sounds to you like mere flattery, it is because you are essentially a modest person who has overcome a lot, and you do not care too much about being praised. Of course, everyone has some negative traits, and in your case, you are fortunate that they are but minor ones. You have a little too much compassion for your loved ones, and you rush to the assistance of members of your family, thus spoiling them to a degree. That is a policy that might be wise to abandon, for each person in this life must learn to stand on his or her own two feet. Homelife represents much comfort to you, even though there are separations, and you are indeed the joy of your partner.

LIFE PATH

You are persevering, tenacious, proud, and conscientious. You are ambitious to raise yourself to a higher plane, both socially and intellectually. You have a slight tendency toward pessimism when your work is not praised, and if driven far enough you will become bitter and caustic. As a rule, you are kind and tender, and the surface of your love is smooth and unruffled.

DESTINY

Let the same standards of ethics that have always guided you in the past with members of your family regulate your relationships with fellow workers. You can be a source of inspiration to someone who is younger than you. You exert a dominant influence, of which you are not fully aware, over the thinking and actions of others. You will find pleasure in metaphysical study and self-improvement.

KARMIC LESSON

You are inquisitive, and during your early childhood you were likely in all sorts of trouble. The weird and mysterious attract you, and when you were young you were always poking about in old corners. You have a great deal of pluck and determination, and nothing ever daunts you or makes you give up. You are quite a rebel and do not make friends easily. What friends you do make are true and loyal, however. You would do well in partnership, and the probability is that you would not make a very great success alone. You are as good as your word in everything you say and do. Study your own nature and character, ascertain any weaknesses, and strive to remedy these.

SECRET

You have a dominant, impetuous nature and are happy mostly when in control, whether in business or at home. You are inclined to get revenge when your will is crossed.

FRIENDS & FAMILY

MAY 7

Love never dies of starvation, but often of indigestion.
—Ninon de L'Enclos

BORN ON THIS DAY

- ★ **Johannes Brahms**
  composer
- ★ **Eva Peron**
  first lady of Argentina
- ★ **Robert Browning**
  playwright
- ★ **Alex Smith**
  football player
- ★ **Aidy Bryant**
  actor

FRIENDS & FAMILY

● PERSONALITY

Outward cheerfulness and inner sobriety combine in the makeup of your personality to form a grand union of traits. You make a good impression because you have decent manners, a pleasant disposition, and a great deal of natural diplomacy. It is always said that the outer person is a reflection of the inner one. Thus, you may deduce that your ingratiating ways are the reflection of intelligence, consideration, and generosity. You possess a well of sympathy, which makes people like you and also seems to draw them to you when they need help or spiritual solace. You can get along splendidly in social life and in the business world, but you have the happy ability to enjoy your own company. A good book, an hour of meditation, or a walk in the outdoors can delight you as much as attending a large party. People like you for yourself, and you should be quite satisfied with the gracious traits that have been endowed upon you.

● LIFE PATH

While your mind does not always act and respond rapidly or brilliantly, you are shrewd, open, and aware, seldom arriving at a false conclusion. You have self-esteem, ambition, and ability. Your married life or partnerships will be pleasant and supportive.

● DESTINY

Mars vibrations rule your birth date and are responsible for the courage you have in your convictions. Do not be afraid to express your opinions, since you cannot ever be content in taking a back seat. You will find cause for satisfaction in both your social and your business lives, but do not abandon your wonderful ability to enjoy being alone. Your associates will find your optimism and cheerfulness contagious.

● KARMIC LESSON

You are fond of being in public life and would shine in the proper setting and environment. You are, at the same time, very reserved and patient, and the superficial side of life does not attract you as it does many others. You are interested in philosophy, metaphysics, and any questions that serve to answer the questions: "Who am I?," "Where did I come from?," and "Where am I going?" Combined with this mystical bent, you also have a very practical side to your nature, and you could probably succeed in accumulating quite a bit of money in your lifetime, just by reason of your steady, solid interests and beliefs. You have strong opinions, which are, however, sometimes not expressed. You like pleasing others and will often put yourself out a great deal to help a fellow sufferer who is in distress. You are really very affectionate, but it is not always easy for you to be demonstrative. You feel very deeply, though, and when you find someone worthy of your love, you will be able to give such a person a great deal of genuine devotion.

● SECRET

You enjoy most being host to friends at feasts and entertainments. You are not one, however, to make many intimate associations.

MAY 8

Books are the ever burning lamps of accumulated wisdom.
—George William Curtis

BORN ON THIS DAY
- **Harry S. Truman**
  U.S. president
- **David Attenborough**
  natural historian
- **Enrique Iglesias**
  singer
- **Olivia Culpo**
  model
- **Don Rickles**
  comedian

PERSONALITY
You can be a great help to others because you have the ability to visualize situations and their likely outcomes. For this reason, you play the role of the builder in the drama of life. Take to heart the words of Richard Bach, "To bring anything into your life, imagine that it's already there." A conflict of emotions sometimes prevents you from fulfilling your highest aspirations. It seems as though your loquacity gets in the way of your ambition. In other words, you are inclined to talk a little too much about your plans instead of actually settling down to the serious hard work of executing them. You really have an infinite capacity for work, and you should make an effort to regulate your hours of work and fun in such a way that you get the maximum return for the energy and time that you expend. Be efficient, cut out waste, and don't gossip and fritter time away watching too much TV and social media.

LIFE PATH
You possess considerable originality, some wit, and could use more self-reliance. You could do many things if you would but make the effort with the proper degree of assurance. You are fond of diversions and light literature. Your disposition is mostly sunny and acquiescent, and you will always be satisfied because that path is the easiest for you to tread.

DESTINY
You will develop the necessary self-confidence to take advantage of the opportunities that will present themselves. You are lucky. Take stock of your talents and develop those that you have allowed to lie dormant. If you are asked to take part in a community enterprise, go into it with enthusiasm and determination. The increased prestige and respect you win will delight you. Do not enter upon such a project with a mercenary attitude, yet neither should you pass up social or financial opportunities.

KARMIC LESSON
You have a romantic point of view. The beautiful in nature appeals to you greatly. You can sometimes have rather a somber, melancholy turn of mind, which gets stuck on the serious side of life and seems at times to bear all the woes of the world. You should learn to conquer this and cultivate your unique sense of comedy—to see the humor in things. One day you will really surprise yourself by the way in which you will burst forth and do something great. You alternately take an interest in worldly things and then seem not to care for them at all. You have a good deal of courage and can overcome many challenges.

SECRET
You are good at manifesting and have a rather charmed life. You will succeed in a confidential capacity to some superior.

FRIENDS & FAMILY

MAY 9

We judge ourselves by what we feel capable of doing, while others judge us by what we have already done.
—Henry Wadsworth Longfellow

BORN ON THIS DAY

★**John Brown**
abolitionist

★**Billy Joel**
singer

★**Rosario Dawson**
actor

★**Candice Bergen**
actor

★**Ghostface Killah**
rapper

FRIENDS & FAMILY

PERSONALITY
You do most things with an intensity of feeling that is individual to you. Because of this, you are liable to a great deal of emotional stress. Although this is your nature, it is within your own control, and control is something you should aim for. It is a waste to spend energy being anxious about matters that are really trivial when seen in their true light. You should develop your natural judgment and keen intellect so that you make no errors along the lines of feeling. Once you have mastered this tendency to exaggerate your feelings, especially your sympathies, you will be on the road to far more abundant and successful living. One field of success that is open to you is dealing with the public—in any capacity. Get out more than you do and see people and do things. By following your innate feelings, your hunches, or your intuition and by using methods to calm down and de-stress, you are more liable to find the road to real happiness.

LIFE PATH
You will be most successful if you give latitude to your natural originality. Attempting to do what others have done, and in the same way, is likely to bring regret and disappointment. You are of an inventive turn of mind, endowed with a dry sense of humor, popular among your friends and acquaintances, and very positive in your likes and dislikes.

DESTINY
A whole combination of fortuitous circumstances will open doors and make possible a remarkable progress toward your most cherished goals. Be ready to answer opportunity's call. You will succeed in your work because you are highly imaginative as well as practical. Continually urge yourself forward through your fears and worries so that you will not waste your talents.

KARMIC LESSON
You usually feel you have to do everything yourself. Not that this is unwarranted, as a rule, but you perhaps underestimate the ability of others. You are cautious and inquisitive, love certain kinds of work, and have strong opinions. You should live in the country if you can, as your best work seems to be brought out by the calm and peace of mind this environment brings. You can live alone and get along by yourself all right, but at the same time you are a lover and like to feel that someone who is fond of you and will do things for you is near you all the time. You must learn to make sacrifices if you would have others make sacrifices for you.

SECRET
You are a lover of fitness and exercise, given to a physically active life. You have great patience in mastering difficult feats.

MAY 10

No person is either so happy or so unhappy as he imagines.
—François de La Rochefoucauld

PERSONALITY
A special set of circumstances makes your birthday a fortunate one, indeed. The heavens have endowed upon you who were born on this date a combination of traits that well qualifies you for living a really full life and enjoying both material and spiritual gifts. You can express yourself well and dramatically. Leadership is one of your outstanding characteristics, and you are original and clever about the way you do things. Strength of purpose qualifies your every deed, and you enjoy persistent effort. You like to start a new project, plan ahead, make a blueprint of your future acts, and then operate with efficiency and intelligence to see them through. Your crowning moments of happiness are those when you see the conclusion of a project you have brought into being. You are warmly affectionate. Family life and friendships mean a great deal to you, and those who love you do so with deep feeling.

LIFE PATH
You are persistent, perspicacious, and levelheaded, never letting adversity lessen your efforts, nor success weaken your stamina. If you make a mistake, you right it immediately to the best of your ability. You are affable, diplomatic, and suave, never showing your inner feelings unless they are optimistic. You have a sweetness and fascination that win many friends for you.

DESTINY
You will achieve your goals because of your creative power and ability to concentrate. The members of your family will depend on your calmness during domestic stress. Some happy friendships may be developed with neighbors. Do not turn a cold shoulder to overtures of friendship from kindly strangers—gold is where you find it.

KARMIC LESSON
You have a very versatile nature, are interested in many things, and are capable of doing several things well. You have good judgment and clear discrimination on many points. Your friends and neighbors will come to you to straighten out many issues that trouble them. You are fond of natural living and all that means. You are also fond of the luxuries of life, though you can do without them whenever necessary. You should have a very distinctive salutation, known at once to all your friends. You are affectionate and must have many close relationships in your life. You are more interested in psychology than anything else, and the problems of the heart and soul have always especially interested you. You will be well-off later in life.

SECRET
You are energetic and capable but a little headstrong. You should be successful in business and a good amateur in music, video, or plays.

BORN ON THIS DAY
- **Bono** — singer
- **Fred Astaire** — actor, dancer
- **Sid Vicious** — singer, bassist
- **Linda Evangelista** — model
- **Donovan** — singer/songwriter

FRIENDS & FAMILY

MAY 11

Every calling is great when greatly pursued.
—Oliver Wendell Holmes

BORN ON THIS DAY
- **Salvador Dalí**
  painter
- **Richard Feynman**
  physicist
- **Martha Graham**
  dancer
- **Louis Farrakhan**
  leader of the Nation of Islam
- **Irving Berlin**
  composer

FRIENDS & FAMILY

PERSONALITY
Enthusiasm and energy mark everything that you do. If you have no interest in a plan, project, or task, you simply pay no attention to it. But if you give your heart and soul to an idea, you do so with a will that allows no frittering away of time or talent. You work with resolve, or you don't work at all. Life holds few secrets for you, for you have a grasp of people and situations that is very masterful. You are very determined, and you can get to the inner core of people you are studying with great efficiency. There is something of the ferret in your nature. You can discover motives, reasons, and secrets almost without effort, but if effort is needed, you are certainly willing to expend it. People like you for your natural sympathy, your quiet understanding, and your soothing personality.

LIFE PATH
You are strong, both mentally and physically. You are versatile, energetic, artistic, and good-natured, happy in your homelife, a leader in your social life, and generally accepted as a comfortable, reliable person. Your love is profound, and you try not to allow anything to cast a shadow upon it.

DESTINY
Your enthusiasm will be stimulated by like-minded friends. This means that together you can make miraculous strides toward the accomplishment of your aims. You are the sort of person who cannot get anything done if you are bored. Look for sparks of interest from others in your new endeavors, and fan them into a flame of zest. You will find your understanding of people an asset in social and business affairs; use this talent without thought of selfish gains, but there will be gains.

KARMIC LESSON
You are inventive and ingenious and have a good head for business. You will never get left far behind on any business deal. At the same time, you are kindly and charitable, and you like doing good for others. You are devoted to improving yourself, and you read everything along this line that you can get hold of. You are very fond of animals—particularly cats. You have strong likes and dislikes and can be a good hater just as well as a good lover, on occasion. You will experience many strange ups and downs during your life and see many strange scenes and places. You should rarely be alone, if possible. You are a good networker and can make friends with most anyone with whom you come into contact.

SECRET
You are generous almost to a fault and will succeed in ventures with a partner. You must guard against your love of luxury and the impulsiveness of your nature.

MAY 12

*Our greatest deeds we
do unknowingly.*
—Elbert Hubbard

BORN ON THIS DAY
★**Florence Nightingale**
social reformer

★**Rami Malek**
actor

★**Rona Jaffe**
author

★**Yogi Berra**
baseball coach

★**Katharine Hepburn**
actor

PERSONALITY
Administrative ability and friendliness make you a successful and popular person when you express your true potentialities. On the negative side, you could express these traits by being domineering and spiteful. Since all life is give-and-take and adjusting oneself intelligently to situations as one finds them, you should make every effort to express only the positive side of these outstanding traits. You enjoy socializing very much—sometimes too much—and you have a tendency to be the life of the party. You can be quite happy when you are alone, too, for you have the ability to be good company for yourself and to find delight in cultural pursuits. You should do very well in any large organization, whether it is a club, a business, or a family. In addition, you have the ability to handle fiduciary affairs. You may not like such tasks as figuring the budget, but if you have to, you do it well.

LIFE PATH
Ambitious for advancement, you are always eager to learn. You have a mind capable of clear thinking and logical reasoning. You love good movies, good food, good music, and artistic surroundings. Your happiness demands love, and you are a demonstrative lover in return. You are prone to writing love notes.

DESTINY
Your adaptability will be of particular value to you in life. While you have never been very fond of detail work, as you mature you will find increased pleasure in seeing your plans carefully outlined and followed. This influence will extend to other members of your family, and a cooperative spirit in business and financial matters will evolve. Do not leave a task unfinished once you have started it, even though new interests sometimes seem more attractive.

KARMIC LESSON
You have an interest in all things that pertain to the mind and the soul. You are independent and live your own life, little caring what others may think of you. You have a strong magnetic presence, are generous, and live a great deal on your emotions and sensations. It is probable that you will rise to a position of power. You are interested in psychic and occult matters, and from time to time you invest quite a bit of research in visiting mediums and astrologers of all sorts. You are intense in your emotions and have a great power of love. For your life partner, you should pick one who is steady and constant, as you can never be satisfied with anything less.

SECRET
You have a strong character and are strong psychically. Unless hampered by early responsibilities, you could go far in business.

FRIENDS & FAMILY

MAY 13

There are no rules of architecture for a castle in the clouds.
—G.K. Chesterton

BORN ON THIS DAY

★ **Stevie Wonder**
singer

★ **Stephen Colbert**
TV personality

★ **Dennis Rodman**
basketball player

★ **Bea Arthur**
actor

★ **Joe Lewis**
boxer

FRIENDS & FAMILY

PERSONALITY

No one could ever deny that you are a multitasker. To use a time-honored expression, you enjoy having your finger in every pie. This is not curiosity or busyness but a genuine interest in people, events, and the life around you. You are a very helpful person, especially in times of need. When a friend is opening a new home, when a hand is needed in decorating, arranging, or moving, you are the first to volunteer. This makes you popular in many walks of life, and you have friends in all of them. Duty is to you a noble thing, not a bore or a punishment. You are quite psychic and seem to delve right into the hearts of people and the motives that make them act the way they do. For this reason, you are liable to extend yourself somewhat unnecessarily. It is wonderful to be noble and generous but foolish to relieve others of their proper duties. Be careful not to spoil the children in your life.

LIFE PATH

You are just, honest, intellectual, of a somewhat retiring nature, slightly subject to moods, and most lovable at all times. You enjoy travel, not because of the change but for the educational value. You make the most of your opportunities for betterment and will always enjoy taking new courses and classes to develop new skills.

DESTINY

You will analyze problems wisely and replace your dreams with acts. Retain your healthy skepticism about untried ways. You will attract others by your friendliness and good manners. However, do not soft-pedal your opinions to placate others when you feel your stand is justified. Do not be hurt by another's unintentional slight or rudeness. Rely on your own judgment in money matters.

KARMIC LESSON

You are dogged and determined. You have an open mind, but you do not use it enough; you must take an interest in the more serious side of life. Try to leave some "footprints in the sands of time" by creating and leaving behind some permanent, substantial work, which future generations will treasure. You can if you try, as you have all the necessary ability. You can be the master of your own fate and fortune and create success if you will it. Begin a life of action; say to yourself, "I will succeed." Think well, and do not marry too young, which might be unwise for one of your nature. Above all, learn to master your will, and you will have learned one of the greatest lessons in life.

SECRET

You are happiest when serving not so much an individual as a higher cause. You are strongly spiritual.

MAY 14

The most beautiful thing we can experience is the mysterious. It is the source of all true art and science.
—Albert Einstein

BORN ON THIS DAY

★ **Che Guevara**
revolutionary

★ **Mark Zuckerberg**
media magnate

★ **George Lucas**
film director

★ **Cate Blanchett**
actor

★ **David Byrne**
singer

PERSONALITY

You have very strong character traits that make you a rugged individual. You want what you want when you want it, and you do everything in your power to get it! This is the spirit of modern times and the expression of strength of purpose and persistence. The negative side of this determination is stubbornness, and you can be that, too, if you feel frustrated in the attainment of your desires. You have quite a strong nurturing instinct and enjoy being surrounded by loved ones, your favorite treasures, and photos, to which you are very attached. When vacation time comes, however, you like to go off by yourself for a change and let the spirit of adventure and romance beckon to you. Before middle life, fun and fooling around are your aims; thereafter, although you settle down, you do not lose your great sense of humor. You can express your thoughts and ideas with accuracy and should do well in writing, publishing, lecturing, and all the areas where words are of significance.

LIFE PATH

You are a loyal friend and a bitter enemy. Your love is for one person at a time, and you demand that kind of love in return. You are dominating, determined, independent, and sometimes headstrong. You have a sharp mind, and you are capable of attaining almost anything you really set your heart upon.

DESTINY

A serene and harmonious homelife, which means so much to you, will be part of your destiny. Because you are fair and honest, others will accept your decisions. The accumulation of lovely possessions will always delight you, and you will be able to add to your favorite collections over the years. Since you are self-sufficient, you do not usually seek out new friends. However, you should never ignore opportunities or invitations to broaden your circle of acquaintances.

KARMIC LESSON

You have a lively sense of humor. You are generally cheerful, bringing happiness and sunshine with you wherever you go. You are smart with money and will probably be successful in all ventures of the kind. You have excellent taste and judgment and can handle a difficult situation to your own credit and the benefit of all concerned. Because you send out positive vibes and are found interesting by those you meet, you must be careful in the selection of your most intimate friends. You must exercise some discrimination, eliminating those who hinder you or drag you down and cultivating those who can help you or will do you good.

SECRET

You like to live close to nature. You get the most out of life in gardening pursuits, where you can draw peace and contentment from your surroundings.

FRIENDS & FAMILY

MAY 15

The first and greatest victory is to conquer yourself; to be conquered by yourself is of all things most shameful and vile.
—Plato

BORN ON THIS DAY
- **Madeleine Albright**
  stateswoman
- **L. Frank Baum**
  author
- **Andy Murray**
  tennis player
- **Brian Eno**
  composer
- **Stella Maxwell**
  model

FRIENDS & FAMILY

PERSONALITY
You have a strong, idiosyncratic character, which means that your likes and dislikes are individualistic and that you tolerate few things that do not live up to your tough standards. It is characteristic of you to say that you love a thing rather than that you like it. The converse holds true, for you don't dislike, but hate. Since, however, you have innate good taste, it does no harm that your likes and dislikes are so extreme. There is much of the quality of a group leader in your makeup. You are good at organizing, and you may express this ability in business, the home, social affairs, and community projects. Once you take the wheel, you are sure to steer the ship to success. Do not allow a tendency to be overgenerous to put you in a bind.

LIFE PATH
You possess great ability and natural aptitude. Fond of learning, you are a constant reader. You are observant, critical, shrewd, and careful; you take very few false steps. You are a giving friend, a loving parent, and the wellspring of wisdom in your home.

DESTINY
New problems do not frighten you. Under the magnetic influence of the Uranus rays, you will find many opportunities to put your original ideas into productive use. Because your language is inclined to be a little too emphatic, you should try to replace the words "love" and "hate" with "like" and "dislike" upon occasion. Moderation in generosity, too, is suggested to protect your pocketbook from unfair impositions.

KARMIC LESSON
You are intuitive, subtle, a good deal of a diplomat, fond of organizing new things, and overflowing with original ideas, which you are always wanting to put into practice. You are inclined to be mystical and are very fond of all that pertains to the occult and the mysterious. You have distinct intuitive ability and should be encouraged to keep a journal. You have a magnetic personality and could hold an audience well. You have eccentric ideas of your own. You have a great deal of patience and your share of tact. While you can appear to be quiet and demure, there is much more brewing within you than the average observer would suppose; you always have a few interests up your sleeve that no one knows anything about.

SECRET
The present is of more importance to you than reminiscing about the past. You are at your best in the library or in front of the computer.

MAY 16

The only safe and sure way to destroy an enemy is to make him your friend.
—Anonymous

◉ PERSONALITY
Rarely out of sorts, blessed with an optimistic nature, you are just about perfect company for anyone you choose to grace with your presence. Because you are so understanding and cheerful, many people like you. Of course, the events of life that must contain some rain affect you as much as they do any normal human being, but you don't mope over life's tragedies for too long; you sensibly try to do whatever you can to alleviate your own troubles and those of your loved ones. Tasteless entertainment holds no charm for you. Your taste is that of an intellectual person, and you display it in your reading, your attendance of lectures and concerts, and the company you keep. Compromise always seems sort of shoddy to you, and you prefer one really worthwhile possession to a collection of cheap articles. You enjoy pleasures but not excesses. It might be truly said that you try to make your life as beautiful as it can be.

◉ LIFE PATH
An independent thinker, you have a good memory, practical ideas, and the ability to carry out your plans. You are cautious, considerate, honest, diplomatic, and self-contained. You have a quick wit and good sense of humor. Your home to you is the most important thing in the world.

◉ DESTINY
You cannot see how something can be right and wrong at the same time. Your definite stands can help others to clarify their own vague ideas. You will find satisfaction in supporting and standing up for your beliefs, whether political or spiritual. Because of your cheerful, understanding nature, you have nothing to lose even if you seem quite stubborn on occasion. People are going to keep on liking your charming company, and you will gain their respect and esteem.

◉ KARMIC LESSON
You have remarkable business judgment, keen insight, and ability. You have a mind capable of dealing in large things and grasping the details of an enormous number of intricate business dealings. You should certainly succeed in business for yourself, as you are throwing away your talents in working for anyone else. You have a keen sense of what is right and just. Learn to make allowances for the shortcomings and weaknesses of others, and you could make a great business success. You prefer intimate gatherings and are a great talker on occasion, when you get started. You are fond of social media exchanges but are always ready to drop it when someone or something more interesting makes an appearance in real life.

◉ SECRET
You understand how things work but are hampered by a desire to do everything yourself, which springs from a lack of faith in others.

BORN ON THIS DAY
- ★Janet Jackson
  singer
- ★Liberace
  musician
- ★Christian Lacroix
  fashion designer
- ★Pierce Brosnan
  actor
- ★Tamara de Lempicka
  painter

FRIENDS & FAMILY

MAY 17

Words are easy, like the wind; Faithful friends are hard to find.
—William Shakespeare

BORN ON THIS DAY

★ **Trent Reznor**
musician

★ **Bob Saget**
comedian

★ **Sugar Ray Leonard**
boxer

★ **Enya**
singer

★ **Bill Paxton**
actor

FRIENDS & FAMILY

PERSONALITY

You have a practical outlook on life that has always stood you in good stead. You like to take a problem, examine it with all your mental prowess, and then go ahead with your idea of how to solve it, doing so resolutely and determinedly. Little in this world can discourage you because you regard everyone, no matter what their position, as human, with foibles and all. With such a philosophy of life, it is natural that you should be cheerful and sanguine most of the time. The cowards of the world have little appeal for you. Your taste runs to individualists and persons with great strength of character, even though they seem to be few and far between. It is part of your concept, however, that everyone should be given the right to develop all their potentialities. For this reason, you are the champion of the common person and the espouser of the real meaning of democracy.

LIFE PATH

You are clever, whole-souled, intellectual, and discriminating. You like people and are much happier when in the whirl of social life. Another integral part of your path is your interest in public activities, civic projects, educational programs, and helping those in need.

DESTINY

The tedium of routine will be reduced through your own inspirations. However, the practical side of your nature will always be expressed effectively. The practice of studying a problem thoroughly, even after the solution has flashed into your mind, will continue to stand you in good stead. The chance for friendly association with and attraction between you and people of admirable character and determination will bring you happiness.

KARMIC LESSON

You have an active, alert, original, and inventive mind. You are not content to follow old truths but must see for yourself what is good and true in new thoughts or movements. You are a natural explorer, whether of things of the mind or in more widely distributed areas. Your independent character never allows you to follow a trend just because the majority do so. Your great love of nature and distinctly artistic bent suggest that you would probably paint or work with your hands, but your work will be tinged with the romantic and the melancholy. You do not understand this despondent streak, for you are usually upbeat and lively enough. Live up to the best in yourself, and yours will be a rewarding life.

SECRET

Born on this day, you can go far in careers that depend upon the subject of freedom. You would make a good motivational trainer.

MAY 18

What other people think of me is none of my business.
—Eleanor Roosevelt

⊛ PERSONALITY

You seem to go through life running the gamut of emotions. Because you are inclined to be very articulate and expressive, you also tend to tell the world your troubles and to spend quite some time in bemoaning your fate, be it real or imaginary. This tendency is a weakness that is within your power to rout out, and it is your sacred duty to do so. There is little in this world that is so ill received as a person feeling sorry for themselves. By taking a greater interest in outside things, by doing some spiritual studies, and by trying to be helpful to others less fortunate than you, you can do a lot to eliminate that time-wasting hobby of self-pity. You do have a wonderful natural sympathy for other people and quite a deep understanding of human nature. Make this the springboard of your resolution to get out into the thick of affairs and accomplish your most cherished wishes.

⊛ LIFE PATH

You like to take a chance and are sometimes venturesome to the verge of foolhardiness. While you are energetic at times, much of your energy is misapplied. You like music and art and have a creative mind. You like children and dearly love hearing stories about your friends and family; you will be instrumental in keeping a family tradition alive.

⊛ DESTINY

Your increased initiative as you mature will conquer groundless fears that have harassed you since childhood. There really is no good time or occasion for defeatism. The natural compassion you have for others can be forcefully expressed by the empathetic counseling you can give to them. Active participation in organizations designed to help those less fortunate than you will bring great satisfaction and serenity in addition to greater self-confidence.

⊛ KARMIC LESSON

You take an interest in a great many things. You are quick and naturally witty and can shine when you want to. You are fond of good stories and of movies. You should cultivate an understanding of psychology and study human behavior and the law of attraction. You can be a good mimic; you have a good sense of humor and see the ridiculous side of things. You have savvy business judgment and a feel for transactions and making deals. You have a strong sense of the propriety of things and do not like people getting too familiar or close if you don't know them very well. Even though you are frank, open, and sincere, you like to keep your distance.

⊛ SECRET

You are a lover of playing games, teatime, and quiet diversions. You succeed by giving more thought to spending wisely than to earning excessively.

BORN ON THIS DAY

- **Pope John Paul II**
  religious leader
- **Tina Fey**
  actor, comedian
- **Chow Yun-fat**
  actor
- **Bertrand Russell**
  philosopher, logician
- **Fred Perry**
  tennis player

FRIENDS & FAMILY

MAY 19

To be happy is not the purpose of our being, but to deserve happiness.
—Johann Gottlieb Fichte

BORN ON THIS DAY

★ **Malcolm X**
civil rights activist

★ **Grace Jones**
singer

★ **Nora Ephron**
filmmaker

★ **Pete Townshend**
musician

★ **Kevin Garnett**
basketball player

FRIENDS & FAMILY

PERSONALITY

To you, there is something beautifully sacred about married life, in reality and in your philosophy. Let no one ever try to talk you out of the joys that homelife and family represent to you. A rather strong character would make this difficult, but one must take the troublemakers of the world into account, too, since they do exist. You can be very clever at running a business and even at making the purchases required for daily routine living, as you know how to strike a good bargain. You develop awareness of progressive trends through constant participation in constructive plans and objective actions. Many opportunities will come to you to do good, for there is an understanding of human foibles that you express in your personality that brings the weaker members of society to your side for help. Don't let them down, for you have strength to spare, morally speaking.

LIFE PATH

A worrier, you are of a nervous temperament and somewhat excitable. You also have considerable humor in your makeup, and a rollicking good time with children is just to your liking. You are kind and affectionate and want your loved ones to be rewarded. Your nature craves affection.

DESTINY

Wise purchasing will make possible the acquisition of some beautiful, valuable objects for your home. Your ability to make things appear attractive to others also will always find expression. Use your fine imagination in some creative work. Opportunities for this will be present if you look for them. The company of younger people will furnish you with inspiration, and, in turn, your example will be a stimulating influence on them.

KARMIC LESSON

You have theatrical ability and are very entertaining. You could also have a good voice, which deserves cultivation and training. Energetic and enthusiastic, you are very fond of design and art and anything to do with the home and garden. You are good with animals. Social and kind, you like plenty of light and can be the life of the party. You are emotional, even passionate in your nature, and are staunch and true to your friends. You could be lucky in speculations of all kinds, but unless you are careful, this interest will lead to disappointments and worry. You could probably make a good deal of money during your life, but unless you are on your guard, you will go through it quickly, so heed the warning.

SECRET

You have a generous nature but are a trifle spoiled by your whims. You enjoy being the boss, with many subjects to command.

MAY 20

Do not worry about tomorrow, for tomorrow will worry about itself. Each day has enough trouble of its own.
—Matthew 6:25–34

BORN ON THIS DAY
- **Cher**
  singer, actor
- **Jimmy Stewart**
  actor
- **Busta Rhymes**
  rapper
- **Iker Casillas**
  soccer player
- **Joe Cocker**
  singer

PERSONALITY
Because you were born on the cusp between two signs, Taurus and Gemini, you share, to a certain degree, the characteristics of both. There is a quality of mysticism in your nature that should be a source of great enlightenment to you. If you have ever felt a certain closeness to nature, and if you have ever felt that certain events you witnessed had a special significance that only you were getting, these are manifestations of the sympathy with life that is part of the makeup of the mystic. You have psychic potentialities that can be developed by study and concentration, and you can bring these to the forefront of your expression by putting your attention on it. Spiritual faith is a solace to you, whether you choose to align with an organized group or to worship at the shrine of nature. You are cooperative, affectionate, and attentive to the needs of those you love. Life should be filled with many soulful moments for you.

LIFE PATH
You are a great reader and have an assimilative memory. You are serious and contemplative in your thinking, your actions, and your love. Your nature demands intimacy and your happiness depends upon it. Where there is reason to make a choice, you decide without hesitation to take love in preference to wealth or fame.

DESTINY
Many of your potentialities will be realized before age forty. Give lots of attention to mysticism and philosophy. Good fortune for you is closely connected with the welfare of people you love. Attention to their comfort and pleasure will promote happiness. Affluence is not limited to money, although you may find a financially profitable career. Be on the alert for new business opportunities that combine your love of philosophy and need for security.

KARMIC LESSON
You have a distinct intuitive ability. You are a good student of human nature and know all the subtle motives and desires that prompt people to do certain things. You have great patience and perseverance and can handle people by appealing to their issues of self-confidence. You are kind and sympathetic, however, and if you could be a little more frank and open you would be very appreciated. You have a sensitive nature and feel slights very keenly. You are capable of a wide range of emotions, from the most frivolous to the most grave. You are active and capable of undertaking a good many different things and carrying them all through to success. You can be quick in temper, strong, and imperious.

SECRET
You have an impetuous nature governed by balance in an emergency. You are the kind who rises to the occasion during a crisis.

FRIENDS & FAMILY

MAY 21

He who has a firm will molds the world to himself.
—Johann Wolfgang von Goethe

BORN ON THIS DAY

★ **Alexander Pope**
poet

★ **Al Franken**
comedian, U.S. senator

★ **Mr. T**
actor

★ **Notorious B.I.G. (aka Biggie Smalls)**
rapper

★ **Naeem Khan**
fashion designer

FRIENDS & FAMILY

_____
_____
_____
_____
_____
_____
_____
_____
_____

PERSONALITY

You have competency, initiative, and courage. Organization is one of your outstanding traits, and where it is needed, there you are to answer the call. Ideas are always flourishing in your active mind. You are creative and original in your thinking and in the way you do things. Tuned-in and alert in your analysis of every problem, you do not hesitate to tackle the most complicated questions, because you have self-confidence from your experience of situations. By developing your cooperative spirit, you will eventually overcome your tendency to be too stubborn or willful. When you work in tandem with others, you have a responsibility, so be sure that you partner with them with the best of intentions. You could have outstanding success in dealing with financial affairs, large organizations, and philanthropic causes.

LIFE PATH

Forceful and compelling, you are quite original and have very big ideas about what you can accomplish. You are a nature lover and fond of water and mountains. You love your home and want it to be beautiful, and you love your family above all else. Sculpting or jewelry making might interest you.

DESTINY

Through the proper carrying out of small responsibilities, you will find yourself in a position to deal with larger matters. That is your gift—your competency and conscientious attention to small duties will be noticed and rewarded. When a situation necessitates a leader, you could be ready to assume the responsibility. The originality of your methods can then be best displayed. Put the same emphasis on cooperation as on self-reliance, and success is enhanced for all your projects.

KARMIC LESSON

You have a very compassionate nature—one that feels things keenly and suffers with the sufferings of humanity. You are probably very interested in social issues or at least have a leaning in that direction. You are sincere and have strong convictions. You are particularly fond of fixing up your home and property. At the same time, you are fond of friends and of shopping, enjoying the artisans of this world. You are naturally modest and retiring but at the same time ambitious, and you have a strong desire to attain the highest rung of the ladder that you happen to be climbing. You will never be in need of admirers; your trouble, in all probability, will be that you have too many.

SECRET

You are an accurate observer of people's true motivations. You would make a good therapist, if you cultivate tolerance, or a dependable vocational expert.

MAY 22

Music is the medicine of the breaking heart.
—Leigh Hunt

⬤ PERSONALITY

Your willingness to cooperate makes you the ideal agent and partner. Given the plan or blueprint of a project, you can be left alone to see that the job is done, and you will not stop work until it is finished to your satisfaction. Demonstrative and emotional by nature, you can easily go overboard in showing another person how much you care for them. While this is honest, it is sometimes embarrassing to those who are not as open-minded as you are. So vivid is your imagination and creative talent that when you are presented with an idea, you breathe life into it. Because your inclination is more to follow than to lead, others may think that you are merely vacillating in nature. Deflate this misconception by asserting yourself. You do not want to be considered weak in character, so this is a necessary step.

⬤ LIFE PATH

You possess great ability, which will lie dormant unless you are so fortunate as to have your true personal ambitions aroused. Do not let your pride gain too great a hold. You are gentle, kind, and generally sincere, and if you are fortunate in securing a love or work partner who will bring out the best in you and believe in your dreams, you will be very successful and happy.

⬤ DESTINY

You will competently carry out the plans of someone else to your mutual benefit. Your effort and conscientiousness will be lauded. Your ability to give life to an idea will make you proud. Be prepared to make some short trips at a moment's notice. These will add excitement to your daily life and give you the chance to meet some interesting new friends, who may be able to help you in the fulfillment of your wishes.

⬤ KARMIC LESSON

Detail work and artistic ability stand out for you, born on this day. You would make a great designer, artist, or musician—whichever you turn your attention to the most strongly. If you cultivate your natural genius, you will achieve success and distinction in whatever line of work you undertake. You are many-sided and could carry out a variety of things well. Your sense of decoration and color is well developed, so you could succeed with this. You have originality and are constantly inventing new ideas and new methods of spending your time. You realize how important proper food is to the human body. Preparing and serving top-notch meals is instinctive to you because you have a natural comprehension of suitable foods and cooking techniques for the maintenance of good health.

⬤ SECRET

You have a good deal of enthusiasm but not enough stability. You would be effective in enterprises that are of short duration; you are inclined to be a little flighty.

BORN ON THIS DAY

- **Richard Wagner**
  composer
- **Lawrence Olivier**
  actor
- **Harvey Milk**
  politician, gay rights advocate
- **Sir Arthur Conan Doyle**
  author
- **Novak Djokovic**
  tennis player

FRIENDS & FAMILY

MAY 23

Poets are all who love, who feel great truths, and tell them.
—Philip James Bailey

BORN ON THIS DAY

- **Joan Collins**
  actor
- **Rosemary Clooney**
  actor
- **Marvelous Marvin Hagler**
  boxer
- **Ryan Coogler**
  filmmaker
- **Jewel**
  singer

FRIENDS & FAMILY

PERSONALITY

You have great success in dealing with large numbers of people, clubs, corporations, and organizations. Contact with the public in some way is always a part of your activity. Popular in social life, you are a real networker. Because of the charm and warmth that you exude, many people consider you their best friend, but you are a close friend to a very few choice ones. Wit and charisma both characterize you, and you don't mind putting yourself out to be charming and to make a good impression. You have so many talents that you are frequently puzzled as to which one to concentrate on or employ to your greatest advantage. This variety of abilities is something of which you must take notice. Since you do not know how to specialize, you might scatter your fine qualities without profit. Settle down to one thing.

LIFE PATH

You are bubbling over with eagerness, and there is nothing you will not try. Failure does not discourage you. You have good self-esteem, assurance, and perseverance. You are animated, funny, and lovable. You can get along well with the members of any group, provided you feel responsive to that particular blend of emotions and intellectual pattern.

DESTINY

Your social success will not be limited to people in your neighborhood. You will find increased pleasure in impromptu parties and congenial associations in your work and may travel to see friends in other areas, as well as meeting virtually. There will be an increasingly large number of contacts with the public through social networking. You are well equipped for such experiences because of your congeniality. Spend some time in developing your writing talents, even if you have no intention of using them professionally.

KARMIC LESSON

You are of a nervous, energetic type, always on the move, and you like to see others active and busy around you. You are too easily influenced by those around you; you should learn to be more independent. Success and failure will probably alternate in your life in a most bewildering manner; they seem to run in cycles. You are a good talker and a mimic and can entertain a whole room full of friends. Never be satisfied with small successes, for you can accomplish far greater things if you set your mind to it. You are too carried away by appearances but not enough inclined to analyze the character of the person before you. You must look below the surface. Study psychology and human behavior.

SECRET

You have natural wit and sharp communication powers, but sometimes you are inclined to think more of a smart-aleck remark than the feelings of a friend.

MAY 24

To see what is right and not to do it is want of courage, or of principle.
—Confucius

BORN ON THIS DAY
★ **Bob Dylan**
singer

★ **Patti LaBelle**
singer

★ **Benjamin N. Cardozo**
U.S. Supreme Court justice

★ **Kristin Scott Thomas**
actor

★ **G-Easy**
rapper

PERSONALITY
You are the master builder, the person who lays the foundations, the mason who sees the project through from start to finish—from the architect's plan to the completed structure. Work is the grist to your mill. You may not always like it, but you never shirk a task that has been assigned to you. Because of this, you have a reputation for being reliable and dependable. Once you give your word, nothing can restrain you from keeping it. You are occasionally liable to take things too seriously and forget that there is a time to play. Do not overlook the importance of having fun now and again, of relaxing so that you may store up energy for the next bout with duty. The driving force in your nature is also concerned with passion, and you are a person who can acquire friends and romantic partners who satisfy your emotional desires.

LIFE PATH
You have a personal magnetism and force of character that enables you to assume a leading role. You are capable of concentrated effort, and you work with enthusiasm and vigor. You are trustworthy and pure-minded and love with the same concentration you apply to your work.

DESTINY
You will find yourself more successful if you sometimes try taking a less serious point of view. Your reputation for reliability and efficiency is secure, so allow a little more time for the pleasantries of life. Take advantage of available opportunities to participate more actively in activities you enjoy besides work. Because you want to be busy all the time, you should cultivate relaxing pastimes.

KARMIC LESSON
You are gentle and kind but also firm. You are farseeing, true, and loyal in your affections. You are a natural diplomat, and tact to you is second nature. At the same time, you are hearty and not a bit of a prude. You are interested in technology, in political questions—in fact, you are an all-rounder. You are a born debater; you shine in an argument. For this reason, you would make a good lawyer. You are handy with tools and are fond of mechanics. You are fond of reading and will probably accumulate a good library. You should have an accomplished life and achieve success and distinction in whatever line of endeavor you undertake. You have very good common sense, a clear, open mind, and good judgment.

SECRET
You are of a generous nature, and you easily attract interesting friends. You would succeed best in careers usually having some connection with technology.

FRIENDS & FAMILY

MAY 25

The power of a man increases steadily by continuance in one direction.
—Ralph Waldo Emerson

BORN ON THIS DAY

- **Ian McKellen**
  actor
- **Mike Myers**
  actor, comedian
- **Frank Oz**
  puppeteer
- **Brian Urlacher**
  football player
- **Demetri Martin**
  comedian

FRIENDS & FAMILY

PERSONALITY

The gift of persuasion is yours by endowment. You can win your way with words where others might fail with mighty deeds. You can employ your talent in public speaking, lecturing, acting, broadcasting, teaching, and coaching. You are quick and mercurial in nature. Sometimes you are prone to tell a lie for someone's own good. Change and variety are the true spices of life to you. Travel and speed have such a strong appeal for you that you are capable of dropping everything at a moment's notice and going off somewhere, just for the sake of being on the move. Never let others know that you think they are slow, mentally or physically; it hurts them unnecessarily, and it does you no good. Speed, which you love so much, can be the cause of a mishap or misunderstanding, if you are not careful, so go moderately and slowly with your emotions, words, and deeds.

LIFE PATH

You always give your best efforts to any undertaking, but sometimes your ideas are impractical and over-the-top. You need to keep your passions and emotions under strong control and be more realistic. You love deeply and require strong displays of affection in return.

DESTINY

Employ your skill with words in public speaking, social discussions, and correspondence. The Mars rays of your birthday favor impetuous action, but do not act thoughtlessly. Although you can do well in a number of different fields, concentrate your efforts toward activities that will bring greater personal satisfaction. Do not allow your defense of the good things of the past to keep you from the progressive ideas for the future.

KARMIC LESSON

You have a strong character—one that is self-sufficient and not at all dependent upon the people with whom you are thrown into contact. Logic and reason are strong within you; you are fond of metaphysics and fascinated by fringe ideas or subtle hair-splitting theories, but you sometimes do not cling close enough to the practical and to material things that are for your own good. The dark and mysterious especially attracts you, and unless you are careful, you could get your wings scorched, like the moth in the flame. You would be happier fixing up a home of your own than anything else you could imagine. You are fond of nature and the country but also of the hustle and bustle of city life.

SECRET

You are a person of precise sensibilities. You could make a success in delicate work, such as painting miniatures or designing small objects.

MAY 26

If you permit your thoughts to dwell on evil, you yourself will become ugly. Look only for the good in everything so you absorb the quality of beauty.
—Paramahansa Yogananda

BORN ON THIS DAY

- **Stevie Nicks**
  singer
- **John Wayne**
  actor
- **Lenny Kravitz**
  singer
- **Peter Cushing**
  actor
- **Miles Davis**
  composer

PERSONALITY

You are the very embodiment of the Universal Law of Building—that is, on a firm foundation. Every experience you have is a lesson from which you profit. As a result, you have learned that the highest values are to be gotten from the highest standards. Right livelihood, partnership, and devotion are your highest ideals, and you aim to have money to make these ideals your very own. Sincere faith protects you, and you reciprocate love, knowing that only in mutual love can there be mutual happiness. You maintain a certain balance in all you do, although there are times when your desire to be kind makes your actions seem a little foolish. Not everyone understands bigheartedness as well as you do. You are the type whose family would take advantage of you because you are so generous; for their sake—their growth, their sense of responsibility—don't let them do it.

LIFE PATH

You are kindhearted, positive, exuberant, and fond of games, and you take great pains to please people. You are affectionate, enthusiastic over valued friendships, and at times obsessive and excitable, though you generally control your emotions.

DESTINY

Experiences of the past will prove to be good foundations for building the future. Realization of the value of your standards will inspire you with the desire to make them generally appreciated. Although you like to appear unassuming, you can be sure that others are aware of the way you attack problems with courage and determination. Continue your habit of silently observing people and drawing conclusions and insights from their actions.

KARMIC LESSON

You are careful, methodical, and prudent. You would make a meticulous manager. You are neat and always careful about your personal appearance. You are fond of psychology and take a great interest in anything that explains human nature. You could excel as an engineer or expert machine operator or computer whiz. You are kind and sympathetic. You are a good observer, quiet, and reserved. When you have something to say, people listen without interrupting because you have a way of describing your adventures or thoughts in a way that sounds alluring. Your code of ethics is directed by your logical ideals and sense of justice. Rely upon your own resources, do not put too much trust in others, and yours should be a productive, creative, and satisfying life.

SECRET

Your chief difficulty will be a lack of accord with what average people think and do. This is due to your very independent mind.

FRIENDS & FAMILY

MAY 27

Every life has its actual blanks, which the ideal must fill up, or which else remain bare and profitless forever.
—Julia Ward Howe

BORN ON THIS DAY
- **Rachel Carson**
  scientist
- **Vincent Price**
  actor
- **Jamie Oliver**
  celebrity chef
- **Joseph Fiennes**
  actor
- **André 3000**
  singer

FRIENDS & FAMILY

_____
_____
_____
_____
_____
_____
_____
_____
_____

PERSONALITY
You have an artistic nature, subtle in its expression and quiet in its manifestation. Not many people know you really well, for you do not bare the secret places of your soul to the world at large. The mystical issues of life have a strong appeal for you, and you have a unique understanding of them. To you, humanity speaks in various languages and symbols, for you see things as they really are beneath their protective covering. All that is mysterious in character has a strong appeal for you, and this goes for the silent beauties of nature as well as spoken and written words. A gorgeous sunset, a moving poem, a touching scene—all play upon your emotions, and you seem to absorb their deeper significance. Sometimes you become quite melancholy. You can take your place among your fellow creatives as a counselor, mentor, and guide, for your empathy and tolerance are as big as your heart.

LIFE PATH
You like to have your own way and are, on occasion, very determined in your efforts to secure it. You are steady and loyal in your friendships; you make few friends slowly but hold them long. Rather exacting and picky, you have a quick wit and pleasant repartee and are somewhat of a homebody.

DESTINY
Your fine sense of taste will play an important part in your business success. Your ability to find the good side in most situations is helpful to your associates as well as yourself. Perseverance will help you accomplish the ambitions you hold most dear. Continue to be sympathetic and kindly to relatives who seek your counsel in times of stress, but do not assume their burdens.

KARMIC LESSON
You are clever with your hands, could draw well, and can undertake delicate operations requiring skill and dexterity. You might be a good artisan. You are poetical with scrapbooking or crafts. You have a good head for business and can take care of money when it is given to you. You are very affectionate but not too inclined to trust others. Unselfish and gentle, you have a love for humanity in general. You are at times despondent, but after a break you can be as lighthearted as possible. You are also quick to forgive. You are very ambitious and desire to reach the top of the ladder of your goals. You must learn to know yourself first, for you can never expect to make a success of your life if you do not.

SECRET
Your talent for both artistic pursuits and commerce will make it difficult at times for you to choose. Concentration, after your choice, will bring many rewards.

MAY 28

If I choose to bless another person, I will always end up feeling more blessed.
—Marianne Williamson

BORN ON THIS DAY
- **Rudy Giuliani**
  politician
- **Gladys Knight**
  singer
- **Elisabeth Hasselbeck**
  TV personality
- **Kylie Minogue**
  singer
- **Carey Mulligan**
  actor

PERSONALITY
It seems to you that when anyone has a serious problem to solve, they run to you for guidance. This is as it should be, because you have a profound understanding of human nature. You can probe humanity's foibles with deep perception, and your diagnosis is usually correct. Therefore, your role in the drama of life is that of the surgeon who must excise the harmful growth that makes for unhappiness and confusion. How does this affect your own life? You take joy in making others happy. You are a good organizer, can see ahead, and can carry out projects with strength of purpose and determination. Because you can both lead and follow in the planning and execution of worthy causes, you are often called upon by your group or community for help, which you render willingly. Yours should be a life full of learning.

LIFE PATH
A self-starter, you are determined, capable of stubbornness, and ambitious. You like socializing and networking if you can move in a circle that feeds your soul, and you have sufficient adaptability to move from group to group. You love your family and will spare no pains or expense for their betterment.

DESTINY
The confidence you have in your own ideas and actions will be translated and communicated to others. You will be respected for your efficiency and ability. Since your judgment is good, feel justified in insisting on doing things in your own way. However, guard against a tendency to become too dictatorial when you are engaged in an undertaking that requires cooperative efforts.

KARMIC LESSON
You have a quick, alert brain—one that sees things in a flash and acts upon them quickly. You have strong impulses, which you are apt to follow too freely at times. You are fond of games of chance and very lucky in that direction. You probably have remarkable dreams, which seem to you to be symbolic, if only you could get them properly interpreted. You are sensitive to slights but appreciative of kindnesses. You are fond of social media interactions and the groups you participate in. You might be able to write well. Try to join a book club or writing group. If you trained your will, there is scarcely anything you could not accomplish, for with your natural gifts, you should be motivated to make a great success in life.

SECRET
Your excess of self-confidence may arouse much jealousy and make rivals bitter. You are a person who believes in the motto "Just do it."

FRIENDS & FAMILY

MAY 29

In family life, love is the oil that eases friction, the cement that binds closer together, and the music that brings harmony.
—Eva Burrows

BORN ON THIS DAY

- **John F. Kennedy**
  U.S. president
- **Annette Bening**
  actor
- **Bob Hope**
  actor, comedian
- **Laverne Cox**
  actor
- **Daniel Tosh**
  comedian

FRIENDS & FAMILY

_____
_____
_____
_____
_____
_____
_____
_____
_____
_____

PERSONALITY
You have a quiet nature and like to be in surroundings that reflect your usual mood of tranquility and peace. Nature has endowed you with a deep understanding of other people, of philosophy, and of all the finer things in life. You really appreciate many various forms of art because your own inner spirit is in harmony with all things that breathe perfection and that represent the creative capacities of humankind. Your own imagination is very vivid, as are your dreams, and you should develop your artistic talents to the greatest extent possible. Even if you think you have no special genius, you should look within yourself for it, because it is there, awaiting its unfolding. You may be likely to have heartbreaks and disappointments in life, which can make you dejected at times, so you had best learn to take things in stride and let go of what you cannot control. Experience will teach you all you need to know.

LIFE PATH
You are fond of children and very loving toward most members of your household. Kindhearted, affable, and very considerate in your treatment of others, you will never intentionally wound another's feelings. Notwithstanding your naturally sweet disposition, you are capable of great bitterness if your trust is flagrantly violated.

DESTINY
Your accomplishments will be due in great part to not allowing yourself to be distracted from the things that you feel must be done. Do not be abrupt when dealing with friends who do not understand your seriousness of purpose. Cultivate tact and take time out to express your inborn compassion for less fortunate individuals.

KARMIC LESSON
You are intense but have a good deal of charm about you, which draws people to you, even though they may not always understand you. You have a flair for getting out of difficulties and awkward situations, no matter how challenging they may be. You have great aspirations to grow and rise to the next level. You are quite a climber, in fact. You are funny and spirited at times; you must learn to take yourself more seriously and make more of a secure business life. Success is won by carefully laid plans and determined effort; it is mostly never due to luck in your case.

SECRET
You can be eminently successful in business, although you are always somewhat suspicious of your coworkers. It is best to have close friends outside of work.

MAY 30

Pleasure in the job puts perfection in the work.
—Aristotle

⦿ PERSONALITY
You emanate power, and the executive branch of life is your field of operation. Financial affairs come within your sphere of influence, and you are able to master them whether they are large or small. Philanthropy and the organizations of charitable institutions could use your services to good advantage. You have the power to put ideas into practical form, and concepts seem to take shape under your hand. Because you are a good analyst, people know that they can trust you with their money as well as their confidences. However, when acting in such a position of trust or guardianship, do not lean too far forward in doing things for others, for you may neglect your own needs and duties. By learning to save and economize, you can accumulate the best things in life for your own comfort.

⦿ LIFE PATH
You are inclined to be dictatorial and could be quick to anger, though filled with remorse immediately if your temper gets beyond control. You are fond of socializing and stimulating conversation, particularly if you can associate with bright, witty people, and are fond of travel. You are faithful to your duties even though they are sometimes irksome. Don't be a martyr.

⦿ DESTINY
A position of trust will give you opportunity to show your reliability as well as your alertness to details and problems. Financial difficulties will not overwhelm you, because of your ability to carefully consider each alternative before you act. Do not hesitate to drop any job or activity that has lost its attraction for you. Continue to put emphasis on security, but do not economize to the point of miserliness. Be generous in expressing your affection for others, as they need to know you care.

⦿ KARMIC LESSON
You have a fair, impartial mind that goes straight to the point. You are quiet, a bit inhibited, and reserved, and while these are not bad qualities, you must learn that when carried to excess they could become faults, a sign of too much self-analysis and absorption. You are original, intuitive, and fond of outdoor activities, especially early in life. Nature is very healing for your spirits. Your interests are mainly business, but you have a taste for good music, too, and probably love concerts and even dancing. You are not overly affectionate or demonstrative, but you have strong feelings and are attracted strongly by sexuality. You are imaginative and should cultivate better self-esteem. Live up to your highest ideas, and you should be able to do great things.

⦿ SECRET
You have an ingenious mind, given to inventing schemes, sometimes without the patience to work them out in detail.

BORN ON THIS DAY
- ★ **Mel Blanc**
  voice actor
- ★ **CeeLo Green**
  singer, music producer
- ★ **Idina Menzel**
  singer, actor
- ★ **Wynonna Judd**
  singer
- ★ **Audrey Flack**
  artist

FRIENDS & FAMILY

MAY 31

Character and personal force are the only investments worth anything.
—Walt Whitman

BORN ON THIS DAY

★ **Walt Whitman**
author

★ **Colin Farrell**
actor

★ **Clint Eastwood**
actor

★ **Azealia Banks**
rapper

★ **Joe Namath**
football player

FRIENDS & FAMILY

_____
_____
_____
_____
_____
_____
_____
_____
_____

◉ PERSONALITY

The pattern of life is a majestic design as far as you are concerned. Petty things, petty people, and minor annoyances are discharged from your field of vision automatically because you have no patience for or interest in them. You have a profound understanding of people and events. Books, tales, music, and occult philosophy appeal to you because you have the key to comprehending them. You are visionary and farsighted. With your powers of visualization, you have vicarious experiences that people who are actually on the spot where things occur may miss. Internet, texting, and all forms of communication over long distances are of interest to you. You have a distinct and unique charm, but you are slow to give your affection to others. Do not become intolerant of the foibles of life and the world because of your critical capacity, as this could easily turn you into a grouch.

◉ LIFE PATH

You are devoted to your good friends but not possessive or jealous. Your emotional balance extends to your relationship with business associates. You let others do as they please, and you expect them to refrain from interfering with you. You would find considerable satisfaction in spending a great deal of time visiting art galleries, reading, or talking with people who have creative talents.

◉ DESTINY

Be realistic in your thoughts, even when you are making idealistic plans for the future. During those rare periods when you feel unsure of yourself, do not let uncertainty become apparent to others. Encourage friends in their endeavors and give credit where it is due. Find pleasure extending hospitality to new acquaintances. You like to dress well and have an artistic home.

◉ KARMIC LESSON

You have a very varied character that is hard to define. In fact, you don't always understand it yourself. You are a good organizer, capable and businesslike. You could have a strong intellectual bent and could write if you tried to do so. You are not very fond of taking classes and often prefer to be alone with your own thoughts, ideas, and reflections. You could be very successful in business and are inclined to ride roughshod over others, as you are very directed in your focus and have no time for small talk. You have a great deal of energy for your interests, which you are inclined to expend lavishly. Find your own faults by self-analysis and determine to conquer them. In this way, success and lasting contentment will be attained.

◉ SECRET

You are clever with words and letters. You could make a successful lawyer or social leader. You understand justice.

JUNE 1

The choicest pleasures of life lie within the ring of moderation.
—Benjamin Disraeli

BORN ON THIS DAY

- **Marilyn Monroe**
  actor
- **Morgan Freeman**
  actor
- **Alanis Morissette**
  singer
- **Heidi Klum**
  model, TV personality
- **Amy Schumer**
  comedian, actor

FRIENDS & FAMILY

PERSONALITY

There is a saying that still waters run deep, and this applies to you. You do not make a fuss about the business of living, but you understand all its peculiar and varying facets. You perform with quiet efficiency each task as it comes up, and you are admired for your skill and aptitude, whatever chore it becomes your duty to do. You are inclined to be optimistic because you understand that destiny never places any obligation on you that is beyond your power to carry out. There are times when you yield to sadness, but you also know that all of life is cyclic in nature and that the low periods will pass on in time and that high ones will appear. The homing instinct is strong in your makeup, and you enjoy the company of your loved ones and the warmth of the fireside, which is a symbol to you of the affection of family ties. Your intuition is right on, and you depend upon it for the conduct of many important events in your life.

LIFE PATH

You are normally optimistic, bright, and cheerful. No one can make you believe that any venture in which you are interested can fail, and your disappointment is very heavy when setbacks do overtake you. You are fond of good movies, like to stay at home, and derive your greatest enjoyment from your private life.

DESTINY

Your good ideas will be accepted by associates, but you will always first have to substantiate and defend them. Make sure your plans are definite and that all persons concerned in their operation have a clear picture of the part each is to play in them. Do not exaggerate the importance of small slights.

KARMIC LESSON

You are very original and come up with fresh approaches to undertakings. You like to have your own way in what you do. You take an interest only in enterprises that involve your talents, and small deals do not attract you in the least. You are independent, caring little for the opinions of others, who are more conventional than yourself. You are intuitive, and a strong spiritual streak runs through your nature. You are not so fond of socializing but love solitude and often walk out into the woods by yourself and meditate. You have a good brain, which needs only practiced training to make you peaceful and calm in your approach to life.

SECRET

You have a sensitive nature and are hurt by small discourtesies. You are happiest when working alone or independently.

JUNE 2

In prosperity prepare for a change; in adversity hope for one.
—James Burgh

BORN ON THIS DAY

- **Marquis de Sade**
  author, politician
- **Marvin Hamlisch**
  composer
- **Awkwafina**
  actor, rapper
- **Sergio Castillo**
  soccer player
- **Andy Cohen**
  talk show host

PERSONALITY
You would make an excellent partner in any financial project because you have the ability to visualize the outcome of fiduciary transactions and the qualifications to work behind the scenes, unobtrusively researching and getting important information. This ability may be manifested just as vitally in the purchase of household goods as in a big business transaction. Because you are seldom wrong in your opinion of other people, you have a distinct advantage in all your associations. Your first impressions are accurate, and you can tell upon being introduced to someone whether this person has qualities or traits that will make them a worthwhile addition to your list of acquaintances. You are very fair in your dealings with your loved ones, but you sometimes will conceal the real depth and warmth that you feel for them because you know that it is wrong to spoil them.

LIFE PATH
You are impulsive and have an intuitive rather than analytical mind. You possess considerable analytical ability and could counsel people successfully if you trained and developed your skills. You care a great deal for your home and would make whatever personal sacrifice necessary to further the happiness of your loved ones. You understand yet can put up with a lot of dysfunction.

DESTINY
You are among the few people who know when to lead and when to follow. Retain your inherent enthusiasm but subdue your tendency toward impulsive action. Respect for established authority will give you the reputation not of a traditionalist but rather of a sensible and substantial citizen. Be proud of your temperance and enjoyment of sane, conventional, and serious pleasures.

KARMIC LESSON
Tactful, ingenious, and clever, you are a diplomat. You are a great reader and fond of TV and movies. Probably detective stories appeal to you, and any story that borders on the fantastic and the weird. You can be narrow in your viewpoints. You need to broaden your perspective, to get a larger, healthier, and more commonsense viewpoint of things and life generally, which only more travel, classes, and contact with all kinds of minds will give you. You do not care much for travel, however, but are quite contented to sit at home and look after your own interests there. You could be successful in business, and few will get ahead of you in any undertaking you enter.

SECRET
You have an optimistic nature and are never down and rarely glum. You have no trouble earning money, as there is quick adaptability, but due to frequent changes, little is saved.

FRIENDS & FAMILY

JUNE 3

Life is a long lesson in humility.
—James M. Barrie

BORN ON THIS DAY
- **Allen Ginsberg**
  poet
- **Curtis Mayfield**
  singer/songwriter
- **Tony Curtis**
  actor
- **Anderson Cooper**
  TV personality
- **Josephine Baker**
  singer

FRIENDS & FAMILY

PERSONALITY
You have a strongly emotional nature, and you are deeply moved by the sufferings of others. This latter experience might bring you down if you permit it to affect you too profoundly. Since you can see into the why and wherefore of the conduct of others, you vicariously go through their experiences with them. But life is designed for you to live it, not to do so for others. You are a lover of things connected with the sea and water. Because you can be very entertaining at social gatherings, you are invited everywhere there is a fun party, but you also know how to have a good time by yourself. The finer things in life attract you, and you enjoy treasure hunting. You can display a sharp temper on occasion and can be very caustic in your comments and criticism. Creative work that can be done in your own home or studio without the supervision of a boss is your best métier.

LIFE PATH
You possess originality, independence, and a fair amount of ambition. Your love of comfort and ease, however, may curb your ambition and prevent you from attaining that degree of success of which you are capable. You give in at times to your moods and spells of feeling defeated. Your heart is big, but you can get hurt easily.

DESTINY
You can use your aptitude for words, both spoken and written, to help you attain your goals. Be sure to carefully consider the duties entailed in accepting new responsibilities or pledging long-range services before you take them on. Your praise of an associate's work will give added incentive to their labors and pay off for you, too. Your critiques and evaluations mean a lot to others.

KARMIC LESSON
You can be strong-willed and independent. You love justice done if it swings in your favor. When opinion goes against you, you are not so anxious to see the letter of the law enforced. You are restless and like newness. You try to make many friends wherever you go. You must take life as it comes and not be so downhearted when things do not go your way. There is usually some bitter with every sweet, and we must take the one with the other and play at life's game with the strengths that we possess. Remember what Shakespeare wrote: "All the world's a stage / And all the men and women merely players." Think of the kind of character you would like to be upon the stage, and see whether you are acting the part.

SECRET
You have an intuitive mind and therefore are a little scornful of logical, patient learning and waiting. You receive much admiration but not enough loyalty.

JUNE 4

Make money your god, and it will plague you like the devil.
—Henry Fielding

⁕ PERSONALITY
An unusual capacity for hard work, problem solving, and manual skills sets you apart. You enjoy tackling a challenging puzzle, whether it involves construction or instruction or is designed for entertainment. Then you wrestle with it until you have it beaten. Such tenacity is indeed praiseworthy. Your home is very dear to you, and you would enjoy a rural life best of all. Nothing delights you more than to putter around in a garden, planting seeds, picking flowers, building an arbor, or making general improvements in the appearance or conveniences of your home. When you are surrounded by the smiling faces of your loved ones, you are at peace with the world. You are better at supervising work than at taking orders, so you should aim for the executive branch of whatever field of endeavor you are engaged in.

⁕ LIFE PATH
You are bright, humorous, and excessively optimistic. You are sure everything will turn out right, even though, when you do take the trouble to look ahead, many times you can see nothing but trouble. You are able to do many tasks very well and thoroughly, and you generally work with enthusiasm. You have many supportive friends and will have the devoted love of a partner.

⁕ DESTINY
Your meticulous attention to detail and ability to follow directions in spite of red tape will be to your advantage. Because you grant favors willingly, you should feel free to ask them of others. Work at an even pace rather than in fits and starts. Make constructive changes only with the approval of associates, or there will be consequences. A long-distance trip or even a tour in your own vicinity can always add to your storehouse of knowledge.

⁕ KARMIC LESSON
You are unselfish and kind but need a little more independence of spirit to make your life the success you desire. Remember that one of the hardest things in life is to say no at the right time, when an occasion really demands it. Do not be so influenced by your friends and other voices around you. You think independently enough; act more in accordance with your own thoughts and wishes. You are always a student, and pop culture attracts you. Born on this day, you would doubtless make a success by somehow dealing with the stage or the movie business, but remember that this is a life of hard work for those who would succeed, and not all roses and glamour, as many suppose.

⁕ SECRET
You have a generous nature and are quickly moved by others' needs. Born on this day, you are a lover of large community or family get-togethers.

BORN ON THIS DAY
★ **Angelina Jolie**
actor
★ **Russell Brand**
comedian
★ **Rosalind Russell**
actor, comedian
★ **El DeBarge**
singer
★ **T.J. Miller**
actor, comedian

FRIENDS & FAMILY

JUNE 5

To feel much for others and little for ourselves . . . constitute[s] the perfection of human nature.
—Adam Smith

BORN ON THIS DAY

★ **Bill Moyers**
talk show host

★ **Kenny G**
musician

★ **Brian McKnight**
singer/songwriter

★ **Mark Wahlberg**
actor, singer

★ **Federico García Lorca**
poet

FRIENDS & FAMILY

PERSONALITY
Action and motion are as essential to you as the very air you breathe. Nothing is so stultifying, in your opinion, as sitting around waiting, doing nothing. You like to organize parties, plan dinners and outings, and keep up a full schedule of entertainment and pleasure. You are particularly efficient at directing activities as if in the theater, for you have a deep instinct for all the things connected with it. Of course, this may sound as though you direct all your energies toward channels of fun and games, but you also have your serious side. In this role, that of the productive, mature person, you enjoy studying, helping others, and seeing that your efforts at your job are not in vain. It does not matter whether you work at home or in an office or on a farm, as long as you know that you are doing a good job, carrying out your tasks from day to day, and getting fair compensation for your work.

LIFE PATH
You love with depth, hate with bitterness, play with abandon, and work with zeal. You are apt to make decisions quickly and to act upon your decisions with equal quickness. While you are usually kindhearted and considerate, you will say very sharp things under provocation.

DESTINY
You take pride in a difficult job well done. You will have strong opinions on controversial subjects but do not press your opinions in discussions when you sense they are being regarded coldly. Take full advantage of labor or time-saving methods. Gauge your capacity for work and timing correctly and without undue strain. Do not let yourself become entangled in financial transactions that hinder you.

KARMIC LESSON
Yours is a very interesting life, full of changes and abrupt transitions, from one plane of life to another, ups and downs fluctuating with astonishing rapidity. You have many surprises in store for you. You are interested in bizarre and odd things, such as medical and psychological questions, collections, and all sorts of out-of-the-ordinary subjects. At the same time, you have a distinctly sane and rational streak in your nature and never get very far away from proven facts. You are a good organizer and can successfully undertake large plans. You are of a motivated temperament and have a large stock of vitality, which you have a rather lavish way of spending. You are very affectionate and like to be on the move at all times.

SECRET
You possess a rare combination of a capacity for detail and an ability to conceive of big plans. You could be successful in event planning.

JUNE 6

Why not try and see positive things, to just touch those things and make them bloom.
—Thich Nhat Hanh

BORN ON THIS DAY
- **Harvey Fierstein**
  actor
- **Thomas Mann**
  author
- **Paul Giamatti**
  actor
- **Björn Borg**
  tennis player
- **Robert Englund**
  actor

◉ PERSONALITY
You have a lot of talents, and you sometimes are bewildered as to how you can best express yourself. In certain respects, you are too much inclined to listen to others and take their advice rather than follow the dictates of your own conscience and the guiding voice of your inner being. Have more confidence in yourself, and don't be afraid to show off what you can do and how well you can do it. However, you should make one decision, and that is to limit your efforts to a single field. Although you might prove to be a success in various activities, you can only cash in most successfully by devoting your time, effort, and energy to the development of a single talent. While you get a lot of pleasure from your family or family of friends, you are prone to do too much for them. This is generous and noble, but it can limit your own life and pleasures, as well as your dreams, if you carry it too far.

◉ LIFE PATH
You can be forceful, energetic, and compelling, a clearheaded thinker and shrewd reasoner. Most of your enterprises are successful unless your judgment yields to some outside influence. Empathetic and very loving, you devote a great deal of your time and energy to making your living space and fashions more interesting.

◉ DESTINY
Friends will admire the patience and courtesy you display when you are confronted by an exasperating situation. Keep your enthusiasm under control, particularly when it comes to buying real estate or getting involved in investments of an unusual nature. Seek the advice of others prior to announcing major business decisions. Be more secretive.

◉ KARMIC LESSON
You are quite original in your thoughts and ideas and would make a good inventor, if you have the opportunity. You are more courageous than you think. A great seeker of truth, you are never content until you have solved a problem or reached the bottom of any difficult question, although you can get distracted along the way. You have a good sense of balance and justice and would make an excellent lawyer. You take things to heart. Slights cannot roll off your mind, and apologies sometimes fail to penetrate. You have a difficult nature to manage; if you master it and make a success of your life, it will be a lasting credit to you for your self-mastery.

◉ SECRET
You have a tendency to procrastinate; you hesitate while others leap ahead. You are more successful when driven by need or stimulated by love.

FRIENDS & FAMILY

JUNE 7

A person who never made a mistake never tried anything new.
—Albert Einstein

BORN ON THIS DAY

- **Prince**
  singer
- **Dean Martin**
  singer
- **Tom Jones**
  singer
- **Liam Neeson**
  actor
- **Bill Hader**
  actor

FRIENDS & FAMILY

PERSONALITY
There is an electrical emanation coming from your personality, figuratively speaking, that makes you a very magnetic, charged person. Placed in strange surroundings, you are soon the center of a group of admirers of your humor, wit, energy, and clever ideas. You possess a social sense that makes your every act seem absolutely appropriate to the occasion. True, you enjoy this popularity, and you revel in the fun of your group every time a party or gathering is held. Nevertheless, there is a side to your nature that you do not always reveal to the world, and that is your attraction to, and understanding of, the mystical. To you, the hidden side of nature and the unrevealed aspects of personality are as an open book. You are as tender within as you are bright and agreeable without. This combination of traits lends great charm and subtlety to your character and should operate to make your life one of super development and attainment.

LIFE PATH
You are impulsive and quick to see a point but rather easily discouraged if those around you are too superficial. You are loyal to your friends, anxious to help those in distress, sympathetic, and sensitive. You are a devoted lover and suffer deeply if love is not returned to you with equal strength.

DESTINY
Your ability to see trying problems as well as trifling annoyances with proper perspective will be responsible for the comparative ease with which you will solve them using both your rational and intuitive gifts. Since the standards you set for yourself are often higher than those most people can attain, you should try to be more tolerant of others' inadequacies. If you are willing to forgive, you will be forgiven.

KARMIC LESSON
You have a smart mind, good judgment, and strong convictions. You also have strong intuitions, which you can usually afford to follow with safety. You are extremely expressive and would make a good performer. You are studious and very fond of taking courses and learning. Your thirst for knowledge is never satisfied. You are caring and understanding of the problems of others. You are quite a philosopher about your own life and manage to get along far better than you otherwise would because of your beliefs, theories, and faith. Entertaining and charismatic, you are a storyteller and can keep a crowd of people amused for hours at a time.

SECRET
You are more interested in the mystical, deep aspects of life than in its superficial problems. You also have a peculiar sense of humor.

JUNE 8

*To know and not do is
to not yet know.*
—Confucian saying

⭐ PERSONALITY
Practicality combined with forward vision makes you successful in whatever field of endeavor you choose to enter. You can run a house, organize a school, manage a business, or succeed as an entrepreneur. The essential qualities are within you, and you are able to use them to seize opportunities that many others might see but never take advantage of. You do not restrict yourself to material objectives, however, because you know what is really important in life. You know that the spirit must also be nurtured and that no person lives isolated in a community. You know how to combine business and pleasure in such a way that you can have your fun and also get your job done and therefore get paid. By weaving a pattern of common sense and idealism into a whole, you achieve a special place in the world.

◎ LIFE PATH
You are quite shrewd. Do not allow it to lead you into manipulating situations. You are also stubborn at times, and you yield ungracefully. You are also honest and ambitious, fond of exploration and travel, and good at meeting people and making friendships.

👁 DESTINY
You may always expect unusual opportunities for self-advancement. If someone hands you the reins, do not be afraid to take them. Do not underestimate the importance of paying attention to small details. Be on the alert for false statements from jealous people, which can later lead to confusion and misunderstanding.

☯ KARMIC LESSON
You can be temperamental, and at certain times in your life you may suffer from "moods." These are largely within your own power, and you must learn to conquer them as best you can. Learn to control and calm your mind by studying yourself and practicing meditation and relaxation exercises. Read some self-help books—they will help you greatly. You have determination and force of character. You are exacting and methodical, to a certain extent, but sometimes get frustrated with the finishing. You are observant of the affairs and foibles of others, but you do not realize some of your bigger goals until you learn to analyze yourself, discovering where your weak points lie. You are thoughtful, honest, and giving. You feel things deeply and are capable of a sincere, abiding love.

🙂 SECRET
You are an omnivorous reader with a genuine interest in research work. You would make a fine teacher.

BORN ON THIS DAY
★ **Kanye West**
singer

★ **Frank Lloyd Wright**
architect

★ **Joan Rivers**
comedian

★ **Nancy Sinatra**
singer

★ **Julianna Margulies**
actor

FRIENDS & FAMILY

JUNE 9

Love is the recognition of oneness in the world of duality.
—Eckhart Tolle

BORN ON THIS DAY

* **Peter the Great**
  leader of imperial Russia
* **Johnny Depp**
  actor
* **Michael J. Fox**
  actor
* **Natalie Portman**
  actor
* **Aaron Sorkin**
  playwright, filmmaker

FRIENDS & FAMILY

PERSONALITY

Your ambition is to transform your surroundings into a place of beauty where you will also be able to conduct either a business or a studio of creative arts. You are interested in the culture of your community and of civilization as a whole, and nothing would delight you more than to have a group of aspiring and talented people around you who are trying to increase the artistic treasures of our times. You have a rather subtle understanding of the occult, and you could well become a leader of a local community or Internet group whose purpose would be to advance the study of a particular philosophy. In any case, your activities should center on your home, for you are a real home-loving type. Much happiness is in store for you, although you may have a rather hard row to hoe in early life. Each experience, however, adds to the store of knowledge you are gathering, and from it will emerge a wise personality.

LIFE PATH

You are determined and concentrated in your work and patient in working out details. You have a seeking, active mind and much ability to carry out ideas. Your disposition is sweet and lovable, and you are very popular in your own circle. You like socializing and are a good host.

DESTINY

Home conditions will be mostly harmonious, and you will realize that you can make a worthwhile contribution to the welfare of your community, either online or in real life. Because new events will often turn up with little warning, try to finish each day's tasks on schedule. Do not think you are inefficient because you prefer to do things the "old way." Also, avoid engaging in chronic petty bickering with family members about subjects not even worth discussing.

KARMIC LESSON

You are generous and sympathetic; there is a good deal that is inspired about you. You might be able to originate designs. You would probably not succeed in business alone, but you might in a partnership, leaving most of the business details in your partner's hands. You are very attached to your home and do not particularly care for travel, except now and then, to see various parts of the world. Careful and thoughtful, you are interested in reforms of various kinds, and suffering humanity inspires you with a genuine empathy and care. You are independent and would sooner starve than borrow. You are proud and would suffer in silence rather than tell others of your problems. Your steady nerves stand you in good stead in a crisis.

SECRET

Born on this day, you generally have a determined temperament. You would be successful in some work connected with social media, video, or websites.

JUNE 10

Life is a quarry, out of which we are to mold and chisel and complete a character.
—Johann Wolfgang von Goethe

BORN ON THIS DAY

★ **Judy Garland**
actor

★ **E.O. Wilson**
biologist

★ **Faith Evans**
singer, actor

★ **Tara Lipinski**
figure skater

★ **Sundar Pichai**
CEO, Alphabet

PERSONALITY

Sometimes there seems to be a war going on in your personality, a conflict between the idealism you feel and the stubbornness you demonstrate in the practical, everyday world. There are times when you cannot resist the impulse to dominate a situation, to take the lead even if it is not rightfully yours. Then there are times when you lean over backward in your efforts to see that everything is fair and square. Such a conflict of desires is less unusual than you think. But a sensible solution to it is the important thing. You should further develop that uncanny judgment with which you have been blessed so that you can tell when a cause is worth fighting for and when it isn't worth the effort of a struggle. In this way only can you emerge the victor. By seeking spiritual guidance, perhaps with the use of an oracle, you will find that there is much help to be attained from this world and beyond.

LIFE PATH

Temper your adventurous spirit by cautiousness, or problems will tend to overtake you. You are inclined to try to overcome difficulties by sheer, misdirected force, where tact, diplomacy, and cleverness would accomplish more. You can be led much better than you can be driven. Your love for another is deep and strong.

DESTINY

Wise investments over the years will increase your sense of financial security. An incident that occurs in public may have great personal significance in your life. Be cautious about accepting advice on professional matters from people not qualified to give it. Reciprocate kindnesses extended by interested friends. Keep alert to a quickly passing opportunity that you can seize; don't miss out. Take the initiative in establishing friendships.

KARMIC LESSON

You are a deep thinker, with a passion for getting at the truth, even if this deprives you of peace of mind. You are not light or frivolous. The serious is clearly marked; even the somber is predominant. You are fond of knowledge and study a lot. You might write a journal. You are very independent in both thought and action, and no one can deter you from a certain line of action when once you have made up your mind. You have a sensitive, feeling nature, and you must consequently expect to experience all the disadvantages of such a disposition as well as the advantages. You are not frivolous, but you have a silly sense of humor. Do not be afraid of being yourself—natural and spontaneous.

SECRET

Often more influenced by people's appearance than by their characteristics, you place your trust too readily in handsome or beautiful people; consequently, you are liable to become disappointed.

FRIENDS & FAMILY

JUNE 11

Your vision will become clear only when you look into your heart. Who looks outside, dreams. Who looks inside, awakens.
—Carl Jung

BORN ON THIS DAY

- ★ **Richard Strauss**
  composer
- ★ **Jacques Cousteau**
  marine biologist
- ★ **Peter Dinklage**
  actor
- ★ **Hugh Laurie**
  actor
- ★ **Gene Wilder**
  actor

FRIENDS & FAMILY

✦ PERSONALITY

You possess the power and the ability to attract success and money. Your soul is filled with dreams of acquiring the great things of life, and you dream of having wealth, fame, and personal success. All of these hopes and dreams are actually within your grasp if you will make the effort to accomplish them. Work, concentration, and will can get you anything you want, for the potentiality for their achievement is already in the composition of your character. Of course, there is a negative side to everything, and there is one to the exceptionally outstanding personality that you possess. Therefore, you should take warning that success of the kind to which you aspire brings with it the temptation to be selfish, domineering, and egotistical. Make up your mind to work hard for the happiness you want, but don't let success go to your head and turn you into someone you don't want to be.

🌀 LIFE PATH

Knowledgeable, you are a great observer and a good conversationalist. You have good judgment and never act hastily or rashly. You form friendships readily and care a great deal for those in your inner circle. You have considerable pride, are careful of appearances, and will be happy in your chosen residence.

👁 DESTINY

Your major accomplishments will be due to the fact that you are willing to do a little at a time and let it add up. Accept delegated assignments without asking a lot of unnecessary questions. When you make big changes, be sure all involved are in agreement before you start. Try to remind yourself and dissatisfied friends of enjoying the pleasures at hand rather than wishing for the unobtainable.

☯ KARMIC LESSON

You are a good talker, lively and entertaining. Energetic, you enjoy outdoor recreation and working out. You are a natural mimic. You should not marry too young. Look well before you leap. You are interested in the occult and mysterious; you like exploring unknown places and getting in difficult situations that tax your ingenuity to the utmost to escape. You are fond of travel and will doubtless see much of the world. A little too prone to pry into the affairs of others, you are curious about all that passes around you. You are a moneymaker, in regular small amounts, more than large investments and big speculations, which earn you a greater return over time. You are not overly domesticated and should cultivate this side of yourself a little more.

🔒 SECRET

You have a quick mind, lacking at times in powers of concentration. You should seek the guidance of a partner with a steady, patient, analytical mind.

JUNE 12

Sow an act, and you reap a habit; sow a habit, and you reap a character; sow a character, and you reap a destiny.
—Anonymous

✦ PERSONALITY

You are always ready when help is needed or when someone dear to you needs consolation, assistance, or advice. The reason for this is that you have a well of sympathy in your makeup that responds immediately to the needs of others. Of course, all of life does not consist in playing the role of the rescuer, and you have good times just as you have trying ones. In fact, you can be the life of any party, and you enjoy the company of good friends and a convivial atmosphere. You have a tendency to interpret events according to your intuitions and instincts, and this is a very dependable part of your natural gifts and talents. Go right on following your hunches, for they are the expression of your best, inner self and should bring results that are rewarding in both the material and spiritual senses.

✦ LIFE PATH

You have a very affectionate nature; you could be happy in a long-term partnership and perfectly contented in your homelife. You are a seeker of culture and refinement as a quality in your friendships. You are greatly admired and quite popular, especially as an accomplished adult.

✦ DESTINY

You will be successful because you enjoy working as part of a team and do not think your own personal gain is more important than the welfare of your associates. Do not shy away from discussing large-scale ideas or goals with trusted friends. You should not procrastinate or put off making decisions—even unpleasant ones. Keep your thinking flexible and be willing to alter your previous stand on an issue when new evidence is presented.

✦ KARMIC LESSON

Determined, stubborn, and assertive, you are generally driven to get your point across, no matter what happens, especially if you think it is for someone else's good. You cannot stand untidiness, and unpunctuality and similar faults anger and annoy you. Be careful that these characteristics do not get the better of you. Rather than trying to make external events and things conform to you, make your life conform to them. You are just and honest, focused and reserved, not given to imparting your wisdom to others unsought. Highly intuitive, you often have thoughts come into your head, and impressions and feelings sweep over you, that you cannot understand. You do not make friends very easily, but when you do, they last for life and nothing can come between you.

✦ SECRET

With a strong ambition for social achievements and honors, you are shrewd in business, yet willing to listen to compliments and flattery, and need many pats on the back.

BORN ON THIS DAY

- **Anne Frank**
  diarist
- **George H.W. Bush**
  U.S. president
- **Chick Corea**
  jazz musician
- **Dave Franco**
  actor
- **Marv Albert**
  sportscaster

FRIENDS & FAMILY

JUNE 13

Though we travel the world over to find the beautiful, we must carry it with us or we find it not.
—Ralph Waldo Emerson

BORN ON THIS DAY

- **James Clerk Maxwell**
  mathematician, physicist
- **William Butler Yeats**
  poet
- **Christo & Jeanne-Claude**
  husband-and-wife artist duo
- **Tim Allen**
  actor, comedian
- **Mary-Kate & Ashley Olsen**
  actors

FRIENDS & FAMILY

PERSONALITY

You may well overlook the ancient superstition that the thirteenth is an unlucky day, for you have been endowed with rather remarkable traits because you first entered the world on this date. As a matter of fact, you have a combination of qualities that it would be difficult to find in the birthdays of many other people. First of all, you derive a great satisfaction from the company of loved ones, both alive and on the other side. Then, you have great ability as a director of people, whether this is in your community or in other social groups. Supervisory ability has been given to you, and you must exercise it to express your full function as an influential member of society. Your greatest happiness is in directing affairs so that they come to a successful or profitable conclusion. No wonder your friends consider you a miracle worker—you are always on the go!

LIFE PATH

You are impulsive, energetic, and slightly combative, depending more upon your intuition than on your linear judgment. You make a good friend and a bad enemy. Your love is fervent and demonstrative, and you will not be happy unless you receive love and support in the same measure.

DESTINY

Your business dealings and social obligations will mostly be pleasant because of your straightforward manner. Your precise and explicit statements are much appreciated by people with whom you come in contact. However, realize that other people are often not as exact as you are, and be sure you do not misunderstand or misinterpret ambiguities. Do not be misled by false boasts. Investigate carefully before you decide to lend or spend money.

KARMIC LESSON

Clever, many-sided, and very creative, you are also original, intelligent, and witty. You go straight to the heart of a problem. You are somewhat psychic and extremely interested in such things. You have a magnetic personality, determination, and force of character. At the same time, you are rather shy at times and afraid to push yourself to the front as you should. You are more independent in thought than in action. Remember that the great rewards come only to the person who acts, and not to the theorist or dreamer. You are affectionate and expect a show of love from those around you. A student of wellness, you are naturally good with food. With your inventiveness and originality, you could be a great success.

SECRET

You have a romantic nature that conceives of love as a diversion rather than a serious, committed matter. You should learn to develop more emotional responsibility.

JUNE 14

Today is your day, your mountain is waiting, so . . . get on your way!
—Dr. Seuss

BORN ON THIS DAY
- **Donald Trump**
  U.S. president
- **Harriet Beecher Stowe**
  author
- **Boy George**
  singer/songwriter
- **Steffi Graf**
  tennis player
- **Alan Carr**
  comedian

PERSONALITY
Cooperation is to you the keynote of life and the greatest factor and motive in the conduct of your affairs. You have an enthusiastic spirit, which you show only to those people whom you really like and trust. Otherwise, you show the world a facet of your nature that seems workaday, sensible, and organized—all of which traits you also possess. However, there is a mischievous child hidden in you, and you surely do enjoy your little jokes, even when there is no one around to share them with. Just as you have a sense of humor, you also have a sense of the dramatic. There is no situation that fails to provide some fuel for you, and you can make a situation funny or dramatic even when it seems to others to lack every element of sparkle. You can assert yourself when necessary, and this is a good thing because you would otherwise allow too many people to take advantage of your giving nature.

LIFE PATH
You are generous, considerate, capable, and reliable. You have a dynamic, active mind and possess considerable tact and diplomacy. You are very fortunate in finding compatible friends and will never make a real enemy. You are generally bright and cheerful and need lots of attention.

DESTINY
You are well equipped to adjust to unexpected events and should find interruptions to your routine a pleasant diversion—you can turn lemons into lemonade. Take advantage of kindnesses extended by a sincere and generous acquaintance—it will take you far. The far-reaching results of original ideas that you set into operation will be extremely satisfying. There is possibility of financial gain from them.

KARMIC LESSON
Kind and sympathetic, you are probably quite psychic and open to impressions of all sorts. You have a restless disposition and will probably travel to many places. You have a good head for business and are private about your own affairs and those of others. No one ever gets a secret out of you that you are determined to preserve. You are probably fond of the sea, and you love to sit by the shore, watching the water and basking in the sun. You have a natural love of excitement and are always at your best when there is anything going on calling for energy and enthusiasm. You are a good conversationalist and can talk a lot once you get started. You are kind, loving, and affectionate—show it even more.

SECRET
Your best success will come from business. You are inclined to be overly ambitious in your career, although you would make a good spouse and parent.

FRIENDS & FAMILY

JUNE 15

Silence is beautiful for wise people; it is all the more beautiful for fools.
—The Talmud

BORN ON THIS DAY

- **Neil Patrick Harris**
  actor
- **Ice Cube**
  rapper, actor
- **Jim Belushi**
  actor, comedian
- **Helen Hunt**
  actor
- **Courteney Cox**
  actor

FRIENDS & FAMILY

PERSONALITY
Cheerfulness and an optimistic outlook on life characterize you, and these traits make you a popular person. You are well aware that life has its ups and downs, and you have evolved a philosophy that makes you able to "take it." This is a very sensible way to look at things, and as a result, you are a pretty balanced person. You bring goodwill with you wherever you go, and you radiate an aura of positive energy. Your interests lie in the direction of group projects, and you are successful in dealing with large numbers of people. Because you can create goodwill, you are chosen to head or participate in charity drives and support causes whose aim is to help the underprivileged. You could be a good public speaker, with some practice, and should be able to move your audience with your oratorical skill. An interest in many things keeps you ever on the alert and makes you interesting to other people.

LIFE PATH
You are creative, intellectual, quick-witted, and diligent. You are very fond of research and possess considerable critical ability. You have many friends, love your home ties, and are pure-minded and sincere. You could be happily partnered.

DESTINY
You should avoid situations that can become too complicated and unpleasant by refusing to let sentimentality influence your judgment. You will benefit from the advice offered by a person with wide business experience. Understandings will be reached with relatives so that obligations will become more pleasant and less burdensome after age thirty. By working with a large group, you can stabilize your finances and lay the groundwork for a secure future.

KARMIC LESSON
The fine arts especially attract you, and you like the life associated with them, as you are a natural bohemian, to a great extent. You are original in style, manner of speech, and thought. You do not like conventionality in any form and have no use for rigid thinkers. You believe that everyone should think for themselves. You are not afraid to express your opinions. You are fair and honest. You should never be content with anything but the best. Do not be satisfied with a mediocre living, as there is all the money in the world at your command; all you have to do is to think of something that you want of this unlimited store. You must realize your own worth and make others feel it also.

SECRET
You could be successful, as you possess drive, intuition, ambition, and a love of creativity, as well as a desire to help others succeed.

JUNE 16

What you leave behind is not what is engraved in stone monuments, but what is woven into the lives of others.
—Pericles

BORN ON THIS DAY
- **Tupac Shakur**
  rapper
- **Geronimo**
  leader of Apache Nation
- **Phil Mickelson**
  golfer
- **John Cho**
  actor
- **Laurie Metcalf**
  actor

PERSONALITY
Quite serious-minded, you have a strong sense of responsibility and a conscientious way of doing things. You accept the chores and tasks of life with equanimity, knowing that if you want a thing well done, you will have to do it yourself. In operating under this principle, you must not allow yourself to assume the tasks and chores rightfully belonging to someone else; don't take on the burdens of others, which you are inclined to do out of pity, sympathy, and sometimes just plain exasperation. Family life means a lot to you. It is your aim and ideal to establish harmonious relationships in your immediate group, and you are forever smoothing things over to the best of your ability. You know how to handle children instinctively, and therefore you are potentially a wonderful parent and teacher. Because you are affectionate by nature and show it, you are sure to have much returned to you in kind.

LIFE PATH
You are inclined to be changeable and restless, although you will apply yourself to the task before you, no matter how annoying. You base your actions more on inward desire than on outward influence. You are affectionate but will not fall in love at first sight. You are cautious and like to have your own way.

DESTINY
You should not harbor grudges. If you air your grievances, you will find that they do not bother you as much as when you suffer in silence. Return calls, texts, and e-mails, and be prompt in answering personal and business correspondence. Try to be conservative when financial considerations are involved.

KARMIC LESSON
Quiet and studious by nature, you love books, art, movies, and good television. You like nature but only for short periods of time in the summer. The city is the place for you: The rush and excitement bring out your best. Many art forms fascinate you, and the occult or mysterious has a special place in your heart. You are sensitive and psychic and take immediate likes or dislikes to people. You could make a lot of money in your life, mostly by your own original work; you must never look to others for support outside of established partnerships, or you will invariably be disappointed. You would do best in chosen partnership; lone ventures in business do not succeed with you. Live up to your ideals, and you will consider your life a success.

SECRET
You attract many admirers by your grace, charm, and cleverness, but you are inclined to be a bit self-indulgent at times.

FRIENDS & FAMILY

JUNE 17

Life is not measured by the number of breaths we take, but by the moments that take our breath away.
—Maya Angelou

BORN ON THIS DAY

- **Igor Stravinsky**
  composer
- **Venus Williams**
  tennis player
- **Barry Manilow**
  singer
- **Will Forte**
  comedian, actor
- **Charles Eames**
  designer, architect

FRIENDS & FAMILY

PERSONALITY

You are quiet and talkative by turns, depending upon your state of mind. Although it may sound strange to you, you are quite good at displaying both of these phases in life. In other words, when you are in the mood for conversation, you are quite loquacious, and when you are in the mood for solitude, you are completely relaxed by being absolutely quiet. Of course, the latter is a remarkably efficient way of restoring energy and strength, and it is lucky you have this ability to concentrate your resting because you are generally a very active person. You like to travel to see new places and faces and learn new concepts and customs in a variety of locales. It would be an excellent idea if you could combine your wishes with a way of earning a living, such as by being a travel reporter or journalist for a newspaper, podcast, website, or magazine, jobs you should be eminently suited for.

LIFE PATH

You have a basically cheerful and optimistic disposition, even though you get anxious at times. You are imaginative, idealistic, and sometimes impractical. You are sympathetic, loving, and very fond of your hobbies and collections. You love planning your vacations and are eager to learn and improve your mind.

DESTINY

When participating in a venture with other people, be sure that your personal interests are protected. Never count on money that you have not received. Do not be too quick to make allowances for unreliable associates. Light reading and stimulating conversation will always add to your enjoyment of the day and help you to relax. You have good reason for strong optimism—you are very lucky.

KARMIC LESSON

You are rather serious by nature, though you can share a joke with anyone. You can be burdened with the realities and cares of the world. You should be more direct and outspoken, because you can be frank and clear-minded, and you have the courage of your convictions. Others come to you with their troubles and look to you to help them out of difficulty. You will probably never become super wealthy, but you will be quite comfortably off later in life and will be able to live how you like and do what you like. You have a loving nature and could be obsessively devoted to your home and family. You are a good and ingenious manager and are creative in making a little go a long way.

SECRET

You are a person interested in antiques and the events of the past. Under the right circumstances, you would make a wise counselor or teacher.

JUNE 18

It's not the size of the dog in the fight, it's the size of the fight in the dog.
—Mark Twain

BORN ON THIS DAY
- **Paul McCartney**, musician
- **Brad Pitt**, actor
- **Jürgen Habermas**, philosopher
- **Blake Shelton**, singer, music producer
- **Isabella Rossellini**, actor

PERSONALITY
Your work in life is to show others the way, and therefore you might make a great or inspiring instructor. Assuming the job you do at your office or business, seeing that everyone is taken care of—these tasks you take upon yourself almost without thinking. It is fortunate that you are endowed with qualities to see you through the difficult situations. Your natural grace, appearance, and inner harmony are a source of constant inspiration. Much kindness is shown to you, and many favors are granted to you because you have a natural magnetism for attracting the gifts of friends and destiny. You know just how to fix things up to look their best, and your home is the artistic expression of your good taste. Exotic apparel and personal adornment appeal to you, but they are never garish. You were made for love and should lead a satisfying and interesting life.

LIFE PATH
You need more self-confidence. You have ability, but your diffidence often causes you to step aside for those with inferior qualifications. Your pleasing manner wins many friends for you, and all who know you hold you in the highest esteem. Your love is devoted, and you will probably select a partner who is accomplished and masterful at what they do and has a compelling personality.

DESTINY
You can expect to get your own way on many occasions if you are tactful as well as firm. Your home will prove a source of great pleasure, both as the scene of harmonious domestic life and as an attractive place in which to entertain. Do not accept rumor as fact without carefully checking the details. You can help a timid, reserved friend obtain the self-confidence necessary for a successful social life—this kind act will benefit you greatly in the future.

KARMIC LESSON
You have a variable and moody nature; you do not understand it yourself at times. You are fond of entertainment and social events, but you also love to be alone—a tendency that could become morbid if you give it too much play. You also have a tendency to irritability, which you must learn to overcome. You have a natural love for history; nothing fascinates you more than the early history of the world. Say nothing about your neighbor unless you can say something kind; all unkind words and actions react upon their originators, causing their undoing later on. Self-assertive, strong, and active, you are loyal but could be a little more sincere. Do not be too inquisitive about the affairs of others; everyone's life is his or her own.

SECRET
You are physically restless; you are fond of outdoor life and prefer personal comforts to success gained at great hardship or sacrifice.

FRIENDS & FAMILY

JUNE 19

Some people grow under responsibility; others merely swell.
—Anonymous

BORN ON THIS DAY

- ★ **Salman Rushdie**
  author
- ★ **Lou Gehrig**
  baseball player
- ★ **Paula Abdul**
  singer, dancer
- ★ **Aung San Suu Kyi**
  democratic leader of Burma
- ★ **Kathleen Turner**
  actor

FRIENDS & FAMILY

PERSONALITY
You try to understand all things by first understanding yourself, and to that end you devote much time and effort. You are rewarded for this self-examination because it results in your intellectual honesty and the tolerance that you develop for all things. Your insight into people and events is as revealing as a flash of lightning in the dark. While you do not care for the tasteless pleasures of commonplace existence, you never criticize others for their way of life. You simply enjoy the finer things more and get more pleasure out of beautiful music, a good show or movie, or watching a thrilling sports event than you do out of pastimes like gambling or using drugs. Vitality, courage, and energy are so much a part of your being that you can hardly restrain yourself when a problem arises. You take all the negative aspects of life in your stride, and you try not to let them get you down.

LIFE PATH
You are sensitive, sympathetic, and loving. While you have very strong convictions, you will sometimes yield to others rather than take a positive stand on your own behalf. You are very affectionate, although you do not have many intimate relationships. You will not be happy if you go through life alone, as a soul-mate partnership will bring out the best in you.

DESTINY
Be thrifty, not lavish, in your spending, and be sure to obtain receipts and keep good records whenever you part with a sizable sum of money. You should not depend entirely on promises that are hastily and thoughtlessly given. Entertainment that is connected with business undertakings should be pursued. You will find that your aims after midlife become more practical and consequently will be more obtainable.

KARMIC LESSON
Not always quite as diplomatic as you should be, you have a strong, independent disposition yet can see others' viewpoints. Your life is bound to have varying fortunes. You have high aspirations, determination, and pluck. You are determined to get ahead in the world, and nothing can stop you except your own limitations. Learn to utilize spare moments, as time is precious. Many forces play upon you, but you must learn to master them. Success brings growing pains, and bad luck brings challenges to overcome. You are a good friend, deep and true in your feelings. You should make a fine life coach, as you have the necessary presence. Look for success, and it will surely come. Remember that every person has their hour; yours will come.

SECRET
Slow to rise to wrath on detecting a wrong but also slow to forgive, you have a passion for fair play. You can be very emotional in your homelife.

JUNE 20

Most of the shadows of this life are caused by our standing in our own sunshine.
—Ralph Waldo Emerson

BORN ON THIS DAY
- **Nicole Kidman**
  actor
- **Lionel Richie**
  singer
- **Javier Pastore**
  soccer player
- **Brian Wilson**
  musician
- **Errol Flynn**
  actor

PERSONALITY
You are instilled with the desire to be on the go all the time because you have so much energy and vitality. Hardly have you finished one project when you get set to start another—and off you go with a bang. Frequent change delights you, and you can visit a dozen people or places in a row without tiring or becoming bored with your own motion. You are vigorous and assertive, for which traits you are rewarded (and sometimes punished) by being given charge of most of the projects of which you are a component part. You are really interested in yourself more than in anything else—a perfectly natural and human trait. However, when your attention is diverted to some other person or to an interesting event, you become completely absorbed in it. You are sometimes a little too frank in expressing your opinion and can get into a heated argument because of this open way of expressing yourself.

LIFE PATH
You have executive ability, originality, and mechanical skill. You think deeply, are closemouthed regarding your deep, dark secrets, are always willing to lend a helping hand, and take a great deal of interest in situations outside of your regular routine. You have many friends and are a lover of sharing your ideas and favorite interests.

DESTINY
While your role in life will involve some hard work, you will find it is an enjoyable one. Avoid friction and clashes with people whom you regard as too aggressive. Be alert to hidden meanings in apparently casual remarks. Associations with family members and coworkers will be generally pleasant, and you will find others pointing to your reliability as a good example to follow. You can always profit by listening to wise and well-informed friends expound on their ideas.

KARMIC LESSON
You have a very good head for business and take a great interest in money matters. You will doubtless acquire a good deal of wealth before old age, but unless you are careful, appreciation of what you have accomplished will not always go with it. Keep your tastes simple; cultivate a desire for study and learning new things. You are levelheaded and a keen observer. Do not be stingy with your money; learn to be more generous. You are intuitive and inclined to do things your own way, even though this way is often opposed to friends' advice. You have a magnetic personality but are apt to dream rather than act on your highest ideals; you do not sufficiently put your plans into operation. You are fond of animals.

SECRET
You possess exceptional mental powers, hampered by a constant passion for change. If concentration can be developed, success will be certain.

FRIENDS & FAMILY

JUNE 21

The question is not what you look at, but what you see.
—Henry David Thoreau

BORN ON THIS DAY
- **Jean-Paul Sartre**
  philosopher, author
- **Prince William**
  Duke of Cambridge
- **Lana Del Rey**
  singer
- **Lana & Lilly Wachowski**
  filmmakers
- **Chris Pratt**
  actor

FRIENDS & FAMILY

PERSONALITY
There is never a dull moment when you are around because you are full of life, always have ideas, and are ready to go anywhere and do anything at any time. This means that you have the imagination and vitality to execute almost any plan proposed, and you are ingenious at suggesting things yourself. You have a vivid sense of the mysterious and the mystical and could become an adept student of occult philosophy, as you have an innate understanding for such things. You are rather easygoing when it comes to your relationships with other people because you understand them so well. It is your belief that a few tried-and-true friends are better than a very large group of casual acquaintances. You could easily become set in your ways, despite your imaginative faculty, because you have a tendency to let things slide. Too much exercise of this tendency can be bad for you, because in difficult circumstances it can make you prey to nonexistent fears or phobias. Keep up an active life, and work on the promotion and manifestation of your highest ambitions.

LIFE PATH
You have a natural gift for mechanics, which demonstrates itself in your occupation and hobbies. You are even-tempered, kind, and inventive, slow to anger and quick to forgive. You enjoy bright, witty friends and are fully capable of taking care of yourself in a battle of wits. You probably will marry young.

DESTINY
You will often have occasion to disprove the old saying that "anticipation is superior to realization." Many of your dreams will become actual. You may be surprised by the speed with which your plans progress once they have been set into operation with your intention. Look for reliable products and guarantees when buying merchandise. Diplomacy will be necessary when dealing with annoying people.

KARMIC LESSON
You have a deep faith and a love of knowledge, and nature in all its branches appeals to you especially. Your strong intellect keeps you interested in all sorts of subjects. You must learn to make the most of your numerous talents. You are imaginative and very interested in the psychic and the occult. You have a great power of concentration in areas of life that interest you. Never speak or write ill of your neighbors, particularly those who can help you or have done so. You are able to regain your smile after many mishaps. You are affectionate, and your passionate nature is very strong. Cultivate your mind; in this way, success will come to you. Always hope for the best and prepare for the worst; this is the way success is attained.

SECRET
You have a diffident nature, sometimes lacking in self-confidence. You should marry or partner with a more aggressive type who can also inspire by their faith, words, and trust.

JUNE 22

Fear not for the future, weep not for the past.
—Percy Bysshe Shelley

⊙ PERSONALITY
Marriage, domestic life and all the love it holds, and being with children are your delights in life. No child could be more attentive to his or her parents than you are or were, nor could there be a parent more loving than you are to your children, nor any more dedicated mentor or guide to children around you. Should this seem like an oversentimental portrait of you, it is because that is the affectionate side of your nature. It does not mean that you lack business acumen or leadership, for you possess both to a very high degree. You have a great ability to plan things very strategically, and you also have the motivation needed to carry out your plans. As a matter of fact, you have been endowed with a special combination of qualities that should enable you to lead a productive and successful life. Exercise, travel, and social networking are your favorite pastimes.

⊙ LIFE PATH
You will be a loyal friend, a fond parent, and a loving partner. You are sensitive and retiring, interested in the beautiful, curious about life, and an engaging conversationalist. You probably love to travel and enjoy outdoor sports, and even yoga, a great deal.

⊙ DESTINY
Acquaintances will realize that they can accept you at face value, because you shun boastfulness and ostentation. Because you are self-effacing, you often underestimate your ability. In the long run, associates will recognize your capabilities, but you should try to think more of your own personal advantage. Do not be afraid of stepping on people's toes when you feel justified in asserting yourself.

⊙ KARMIC LESSON
Real-life stories fascinate and attract you, and you have storytelling ability yourself. Your strong imagination is inclined to run away with you at times. You could write well if you tried; your work would be tinged with quirkiness and full of odd happenings and imaginings. A good raconteur and an entertaining companion, you are fond of the natural world. You probably like visiting friends and traveling around the country, actually or virtually, studying the people. You are a great explorer and will see many foreign lands during your full and eventful life. Interested in many subjects, you have a wide range of information. You are fond of living your life and are deeply affectionate, taking life as it comes. You are a natural linguist. Sympathetic, yet discriminating, you have remarkably good judgment.

⊙ SECRET
You are one who delights in nature study and particularly in floral manifestations. You could achieve success in specialized forms of gardening and horticulture.

BORN ON THIS DAY
★ **Cyndi Lauper**
singer

★ **Dan Brown**
author

★ **Meryl Streep**
actor

★ **Kurt Warner**
football player

★ **Stephen Chow**
comic actor, filmmaker

FRIENDS & FAMILY

JUNE 23

Let our lives be pure as snowfields, where our footsteps leave a mark, but not a stain.
—Madame Swetchine

BORN ON THIS DAY

★ **Clarence Thomas**
U.S. Supreme Court justice

★ **Alan Turing**
mathematician, computer scientist

★ **Bob Fosse**
dancer, choreographer

★ **Frances McDormand**
actor

★ **Wilma Rudolph**
Olympic track and field athlete

FRIENDS & FAMILY

PERSONALITY
Life requires that you make important decisions before you settle down. You like to enjoy yourself, and you are rather easily prey to temptation. If some party or project appeals to you, you will gladly defer the task you should be doing to join in the fun. Money seems unimportant when you have it and terribly important when you don't. This attitude denotes that you must define your own philosophy of life before you can accomplish anything worthwhile. It would appear that you really settle down to the serious business of living around the time you reach middle age. However, many people who are lighthearted and high-spirited like you attain remarkable success because they have learned the contrast between fun and accomplishment. Thus, you will be able to regulate your life when experience has taught you its valuable lessons. Develop your judgment by constant application.

LIFE PATH
You enter upon new projects with spirit and determination but often tire of them quickly and want to change. You are excellent at planning but sometimes need motivation to execute. You are fond of pleasure—fine dining, wine, sex, parties—and can let it interfere with your business. You are, at the same time, loving, caring, and kind. You will have a very understanding partner.

DESTINY
You may expect an exciting life, always filled with new projects and outstanding accomplishments. However, do not carry business problems around with you after working hours. Social engagements will keep your leisure hours well filled. Be willing to listen to advice offered by interested friends, but make your own decisions. When passing on news, be sure your facts are substantiated.

KARMIC LESSON
You are fiery and impetuous, mercurial, unsettled, and shifting; you cannot stay at home or in any one place for very long. Creative and original, you are extremely fond of conceiving ideas. Your passionate nature is strongly developed, and you must be careful to keep it within bounds; otherwise, it will cause you problems. You demand much of others, but you are always ready to give it back to them with interest. You are a good storyteller. You are impressionable, often led by your feelings rather than your reason. You are strong-willed but sometimes too swayed by the bad habits and influences of others. You are fond of nature and animals, and they like you in return. You have many talents. Overall, you are a very appealing person.

SECRET
You have a savvy nature and strong financial shrewdness. You are one who can scrimp and save for the purpose of investment.

JUNE 24

A thousand words will not leave so deep an impression as one deed.
—Henrik Ibsen

BORN ON THIS DAY
- **Henry Ward Beecher** — minister, abolitionist
- **Lionel Messi** — soccer player
- **Mindy Kaling** — actor
- **Robert Reich** — economist
- **Mick Fleetwood** — musician

PERSONALITY
Because you prefer not to always show your true feelings, you are sometimes misunderstood. You have a great deal of pride, and you dislike having others know when your feelings are hurt. For this reason, you are sometimes taken to be colder by nature than you really are. Actually, your idea is that for all people to express their true selves, real happiness in life must be universal. Since this is quite a difficult dream to realize, it is little wonder that you find fault with things as they are. However, you should adapt yourself to your social and business group in such a way that you get the most out of your efforts. Do not waste your time with frivolous people. You like fun, but you can enjoy yourself just as much with a select few who are worthy of your character as with a lot of time wasters. You are devoted to several members of your family and loyal to your closest friends. You will grow in wisdom and tolerance over the years.

LIFE PATH
You are determined, persevering, somewhat opinionated, and rather prone to putting and seeing yourself in a critical light. You need to cultivate cautiousness in action and speech. You have a remarkable ability to secure and hold long-lasting love and friendship.

DESTINY
Because you are always eager to learn and are adaptable in your methods and ideas, you will be able to take advantage of opportunities as they arise. Be guided by reason rather than emotion. Your practical and moral support of friends who deserve assistance will be returned many times over. Be willing to make concessions that will contribute to domestic harmony.

KARMIC LESSON
A good conversationalist, engaging, and clever, you have a lot of personal magnetism. You have a sound business sense, too, and will succeed in making money. You have an excellent memory for details, yet you can think big thoughts and carry out big enterprises. You are a little stingy in money matters and should learn to give gracefully and be a little more open in your dealings. You are fond of collecting, and one of your weaknesses is your attachment to material things. Proficient in law and finance, you are observant and diligent and have clever viewpoints. You think it's a virtue to induce others to give rather than to give yourself. Learn to trust your intuitions more and rely on the guidance of your heart.

SECRET
Born on this day, you are graceful in your movements. You are fond of dancing and would get a lot out of foot massages and reflexology.

FRIENDS & FAMILY

JUNE 25

The miracle is not to fly in the air, or to walk on the water, but to walk on the earth.
—Chinese proverb

BORN ON THIS DAY

★ **George Orwell**
author

★ **Sonia Sotomayor**
U.S. Supreme Court justice

★ **George Michael**
singer

★ **Ricky Gervais**
comedian

★ **Carly Simon**
singer

FRIENDS & FAMILY

✸ PERSONALITY
You are a hard worker, conscientious, and practical. Although you enjoy a good time as much as anyone, you know that not all of life is made up of parties, and you willingly perform the jobs you are called upon to do. Life's obligations find you cheerfully ready to assume them. This makes for a very sensible outlook on life, one that will carry you far. You know that by taking things in your stride, you will get further and accomplish much more than by working in spurts. People like you for your dependability, and you rarely lose a friend through any action of your own. There may be misunderstandings that arise between you and other people, but they are not likely to be of your making. You enjoy constructing things and have a rather good sense of design. Rural life has a strong appeal for you, and you visualize yourself happily dwelling where you can have your own house and garden.

✸ LIFE PATH
You are lighthearted and happy-go-lucky, and when you get into trouble or experience a setback, your friends always help you out. You are inclined to rush into tricky situations without due consideration. You are charitable and tolerant in your judgment, and you care strongly.

✸ DESTINY
You will always be examining various moneymaking opportunities that offer the possibility of profits. Find out the reactions of friends to your ideas and accept the consensus of opinion even if it disagrees with your own conclusions. Use tact to avoid open clashes of temper over trivial matters.

✸ KARMIC LESSON
One side of your nature is strong, active, and self-reliant. The other side procrastinates and puts things off—you can be a dreamer, desiring everything to be more harmonious. You hate to say no. While this springs largely from a well-meaning nature, remember that the first key to success is the ability to say no, and those who have not learned to say it will never succeed. You crave honor and rewards. You like to have a lot of fuss made over you. At the same time, you are shrewd and economical and take great care in the matter of expenses. Sensitive to slights and easily offended, you are sometimes jealous or insecure. You should cultivate greater frankness toward others; if someone offends you, politely tell the person at once—don't brood in silence.

✸ SECRET
Rid yourself of shyness, but at the same time, see to it that you are not too assertive. You are firm, yet gentle.

JUNE 26

Great necessities call out great virtues.
—Abigail Adams

⁂ PERSONALITY
You are lured by the call of travel to romantic places. If you could arrange your life the way you really want, you would take frequent trips and enjoy meeting new people, seeing colorful scenery, and mixing with different types of people and cultures. Books and movies give you the vicarious thrill of such experiences. In your contact with individuals, you make quite a strong and lasting impression, because you are able to talk interestingly about subjects that you like. With a little practice, you could become quite an excellent raconteur, being endowed with the attributes of an actor. You have a good vocabulary, stimulating ideas, and an active mind. It seems as though you are always thinking up new ways of doing things, and people like to have you around when they are planning or giving a party or event because you are so ingenious at thinking up innovative ways of entertaining. Do not neglect any interest you have in digital businesses, social media, and the tech world.

◎ LIFE PATH
You have a brilliant mind; you love to explore ideas and to associate with intellectual people. You have a sophisticated sense of humor, and your friends look to you for good company. You will have an unusually satisfying love life.

◉ DESTINY
Although you will attract new friends, you will always appreciate the old. You can obtain help when it is needed to finish a task, and you should not hesitate to ask for it. Never agree to participate in an activity that you do not enjoy simply because you feel obliged to do so. If you find that your opinions are misunderstood on occasion, be patient in explaining carefully and exactly what you meant.

☯ KARMIC LESSON
Serious-minded, you have a good head for facts and figures and a very good memory. Philosophy and psychology attract you above everything, and you feel, at times, that you devote your entire life to the pursuit of these subjects in an attempt to discover some hidden secret of nature that no one has yet unearthed. The occult and mysterious attract you but only insofar as you think you can explain them and find natural causes for the phenomena you see. You are inclined to be irritated by trivial things—a habit of which you must cure yourself. Keep trying to find yourself, for once you accomplish this, all your goals will manifest of their own accord. Trust your Higher Self and live up to it, and all will be well.

◉ SECRET
You are easily discouraged by opposition or adversity. When the wind is with you, you are a dedicated worker.

BORN ON THIS DAY
★ **Ariana Grande**
singer
★ **Derek Jeter**
baseball player
★ **Mick Jones**
guitarist
★ **Aubrey Plaza**
actor
★ **Sean Hayes**
actor

FRIENDS & FAMILY

JUNE 27

Defeat is not the worst of failures. Not to have tried is the true failure.
—George Edward Woodberry

BORN ON THIS DAY

★ **Helen Keller**
disability rights advocate

★ **Vera Wang**
fashion designer

★ **J.J. Abrams**
filmmaker

★ **Tobey Maguire**
actor

★ **Khloé Kardashian**
media personality, socialite

FRIENDS & FAMILY

✦ PERSONALITY
You like the finer things in life. By preference, you live in pleasant surroundings, and you enjoy having your home furnished artistically, with functional beauty as the motif. In other words, you want your furnishings to combine loveliness with usefulness. This is, in fact, the motif of your pattern of life; you want it to be a thing of beauty that is also useful. This is a good philosophy to have, for you can attain the most by striving for the best. You like family life, and you accept its joys with pleasure and its troubles with equanimity. Music, movies, and photography give you much pleasure. You would make an excellent instructor, and you aim to be a model parent. Your respect makes you the beloved child of your own parents. You are affectionate, tender, and true. Happiness should be yours in a useful and peaceful life.

◉ LIFE PATH
You are kind, loving, and tender. You are very demonstrative in your love for your partner, rendering a devotion that causes your friends to look upon your homelife as model and ideal. Your aims are high, and you generally can succeed in their attainment. Don't be so hard on yourself.

◉ DESTINY
Your good sportsmanship and sense of fair play will stand you in good stead in both the business and the social worlds. Do not be too gullible. Accept extravagant statements and promises with a grain of salt, and be sure your sympathy is warranted before you bestow it. Guard against careless loss of personal possessions. Do not fall for high-pressure sales talks, for to do so may prove costly.

☯ KARMIC LESSON
More emotional than intellectual in your life and interests, you live a good deal according to your senses and sensations. You are temperamental and would make a fine painter, sculptor, or musician. You are very affectionate and passionate, but you allow yourself to be swayed too readily by your feelings, forgetting the better part of discretion. Independent in thought and action, you can live your life quite contentedly without others' meddling or counseling. You must keep your strong imagination under control. You are fond of reading and can often spend a whole day with a book, checking your cell phone, browsing the Internet, and pondering over things you have discovered. You are fond of a good time; you like entertaining. You are exacting with details, methodical, and mostly tidy in all that you do.

☺ SECRET
Charming, and more courageous than you think, you are a warrior when you are fighting for an idealistic idea, whether in business or personal relationships.

JUNE 28

Men and nations can only be reformed in their youth; they become incorrigible as they grow old.
—Jean-Jacques Rousseau

BORN ON THIS DAY
- **Elon Musk**
  business magnate
- **Mel Brooks**
  actor
- **Kathy Bates**
  actor
- **Gilda Radner**
  comedian, actor
- **Kellie Pickler**
  singer

FRIENDS & FAMILY

✦ PERSONALITY
By training yourself to avoid worry, nervous tension, and strain, you can reach the heights of satisfaction in your life. However, you have a tendency to let little things get under your skin and to allow the petty annoyances everyone has to contend with to upset you. Your sensitivity is the cause of this nuisance department of your life. There is nothing that cannot be overcome by determination and concentration, so make up your mind that you are going to stop fretting over the minor anxieties of day-to-day existence. You are very hospitable by nature, generous to your family and friends, and receptive to the environment in which you find yourself. You dislike offending anyone and go out of your way to spare people's feelings—even when it means sacrificing to do so. The cares and responsibilities you have are those that you have willingly assumed. Therefore, your life can be as peaceful and free of drama as you wish to make it.

✦ LIFE PATH
You are changeable and may at times be too easily influenced by your friends, who are not always the best influence. But you are a steadfast friend, of the self-sacrificing, helpful kind. Your love flows in deep channels, and while you may be changeable in some things, in friendships you are loyal.

✦ DESTINY
Success can reward your efforts since the fear of failure does not keep you from trying out feasible ideas. The trusted opinion of an influential person will contribute greatly to advancement in your career. If you and a family member are involved in a dispute, seek the opinion of a third person. Resolve all disagreements as soon as possible, as it is not healthy for you to hold resentments.

✦ KARMIC LESSON
You are a good observer of human nature, which interests you immensely. You are caustic at times, and cynical, but you have a good sense of humor, which entertains you and those close to you. Bighearted, generous, and sympathetic, you are bright and very good company. You have a strong interest in writing and should be able to write fiction, essays, a blog, or a journal. You are a good mimic and appreciate the craft of acting. You are artistic and display great originality and taste in your dress or decorating. You probably would not make a great businessperson as you are more of an art type. You may not utilize your mind power enough and should develop the talent of concentration more fully. Cultivate greater independence and strength of purpose, and you could make your life a greater success.

✦ SECRET
You possess a philosophic mind, leading you away from the bustle of the complications of modern life. You are a person of strong principles.

JUNE 29

The person who says it cannot be done should not interrupt the person doing it.
—Chinese proverb

BORN ON THIS DAY

- **Stokely Carmichael**
  civil rights leader
- **Nicole Scherzinger**
  singer
- **Gary Busey**
  actor
- **George Ellery Hale**
  astronomer
- **Colin Jost**
  comedian, actor

FRIENDS & FAMILY

PERSONALITY

You are enterprising by nature, and you go about fulfilling your ambitions with persistence and determination. Poise characterizes everything you do, and you also inspire confidence in others. Because you have this quality, you are generally entrusted with responsibility in any project with which you are allied. It might be a good idea not to act too forcefully, however, as in that way you might make enemies. From your point of view, you are practical and matter-of-fact. You like to get good value for your money and fair compensation for your efforts. You are always ready with a quick and witty answer and are known for this trait. Sharply perceptive, you see through fraud and sham as though with an X-ray eye. You respond to praise, and you try to lead a life that will bring you acclaim for your way of living it.

LIFE PATH

You are forceful, resolute, and realistic, and you possess sound judgment. You are not so very talkative, unless the subject is one you are passionate about. Your passions are deep-seated, and your anger is rather explosive when you give in to it. You will never be quite happy unless you have a special someone or pet upon whom you can lavish your affection.

DESTINY

There will be nothing humdrum about your life, even though you devote the major portion of your time to duties and obligations. Your willingness to abide by rules and regulations will prove a valuable asset. Get routine matters out of the way as soon as they arise so you have as much time as possible for more interesting tasks. Guard against hasty speech or action.

KARMIC LESSON

You are always hoping something will turn up and make life easier for you, but it never will unless you set the ball rolling by your own efforts. You are somewhat defensive, sensitive to slights or rude behavior and anything that insults your sensibilities. You are sentimental without being foolish about it but are capable of strong and lasting love, and you expect the same in return. Psychology is a subject that never grows old for you; you ponder people's behavior and never tire of trying to figure them out. You have good powers of discernment but are more perceptive about the affairs of others than your own. Cultivate greater self-control and a stronger will and purpose.

SECRET

You possess a clever mixture of seriousness and fun, with a talent for mimicry. You are a good joke teller and are always fun company at a dinner party.

JUNE 30

Pleasure comes through toil, and not by self-indulgence and indolence.
—John Ruskin

PERSONALITY
There is much latent power in your makeup that you must try to recognize and cultivate for your advancement. You are quite psychic, receiving impressions that are piercing and accurate. However, to make use of this power, you must practice, study, and develop it. There are times when this quality can be a drawback for you, such as when it makes you feel so sorry for people—then you extend yourself for them instead of attending to your own affairs. Once you have made up your mind what you want, there is no barrier in your character to prevent you from getting it. You must be determined, however, and you must not allow other people to get you off the path. The pursuit of truth and knowledge is ever a source of joy to you. Handmade items especially delight you. There is a tendency in you to overindulge yourself when you are nervous; avoid this carefully.

LIFE PATH
You are remarkably adept at making things. You are self-reliant, eccentric, and absolutely indifferent to the opinions of others, at times displaying an independence that is challenging to your friends. You have a great capacity for acquiring knowledge and possess the rare ability of imparting it to others. You have a very compassionate nature.

DESTINY
Many fields of endeavor are so well indicated for you that you may have difficulty choosing or limiting yourself to your favorite activities. However, you should restrict your activities so that you can give each undertaking the attention it deserves. Be sure any instructions that you give or are given are clear and definite.

KARMIC LESSON
You are distinctly crafty—making things is what you love to do. Self-reliant, you have a pretty strong will. You are generally successful in what you undertake, and people learn to trust and rely upon you, knowing that your work is as good as done. You have a clear vision about life and are probably quite popular with your group of friends. Happily, you possess a temperament balanced between intellect and emotion. You are very affectionate but have a good sense of humor and can be full of fun when around the right people. You are fond of taking classes. Also, find a way of working out that suits you. You are probably a good conversationalist, but if you are too shy you should cultivate the art of self-expression.

SECRET
You are quick to thought but sometimes slow to action. You are impeded by a stubborn streak that refuses to yield to the opinions of others.

BORN ON THIS DAY
- **Lena Horne** — singer, actor, civil rights advocate
- **Mike Tyson** — boxer
- **Michael Phelps** — Olympic swimmer
- **Vincent D'Onofrio** — actor
- **Fantasia Barrino** — singer

FRIENDS & FAMILY

JULY 1

Whether you think you can or think you can't, you're right.
—Henry Ford

PERSONALITY
Your birth date gives you mental strength, much grit, and fortitude. You are also curious, knowledgeable, and somewhat inclined to be fickle. Concepts and logical ideas seem to have a greater role in your opinion than feelings. You are motivated to action by what you think far more than by what you feel. For this reason, some people may consider you somewhat self-centered. Because you are determined to have your way, you are liable to be a bit devious about getting it. You might, for example, exaggerate circumstances or facts to make the kind of impression that will alter situations to your liking, though you would never do so to hurt another person. You think quite clearly, and your perceptive powers are keen. Once success is yours, your personality mellows, and you become popular and well-liked.

LIFE PATH
You are ambitious to get ahead, and your will is strong enough to bring you success. You can be charming when you want to be and are fond of music and concerts, sewing or knitting, and even horror movies. You are careful about appearances, very adaptable, popular in your own circle, and admired by your family.

DESTINY
Your ability to penetrate to the heart of any situation is always apparent in conversations. Your mind is sharp. Concentrate on tasks at hand, and then you will not get anxiety attacks and anticipate troubles that will not materialize. Try to finish one job completely before you assume new ones. Try not to become impatient when you have to put up with temporary inconveniences. Plan and save for purchases that will add to your home's value and comfort.

KARMIC LESSON
You are individual, organic, and natural in your tastes. You are fond of selling and clever at marketing. You have a practical insight into the suffering of humanity, and this would make you interested in politics, on the one hand, and medicine or healing, on the other. You have a great deal of tact and patience. You are funny at times, with a dark sense of humor. You are shrewd and should learn to trust these instincts more fully. Listen to what your wisdom is telling you. You like to be organized and dislike seeing anything out of its place. Cultivate more concentration and determination.

SECRET
You are an all-rounder, and you always have opportunities offered to you. You would make a capable manager.

BORN ON THIS DAY
★ **Diana Spencer**
Princess of Wales

★ **Olivia de Havilland**
actor

★ **George Sand**
author

★ **Debbie Harry**
singer

★ **Missy Elliott**
singer

FRIENDS & FAMILY

JULY 2

Conscience is the voice of the soul; the passions are the voice of the body.
—Jean-Jacques Rousseau

BORN ON THIS DAY

- **Thurgood Marshall**
  U.S. Supreme Court justice
- **Larry David**
  comedian
- **Lindsay Lohan**
  actor
- **Johnny Weir**
  Olympic figure skater
- **Jose Canseco**
  baseball player

FRIENDS & FAMILY

PERSONALITY

There is a balance in your makeup, which consists of you allowing your heart and head to share rule over your conduct. In this way, you direct things from both your thinking and your feeling, which is a fair way of doing it, and it works for you. While you are thoughtful and intellectual, you are also hospitable, kind, and considerate of the welfare of others. You have the soothing qualities that make people born on your birthday good doctors, nurses, social service workers, and healers. By developing this trait, you may make an unusual career for yourself. Of course, everything in life has two sides. The negative side of your personality is that you could easily give in to the temptation to procrastinate or vacillate, to overindulge emotionally, and to do so also in eating and drinking. Knowing this potential weakness, however, is as good as being insured against it, for you can avoid what you know to be risky behavior.

LIFE PATH

You have an active mind, much originality, considerable pride, and a tender, compassionate conscience. You try to be scrupulously honest and never overstep your bounds. You are affectionate and kind to others, and your friends seek you out a great deal to join in their entertainment and pastimes.

DESTINY

Do not be afraid or reluctant to enter into new endeavors. There can usually be success for undertakings that you are enthusiastic about. Listen to the advice of older members of your family when it comes to financial matters. Express proper appreciation for the accomplishments of associates. Sparkling conversation, in which you take an active part, will always add to your enjoyment of social affairs, and therefore you will not be bored.

KARMIC LESSON

You have a restless, roving disposition, which will cause you to move a great deal and probably see many parts of the country. You crave excitement, and nothing annoys you more than a regular, boring life, in which nothing of interest happens from one year to another. For this reason, a city would be far better for you than the country, to which you are not as well suited. You have a natural business ability and can be successful as an entrepreneur. You are capable of handling an unusual business enterprise, and one of your talents ought to make a considerable success for you—enough to travel anywhere you want and to do as you please.

SECRET

You are a proud person, a stickler for some conventions, and fond of some of the artificial and glamorous. You like to impose your tastes on others.

JULY 3

The most terrifying thing is to accept oneself completely.
—Carl Jung

⁂ PERSONALITY
You have a lot of initiative and never need to wait for someone else's suggestions to get to a good start on a creative idea. You like to think things over, look around for the best possibilities, and then make a sensible and practical choice among the alternatives on offer. Once you have come to your decision, you work with a will to make your goal manifest. However, you're not an "all work and no play" type of person. You enjoy the company of good friends, and you like to entertain in your own home and go out visiting. Your special talent lies in devising efficient ways of performing your daily tasks. This is where your ingenuity comes into play, for you can make the most tiresome, boring job into a game.

◎ LIFE PATH
You are intuitive, independent, self-contained, and rather opinionated but also sympathetic and kindhearted. You may not be as well-liked by your own sex as by the opposite. You are a convincing talker, studious, and fond of intellectual banter, and you get much enjoyment out of the small things in life.

◉ DESTINY
Your goals will be reached more easily if you ask questions when you do not understand exactly what is expected of you. Sentiment will play an important part in your life. Consideration for the comfort and happiness of others will make your own life more pleasurable. If someone of your acquaintance proves to be dishonest, do not harbor resentment. Do not discuss your plans with others until they are completely worked out in your own mind, or you will be misjudged.

☯ KARMIC LESSON
You are independent and reserved. You are sometimes almost too retiring and should be more willing to come forward and share your inner life with others. True, they do not have the same thoughts and interests as you, as a rule, but you must not become self-centered for all that. Learn to be confident and show it. It is a duty in life. Your self-esteem can add life, power, and worth to all those around you. It is most important, therefore, that every moment should be full of contentment. While you are waiting for an opportunity to improve your time, improve yourself. Learn to see your true beauty.

◉ SECRET
You are intrigued by the creators of interesting art, movies, and music. You will become disappointed unless you are engaged in your own business.

BORN ON THIS DAY
- ★ **Franz Kafka** — author
- ★ **Tom Cruise** — actor
- ★ **Julian Assange** — publisher, activist
- ★ **Audra McDonald** — singer, actor
- ★ **Dave Barry** — humor columnist

FRIENDS & FAMILY

JULY 4

It's faith in something and enthusiasm for something that make a life worth looking at.
—Oliver Wendell Holmes

BORN ON THIS DAY

★ **Calvin Coolidge**
U.S. president

★ **Nathaniel Hawthorne**
author

★ **Geraldo Rivera**
talk show host

★ **Stephen Foster**
songwriter

★ **Gina Lollobrigida**
actor

FRIENDS & FAMILY

◉ PERSONALITY
The birthday of the United States is indeed a day of significance on which to be born. This date endows the same interests upon you, and you live your life as an example of the principles of freedom and liberty for all. You represent the spirit of cooperation and are very helpful in all community, group, and family activities. You are able to command respect and confidence because you are fair, intellectual, and considerate. Strength of will and forcefulness of personality make you an outstanding member of your community. You are a good friend because your tastes in people, as in other things, are diverse and eclectic. You are clever at getting people to cooperate with you in ventures where group activity is needed. You are a leader in your workplace and a power in your home; yours will be an eventful and full life.

◉ LIFE PATH
You have a strong personality, generally trying to rule by sheer force of will when you are driven to succeed. You are also cautious and careful, always mean what you say, and are worthy of all the confidence people have in you. You make many friends and very few enemies. You love deeply but are not always very demonstrative with affection.

◉ DESTINY
You should be ready to seize a quickly passing opportunity. You need never be bored if you are alert to the numerous opportunities for your self-expression. Your ideas will usually receive support if you present them forcefully. Do not be satisfied with mere flattery but seek sincere comprehension of your aims and ideals. Never let the remarks of others about your plans dissuade you from undertakings in which you have a strong faith.

◉ KARMIC LESSON
You are strong and self-controlled, never afraid, and quite capable of governing your own life without much help from outside sources. You are a thinker with good instincts and exceedingly fond of the psychic and mystical. You never tire of dabbling and investigating along these lines. You are also fond of philosophy and history. You may have failed several times in your life, in projects you have attempted, but this should not discourage you. The fact that you have failed to get the lesser yet may prove conclusively that you deserve the greater. Know what you want and continue to want it. You will get it if you combine desire with faith. Learn to look on life in a broader way, seeing in it many persons of many differing temperaments.

◉ SECRET
You are an avid life sleuth, destined to be successful. You have an inquisitive nature and are unafraid of having your own original way of thinking.

JULY 5

The thing always happens that you really believe in; and the belief in a thing makes it happen.
—Frank Lloyd Wright

BORN ON THIS DAY
- **P.T. Barnum**
  showman
- **Edie Falco**
  actor
- **Pauly D.**
  reality TV personality, DJ
- **Susan Wojcicki**
  CEO, YouTube
- **Paul Smith**
  fashion designer

PERSONALITY
You have personal magnetism of the kind that can draw people and goals to you, so that should you choose to espouse some important cause, you could acquire a number of powerful adherents to help you spread your idea. You have the type of mind that sees the far horizons and a future scenario toward which a situation may be headed. You are always busy and do not let the grass grow under your feet. Because you desire to live up to your ideals, you are sometimes willing to sacrifice personal gain and glory, choosing to see the group benefit rather than to make a profit on your ideas of how to ameliorate the state of humanity and world problems. Other thinkers of this type have been born on your birthday. Popularity and respect are your due, and a willing group of admirers gives you both.

LIFE PATH
You are persevering, plodding, and faithful; you do not allow reversals and setbacks to deflect you from your course. While your foresight is very great, you can profit by experience and do not have to learn a lesson twice. You like to have attention shown to you, and when you love, you love with your whole being.

DESTINY
If you have to work hard to gain what you want, do not be discouraged. Your goals can be achieved if you are determined and stick to your plans. Financial remuneration may seem inadequate at times, but this situation will be made right in time. Slow progress is sure progress, and after age thirty-five you will see increased payoffs. Make agreements tentative so that they can be altered to fit changing conditions.

KARMIC LESSON
You have a many-sided, varied life, containing many ups and downs. On the whole, you will get much more out of life than the majority, however. You have a great deal of natural talent and ability as a writer. You are fascinated by the occult. You, yourself, are probably somewhat psychic. You are never beaten, for the more often failure comes, the more determined you are to succeed. You are kind to others—at times too kind, and advantage is sometimes taken of your sympathetic nature. You believe in yourself, as everything you desire depends upon you. You have good business judgment and will undoubtedly be successful when you set up in business, as long as you are in control. You are too independent to listen to many others.

SECRET
An enjoyable companion when everything is running smoothly, you are given to sulking when the clouds appear.

FRIENDS & FAMILY

JULY 6

Hurt not others with that which pains yourself.
—Buddha

BORN ON THIS DAY
- **George W. Bush**
  U.S. president
- **Dalai Lama**
  Tibetan spiritual leader
- **Sylvester Stallone**
  actor
- **Frida Kahlo**
  artist
- **Merv Griffin**
  media mogul

FRIENDS & FAMILY

PERSONALITY
You are a hard worker, a conscientious performer of your duties, and a thoroughly dependable personality. You have a deep affection for those you have chosen to love, as well as for people attached to you by ties of blood. Occasionally, you like to escape, get away from it all, and have a complete change, but in general your gratification comes from familiar things like your home, family, and friends. Self-help books, good movies, and soothing music are sources of inspiring delight to you. You would rather be denied the physical exercise most folks enjoy than be denied your appreciation of the culture of your times. You know the right time to do the right thing, and consequently you can succeed in almost any field of activity that appeals to you. It could never be said that you fail to hear when opportunity knocks at your door. Always stick to your own principles, and you will never go wrong.

LIFE PATH
You are not comfortable with halfway measures. What you do, you try to do to the best of your ability, and what you have, you try to make the most of. You are a serious student, a great reader, and a profound thinker. Culture and refinement mean a lot to you. You are calm, sensitive, and giving in your love, as in other things.

DESTINY
Interesting, weird experiences are always going to add color to your life. Without being unpleasantly suspicious, check the motives of those with whom you are associated in a business when a new financial venture needs looking into. Make sure your intentions are not misunderstood by people who have known you for only a short time. Sacrifice quantity in favor of quality when purchasing.

KARMIC LESSON
Loyal, generous, and true, you have an interest in and sympathy for the sufferings of others, which makes you interested in psychology. You are especially interested in many philosophies. You are not always sufficiently awake to opportunities that are presented to you, so stay more aware. You like the countryside, yet you are also fond of the buzz and excitement of a great city. You have excellent taste in arranging things, and you try to keep your home neat. You also like going out to dinner and to have a good time. You must take life a little more seriously and remember that you are alive for a definite purpose, as well as just to enjoy yourself. Look on the sunny side and try not to allow yourself to fall into self-pity or gloom.

SECRET
Sometimes you are timid about displaying your emotions, as you don't like to be judged. Enjoy your daily round of duties and routine business matters.

JULY 7

It is absurd to divide people into good and bad. People are either charming or tedious.
—Oscar Wilde

BORN ON THIS DAY
- **Gustav Mahler**
  composer
- **Ringo Starr**
  musician
- **Lisa Leslie**
  basketball player
- **Jim Gaffigan**
  comedian

PERSONALITY
Some brilliantly creative people have been born on this day, which confers imagination, creative talent, and virtuosity. You have a particular talent with words. This is a very inclusive statement, and intentionally so. Wherever words are used—such as in writing, speaking, blogging, teaching, and lecturing—you have the potential to be successful. Do not neglect this innate ability, and do all within your power to develop it so that you may claim the reward of your efforts on behalf of your own improvement.

You like all forms of motion, dancing, and especially travel. Speed is your element, and you inject it into everything you do. Try not to always be in such a rush.

LIFE PATH
You are inclined to be domineering and not always as considerate of or as patient with other people in your family as you might be, although in important matters you are generous, kindly, and sympathetic. You are ambitious, capable, and held in high esteem. You will be reasonably happy in your homelife, once you settle down.

DESTINY
Your inclination to "live and let live" at your place of business is highly regarded by associates. Your time should not be monopolized by any one activity or project. Domestic life also offers you chances to use your executive ability. Take pride in efficient home management. Use your organizational skill socially, by joining community groups in addition to planning private entertainments.

KARMIC LESSON
You have a good head for business and should accumulate a good deal of money by saving and by your natural shrewdness. At the same time, you are kind and supportive to those who deserve it and can often help those in trouble or distress. You are rather curious and inclined a little too much to gossip, interested in the affairs and problems of others. You are rather matter-of-fact and not easily moved to silliness or excitement. Do not worry, as everything in your life will certainly come out for the best in the end. You are fond of animals, and they comfort you. You would make a good nurse or healer and a splendid parent. Learn to be a little more enthusiastic, and greater happiness will be within your grasp.

SECRET
You have a great capacity for concentration, particularly in reading and writing. You are a true parenting type.

FRIENDS & FAMILY

JULY 8

*I am not what happened to me,
I am what I choose to become.*
—Carl Jung

BORN ON THIS DAY
- **John D. Rockefeller**
  businessman
- **Toby Keith**
  singer
- **Kevin Bacon**
  actor
- **Angelica Huston**
  actor
- **Wolfgang Puck**
  celebrity chef

FRIENDS & FAMILY

PERSONALITY
You have a vivid, creative imagination, and you know how to put your ideas into practical forms that can bring you cash rewards. You could succeed in politics, because you know how to win adherents to your side and because you are a natural organizer and administrator. Even in the home, you express this ability, which is such a valuable asset. However, your natural bent is toward artistic things, and you can be creative in any area of the arts that you choose to develop as your special interest, especially working with textiles. Because you also have such good taste, you are a rather perceptive connoisseur and would make a fine critic. Yours is an auspicious birthday, and you will have many happy returns.

LIFE PATH
You are quick, alert, and energetic, a resourceful schemer and shrewd manipulator. You generally succeed in having your own way and in getting others to do what you want them to do. You love art and crafts and would become proficient in the latter field if you developed your talent.

DESTINY
If a relationship with a friend becomes disappointing, do not dwell on it. Better use of your time can be obtained by always following a schedule and a plan. This helps you to focus on the positive. Try to make your goals a little more realistic, and you will find them obtainable. Sidestep controversy in discussions or you will find yourself frustrated, particularly in political discussions.

KARMIC LESSON
You can be shrewd and calculating in business transactions and have a good head in managing business affairs. You have solid judgment. You are cool and do not get easily disturbed over trifles. You are not naturally enthusiastic but rather reserved. You may be fond of athletics and outdoor sports and pastimes. At times, you are inclined to be pessimistic. Do not allow this to influence you; forget the mistakes of the past and enjoy the present while looking to the future. Cultivate cheerfulness. Develop a special hobby, as it will always be a healing process and soothe your anxiety. You are capable of loving, but your head never lets your heart get very far away. If you live close to your ideals, life can be far richer for you.

SECRET
You are an unconventional person of considerable daring. You might make a flashy and quick success with a quirky idea.

JULY 9

A great deal of talent is lost to the world for want of a little courage.
—Sydney Smith

⭑ PERSONALITY
You have a deep interest in things that are mystical. The philosophy of the East has a profound attraction for you, and you live up to the standards or code of ethics of your personal spiritual practice. Your hunches and intuitions are so remarkably astute that your friends often say you must be psychic, and indeed you have that power to a highly developed degree. You have a deep sympathy for human suffering, and your highest ideal is to see the many freedoms established for the entire world—and a world at peace, at that. Although you are a powerful fighter for your own and everyone's rights, you seek to accomplish them through tactfulness and diplomacy.

⭑ LIFE PATH
You are ambitious and idealistic but cool and calculating rather than dominating. You are very conscientious in the performance of duty, original and resourceful in your methods, and generally accurate in your calculations and deductions. You love children, enjoy your home, and spare no pains to make it pleasant and happy.

⭑ DESTINY
Although it usually is considered wise to keep business and friendship separate, you will find that with the rays of Jupiter in a power position on your birth date, you can work out a happy and profitable combination of the two. Thoughtfully consider suggestions made by relatives, even if the ideas do not strike you favorably at first. Do not pin your hopes on get-rich-quick schemes but be content with steady and dependable progress.

⭑ KARMIC LESSON
Strongly drawn to the psychic and the occult, you are a natural investigator. Sensing things that others never seem to feel or articulate, you are governed a good deal by your impressions and intuitions. Original and inventive, you have an inner life that others cannot reach, and when you take time in your inner sanctuary, you think out the problems of life and contemplate your own and others' fate. You have a good head for business and will succeed if you stick to it, not becoming downcast by slights and difficulties. You endure a good deal of mental anguish in your life, owing to your oversensitivity. Learn that other people, whose skins may be thicker than yours, do not always mean things as they sound to you.

⭑ SECRET
A versatile person, you must be wary of scattering your talents and energies in too many fields. You sometimes tire of a project as soon as you have mastered it.

BORN ON THIS DAY
- **O.J. Simpson** — football player, actor
- **David Hockney** — artist
- **Dean Koontz** — author
- **Jimmy Smits** — actor
- **John Frieda** — celebrity hair stylist

FRIENDS & FAMILY

JULY 10

The more I give to thee, the more I have, for both are infinite.
—William Shakespeare

BORN ON THIS DAY
- **Nikola Tesla**
  inventor
- **Marcel Proust**
  author
- **Sofia Vergara**
  actor
- **Jessica Simpson**
  singer, actor
- **A.O. Scott**
  film critic

FRIENDS & FAMILY

PERSONALITY
You have the adventurous spirit of the pioneers. Fear doesn't deter you, and you are brave enough to investigate places where angels might fear to tread. Sometimes such courage is yours that you do brave deeds without thought of the chance you might be taking. In the course of everyday life, this is expressed in your saying what you think and in your doing what you want. Because you are impelled to word and act by only the highest motives, no harm should ever come of your natural way of handling funds, in business, in shopping, or in any position of trust or guardianship. You are a natural-born motivator and can get followers and volunteers for any project or undertaking that you have faith in. You are independent in thought, and you live your own life—irrespective of the opinions of others.

LIFE PATH
You have a great deal of natural leadership ability and self-confidence. You are also faithful and trustworthy in the performance of anything directed by others, as you offer strong support and service. You are kind, tender, sympathetic, and very loving when you respect a partner or friend.

DESTINY
Your intuitive reluctance to make a big, sudden, drastic change will prove wise. Loyalty to ideals and tenacity of purpose will pay off well in the long run. A job where the monetary rewards seem slight can be well worth your effort and eventually pay off. Look into new activities that you would enjoy as a recreation, as they will probably lead to lifelong practices. Do not start an old argument all over again even if strongly tempted to do so, as you might regret the legal consequences.

KARMIC LESSON
You have a good deal of the teacher in you, if not the authority. Often your way is the only way anything can be done, you believe. While it is many times a good way, there are other ways too, and you must never think that you are the only competent person in the world. You are not consciously trying to be arrogant, but you are proud. You have a good logical mind and good business ability. Learn to be more openhanded with money when you have acquired it. You sometimes talk and share too much for your own good. Learn to think more deeply and to concentrate. Life will then mean and hold much more significance for you. Pay less attention to the faults of commission and look more at the faults of omission.

SECRET
You are one who should interpret success in terms of contentment and peace, rather than money, fame, and power.

JULY 11

Always vote for a principle . . . and you may cherish the sweet reflection that your vote is never lost.
—John Quincy Adams

BORN ON THIS DAY
- **John Quincy Adams**
  U.S. president
- **Lil Kim**
  rapper, actor
- **Giorgio Armani**
  fashion designer
- **Cassi Davis**
  actor
- **Richie Sambora**
  guitarist

PERSONALITY
Oversensitivity makes you rather difficult to understand and sometimes tough to get along with. Because you are so independent in your actions, most people know only the surface of your personality. You really put on this appearance because you do not want to be slighted or hurt by other people. Those who know you are very fond of you for your deep well of knowledge and understanding, but you don't let a great many people know you as you really are. You need very calm and supportive surroundings to feel secure, preferring quiet and thoughtful companions. The night hours seem much happier to you, and you can do your best work while others are asleep. Although you would never hurt anyone, you are deeply wounded by even imaginary slights.

LIFE PATH
You basically have good judgment and a kindly spirit that draws people to you. Your close friends are staunch and true, and many may make you their confidant. You like a pleasant environment, and you are forceful enough to eliminate what is unpleasant. You may have an ideal, contented homelife and receive a deep, shared love.

DESTINY
You may at some point consider a drastic change of occupation under the rays of Mercury, which favor new ideas and decisive action. However, if you contemplate this step, be sure that every angle of the situation is taken into consideration. Added prestige will be yours, and your association will be with people of determination. Your mental alertness will preclude the possibility of anyone taking serious advantage of your good humor and easygoing ways.

KARMIC LESSON
Clear and focused, you have a good, practical head for business. You are naturally kind to those around you, but you cannot bear anyone making a fool of you—you are quite sensitive. You could be successful, particularly in partnership. You are progressive and determined. You have a great deal of originality and often take people by surprise with your witty and original sayings. You are a good mimic. You are interested in politics and world affairs. You are sincere and affectionate, almost too much for your own good. Cultivate your boundaries more, and practice greater self-restraint.

SECRET
You have an unusual personality and are helped considerably all through life by people who are attracted by this quality, even though you do not ask for help.

FRIENDS & FAMILY

JULY 12

In all things it is better to hope than to despair.
—Johann Wolfgang von Goethe

BORN ON THIS DAY

★ **Bill Cosby**
actor, comedian

★ **Oscar Hammerstein II**
musical theater songwriter

★ **Malala Yousafzai**
human rights activist

★ **Richard Simmons**
fitness advocate

★ **Julio César Chávez**
boxer

FRIENDS & FAMILY

PERSONALITY
A peaceful philosophy of life combined with the necessary aggressiveness to live in the modern world makes you a well-rounded individual. You know when to draw fire, but you also know that it is foolish to do so unless necessary. You were born with very high ideals, but contact with reality has made you aware that you cannot attain all of them. You therefore compromise with a hectic environment by playing the game fairly and reserving your dreams and aspirations for your hours of leisure and your most trusted confidants. Your air of assurance makes you popular because people like others who give off an aura of self-confidence and success. At home, everyone comes to you for advice, and in your business dealings, you command great respect. Your eventual aim is a quiet home in the country where you can have your friends visit you and where you can develop your ideas and dream your dreams in tranquility.

LIFE PATH
You are moral and decent in action, fastidious in taste, sound in judgment, and capable of attaining a high degree of perfection in any area to which you faithfully apply your energy and ability. You are dependable, altruistic, and lovable, always seeking harmony and pleasant surroundings. Discord in your home would be most trying to you, but you must let go of trying to fix everyone.

DESTINY
You avoid asking others for financial concessions and expect others to do the same. Do not allow daydreaming to result in foolish mistakes while you are working. You can acquire a lot of valuable information by listening, but when you can help clarify the ideas under discussion, do not hesitate to do so. You will discover a more efficient way to deal with routine tasks and might make a business of it.

KARMIC LESSON
You are a natural student and a deep thinker, original and quiet. You understand yourself well. You have a good voice and are naturally persuasive. For this reason, you would make a good lawyer. You have a good head for business and will doubtless succeed in that direction and make money. You are original and would make an excellent inventor. You are fond of animals, and they are fond of you. You are a home lover, and nothing pleases you more than settling down in a cozy corner with a book or watching your favorite TV show with someone you are very fond of. You are very affectionate, and you must keep guard over yourself in this direction. Cultivate more discipline.

SECRET
You desire absorption in an enterprise on a huge scale. You could be skilled in a particular talent, with a genuine interest in pottery or jewelry making as a hobby.

JULY 13

Our chief want in life is somebody who shall make us do what we can.
—Ralph Waldo Emerson

BORN ON THIS DAY
- **Julius Cesar**
  Roman emperor
- **Patrick Stewart**
  actor
- **Harrison Ford**
  actor
- **Cameron Crowe**
  screenwriter
- **Chani Nicholas**
  astrologer

PERSONALITY
Although you would rather lead a quiet and undisturbed existence, life seems to have drawn you into all the complexities that invention, technology, and modern life spell out. You sensibly take your part in the world drama, lending your aid where needed, giving your advice, and adding your cooperation to the group project that we call family life. You have the qualities of a builder—vision, strength, foresight, and practicality. To these you add imagination, and the combination makes you a fine, dependable personality. Provoked, you can flare up to a show of usually hidden temper. Left undisturbed, you prefer to be contemplative and mindful. You are naturally friendly but not a party type. You like a quiet evening with your friends but can do very well without hilarity, drunkenness, or noise. You enjoy friendly, like-minded people with whom contact is easy and open.

LIFE PATH
You can be energetic and enthusiastic about your own projects. You usually think with clarity and reason, decide quickly, and act impulsively. You are a student of causes and conditions, ambitious for intellectual betterment and self-discovery. Your love and affection are strong and enduring.

DESTINY
There will usually be a lack of hindering restraints once you decide to take action. It's as if doors open for you. You are wise to retain a little caution regarding your speech. There is danger of misinterpretation. The harvest you reap will be in keeping with the conscientiousness with which you perform your duties and your willingness to help others.

KARMIC LESSON
Naturally refined in your tastes, you are democratic all the same. You have a strong desire for learning and can be quite a recluse when you are studying or researching. The practical side of things does not escape your notice. You have a great love of exploration; you like odd and unusual places, and in a foreign country, you prefer out-of-the-way and little-known places, which the ordinary tourist might skip. You are quick and adaptable. You are fond of exploring the world, and you like to collect interesting things. You can be lively and entertaining on occasion, yet you always feel that you have an inner life that no one can ever reach or touch, unless, perhaps, one comes along who can understand and appreciate the real you.

SECRET
You possess an idealism that makes it difficult to live in a world where compromise is a necessity. You would be very successful in philanthropic work.

FRIENDS & FAMILY

JULY 14

When someone shows you who they are, believe them the first time.
—Maya Angelou

BORN ON THIS DAY
★ **Gerald Ford**
U.S. president

★ **Gustav Klimt**
painter

★ **Ingmar Bergman**
filmmaker, playwright

★ **Jane Lynch**
actor

★ **Conor McGregor**
MMX fighter

FRIENDS & FAMILY

☸ PERSONALITY
Intensity, excitement, and activity seem to surround you at all times. You have a stimulating personality that draws interesting people to you. If there is a new show, you want to be at the opening. If there is a new person at work, you want to meet him or her. And because you are the center of attraction of your own group, you are often asked to be present at important and interesting events and parties. At your place of work, your opinion is sought after because you have good judgment. At home, you always know the latest and best way of doing things. You can tell others what the fashion is, how to cook a special dish, or which new gadget to use. You believe in the full life, and you surely lead one. Romance is important to you, and you give your whole heart when you fall in love. Your life is marked out for a great deal of material success.

☸ LIFE PATH
You are optimistic, generous, extreme, and adventurous. It is hard for you to believe that everyone is not as straightforward and trustworthy as you are. Your love is spontaneous, whole-souled, and pure, and you need the constant and steady devotion of your partner. It would take you a long time to recover from the shock of a shattered relationship or ideal.

☸ DESTINY
Protection of the gains that you have worked hard to secure is essential. This consideration is sometimes more important than the initiation of new projects. You can always rely on the loyalty of old friends. Concentrate on financial security rather than on the accumulation of extravagant possessions. Live up to your natural sincerity, and your life should be full of reciprocity.

☯ KARMIC LESSON
Your nature is simple, childlike, and trusting. If you have been changed, it is the result of cruel disillusionments, and you are living in a world that is not natural to you, not of your own choice. You must break away from an environment if it is unpleasant and unsuited to you, for you will never be happy until you do. You are considerate and kind, and good manners and healthy boundaries mean a lot to you. You have strong convictions and generally live up to them. You are fond of the country, and the business, crowds, and noise of big cities do not appeal to you as much. You must avoid the habit of gossiping or being around gossips, as this is one of the most toxic traits a person can possess.

☸ SECRET
Born on this day, you are given to excessive planning. You are clever at forming plans but sometimes have no energy left to put your schemes into action.

JULY 15

Strength of character may be said to consist of two things—power of will and power of self-restraint.
—Anonymous

BORD ON THIS DAY
- **Rembrandt**
  painter
- **Forest Whitaker**
  actor
- **Linda Ronstadt**
  singer
- **Arianna Huffington**
  media mogul, columnist
- **Burak Yılmaz**
  soccer player

PERSONALITY
Whatever you do, you try to do to the best of your ability. You have talent in many directions, particularly in creative and artistic fields. Yet it doesn't matter whether you like to sew, cook, paint, play music, write, or perform. There is within you that which takes pride in perfection and will never be satisfied with second best. You are dependable and conscientious. Be open, frank, and honest, and you can have peace of mind. When you give your word, you are sure to keep it, no matter what personal inconvenience it may cause you. Fond of your family and friends, you also like to be shown that they like you. Life is cold and empty for you without mutual love. The true ardor of life is in living it fully, and at this you are a master.

LIFE PATH
You have wonderful intuitive and psychic powers, uncanny perception, and a vivid imagination. Although you are inclined at times to fret and worry, you are generally even-tempered, loving, and kind. You possess a quick wit and are fond of collaboration. You probably will be fortunate in finding a compatible partner who supports your endeavors.

DESTINY
Seek the advice and help of wise relatives. You can accomplish a brilliant piece of work with little strenuous effort if you channel your dreams into productive avenues. Do not reject systematic methods. A well-planned routine, strictly followed, will bring the best results. Guide others by example rather than by too much verbal direction.

KARMIC LESSON
You are a good networker and could have the excellent ability to make and keep friends of all kinds. You have a good head for business but are a dreamer in your early youth, a trait you outgrow as you become somewhat more practical. Your wicked sense of humor is a saving grace that will help you out of many difficulties. You are prone to being sensitive and psychic, but it is probably not wise for you to depend only on this, as you are never sure of it. An extremist in all that you do and think, you have a lot of gratitude for your many blessings. You will have great success along certain lines, but whether it is financial success or not depends upon whether you make it your chief interest in life.

SECRET
You have a quick mind and a strong personality, with little tolerance for those not so well equipped. You should cultivate more patience.

FRIENDS & FAMILY

JULY 16

I have a simple philosophy: Fill what's empty. Empty what's full. Scratch where it itches.
—Alice Roosevelt Longworth

BORN ON THIS DAY

★ **Ida B. Wells**
civil rights leader

★ **Will Ferrell**
comedian, actor

★ **Ginger Rogers**
dancer, actor

★ **Barry Sanders**
football player

★ **Michael Flatley**
dancer, choreographer

FRIENDS & FAMILY

PERSONALITY
Action and motion delight you. You are a real dynamo of ideas and energy and are miserable when you are confined to one place, one job, or one errand. You like to see, text, or call a number of people every day, to go visiting, and to have many followers or message exchanges. Conversation is a source of fun and learning to you, and you never tire of a good conversation. Physical exercise is one of your favorite pastimes, and you prefer those games and sports in which you can participate with other people or a team. You don't care especially about winning the game or the contest, as long as you enjoy the company of the people you are playing with, and as long as they play the game as fairly as you do. Life holds many treasured moments for you.

LIFE PATH
You possess a tenacity of purpose that borders on stubbornness at times, although it never appears so to you. To you, right is right and wrong is wrong, and you are not very tolerant of any deviation from the straight and narrow path. It is your aim to do everything correctly, and you try to have your friends and teammates do the same.

DESTINY
Mutual interests will attract you to new acquaintances. You will do better if you rely on your first impressions. Be sure to give your work priority over pleasure when seeking success, no matter how appealing the latter may seem at the moment. Many of your theories can be put into action, while other ideas may be colored by wishful thinking. Ignore, rather than challenge, statements you cannot accept.

KARMIC LESSON
You have a strong, influential nature and are inclined to be imperious and commanding to those about you. You have a strong will and generally make things come round your way. You have lusty, physical passions and ardent emotions, and if you were as frank as you appear to be, things would be better for your inner soul life. However, sometimes you are a little sly and evasive in this direction—not that you do so consciously, but you do not want to be hurtful to others in any way. Simply, there is another self working within you who you cannot always master and who is not as noble as the one you would like to express. You have a good head for negotiations and seldom lose on a business transaction.

SECRET
You are a distinct pioneer type who most enjoys doing new things or doing old things in a new way.

JULY 17

People rarely succeed unless they have fun in what they are doing.
—Dale Carnegie

⊛ PERSONALITY
You possess the unique ability to turn a small idea into a big and profitable project. From the type of dreams you have, fame and fortune can evolve and be realized. You are especially good at starting new ventures and putting so much enthusiasm, concentration, and vitality into them that they turn out to be successful, although you may not be satisfied. There is something of the explorer about you, and you like to travel to distant places or study them, seeking unusual opportunities or creating them for yourself. You have a great deal of family pride, and you want your name and reputation to be respected. You would never do anything that would put it in bad repute or cause shame to anyone. Because you are generous and considerate, a lot of people try to take advantage of you. You should be more discriminating in the help you give others, because there are a lot of people to whom you are kind who do not always deserve what you do for them.

◎ LIFE PATH
Your powers of understanding are penetrating and comprehensive, and you do not need much guidance from others. You like colorful surroundings and will spend a great deal of energy in making your home attractive. You are a good entertainer and a fluent conversationalist. You smooth over the unpleasant spots in life with calm assurance and an optimistic spirit.

◉ DESTINY
The harmony of your home will make all of your problems easier to solve. Let the bulk of your concern be for present affairs—don't dwell so much on the past. The future will work out very satisfactorily if you attend to things one at a time. When a number of people are involved, subordinate your wishes to those of the majority. Do not hesitate to answer a call for help, but be discerning about how much help you give or for how long. Your consideration usually enables your friends to solve perplexing problems.

☯ KARMIC LESSON
You have a great deal of personal magnetism about you, attracting people wherever you go. You are an idealist, living in a world you create for yourself rather than in the world as it actually exists. At the same time, you are no absolute dreamer. You can be very practical when you want to be, and you have a great deal of force and determination when you focus your mind. You have a good idea about your own position and rights. You are not by nature super affectionate, yet your sexual nature is strong. Financial success will be yours, as you have the ability to make people do your bidding to a remarkable degree. You have a very curious mind; let your heart have greater sway and influence over your life.

☻ SECRET
You have a passionate nature that will slowly rise to its climax in one very important deed, something that may affect the welfare of many people.

BORN ON THIS DAY
- **Angela Markel**
  former chancellor of Germany
- **David Hasselhoff**
  actor
- **Phyllis Diller**
  comedian
- **James Cagney**
  actor
- **Donald Sutherland**
  actor

FRIENDS & FAMILY

JULY 18

The most beautiful thing we can experience is the mysterious. It is the source of all true art and all science.
—Albert Einstein

BORN ON THIS DAY

- **Nelson Mandela**
  president of South Africa
- **Richard Branson**
  business magnate
- **M.I.A.**
  rapper
- **Hunter S. Thompson**
  author
- **John Glenn**
  astronaut

FRIENDS & FAMILY

PERSONALITY

Astrologically speaking, this is an auspicious birth date. You who were born on this day are endowed with courage, leadership, and initiative. However, you are not aggressive when it is unnecessary, not domineering when you know it is futile. The interest of people born on this day in things of a mystical or occult nature is attested to by the fact that Dr. John Dee, the great English astrologer, is a native of this month and date. His predictions were so clear and worked out so accurately that he was questioned publicly by Parliament as to whether he had previous knowledge of the facts he forecast. You also have this prophetic power, although no doubt to a lesser degree. However, your psychic flashes are uncanny, and your intuition is very on target. Trust your hunches and record your dreams.

LIFE PATH

A great lover of beauty, you are ingenious, studious, and generally amiable in your disposition, and although you can lose your temper quickly, you also recover quickly and move on. Your tastes are fastidious, and you like to dress well and appear fashionable. You are affectionate and kind and fond of good design.

DESTINY

You will often look "behind the scenes" and discover more activity than first meets the eye. Although the real motives may be different from the declared ones, you will grasp the true situation. The advantages that you will gain from being polite and gracious even when pressed for time are considerable. The opportunity to begin a lucrative new business should not be overlooked.

KARMIC LESSON

You are active and dynamic and have a great deal of energy to put into something you care about—whether mental or physical pursuits. You have the power of concentration. You could attain success at whatever you apply yourself to. You are very intellectual and a great reader, student, and lover of culture and education. You are an indefatigable worker, never tiring of doing those things that interest you. You probably also absorb facts quickly. You like to take breaks to chill out and have a good time. You are imaginative and seek inspiration. Movies and good TV will probably exert an irresistible attraction for you—you like to see everything.

SECRET

You have a sense of humor and unusually accurate powers of perception, particularly in reading the characters of people.

JULY 19

We are all faced with a series of great opportunities brilliantly disguised as insoluble problems.
—John W. Gardner

BORN ON THIS DAY
- **Edgar Degas**
  painter
- **Benedict Cumberbatch**
  actor
- **Lizzie Borden**
  acquitted axe murderer
- **Topher Grace**
  actor
- **Brian May**
  guitarist

FRIENDS & FAMILY

PERSONALITY
Throughout life you experience a wide divergence of ups and downs and many moods of differing and contrasting natures. It is as though you were born to touch each of the facets of a dome of many-colored glass that symbolizes life as you see and live it. Your reward or compensation is that each experience you have increases your knowledge, widens your mental horizons, and enhances your tolerance. The whole gamut of emotions will be yours, and each will leave its mark upon you. After middle life, you will succeed in your chosen field, and you will have the acclaim for which you secretly hanker. Although you may not become famous in your own right, your name could eventually be known because of a relationship to some famous event or personality.

LIFE PATH
You are original, ambitious, and energetic. Your love is deeply caring and constant, and your happiness demands an adequate return of affection. You are fond of travel and cruises, and you love to be outdoors.

DESTINY
You will be sought as a confidant by a famous acquaintance who respects your judgment. Your completed tasks will usually be satisfactory because of your desire for perfection. Contentment, rather than drama, will be your reward for conscientious endeavor. Accept sincere advice gracefully. Delve into the study of occultism and philosophy for enlightening experiences—you will enjoy it.

KARMIC LESSON
You are composed and poised. You are resourceful and self-sufficient. You have certain whims and quirks, but they are your own, and you are not readily influenced by the views of others. You are capable of undergoing many hardships, and nothing deters you from a certain course of action once your mind is made up to undertake it. You have a roving nature, which will take you to investigate many subjects. You want to see everything and do everything. You are a capable worker, and you love making the most out of any job placed in your hands. You are lively and good company. Yours should be a life full of important events, and one full of promise, which it depends upon you alone to fulfill.

SECRET
Energy and enthusiasm govern this day. You have a distinct love for helping others in an unostentatious way.

JULY 20

Love is the crowning grace of humanity . . . the golden link which binds us to duty and truth.
—Petrarch

BORN ON THIS DAY

* **Sandra Oh**
  actor
* **Carlos Santana**
  musician
* **Chris Cornell**
  singer/songwriter
* **Natalie Wood**
  actor
* **Ray Allen**
  basketball player

FRIENDS & FAMILY

PERSONALITY
Your whole life proceeds on the principle that the finest thing you can do is a good deed for another person. You can be completely unselfish and altogether considerate of the feelings and desires of your friends and relatives. To those you have chosen to love, and to your life partner, you display a generosity unparalleled. As a practical person working out your destiny, you do your best work when you are carrying out the plans that someone else has conceived. In this, you are remarkably efficient. You do the job better than the person who thought it up. You have a special ability to know what people are thinking and feeling. Because you have this special talent, however, you do not take advantage of your associates but lend your sympathy and helpfulness most of the time. You have it in you to be the best friend anyone ever had.

LIFE PATH
You are industrious, shrewd, upright, and studious. You are candid and straightforward but tactful. You are fond of socializing and are well-liked by many in your immediate circle. You will probably be happily partnered and will always strive to make your home organized and convenient.

DESTINY
Mental and emotional inertia have no part in your future. A dear friend will face problems similar to ones that confronted you in the past, giving you an opportunity to pass on the benefits of your experience. You will always do well to discuss business details with a trusted associate—success will be the result. Partnerships in business will benefit you.

KARMIC LESSON
You have a good mind—which, however, is prone to becoming engrossed in trivial concerns instead of concentrating on one subject or study of great interest and value. Your interests probably lie in odd and out-of-the-way things, and for this reason you will not make as much money as you would like until later in life, when you determine to put these aside for a time and devote yourself more to the practical side of life. You are possibly retiring and a bit shy in the company of those who attract you, but this you can learn to overcome. You do not utilize enough the great opportunities that are offered to you or make use of your own latent powers and potentialities. Use your will; success can be easily attained by you.

SECRET
You are one who cares too much for the concern, judgment, or critique of others. You should learn to exercise independence of your own decisions, for greater success.

JULY 21

Just as a candle cannot burn without fire, men cannot live without a spiritual life.
—Buddha

◉ PERSONALITY
This is a date that marks the birth of some very artistically talented people. Among those born on this month and day are Robert Burns, the great Scottish poet and songwriter, and Ernest Hemingway, among the foremost writers of fiction. Born on this date, you are able to express your thoughts and feelings in a manner that shows their innate power. You have a high degree of aggression, with the strength to make your voice heard, to give wing to your thoughts, and to put across the thoughts and the original concepts that your mind produces. You like many people, and they like you in return. Do not hesitate to offer help when needed—it's good karma!

◉ LIFE PATH
You love travel, are adventurous, daring, and active, and enjoy taking care of your body when in the mood to. You should try to overcome any addictions. You are quite logical, independent, and self-sufficient and like to assume a leading role. You have the courage of your convictions and will not yield a point you are trying to make without good cause.

◉ DESTINY
Gracious living will be a part of your life goal. You will be mostly lucky. You enjoy receiving or purchasing desirable objects that will add to the charm and value of your dwelling. Invitations will always be plentiful. Material resources will be available, making possible additional expenditures for gifts, expansion, and entertainment, which you love. Learn the value of concentration. Strive and never stop working on the things you are passionate about.

◉ KARMIC LESSON
You have an innate common sense and are very intuitive. You would do well to follow these intuitions more and accept the advice of others less. You are good at an argument, and this would suit you for the law, at which you would make an undoubted success. You will be more or less successful at whatever you undertake, and it is rare to find one of your nature who is not fairly well-off. You have good directorial ability and can manage others and their affairs so well that rapid advancement can be yours. You are eminently levelheaded. You would not willingly hurt anyone. You are a lover of justice and cannot bear to see the weaker oppressed by the stronger.

◉ SECRET
There is power in your nature that should raise you to a position of high authority. With it is a desire to exercise this power for the greater good.

BORN ON THIS DAY
- **Alexander the Great**
  ruler of ancient Macedonian empire
- **Ernest Hemingway**
  author
- **Robin Williams**
  comedian, actor
- **Cat Stevens**
  singer
- **DeAndre Jordan**
  basketball player

FRIENDS & FAMILY

JULY 22

The goal of life is to make your heartbeat match the beat of the universe, to match your nature with Nature.
—Joseph Campbell

BORN ON THIS DAY
- **Selena Gomez**
  singer
- **Oscar de la Renta**
  fashion designer
- **John Leguizamo**
  actor
- **Danny Glover**
  actor
- **Prince George**
  eldest child of Prince William and Catherine, Duchess of Cambridge

FRIENDS & FAMILY

PERSONALITY
Your birth on this date indicates that you were born on the cusp, that is to say, astrologically speaking, when the Sun was at a degree between two signs of the zodiac. You therefore share the traits and fortunes of those people who were born under both Cancer and Leo. There is great strength and courage in your nature and also great gentleness. This combination of qualities makes you a very resolute person, one who will not give up without a struggle. You like best to be of help to others, but you are not lacking in initiative. When it is necessary to dominate a situation in order to bring about a satisfactory conclusion, you can assume the necessary potency even though the fight may cause you pain in an emotional sense. You must learn to finish one thing before beginning another, and you have a fault of attempting too many things at once.

LIFE PATH
You are versatile and resourceful, of an expressive temperament, and rather proud, and you have a perceptive, penetrating mind. You are quick to see the good in others and are fair and generous in your dealings. Your love is strong, you may marry young, and you will probably select an emotional, sensitive partner.

DESTINY
An unanticipated change in circumstances may give you the opportunity to further your ambitions—it is a blessing in disguise. A long-term, worrisome misunderstanding will likely be cleared up, reestablishing a close relationship with someone who was important to you and will again be a trusted companion. Your adaptability may be called into use on more than one occasion. You will appreciate the outstanding devotion and loyalty of your loved ones.

KARMIC LESSON
You are a well-meaning character, one that a friend can trust to do exactly as you say you will. You take things to heart and are very sad when you are disappointed by one whom you esteemed highly. A great worker, you are practical, brave, and energetic. You are frank and true. At times, you are moody, and then you can feel hurt so much that you hardly know what to do with yourself. You can be quiet and reserved. You have a way of going ahead and doing things without telling anyone about them until they are done. You are not always understood, and many of your thoughts and actions are often misinterpreted. You may be blessed with many of the material comforts of this life.

SECRET
You have a highly emotional nature and are a little too prone to disregard what is best for your own good, at times.

JULY 23

Life is far too important a thing ever to talk seriously about.
—Oscar Wilde

BORN ON THIS DAY
- **Anthony Kennedy**
  U.S. Supreme Court justice
- **Daniel Radcliffe**
  actor
- **Woody Harrelson**
  actor
- **Don Imus**
  radio personality
- **Monica Lewinsky**
  former White House intern, activist

PERSONALITY
You are very hospitable by nature, and you enjoy cooking and entertaining in your home. Nothing gives you as much pleasure as being the host to a large group of your relatives, friends, and neighbors. "The more, the merrier" is your slogan. Nothing seems to be too much trouble when you plan a good time. You prefer the kind of freelance job that allows you to regulate your hours yourself and that leaves it to you to use your judgment as to how and when things should be done. Your family and friends all appreciate the fact that you never forget a birthday or anniversary and that your choice of cards, events remembrances, and gifts is in perfect taste.

LIFE PATH
You are nervous, vivacious, rather talkative, and full of energy. You like to laugh and have fun, and your social life is busy—you like to take an active part in all that is going on around you. You demand attention and love, and you love deeply. You do not like people who do not take the trouble to show love as intimately as you do.

DESTINY
Remember the old saying "A person is either on top of their job, or it is on top of them." This is just as applicable to domestic life as it is to business matters. Be optimistic. Do not wait until boredom has wounded your initiative. If you want to take a trip or make a big purchase, and you have the time and resources necessary, do it.

KARMIC LESSON
Born on this day, you are mostly self-reliant, determined, and self-confident. You like excitement of all kinds. To you the motto "Any means to an end" is a good one. Once you get your teeth in a thing, nothing can induce you to take them out. You have good taste, and you display originality in many ways. You have an eye for color and would make a good decorator or designer. You have a curious mind and are fond of fashion, food, and fun. You have a good head for details and are a natural salesperson. You are magnetic and can persuade others, converting them to your views. You are frank, open, and true. As a rule, you are a charming individual.

SECRET
You possess the quality of retaining the spirit of youth all through life. You have a nature that takes nothing seriously, except personal surroundings.

FRIENDS & FAMILY

JULY 24

We enjoy thoroughly only the pleasure that we give.
—Alexandre Dumas

BORN ON THIS DAY

★ **Amelia Earhart**
aviation pioneer

★ **Jennifer Lopez**
singer

★ **Chief Dan George**
native activist, actor

★ **Barry Bonds**
baseball player

★ **Karl "Moses" Malone**
basketball player

FRIENDS & FAMILY

● PERSONALITY
You enjoy puttering around the house, working with tools, cooking, sewing, and making general improvements. Your nature is such that you see the beauty in the practical, and you like to express this by making things of functional loveliness. You have a masterful capacity for organizing and are constantly called upon by your employer, your community, and your family to form committees and group activities, to seek new ways to improve conditions. Because you are cooperative, you never let your friends or coworkers down. You are studious by nature, and you enjoy discovering solutions to problems. There is a lot of talent in your makeup, and you could succeed in life in some inventive or creative capacity.

● LIFE PATH
You are intense, emotional, and sometimes explosive, so you need to cultivate more self-control. You are devoted to your family, but they can drive you crazy. You are inclined to combativeness and are very persistent in maintaining your position, especially when you think it is for another's good. You are generally well-liked because you really care so much.

● DESTINY
Your sense of discrimination will be used in deciding where lies the best opportunity for future success in your business and in other people's businesses. You would make a good coach or consultant. Accept the competent assistance offered by an associate when you have a difficult assignment to complete, as it will lead you to greater success. Supply determination, and you will then be pleased with the results of your labor. Always beware of acting too impulsively, as this is your nature.

● KARMIC LESSON
You are strongly imaginative, capable, and enthusiastic. You are fond of color and warmth and cannot endure people who are lazy or who enjoy a sort of half-hearted existence. You must always be up and doing. You take a great interest in humanity and have a remarkable understanding of the motives that govern human nature. You are an excellent judge of character. You have a marvelous memory, which needs only training and exercise to render it truly phenomenal. You are also intuitive, interested in all things relating to the psychic, occult, or mysterious. These subjects have always had a secret fascination for you. You are original, inventive, and wired to produce. You have a good sense of humor. You are resourceful. You need your own home sanctuary and comforts.

● SECRET
You have fine powers of intuition. You should exercise more your own individual judgment in public as well as in private affairs.

JULY 25

Believe that life is worth living and your belief will help create the fact.
—William James

PERSONALITY
You are quick at repartee and always have the attention of your crowd because they know that once you get started, the clever remarks will flow freely. You have artistic taste, and you are attracted to anything that is dramatic, exotic, vintage, or bizarre. The theater, acting, and movies and all their various branches interest you, and you would be very good at participating in those professions. Your professionalism, humor, and intelligence give you the necessary poise for appearing in public; it would also be good for you to study the basic elements of drama. As it is, you would be a good marketing professional and could build a career around a job that requires contact with groups and the public. Variety is necessary for your happiness because you soon become bored with sameness.

LIFE PATH
You are competent and versatile. Your personality is magnetic, and you make contacts easily and are a general favorite with your friends. You are an excellent manager, have a keen insight in business dealings, and seldom come off second best. You are warmhearted and noble-minded and give your love with great strength and devotion—but sometimes your enthusiasm can scare people off.

DESTINY
The nature of your work may change, but never give up the earnestness and sincerity with which you handle your job. Carefully look into suggested investments before deciding definitely one way or another. Your hospitality may often be imposed on, but it will be due to thoughtlessness rather than intent. You can be a clever and witty conversationalist, but do not become sarcastic, or you may hurt people's feelings. Give full credit or praise to anyone who shows it has been deserved. Emphasize compliments rather than criticism in what you say.

KARMIC LESSON
You have a great deal of talent in various directions. You are artsy and have a certain ingenious gift that renders you an all-rounder. You are sensible and fair-minded. You have a good speaking voice and should be able to address an audience. You have a good deal of personal charisma and might be onstage or in front of others in some way. You doubtless have a special psychic power. At the same time, you are distinctly practical and will probably be successful in a material way. You are imaginative and responsive to the ideas of others. Cultivate your sense of humor, which is often helpful in the battle of life.

SECRET
You have a deep, spiritual nature but are not exactly religious, which is wise and comforting to those you care for.

BORN ON THIS DAY
- **Alicia Keys** singer
- **Estelle Getty** actor
- **Walter Payton** football player
- **Iman** fashion model
- **Rosalind Franklin** molecular biologist

FRIENDS & FAMILY

JULY 26

Any idiot can face a crisis—it's day-to-day living that wears you out.
—Clifford Odets

BORN ON THIS DAY

- **Aldous Huxley**
  author
- **Carl Jung**
  founder of analytical psychology
- **Mick Jagger**
  singer
- **Helen Mirren**
  actor
- **Sandra Bullock**
  actor

FRIENDS & FAMILY

PERSONALITY
The old popular song title "There's No Place Like Home" is a real slogan to you, for you feel just that way about your home, "no matter how humble." Nothing delights you more than to have all your family around you, having a good time. You are generous to a fault in giving them anything that you think will make them happy, and you succeed in spoiling them as you were never spoiled. You are crafty and talented, being able to do a lot with little. For example, you can switch furniture, change drapes, or repair things so that everything looks new and attractive. You are a good bargain hunter. You are probably what is called a "handy person." You have strong common sense and are firm in your ideas and opinions.

LIFE PATH
You are capable, dependable, rather imperious, and sometimes headstrong. You are fond of good design. A fluent talker and a good comedian, you are always interested in improving yourself, especially along cultural lines.

DESTINY
Keep your imagination under control, and you will build the foundations of security. Let it run away with you, and you will build nothing but castles in the air. Although you may lose your temper when exasperated, you find it almost immediately. Most people realize this and just wait until your usually agreeable manner has returned. An associate who admires you could get deeply hurt by the remarks you make, so be aware.

KARMIC LESSON
You have a generous nature. You see the better side of things and of people and even make the best you can of unpleasant events. You are tolerant and sympathetic. You have a simple nature, but you are not easily taken in, all the same, in a business transaction. You are a talented raconteur, popular wherever you go. You have a knack of doing a lot of work without appearing to do anything at all. You are a great hustler and have an untiring fund of energy. You will have several good positions offered you during your life, but you will probably make a greater success by working for yourself. You will enjoy yourself no matter what. You are very loving in your nature and seek the same in return.

SECRET
You have a generous streak and a tendency to sometimes do too much for others, causing self-neglect.

JULY 27

A man is not old until regrets take the place of dreams.
—Anonymous

◉ PERSONALITY
Because you have a rather peaceful, kind, and sympathetic nature, people find you good company. You never get on their nerves, because you are not jumpy, do not suffer from the common modern tensions, and have a sort of soothing effect. This condition exists because you are that way by nature, and also because you have the kind of mind that can control the body at will. You have a strongly developed intuition, and most of the time you know just what another person you are with is thinking about. This gives you an advantage over people that can take you far along the pathway of success if you use it to your own advantage. Still, there are times when you become irritable. When you do, it is time for a change. Just pick yourself up and get out where things are happening.

◉ LIFE PATH
You are capable of concentrated, earnest effort, and your quick mind and insights, coupled with ambition and determination, bring you more than ordinary success. You are mostly cheerful and lovable, and your friends are very tied to you. You love with unusual strength of expression, and you will never be contented with half-hearted affection in return.

◉ DESTINY
Government matters may interest you considerably, although your connection may not necessarily be personal. Intensity will characterize your attention to all matters. This can be good, but you must expect some letdown when the task is completed and the tension released. Seek the companionship of younger people when you are feeling glum, but do not exclude older ones from your circle of friends.

◉ KARMIC LESSON
You will have many ups and downs in life and many hard battles, especially with yourself, but you will be victorious, if only you determine to undergo certain periods of unpleasantness and stay positive. You have two very different sides to your nature. You are fond of writing, art, music, and film. You are rather too fond of the good things of this life; be careful that this does not lead to dependency. Learn about the power of habits and addictions—good or bad. If you wish to succeed, you must learn the value of money and how to save. If you do this, you will attain great returns in the long run. You are magnetic and have a peculiarly fascinating personality. Above all, learn to focus.

◉ SECRET
You are a rebellious spirit, desiring to remake everything according to personal beliefs of perfection.

BORN ON THIS DAY
- **Alex "A-Rod" Rodriguez** — baseball player
- **Jean Baudrillard** — sociologist, cultural theorist
- **Norman Lear** — TV producer
- **Jonathan Rhys Meyers** — actor
- **Maya Rudolph** — comedian, actor

FRIENDS & FAMILY

JULY 28

The years teach much which the days never know.
—Ralph Waldo Emerson

BORN ON THIS DAY
- **Jacqueline Kennedy Onassis**
  U.S. First Lady
- **Simon Kirke**
  drummer
- **Beatrix Potter**
  author
- **Marcel Duchamp**
  painter
- **Sally Struthers**
  actor

FRIENDS & FAMILY

PERSONALITY
You are a very active person, and you must always be on the go to be happy in this life. You find nothing more stultifying than to be kept locked up in one place or to have your activity limited in any way. Of course, this also applies to the life of your mind. If you had to live in an atmosphere where your conduct was regulated by public opinion, or where freedom of expression was frowned upon, you would soon make a break and run for it. You like a friendly crowd of up-to-date people to associate with, and you want action, freedom, and liberty at all times and for everyone. You have great moral and physical courage to do your own thing. Nothing will frighten you because you have great self-confidence, or at least you go forward even if you are afraid.

LIFE PATH
Your mind is sharp, incisive, and active. You are energetic, slightly edgy, and petulant when working under a strain but pleasant, kind, and sympathetic when your mind is free. Your interests are toward culture and all that is uplifting. You are fond of working with children and will be very happy making your environment attractive.

DESTINY
The time for you to make important decisions is when you are prepared for them—with calm nerves and a spirit of resolution. Do not jump to hasty conclusions. Consider the council of elders. Analyze the advantages to be gained and the potential losses in security and contentment before taking a definite step. Then be satisfied to forget the past and concentrate on the future.

KARMIC LESSON
You have strong intuitions and impulses. You have a mercurial temperament, which sometimes runs away with you. You are emotional and feel things deeply. You might be successful if you decide to perform in some manner. You have a good deal of natural ability and are probably a fine impressionist. You take a great interest in people's lives, and this is to you always a topic of interest. The latter part of your life will be very happy and possibly prosperous; the earlier years stand a chance of being challenging unless you are especially careful in your actions. Remember that every day begins a new life, and it is your duty to get in touch with your traumas, then forget the unpleasant things of the past and think happy thoughts to move forward.

SECRET
You require continual encouragement in order to do good work. You are susceptible to flattery, and your spirits are easily dampened by adverse criticism.

JULY 29

Good words are worth much, and cost little.
—George Herbert

PERSONALITY
You have a pioneering spirit. You don't have to go into the wilderness to express this, for a person can be just as daring and original in a creative way as he or she can in actual motion or by doing deeds of courage. And this is what is meant by your having the pioneer spirit, that you dare to think as you please, you dare to express your thoughts to the world at large, and you dare to live your own life just as you want and not according to any limiting or petty standards that you consider hypocritical. You should find the study of occult philosophy and metaphysics enlightening and interesting. You have good intuitions about your family and your business, and you will succeed, slowly but surely, by reason of your ability for organization and control, once implemented.

LIFE PATH
You are idealistic and imaginative but often fill your head with worry. You like excitement, have a funny sense of humor, and are generally well-liked. You will do anything for a friend, and you have many of them. You are domestic, nurturing, and very affectionate but tend to overdo.

DESTINY
The benefits you can obtain using the written and spoken word will have an important bearing on both social and business life. With Mercury rays in control of your birth date, you have reason to expect plenty of action. Take a chance now and then. Do not expect all of your endeavors to work out perfectly unless you give them the impetus of practical effort.

KARMIC LESSON
You are strongly drawn to the strange and weird. Everything of an odd and out-of-the-way nature fascinates you. You are fond of old ruins and castles and anyplace where the great once lived and loved—such as Egypt, Greece, and Rome. You are naturally investigative, and you apply this to all you do, including to life in general and the lives and motives of others. Learn the great lesson that too much exactness and analysis destroy naturalness and spontaneity and hence rob life of half its charms. You are curious and have a thirst for knowledge, which is not always easily satisfied.

SECRET
Because of your bold spirit, you will try many paths. You have the strength of purpose, however, to overcome all obstacles.

BORN ON THIS DAY
- **Ken Burns**, documentary filmmaker
- **Will Wheaton**, actor
- **Martina McBride**, singer
- **Tim Gunn**, fashion designer, TV personality
- **Josh Radnor**, actor

FRIENDS & FAMILY

JULY 30

You're either part of the solution or you're part of the problem.
—Eldridge Cleaver

BORN ON THIS DAY
- **Emily Brontë**
  author
- **Henry Ford**
  industrialist, business magnate
- **Arnold Schwarzenegger**
  actor, politician
- **Christopher Nolan**
  filmmaker
- **Vivica A. Fox**
  actor

FRIENDS & FAMILY

PERSONALITY
You combine the qualities of possessing a vivid, creative imagination and the ability to put the product of your mind into such a form or shape that you can market it to the world and realize profits from it. Thus, you might make a good inventor, novelist, playwright, artist, financier, broker, or producer. Many geniuses of invention were born on this auspicious day. You like to be the leader in whatever project there is, and you make quite a good leader, too, having initiative and spunk. You are willing to take a chance, and you have such good judgment that you rarely come out on the short end. Use your original ideas; they are valuable. You are probably more than generous to your loved ones, but that can hardly be listed as a fault. You like to be loved, and because you make yourself worth it, you should have a rewarding emotional life.

LIFE PATH
You are ambitious, energetic, persevering, adaptable, and very definite in your likes and dislikes. You do not form many close friendships, but the friends you have are staunch and true. Love of family is very strong in you, and you are very demonstrative in your love. You do not have many interests outside of your home and your personal projects.

DESTINY
Satisfying emotional experiences are what you look for in a friend and partner. In time there will be a lessening of worry over home, finances, or marriage. Mental and spiritual serenity is signified. Younger people will play increasingly important roles in your life. An intimate circle of friends will add to your joy. Delegate some of your leisure hours to reading, yoga, or just resting.

KARMIC LESSON
Born on this day, you have a sly sense of humor that sees something funny in nearly everything that transpires. You are good-hearted and generally happy. You are picky in your tastes and have a love of detail. You can fit yourself to your surroundings if you have to. You are very full of imagination, and you often keep your close friends and family amused and entertained by your humor and originality. You are very fond of animals, and they in turn take to you. You are psychic and open to impressions. You have a good business sense, which is rather exceptional in someone of your talents. On the whole, you are a very original and likable personality and deserve the best of everything.

SECRET
You would make an ideal companion, as you accept most conditions with cheerful grace.

JULY 31

No one is useless in this world who lightens the burdens of another.
—Charles Dickens

PERSONALITY
You are very idealistic in your outlook on life, and it disappoints you to observe people acting from low, rude, and selfish motives. To you, the only way to live is according to the Golden Rule. When you see that people whom you know are conducting their lives from purely selfish aims, you are impelled to drop them at once because you just don't want to see what they are doing. You are quite eclectic in your taste, and you hate to have to compromise by accepting what is only second best. In fact, you would prefer to do without a thing rather than take a substitute for the very best of its kind. As long as you feel that way, you would do best to have a few fine things instead of a collection of poor-quality things. You are very positive in your opinions, and you will not take arguments from anyone on subjects on which you consider yourself an authority.

LIFE PATH
You are fastidious, exacting, careful in your plans, and capable in their execution. You have wonderful foresight, and many come to you for advice. You are scrupulously honest and severe in your judgment of others. You should exercise care in the selection of your partner and not marry hastily. You demand undivided attention and affection.

DESTINY
Avoid arguments that will get you nowhere with those in authority. You will have ample opportunity to put your advanced ideas into operation. When these ideas are opposed to established procedures, be diplomatic and patient. Voluntary service in an organization can give you added chances to display the originality of your mind and your organizing ability. The promise of a bright future can be yours.

KARMIC LESSON
The restlessness and wandering spirit of those born yesterday is often accentuated in those born today. You can be a great wanderer—rough and ready but kind and sympathetic. You have ideal aspirations, and you look for the best in everybody, but you are often disappointed if you do not find what you seek. You take a broad and comprehensive view of everything, and in your intuitional grasp you are seldom wrong. Show your inner kindness and affection to those you love, and these qualities will be shown to you in return. Someone of your nature should succeed in accumulating quite a small fortune, if you do not spend it all in your travels or give it away while it is being made. Learn the value of saving, if only a little.

SECRET
You are a lover of speed, frequently marring success by hastening the development of plans before they mature, naturally, in their own time.

BORN ON THIS DAY
- **J.K. Rowling** author
- **Milton Friedman** economist
- **Mark Cuban** entrepreneur
- **Wesley Snipes** actor
- **DeMarcus Ware** football player

FRIENDS & FAMILY

AUGUST 1

What a man does for others, not what they do for him, gives him immortality.
—Daniel Webster

BORN ON THIS DAY
- **Herman Melville**
  author
- **Jerry Garcia**
  musician
- **Jason Momoa**
  actor
- **Chuck D**
  rapper
- **Yves Saint Laurent**
  fashion designer

● PERSONALITY
To use a time-honored expression, you are very often thought of by your friends as a "lone wolf." The reason is that you are very independent in thought and action. You prefer to do things your own way, and you won't allow anyone to influence you. Of course, the negative expression of this independence is extreme stubbornness. That is a trait you want to try to avoid; be careful that in keeping your head up in the world, you are not knocking it against a wall. You have very fine perceptive powers; you seem to pierce the armor of superficiality that people usually wear, getting right to the heart of who they are and understanding them completely. Despite the fact that you won't do anything you don't want to do, you will make sacrifices for your loved ones very willingly. You are inclined to spoil them, in fact, with too much attention and loving care. Develop your tenacity and perseverance so that you can bring out the very best that is in you.

● LIFE PATH
You are intuitive, cautious, fastidious, and bold even to the verge of sometimes being foolhardy. You are generally successful in surmounting difficulties, persevering, fond of out-of-door life and sports events, and a great lover of playing games. You are affectionate, good with children, and empathetic and kind to those in need.

● DESTINY
Being a positive person always helps to keep your enthusiasm at a high level. You will meet people to whom you are immediately attracted because of common interests—so always listen to those hunches you have about people. Do not let sentiment run away with your good judgment. Extensive reading will be helpful in establishing a workable and happy philosophy of life.

● KARMIC LESSON
Impulsive, original, stubborn, and clever, you will have many friends and a few jealous competitors. You are many-sided; you may be perfectly sincere in your attachments to several people at one time, and you present a number of sides to a number of people. Each one of them is different. Each of them meets and gratifies a certain side of you. You are inclined to hold two opposite opinions on a certain subject, sometimes not knowing which one to choose. You must learn the value of immediate choice by listening to your first hunch. When once you have learned to do this, you can make a great success out of your life, as you have many original talents.

● SECRET
You have a rather lustful temperament, devoted to sensual and sexual recreations.

FRIENDS & FAMILY

AUGUST 2

Everyone has been made for some particular work, and the desire for that work has been put in every heart.
—Jalāl ad-Dīn Rumi

BORN ON THIS DAY

- **Peter O'Toole**
  actor
- **James Baldwin**
  author
- **Wes Craven**
  filmmaker
- **Mary-Louise Parker**
  actor
- **Sam Worthington**
  actor

FRIENDS & FAMILY

PERSONALITY

Born on this day, you are among the architects of modern thought. Your natural processes of concepts, analysis, and logic are so clear that you see the right thing to do without effort, and you carry out a plan of life that is reasonable, satisfactory, and sensible. Of course, you have the same disturbances and emotional challenges that others do, but you regulate your feelings with a rational point of view that prevents unhappiness and disappointment to a large degree. You direct the affairs of your family life in such a way that there is a minimum of friction and a maximum of goodwill. You can develop the spirit of cooperation among those with whom you work and live such that things go smoothly and efficiently. You really like the finer things life has to offer, and you indulge your good taste by purchasing the best that you can afford, in the material world.

LIFE PATH

You have business ability, aptitude in the handling of details, application, and progressiveness. You are hopeful, buoyant, and sincere in your modern way of thinking. You admire talent and prefer the company of cultured and refined people. You are a good conversationalist and are rather fond of new inventions, trends, gadgets, and theories. You love to be on the cutting edge.

DESTINY

You will usually be able to crystallize your ideas and use them as a basis for action. You should take upon yourself the responsibility of avoiding unnecessary disputes. Do not allow even the smallest misunderstanding to continue, since more serious troubles may result. Emotional reactions should be tempered with wisdom. Try to rid yourself of prejudices that do not have a basis in fact. You should put your emphasis on thoroughness, not speed.

KARMIC LESSON

You are smart and have a considerable ingenuity. You can think of things no one else would conceive. You are also a hard worker and believe in succeeding through sustained effort. But this work should be devoted to your own betterment and advancement and not simply given for the advancement of another. You are scientific and interested in philosophical problems. You are not naturally a bohemian, though you can be on occasion. You prefer something more solid, practical, and substantial. You are very devoted to your family unit and to the young people around you, and one of your chief objectives in life is to provide a comfortable home for your old age. You are capable of deep feelings and are naturally sincere and loving in your regard for your partners.

SECRET

You are a person quick with words, and you have great confidence in addressing others. You could succeed as a trainer, coach, or teacher.

AUGUST 3

A journey of a thousand miles begins with a single step.
—Lao Tzu

◉ PERSONALITY
Diplomacy, tact, and sincerity mark the manner in which you conduct your life. You rarely, if ever, get embroiled in emotional situations that are damaging and upsetting, because your clever and rational planning prevents them from happening. You never enter a situation without thinking out in advance what the involvements and repercussions might be; in this way you avoid the friction and flare-ups that others with less forethought than you must undergo. Tolerance is another trait you have developed, which allows you a certain peacefulness in your life direction that is very enviable. As long as other people don't interfere with your choices and way of life, you are perfectly willing to let them live their lives without criticism or interference. You have a highly developed social sense, and you enjoy entertaining and being entertained.

◉ LIFE PATH
You are self-contained, independent, and persistent. You do a lot of pondering and thinking and form very definite opinions, although you never force your views upon others. In a quiet, unassuming way, you go ahead and do things in your own way, regardless of advice, and your way is usually a positive one. You are affectionate and demonstrative, and your happiness requires the steadfast devotion that is your true nature.

◉ DESTINY
Your independent endeavors will be rewarded. You appreciate established routines but are open to upgrades to new methods. Activities in which you have always desired to participate will eventually become a part of your life and leave their mark on all your undertakings. You will find that your creative urge may be expressed both mentally and manually. Take pride in achievement, and help others develop their talents. Favors you grant will usually be returned in full.

◉ KARMIC LESSON
You are quiet and reserved and not usually inclined to entrust your private thoughts and ideas to others. You can be good at debates, and for this reason you could make a good lawyer. You can handle large business enterprises if you have the chance to do so. You could gain power, though possibly not until later on in life. You are orderly and tidy and almost militant in your precision. You are idealistic in your aspirations and never satisfied with anything short of the best, yet you can go without if you have to. You are not easily moved, but when thoroughly convinced that you are in the right, you will fight for truth so long as you have the energy for it. You have a strong sense of justice.

◉ SECRET
You are one who will endure many trials and reversals of fortune for your ideals. If sufficiently driven, you might leave your imprint on history.

BORN ON THIS DAY
- **Martha Stewart** — retail businesswoman
- **Tony Bennett** — singer
- **Tom Brady** — football player
- **Martin Sheen** — actor
- **Ryan Lochte** — Olympic swimmer

FRIENDS & FAMILY

AUGUST 4

Limitations are merely opportunities to grow. I use them as stepping-stones to success.
—Louise Hay

BORN ON THIS DAY

- **Barack Obama**
  U.S. president
- **Louis Armstrong**
  trumpeter, vocalist
- **Billy Bob Thornton**
  actor
- **Jeff Gordon**
  race car driver
- **Anna Sui**
  fashion designer

FRIENDS & FAMILY

PERSONALITY
Originality and a good sense of humor make you very popular in your social circle, among your friends, and in your family. You have a flair for getting people together in an entertaining atmosphere and bringing about connections between individuals that really promote a good time wherever you are. This is not meant to imply that your sole ideal in life is to network and make your existence a mere party for pleasure, for you have your serious side, too. On that side, you pursue the illumination that comes from a sharp observation of life and the study of the works of the great thinkers of all times. You enjoy good books, both fictional stories and philosophies of life by the great thinkers of the past and present. You tend to have a balanced mind and to lead a well-rounded existence, enjoying a delightful equilibrium between your emotions and your intellect. When you express your higher nature, few people can lead as productive a life as you.

LIFE PATH
You are shrewd and intellectual, with refined tastes and high ideals. You are positive, somewhat opinionated, and willful but fair and generous. You would do a good deed and use your best efforts to keep others from knowing about it. You are well-liked and have many trusted contacts and helpers. Your ancestry and family tree mean a lot to you.

DESTINY
Although strenuous effort will be necessary, you can accomplish wonders because you have the required will and self-confidence. Concentrate on your own interests rather than on the activities of your friends, which may be a distraction at times. Do not feel obliged to "keep up with the Joneses." Sometimes be a little bit more secretive and keep your immediate, as well as your future, plans to yourself. Decisions to purchase anything of value must coincide with your ultimate goals in life, not just temporary desires.

KARMIC LESSON
Quick to accurately perceive a situation, you see which way events are trending. You have good common sense and an alert, active mind. You possess a wealth of funny stories and are naturally witty. You are probably fond of the country, seeing in it many beautiful details that escape others. You are poetical, possessing marked ability in the line of art and design, if you cultivate your talents in that direction. At times you are a dreamer, yet at other times you possess an intensely practical nature. You often do not devote enough time, study, or concentration to one effort. You must take your own time in anything, and you cannot be hurried into doing anything you do not want to. You will have many ups and downs but ultimate success.

SECRET
You are a natural peacemaker who can see both sides to a disagreement. You would make a good judge or arbitrator.

AUGUST 5

Receive your thoughts as guests but treat your desires as children.
—Chinese proverb

BORN ON THIS DAY
- **Neil Armstrong** — astronaut
- **Shirley Ann Jackson** — physicist
- **Patrick Ewing** — basketball player
- **Loni Anderson** — actor
- **Peter Burns** — singer

PERSONALITY
Nothing could give you greater pleasure in this life than to make all the people in your circle happy. Although this is quite a big dream, you visualize yourself as a messenger of happiness who, through education and goodwill, would give this gift to civilization. Limited as any single individual must be, you try to put this ideal into practical expression by doing all you can for the people with whom you associate, and you also try to extend your associations to wider circles. Because of this personality trait, you could be an excellent social service worker, a director of an educational, charitable, or philanthropic institution, and an ideal parent. You are curious and have a desire to experience everything in life that a human being can experience. You can be quite a leader of your social circle because you have original ideas and a great sense of humor.

LIFE PATH
Your judgment is good; you are clever, capable, and observant, and you have the knack of always appearing in a beneficial position for advancement. You are neat and fastidious most of the time. Of an artistic temperament, you are a creative storyteller, popular in your circle of friends. You are not overly demonstrative in your love, but you tend to make your homelife peaceful and harmonious.

DESTINY
From your associations with qualified and gifted people will arise opportunities of which you can take advantage. Enthusiasm will work to facilitate your tasks. Try to merge personal interests with the welfare of the public. Do not let outward appearances blind you to the real worth of an individual. Your daily life will be rich and satisfying because of your spiritual outlook on life.

KARMIC LESSON
You are artistic and very idealistic. You are clever and versatile, taking responsibilities in stride without feeling weighed down under the burden. You have great aspirations and hopes for the future, if only you will stick to your guns and determine to succeed in the line you have chosen as that most suited to you. You are impressionable and psychic and greatly interested in all that pertains to the occult and mysterious. You often have strange dreams that appear to you as symbolic, and in this you are quite right. Work with an expert, and you will gain a great deal of insight into your psyche by learning to understand archetypes and universal myths.

SECRET
You are a person of high ideals, but you are frequently disappointed in life because the conduct of others does not measure up to your own standards.

FRIENDS & FAMILY

AUGUST 6

Life is like a ten-speed bicycle. Most of us have gears we never use.
—Charles M. Schulz

BORN ON THIS DAY
- **Alfred, Lord Tennyson**
  poet
- **Lucille Ball**
  comedian, actor
- **Andy Warhol**
  artist
- **Elliott Smith**
  singer/songwriter
- **M. Night Shyamalan**
  filmmaker

FRIENDS & FAMILY

PERSONALITY
There is an old saying that "variety is the spice of life." Perhaps you have never thought of this phrase in connection with yourself, but it is the real slogan of your life. You like change more than anything. Staying in one place too long becomes a terrific bore to you, and staying anywhere that lacks a lot of action seems to you a real torment. You want to be going and doing all the time. Fortunately, your mental makeup has stamina, and you have the vitality to go through a schedule that others might find absolutely exhausting. You like to direct things logically, and you try to regulate your life with your head rather than your heart. There is one important rule to remember—you must get enough sleep, as your nervous thinking process can keep you wide awake at night.

LIFE PATH
You are emotional and at times tempestuous. You are ambitious for social and intellectual betterment, read with avidity, converse fluently, and take a great deal of interest in planning your social life. You like to lead but will also readily follow anyone whom you regard as a capable leader. You could marry young, selecting a partner who is both positive and self-assertive.

DESTINY
Some of your life gains will seem to be just luck. Actually, they are the rewards you earned over a period of time by constantly applying yourself to the best of your ability. Do not relax your efforts, and do your best on every job you undertake. There are always more rewards than just financial ones for work well done. Jot down the ideas that occur to you for future development into successful endeavors. You can be a source of encouragement to others who may find the going a little rough.

KARMIC LESSON
You are perhaps inclined to talk too much, though what you say is generally interesting. You are studious and love learning new things. At the same time, you like the material plane, enjoy a delicious dinner, and love ease and comfort. You have high aspirations, and with enough stick-to-itiveness, you should succeed. You must learn to keep your word—not that you are untruthful in any way, but it is sometimes difficult for you to keep your promise. Do not procrastinate. You have many hobbies that interest you. Learn to concentrate on one project at a time. Your greatest happiness will come through a partnership with someone whose intellectual capacity matches your own.

SECRET
You are a tireless seeker of romance, with a highly amorous nature. You should marry after a long courtship and certainty of heart, and not on impulse.

AUGUST 7

What is becoming is honest, and whatever is honest must always be becoming.
—Marcus Tullius Cicero

BORN ON THIS DAY
★ **Charlize Theron**
actor

★ **David Duchovny**
actor

★ **Garrison Keillor**
author, humorist, voice actor

★ **Helen Caldicott**
physician, author

★ **Louis Leakey**
paleoanthropologist

PERSONALITY
Quiet and reserved by nature, you seek to establish a way of life that represents reason and sanity, as you probably come from a dysfunctional background. There is nothing unsubtle about your makeup, for you see right through people's actions and right into their hearts and motives. Although this may sound as though you are uncompromising and controlling, you still have a sense of humor, and you can laugh at the mistakes you make. To err, as you know, is human, so continue to tolerate your own errors as much as you do those that other people make. You are very loyal to your friends. Generous in your outlook, you are also unselfish with material things, and you love to make people happy by giving and entertaining. You have a soothing influence, and many people ask your help, your advice, and often your consolation.

LIFE PATH
You are somewhat authoritative but also charming, magnetic, and lovable. You have a sense of humor that enables you to enjoy a joke even when it points your way. You are energetic, always wanting to be doing or making something, and you possess a considerable originality of ideas. While you are capable of deep affection, you do not often let it appear on the surface.

DESTINY
Give ample attention to matters affecting the comfort and beauty of your home, as that gives you great satisfaction and fulfillment and a sense of protection. Proper budgeting will make possible your financial security and the purchase of possessions that will give lasting pleasure. Try to handle your problems by yourself rather than putting yourself under obligation to another.

KARMIC LESSON
You are lively and active, full of efficiency and enthusiasm when you wish to be. You cannot bear to be cooped up all day indoors. You have very high ideals and lofty aspirations, spending a good part of your time in daydreams and imaginary worlds. Yet when you force yourself, you can be eminently practical. You have a great deal of personal magnetism and can usually control those with whom you are thrown into contact, although boundaries are important to you. You are a bit of a "bluff" in spite of the fact that you usually make good on what you say. You are fond of reading, but the quality of books you read is not always the best. You need a little more tidiness and concentration in your makeup. Always stay busy!

SECRET
You may spend much of your life in preliminary work before you discover the field for which you are best suited. Then success will be quick.

FRIENDS & FAMILY

AUGUST 8

The true way to render ourselves happy is to love our work and find in it our pleasure.
—Françoise Bertaut de Motteville

BORN ON THIS DAY
- **Dustin Hoffman**
  actor
- **Shawn Mendes**
  singer
- **Roger Federer**
  tennis player
- **Dino De Laurentiis**
  filmmaker
- **The Edge**
  guitarist

FRIENDS & FAMILY

PERSONALITY
You are a wonderful organizer. This ability is best expressed in material ways along the lines of money management. You can plan the home budget, arrange salary schedules, or make investments—all with equal ease and with profitable results. Because of this unusual capacity for seeing things clearly and with farsightedness, you should devote your talents in directions where they will do the most good. It is therefore better for you to work alone at the head of your household or business, rather than for someone else. You are generally calm in your outlook, but you can become very excited when you think that someone is taking unfair advantage of you. Because you are usually so easygoing, some people think that you can be walked over. That is far from true. You have much pride, and you will not tolerate any indignity to your personality. Don't be cheap.

LIFE PATH
In your immediate circle, you are looked upon as somewhat of an oracle. Your intuitive judgment is wonderfully correct, and you have a positive, convincing way of making people see things as you do. You have great people skills, particularly in the handling of arguments. Your wishes will carry the greatest weight in the family counsels.

DESTINY
Increase in revenue can result from your own efforts. The good opinion of you held by an old friend or distant member of the family may pave the way. Heed well-intentioned advice in all financial matters. Continue your detached attitude toward associates, but lend a sympathetic ear to their problems, if serious. Courtesy is important at all times, and more will be accomplished by arbitration than by dogmatic insistence.

KARMIC LESSON
You love law and order and sometimes can even have a touch of military sternness about you. You might be a natural linguist. Fond of foreign travel and exploration, you are destined to see many places in this world, at different times, and under different circumstances. You have a deep love of nature, which is sincere and capable of great heights of emotion. You want to be always up and doing something. You are also interested in things beyond the realm of the known—the occult and psychic. But you are also a skeptic, critical and cautious and not at all credulous. You are kind and like to help others out of their difficulties. You can be a bit of the jealous type, and your passion is strong.

SECRET
You have a natural charm, which is likely to be a turn-on and to attract many. You should discount such superficial attention and devote yourself to your higher ideals.

AUGUST 9

In the midst of winter, I finally learned that there was within me an invincible summer.
—Albert Camus

BORN ON THIS DAY
- **Whitney Houston**
  singer
- **Anna Kendrick**
  actor, singer
- **Kurtis Blow**
  rapper
- **Michael Kors**
  fashion designer
- **Deion Sanders**
  football player

PERSONALITY
The outstanding traits in your character are your independence, cleverness, and decision-making ability. You like to do things your own way, and you won't be imposed on by anyone. Since you are generally right in the way you figure things out, you should continue to act as an individualist. You also know that it is not fair to try to impose your way of life on anyone else, and so you never take advantage of those who are weaker in character than you are. The mystical side of life interests you quite strongly. You are attracted to psychic phenomena, and you should have aptitude in the study of metaphysics. You undergo periodic moodiness, which can get you down, but as you grow older and your understanding of life evolves, you learn how to overcome such cycles by developing greater compassion and deeper gratitude.

LIFE PATH
You are adamant and insistent, sometimes disagreeable under opposition. You give way to moods at times but recover quickly. You have a keen sense of justice, chafing under the wrongs of others. You are very definite in your likes and dislikes and wholehearted and vigorous in your relationships. Weird art, music, and movies interest you greatly.

DESTINY
Learn to utilize your self-reliance and your intuition in money matters. You can expect ample reward for conscientious business endeavors and responsibilities. Take the initiative in establishing friendships. Do not become overconfident and make careless mistakes. When money is involved, be sure your information is accurate. Most social activities will be enjoyable, but do not spend more than you should on entertainment.

KARMIC LESSON
You have a very good head for tuning in to people's true motives; you are seldom disappointed in your estimate of a person. Observant and intuitive, you are a good judge of human nature. You see people's intentions and can easily pick out an honest person in a crowd. You are a great schmoozer and a flirt, especially in your younger days. You might not be as great a student as you could be. You are a good host and an entertaining companion. You like the best of everything, and you like to live luxuriously. You have a great deal of concern for those in distress, but you do not allow your heart to run away with your head. Yours is a strong, rather than a sweet, nature.

SECRET
You may be destined to succeed in a land other than the one in which you were born. Fortunately, you have the courage to make the change.

FRIENDS & FAMILY

AUGUST 10

Life is not so short but that there is always time enough for courtesy.
—Ralph Waldo Emerson

BORN ON THIS DAY
- **Herbert Hoover**
  U.S. president
- **Antonio Banderas**
  actor
- **Andrew Sullivan**
  author
- **Kylie Jenner**
  media personality
- **Rosanna Arquette**
  actor

FRIENDS & FAMILY

◉ PERSONALITY
You know how to regulate your life in such a way that you achieve eventual happiness and success. Your mental acumen is strong, and your emotional impulses are sensitive and compassionate. You will usually succeed in making the most of every opportunity that comes your way for development, self-improvement, and the establishment of a rational and satisfactory philosophy of life. Opposition and hard knocks are part of life, and you will face those in your experience with courage and determination. It is possible for you to rise from obscurity to fame, because you have tenacity and farsightedness. Good judgment and a businesslike attitude guarantee your attaining many of the goals and ideals that interest you and spur you on.

◉ LIFE PATH
You have good managerial ability and sound judgment, and you like to take a prominent part in anything in which you are interested. You are a good negotiator and are convincing in an argument, which you get into more than you would like. You have generous impulses but look out for your own interests very carefully. Your work life is interesting to you, but you also have many outside, independent interests.

◉ DESTINY
Do not hesitate to volunteer your services when a job comes up that you know you can handle well—it will lead to an award or reward. You can talk about your abilities without being conceited. The rays of Mercury's energies on your birthday favor mental alertness and the turning of theories into action. Keep public and personal matters separate so that there cannot be any possible discord between the two.

◉ KARMIC LESSON
You are very persistent and persevering. You are clever and resourceful, seldom beaten down by circumstances. For yourself, you want the best things in life. You have great determination and never know when you are beaten. You are also very dramatic and might like to complain. You have a strong imagination and good taste and may be able to critique well. You can hold a circle of listeners when you tell a story better than most people you know. You are never more at home than when taking in life at its best and in its rainbow of experiences.

◉ SECRET
Control your impulses and conserve your resources, and you will be happy. You love the free, uncommitted life.

AUGUST 11

Some people are always grumbling because roses have thorns; I am thankful that thorns have roses.
—Alphonse Karr

BORN ON THIS DAY

- **Chris Hemsworth**
  actor
- **Viola Davis**
  actor
- **Hulk Hogan**
  wrestler, actor
- **Steve Wozniak**
  tech entrepreneur
- **Jerry Falwell, Sr.**
  televangelist

PERSONALITY
You are likely to have a life filled with many and varying experiences and unexpected changes. As you go along from year to year, you learn how to handle situations with tact and intelligence. The ups and downs that everyone must face in a world of competition eventually become experiences that you find a challenge rather than a torment. The main trait you should develop in your character is your confidence in yourself. By making each experience a stepping-stone to greater wisdom, you will evolve a way of life that gives you ever-increasing determination, courage, and tenacity. These traits bolster your self-confidence to the point where you can act independently. Life for you will seem much richer and more significant after you have passed middle age. Because you have a strongly emotional nature, you express yourself demonstratively by "acting out." Be sure that you do not waste your affections on someone who is undeserving; pick your companions and choose your life partner with great care.

LIFE PATH
You have clear-cut ideas and opinions, but you are somewhat diffident, too. You are determined, persevering, and energetic, fond of physical activity and recreation, kind and affectionate, empathetic, and generally good-natured. You will not fall in love easily, but when you do love it will be with much commitment.

DESTINY
You will have challenging possibilities. Rely on your logical thinking, and use time-tested methods to get the best results, even though you often have strong intuitions. Do not force issues, but be on the lookout for chances to advance the causes you believe in. You may make considerable financial gain in your life from a small product you invent.

KARMIC LESSON
You are sincere and honest and have strong convictions, which you feel it is your duty to express. You have a wide and deep sympathetic nature, which makes you interested in humanity and will probably place psychology and healing therapies among your main focuses in life. You are kind and extremely fond of teaching children. You would make a good parent. You are intuitive, fearless, and brave. You have inventive abilities and could make a success of whatever you undertake. You are at times dogged and persevering but need lots of encouragement, too. You are an original, and you detest copying thoughts or ideas from others.

SECRET
You are a person with a love of rhythm. If you manifested an early flair for dancing or music, you could make your mark with that talent.

FRIENDS & FAMILY

AUGUST 12

The punishment of the liar is that he eventually believes his own lies.
—Elbert Hubbard

BORN ON THIS DAY

★ **Erwin Schrödinger**
physicist

★ **George Soros**
billionaire philanthropist

★ **Cecil B. DeMille**
filmmaker

★ **George Hamilton**
actor

★ **Pete Sampras**
tennis player

FRIENDS & FAMILY

PERSONALITY

You are very creative. You possess more than an ordinary ability in a certain area. A brilliant imagination, a good vocabulary, and natural talent make it possible for you to acquire prominence in the world of culture if you develop the innate abilities that have been endowed upon you. If you have not discovered the creative talent in your makeup, you should certainly get some coaching to help bring to your attention the type of work to which you are best suited. Also, if you have brought out your ability to some small degree, you should make up your mind to develop it further. You can help others along their own path of development because you see their problems, and you have an analytical mind that can find the solution to abstruse and puzzling knots.

LIFE PATH

You are sometimes abrupt and quick in your speech, but it is not your intention to hurt anyone's feelings. You are methodical and careful in your plans. You love travel but want your loved ones to have the same pleasure. You are quite a romantic and are creatively demonstrative in your personal relationships. You like most people, and they in turn find you interesting and helpful.

DESTINY

An unusual opportunity can result from an important but unexpected interview. Constructive Uranus rays favor new ways of doing things, so do not be afraid to take a step just because it is in an unaccustomed direction. Cooperative undertakings with family members can be profitable for all concerned. Tackle difficult problems as soon as they arise as a preventive measure, so that you do not get overwhelmed. Do not wait for them to work themselves out.

KARMIC LESSON

You have a dramatic ability and a good voice and could make your mark as a speaker or lecturer. Politics also may have a great attraction for you. You are obstinate and at times cannot be made to see another point of view. Try to see things from the other standpoint. You are very cautious in all your undertakings and cannot be led into anything until you have investigated it thoroughly. For this reason, you will probably succeed in business, and there is every probability that you will be good at making money. You can mix with all kinds of people equally well. You are inclined to be a seducer, but you are capable of great love and affection, just the same.

SECRET

You possess the rare combination of an intuitive and analytical mind. You could be successful both in business and in your private life.

AUGUST 13

It's not how much talent I have, but how I will use the talent that I have.
—Anonymous

◉ PERSONALITY

You dislike the run-of-the-mill, humdrum variety of experience and have a penchant for finding the different, the unusual, and the colorful. You like to associate with extraordinary individuals; you like designs and patterns and objects that are different and not easily obtainable; and you want to lead a life that will make a lasting impression for its individuality. No one can blame you for having these standards or hopes, for you have been born with a mind that is tantamount to genius. You have many talents; in fact, you are so versatile that you frequently wonder just which field of endeavor you should conquer. This can be a serious drawback to your progress, for vacillation and indecision can defeat you. Therefore, it is your solemn duty to consider the one thing you like best and then specialize in that. You can, in this way, become a groundbreaker, get noteworthy attention, and achieve your highest ambition.

◉ LIFE PATH

You are trustworthy, energetic, and determined. You desire to excel in any undertaking, and your aims and ideals are high. You possess a very sentimental nature, are very loyal to your friends, and love your family above everything else. Sympathetic and bighearted, you are adored by children.

◉ DESTINY

When you are in contact with people who waver in their ideas, you can help them make up their minds by giving them insights into the best direction to go. Because you are convincing in a tactful way, you convert many associates to your way of thinking. Give your duties sustained and undivided attention until they are finished in every detail. You are probably a perfectionist, which can sometimes stop you from finishing a project.

◉ KARMIC LESSON

You have an unusual penetration of perception. You are a good judge of human nature. You are diplomatic and tactful. There is a strong spiritual streak in your nature that seeks to find expression. At the same time, you have a way with finding bargains, and it is rare that someone gets the best of you in a deal. You are naturally affectionate, kind, and sympathetic. You must never backbite or whine, as you will regret it for days. You are original and inventive, very fond of different cultures and ways of thinking. You have a wide range of interests—perhaps too wide, for concentration is the secret of all success. Do not scatter your forces over a variety of topics.

◉ SECRET

You have a refined nature and dislike egotists and bragging. You would do well with gardening or cooking for a hobby, as it calms you.

BORN ON THIS DAY

★ **Fidel Castro**
Cuban revolutionary

★ **Alfred Hitchcock**
filmmaker

★ **Annie Oakley**
sharpshooter

★ **Alan Shearer**
footballer

★ **Phil Taylor**
darts player

FRIENDS & FAMILY

AUGUST 14

He who promises runs in debt.
—The Talmud

BORN ON THIS DAY
- **Magic Johnson**
  basketball player
- **Steve Martin**
  actor, comedian
- **Halle Berry**
  actor
- **John Henry "Doc" Holliday**
  gunfighter, gambler
- **Mila Kunis**
  actor

FRIENDS & FAMILY

PERSONALITY
Your highest ideal in life is to see justice and fairness established for the world's less fortunate people. Although you know that you cannot attain this single-handedly, you do everything in your immediate power to achieve this wonderful goal. In your family, in your relationships, at work, and in your social life, you make every effort to see that people are treated with equity and that all get a fair-and-square deal. You have a highly developed power of persuasion, and you use it to promote better relationships all around you. In your working life, you do not neglect yourself as some others with your workload might do. You know that money and other material things are needed to lead a full and satisfactory life, and you combine your idealism with a practicality that is very sensible. You should go far in life no matter what you choose for the expression of your talents.

LIFE PATH
You have good organizing ability and possess lots of vim and vigor. You are spontaneous, soulful, and optimistic. Culture and refinement mean a great deal to you, and you are fond of the arts and of artists, too. Things superficial, temporary, and frivolous do not interest you. You care a great deal for people, and when you love, your love is deep and profound.

DESTINY
Financial prospects will be good along the path of your career, and you should take advantage of them. Your accommodating nature makes it hard for you to say no to friends who seek your companionship. However, you should be careful to not sacrifice your own welfare to the desires of others too much. One of the best fields of endeavor for you is that of social service or any of the helping professions, as you have the sympathy and understanding to be of use to those in need.

KARMIC LESSON
You are firm and determined in your actions and in your life, going into everything in a hearty, enthusiastic manner. You have a fresh, breezy way about you, which should win you much popularity wherever you go. You are sincere, affectionate, and capable of feeling very deeply. You are generous, and so long as you have a dollar, you are glad to share it with your friends. You are fond of children and understand them, and they in turn understand you. You could make money easily, if you approach it in the right way, as with your large group of acquaintances and magnetic personality, you should be able to find a satisfying livelihood wherever you are. Learn the value of healthy habits and living as if you were in nature.

SECRET
You have an aggressive spirit, marching without deviation toward a fixed goal. This nature, when moved, can generously win you material resources.

AUGUST 15

The most unhappy of all men is he who believes himself to be so.
—David Hume

PERSONALITY
You have unusual strength of character. Because you have so much determination and tenacity and a militant attitude, you will let very little stand in the way of attaining any goal that you have set up for yourself. You are especially talented in the fields of endeavor in which words are of importance in the process of changing people's minds. You should do well in the communication field, in the vocal professions, such as movies, TV, teaching, and lecturing, and in the silent professions, such as creative writing. You have tact, patience, and discrimination. You can sway others to your way of looking at things and might make a good motivational speaker. You never forget a friend. You have a deep well of love within you, which demands expression at any cost.

LIFE PATH
You are aggressive, aspiring, versatile, and adaptable, which to those less sure of themselves sometimes makes you seem arbitrary. You are not easily disheartened, even though your plans often go wrong. You come right back with some different method of accomplishing your purpose. You love to create sanctuaries and gardens and are most content when surrounded by beauty in all forms.

DESTINY
Associates impressed by your determination will help you go to the next level and attain a position of prestige and influence. Cooperation is important in social and business relationships, but maintain your independence of spirit and action. Risky financial speculation is unwise for you, but you can gamble instead with your talents and time. Always work to improve your proficiency in activities that interest you, whether or not this seems practical.

KARMIC LESSON
You have great natural gifts, which you should appreciate and prize. Earlier in life than most, you must learn to conquer your bad habits, find yourself, plan out what you want to do in life, and then set about accomplishing your aim. Never let side issues interfere with the main objectives of your life. You are one of the born cultural creatives. Do not disappoint yourself by neglecting the cultivation of the gifts you have; grasp the opportunities that come your way. You will have great staying power and the ability to work. You like work, but it must show measurable results. You have force of character and personal magnetism.

SECRET
You are a lover of harmonious living and will surprisingly give in even when right to preserve peace. You make a devoted partner to a person you deem worthy of respect.

BORN ON THIS DAY
- **Napoleon Bonaparte** French military and political leader
- **Julia Childs** cook, TV personality
- **Jennifer Lawrence** actor
- **Ben Affleck** actor
- **Deborah Messing** actor

FRIENDS & FAMILY

AUGUST 16

The solution of the problem of life is life itself. Life is not attained by reason and analysis, but first of all by living.
—Thomas Merton

BORN ON THIS DAY

★ **Madonna**
singer, actor

★ **Steve Carell**
actor

★ **Angela Bassett**
actor

★ **James Cameron**
filmmaker

★ **Kathie Lee Gifford**
talk show host

FRIENDS & FAMILY

PERSONALITY
If you had your way, you would bring prosperity to everyone you know. Your philosophy of life is that people were born not to suffer but to be happy. You live up to this philosophy in your personal life to the greatest extent that you can, and you do your best to bring joy to others. When you face disappointments and delays in your plans, hopes, and dreams, you never let it discourage you or get you down. You pick right up again and resume your efforts. Because you are efficient and methodical, you usually get the most done with the minimum of effort. In this way, you can arrange your daily routine in such a manner that you have time left for the working out of your aspirations after the chores of the day have been done.

LIFE PATH
You are systematic, attentive to details, painstaking, and generally accurate. You are not in a hurry and will not be driven or pushed. You will be an indulgent parent, a loving partner, and a loyal friend; you are well-liked by your circle of associates. Surprisingly, you have a quick temper, at times, and are easily upset over trifles. But you get over such situations quickly.

DESTINY
You work to ensure that your reputation is above reproach. You will discover that to be successful in business, the esteem of your associates is as important as good work. Mull over personal problems in your mind, but be careful not to become too introspective. Arrange for plenty of happy social gatherings with friends and family, as this gives both you and them pleasure. Make plans for your financial future with specific targets and goals in mind.

KARMIC LESSON
You are penetrating and able to focus, and you have a good mind for facts and figures. You might shine in construction or as an engineer. If you go into science, you will doubtless attain a high position, probably in some physical science, since you are very material and matter-of-fact in your view of life and of this universe. You are many-sided and take an active interest in a variety of topics. You are too sensitive to slights and should not feel hurt so easily. You may not have a regular life, as you are fitted for one filled with ups and downs and variety of all kinds. At some point in your life, you are destined to travel a great deal for your job.

SECRET
Avoid the arrogance that comes with being born with too many talents, and cultivate the one that can bring the highest financial returns.

AUGUST 17

The mind is not a vessel to be filled but a fire to be kindled.
—Plutarch

PERSONALITY
You prefer to get your way in life by being subtle, diplomatic, and tactful rather than by being aggressive or pushy. You can go much further along the path of success by using your judicious methods than by being domineering. You do not care to reveal your mental processes or your feelings to strangers or even to relatives unless the latter are very close to you. You believe in letting actions speak louder than words. One of the great pleasures in your life is a communion that you have with natural beauty, the scenery of the countryside, and the pet animals you bond with. The little things in life can give you much more pleasure than most. It is not necessary that an experience be exciting for you to enjoy it. Your sense of humor is typical of your outlook.

LIFE PATH
You are fair-minded, charitable, kind, often shy, and always modest. No matter how capable you are or how sure of success, you will never assert yourself or push others out of the way to get to the forefront. You need a bit more concentration, more and more confidence, and compatible friends. You can be very affectionate but are undemonstrative until you really trust someone.

DESTINY
Added responsibilities, even though they may occasionally seem overly demanding, will add to the development of your character. Equally important, they will give you the opportunity to reveal your hidden capabilities. Financial remuneration will follow. Expressions of generosity will be well repaid. There are pleasant and worthwhile experiences for you in the form of long-distance relationships; do not pass them up.

KARMIC LESSON
You are kindhearted and have much talent, but you do not always make the most of your abilities and opportunities. You are inclined to wait for something to turn up, instead of turning it up yourself, not realizing that "God/dess helps those who help themselves" and that you must keep things moving to make a success in life. So long as you drift, you will never succeed. Make up your mind to do this once and for all, and your desires will begin to manifest, as you have the ability to do a great deal once you make up your mind to. Do not be too eager to please, as you will be imposed upon until you learn the art of saying no when occasion demands.

SECRET
You have a curious mind. You are creative, though you would not use that word to describe yourself and would be most successful in writing or working with writers.

BORN ON THIS DAY
- **Robert De Niro** — actor
- **Sean Penn** — actor
- **Mae West** — actor
- **Maureen O'Hara** — actor
- **Jon Gruden** — football coach

FRIENDS & FAMILY

AUGUST 18

Great minds master their circumstances.
—Paul Leicester

BORN ON THIS DAY
* **Robert Redford**
  actor
* **Meriwether Lewis**
  explorer
* **Roberto Clemente**
  baseball player
* **Patrick Swayze**
  actor
* **Christian Slater**
  actor

FRIENDS & FAMILY

PERSONALITY
Although you are generally agreeable and tactful, you can be very stubborn. There are streaks of obstinacy latent in your makeup that can make you very hard to get along with. These traits come out when you are roused to anger or when you think that someone is taking undue advantage of you. Pride is one of the mainsprings of your character, but this also has its negative side, and you should carefully avoid letting your pride develop into being overbearing. There are times when you will dare to take almost any kind of chance. Now, that may be considered courage, but it may also be plain foolishness. Use your intense and lively mind and your sharp sense of judgment to help you avoid plunging into experiences that might prove costly and painful in the long run.

LIFE PATH
You are courageous and stronghearted, opinionated in your tastes, resourceful, and intellectual. You read good books, see people involved in education as friends, and strive to improve your condition. You are of a philosophical turn of mind and always want to know "Why?" You will have fulfilling relationships with a few who really understand you.

DESTINY
Draw up a practical plan of operation and stick to it. You will be able to hurdle barriers with grace and speed if you take them one at a time. Do not be afraid of hard work. Tasks well done will be followed by success and rewards. Although you may have envied others in the past because they had an easier life, you will realize that one gets out of life what one puts into it.

KARMIC LESSON
You are quick, original, and emotional in your speech and actions. You are a good judge of human nature, witty, resourceful, and intuitive. You have a good grasp of details, but your specialty is your ability to manage large enterprises and long-range schemes. You feel that you could do great things if only you were removed from your present cramped environment. You are apt to trust others too easily at times and must be careful that you are not led astray in this manner when you are feeling insecure. You will doubtless make a very happy and successful partnership, early in life, with one who understands your stubborn streak. Your love nature is strong and will be gratified fully only when you meet your match.

SECRET
You tend to weigh things carefully before a decision and then to be fixed in your determination. But sometimes you wait too long.

AUGUST 19

Love can live without language, but words alone keep hate alive.
—Anonymous

◉ PERSONALITY

Although you feel that you possess rather unusual qualities, you have a natural modesty that keeps you from being very vocal about them. You prefer to show your good traits by actions rather than by words. This also applies to your feelings, for you don't talk a lot about how you feel toward people you are fond of but show how you feel by kindnesses and polite attention. You have a great deal of pride and independence, and you hate having to ask anyone for a favor. You would rather do everything for yourself than ask someone to help you. As time goes on, your disposition mellows. A love of reading, study, and carrying on the activities connected with your favorite hobby keep you at home a lot. The life of the social butterfly doesn't appeal to you very much, although you enjoy inviting your old friends to your home whenever you can.

◉ LIFE PATH

You are self-reliant, observant, and systematic. You can, at times, be impulsive, sometimes even quick-tempered, but you are always willing to listen to reason. You take great pleasure in making healthy food and devising recipes and will give your partner and friends your undivided attention, nurturing, and devotion.

◉ DESTINY

Your analytical ability will be put to good use exposing false motives and unsound ideas in your workplace. You can periodically indulge your curiosity to see new places and try different things. However, loyalty to family and old friends will always be of equal importance. Politely but firmly decline the favor of any powerful person who may wish to put you under obligation. You are not the kind of person to permit yourself to be imposed on.

◉ KARMIC LESSON

On the outside, you have an impetuous and imperious nature, which causes you to appear, at times, puffed up to those around you, but it is only your habitual way of presenting yourself. You are often misunderstood because of this, as you can be surprisingly shy. Try to be more clear, open, and democratic. Never hold a grudge but deal with people's actions that you do not like honestly at the time they occur and state your grievance. You are very fond of reading and might make your living from communications or in publishing. You are affectionate and home loving. You demand a great deal of honesty from others but are willing to give the same in return. You must develop more emotional stability and poise.

◉ SECRET

Your skills reside in your fingers, and when these skills are accompanied by desire and instinct, you would make an excellent musician, jewelry maker, or sculptor.

BORN ON THIS DAY

- **Bill Clinton**
  U.S. president
- **Coco Chanel**
  fashion designer
- **Renée Richards**
  tennis player
- **Gene Rodenberry**
  TV screenwriter, producer
- **Ogden Nash**
  poet

FRIENDS & FAMILY

AUGUST 20

All our dreams can come true, if we have the courage to pursue them.
—Walt Disney

BORN ON THIS DAY
- **Benjamin Harrison**
  U.S. president
- **H.P. Lovecraft**
  author
- **Demi Lovato**
  singer
- **Robert Plant**
  singer
- **Isaac Hayes**
  singer/songwriter

FRIENDS & FAMILY

PERSONALITY
You are somewhat demanding in most respects. It is not in your philosophy of life to compromise with any person or any situation. You think you know the best way to do things, the proper way to handle people, and the right thing that should be done. Putting all of these concepts together, you can understand why life to you is a matter of black and white, right or wrong, with no in between. This does not make for popularity with people who won't agree with the way you think, but you feel that anyone who regulates his or her life according to standards lower than yours is not worth knowing anyhow. You could go far in life as you define success, and you should have a very good influence on your life partner, your relatives, your children, and most of the people whom you allow to become your intimate friends.

LIFE PATH
You are fond of going on distant journeys, both in reality and in your daydreams. You want to be sure that the people you associate with are worthy of your attention and love before you confer it on them. You will be well-liked by people of every persuasion. Act on your ambitions, for your aims are high, noble, and attainable.

DESTINY
Homelife and friendships will receive positive stimulation under the rays of Venus on this birthday. Your moments of great contentment will include periods of leisure when you are relaxed enough to appreciate the beauty and comfort of affectionate, nurturing relationships. You also will know the satisfaction of work well done, and financially rewarding transactions may often be completed more efficiently by distance than by in-person meetings. You make the most of technology in your business. Do not indulge your tendency to lend money without proper collateral.

KARMIC LESSON
You are many-sided and interested in a variety of subjects. You are forceful and energetic. While your lifework may be something entirely different, you are distinctly interested in politics. You have good taste and discrimination. You have a good head for organization and supervision. In this line of endeavor, you could prove to be very successful and could make a good deal of money during your life. You are kind and sympathetic to those who deserve it and can cut off those who you feel do not. A lot of people envy your honesty and directness. You are very straightforward in all your dealings.

SECRET
You are effective in understanding legal matters and could make a good lawyer. You also have a talent for getting people to buy what you are selling.

AUGUST 21

You have not fulfilled every duty unless you have fulfilled that of being pleasant.
—Charles Buxton

PERSONALITY
You like to have good times, but you make a sensible balance between your social life and the tasks and chores that fall to everyone. Because you have a naturally sunny disposition, most people like you, and you get along well with your friends, neighbors, and relatives. There is a high degree of originality about you. For example, you can think up new and efficient ways of doing things. When you are enthusiastic about your work, a person, or a hobby, you can devote your entire attention to your enthusiasm, and you seem to fire up others with the same feeling. Inspiration runs high in your makeup, and you can be very creative when you are in the right mood. Because you are known never to break a confidence, many people tell you their innermost secrets. You should be careful about the way you handle money, because in your moods of generosity, you can give too much and be a very big spender.

LIFE PATH
You are critical, somewhat opinionated, aggressive, adaptable, and very unselfish. Your judgment is generally good. You are very magnetic and have great power for good or evil. People instinctively follow your lead. You are fond of music and like your home to be bright and attractive. Your married life will be pleasant and happy—but you are unconventional in your relationships.

DESTINY
The big changes that will come into your life will mostly be fortunate ones, even if they do not appear to be so at the time. Your career is one of innovations and departures from established practices. Beneficent Uranus vibrations on your birthday ensure progress and good results from independent action, so try to work for yourself if you can. Do not be goaded into useless disputes.

KARMIC LESSON
You are tireless in your pursuit of esoteric knowledge. You are a hard worker and have a great deal of patience. You are original and inventive. You will have many ups and downs in your life, and you will probably find that the month of June is sometimes not always a fortunate one for you. December could probably be the happiest month. You have strong emotions and are rather too ready to fly into a rage when things do not go right with you. You have a peculiar form of common sense combined with innate perception, which is called the possession of the third eye. Live up to your ideals and goals, and yours should be a successful life.

SECRET
You have a commanding nature and always appear to be in charge. You can be stern in professional or business activities but tender and emotional in your homelife.

BORN ON THIS DAY
- **Kenny Rogers**
  singer, actor
- **Wilt Chamberlain**
  basketball player
- **Usain Bolt**
  runner
- **Robert Lewandowski**
  soccer player
- **The Winklevoss Twins**
  investors

FRIENDS & FAMILY

AUGUST 22

We must wake up knowing we have work to do and go to bed knowing we've done it.
—Audre Lorde

BORN ON THIS DAY
- **Claude Debussy**
  composer
- **Ray Bradbury**
  author
- **Tori Amos**
  singer
- **Dorothy Parker**
  poet
- **Giada De Laurentiis**
  celebrity chef

FRIENDS & FAMILY

PERSONALITY
You have wonderful willpower, which you can use to command any situation in which destiny places you. This ability makes you a role model for more people than you know and can take you right to the top of the ladder of success in your chosen field of activity. No one will ever misunderstand you, because you are so definite in the traits that make up your character and you are so clear in your manner of expressing yourself. You enjoy being with people, and you give them a lot of pleasure because you have a great sense of humor. As a matter of fact, you may easily be tempted to let this social popularity lead you from your goals because you enjoy good times so much. You should be very careful to avoid frittering away your time and talents on circumstances that hold no returns for you. Natural diplomacy and innate intelligence can bring you rich rewards; don't waste them.

LIFE PATH
You are fastidious, self-reliant, popular, and amiable. You have winning ways and offhand, humorous methods of doing the things you want to do and of avoiding trouble when most people would find it. You have the knack of making other people see things as you do. You will inspire deep love and tender devotion.

DESTINY
Do not confuse impatience with impetuosity. It will usually be to your advantage to seize passing opportunities for advancement—don't let them get away. But you should not barge into unfamiliar undertakings just because you want a change of pace. Occupy part of your leisure time with reading and personal correspondence—stay up to date with your social networking. More exciting recreations also are good. However, limit them, and be conservative in your spending.

KARMIC LESSON
You have force of character, usually succeeding in getting your way. You are many-sided and can be all things to all people, like a mirror. You are good at figures and would excel at investments, professional gambling, or as an accountant. You can make and keep many friends. You have the ability in you to make or break another person, so be kind to those who deserve it. You are resourceful and ingenious. You feel things very keenly and should train yourself to be less sensitive to behavior you find offensive, which you may find is not intentionally so, if you take the time to understand where the offender is coming from. You must use your mind more and be more intellectual. You are passionate and lustful by nature and must learn to keep this under control.

SECRET
You have nurturing impulses but are more inclined to be hypercritical of the conduct of others. You would make a thorough, if unpopular, teacher or trainer.

AUGUST 23

Nothing in life is to be feared. It is only to be understood.
—Marie Curie

PERSONALITY
You were born on the cusp between two signs, Leo and Virgo. This means that you share, to a certain extent, the traits and characteristics of both, as the Sun was on the borderline between these two segments of the zodiac when you were born. Courage and ambition mark your character very strongly. You are deeply motivated by your intellect, and you rarely act from impulse or strong feelings alone. You analyze and think things out before you act, and as a result, you rarely get into scrapes or embarrassing situations. You are generally economical but not a penny-pincher. You want value for what you spend, whether that is money, time, or effort, and you're right in having this attitude. You are very selective in choosing your companions, and you are inclined to be loving but also critical of your close friends.

LIFE PATH
You have a keen, inquiring mind and balanced energy. You probably take care of your body, are fond of out-of-door life and sport, and skillful in many athletic contests. You are resourceful and discriminating, form very select, close friendships, love your home and pets profoundly, and will be unusually compatible with your partner, especially later in life.

DESTINY
You will benefit from relying on your intuitions. Cultivate friendships only with people who are open-minded in their outlook. Combine your ideas with theirs. The resulting compilation can be profitable to all concerned. Before any action is taken that will involve financial expenditures, consult someone with proven success and experience in such matters.

KARMIC LESSON
You have a strong desire for power, and if you crave a lot of money, it is largely because of the power it would bring with it. You cannot stand being scolded, but while young it was necessary to get your attention, and it has led to your noteworthy self-discipline and good character. You are extremely fond of art, literature, good cuisine and wine, fine clothing, and all the joys and comforts. You love all the good things of this life, which you can attain. You cannot stick to one occupation and sometimes cannot stick with one lover for long. You must learn to concentrate above all else and not get so easily bored or distracted. Develop your mind more, and do not allow yourself to be overwhelmed by emotions and impulses as you do.

SECRET
You have a natural interest in research and investigative affairs. To be happy, you must find a partner of similar desires.

BORN ON THIS DAY
- **Kobe Bryant** — basketball player
- **Gene Kelly** — actor
- **River Phoenix** — actor
- **Keith Moon** — drummer
- **Seth Curry** — basketball player

FRIENDS & FAMILY

AUGUST 24

There is something better than getting on in the world—that is getting above the world.
—Anonymous

BORN ON THIS DAY

- **Dave Chappelle**
  comedian
- **Paulo Coelho**
  author
- **Stephen Fry**
  actor, comedian
- **Marsha P. Johnson**
  gay rights activist
- **Howard Zinn**
  historian
- **Cal Ripken, Jr.**
  baseball player

FRIENDS & FAMILY

PERSONALITY

You are distinguished by a quick wit and a ready use of words to make an impression or make someone who is acting foolish regret doing so. You would be a splendid critic of drama, movies, art, or literature because you see the ridiculous so clearly and so quickly. You never go to extremes in anything you do, because you can so readily see how extremes cause problems. In fact, your own sense of humor always saves you from appearing foolish because you can visualize yourself as others see you. You are known for being practical, methodical, clever, and industrious. You could be a success in business, but in managing the home or real estate issues, you are also sensible, matter-of-fact, and not by any means a dreamer. You know how to get things done.

LIFE PATH

You are affectionate and farsighted, accurate in your judgment, and fair and honorable in your dealings with others. You love to be creative and may possess considerable talent. You are bright and humorous, and people like to have you around. At home you are kind, loving, and solicitous for the happiness and welfare of the ones you love.

DESTINY

You can expect the fulfillment of many of your dreams. Success will be always accompanied by new ambitions. You love to dream and plan. Do not be content to take a selfish attitude regarding optimism. Share your faith in the future with others. An abundance of good things will whet your appetite for more. The joy of achievement will be experienced in both domestic and social undertakings.

KARMIC LESSON

You are peace loving and desire to lead a calm, contented life, free from strife of all kinds. You would make a good speaker, as you have a pleasant speaking voice, a good presence, and a magnetic personality. You are intellectual and want to know everything about everything. You are tender, faithful, and loving and would be very good at home design if you have a place of your own. Yet, yours is a life full of longings and yearnings. You are very idealistic in your aspirations, and perhaps for this reason you find it so hard in your present environment to obtain what you crave. You are softhearted and sympathetic.

SECRET

You have a sharp wit, which would be placed to the best advantage in motivating others to be their best. You are moved to take action chiefly by materialistic impulses.

AUGUST 25

We must learn to live together as brothers or perish together as fools.
—Martin Luther King, Jr.

BORN ON THIS DAY
- **Leonard Bernstein**
  conductor
- **Sean Connery**
  actor
- **Elvis Costello**
  singer/songwriter
- **Gene Simmons**
  singer
- **Rachael Ray**
  celebrity chef

PERSONALITY
In the quiet of your own home, studio, or workshop, you like to make meticulous plans and work on them uninterrupted. Noise and rackets distract you more than most people and you feel that your time is being wasted with every interruption. You may not be seeking fame or fortune, but you want all the conveniences of modern life for yourself and your family. You feel that you and yours should not have less than others. Temptation along the lines of overindulgence, emotionally or in other appetites, fails to lure you from the rather simple life you choose to lead. You hardly ever act from impulsiveness, and this is a good thing, for you have been endowed with a creative mind, and it would be a shame to waste your brilliance.

LIFE PATH
You are fond of small gatherings with good friends and like to be amused by their quirks. You are careful of appearances, able to discuss many topics, prone to making sudden changes that surprise everyone, demonstrative in your love, and bitter in your hatred. You are affable, pleasant, and diplomatic and seldom allow any perturbation to show on the surface. You should not be in any hurry about marrying, but when you do marry, you will be very loyal.

DESTINY
You will appreciate the security and warmth of your home and work hard to make it cozy and function well. You will often be remembered by the gifts you buy and not just because you will sometimes allow sentiment to cause you to ignore practical considerations. It is your thoughtfulness, and not the cost, that makes them precious. Business matters will be conducted with goodwill on all sides, as you are trustworthy and have a good track record.

KARMIC LESSON
You are a careful observer of human nature but inclined to be surprisingly cynical and caustic about people you feel are cheap or cruel. Try to look for the best instead of the worst. Both sides are there; it remains only to choose which side we wish to see. Realism is all right in its place, but ideals have a place also. You have a retentive memory and a great capacity for work. You are cautious and would make a great healer. You are extremely affected by nature, plants, and animals and like nothing better than spending a day in the country. You have a good deal of patience and would be perfectly suited to being a teacher of students who genuinely want to learn, as you have the gift of making things clear, and younger people respond well to you.

SECRET
A love of games will take you away from your more important work. Avoid an "I told you so" attitude.

FRIENDS & FAMILY

AUGUST 26

Life is an adventure in forgiveness.
—Norman Cousins

BORN ON THIS DAY
- **Mother Teresa**
  Catholic nun
- **Melissa McCarthy**
  actor
- **Thalia**
  singer
- **Macaulay Culkin**
  actor
- **John Mulaney**
  comedian

FRIENDS & FAMILY

PERSONALITY
You have a very receptive nature. In other words, you have a sensitivity that is so highly developed that you respond to vibrations emanating from people and places that can make you very happy or very miserable, depending on your reaction. You must be careful to avoid living near emotionally disturbed people. The word "hypersensitivity" can all too often capture exactly what your mental state is like. You are inclined to worry needlessly and must try very hard to overcome this tendency. As far as health is concerned, you can have a vigorous constitution but one affected by your emotional and mental state. When you are at ease or calm, you feel fine, but when something upsets your peace of mind, you seethe inside. Calm your mind by meditating so that you learn to take things in your stride.

LIFE PATH
You are curious, artistic, versatile, whimsical, and headstrong. You are usually dependable, trusted, and looked up to by your friends. You seem more cool, calculating, and reserved than you actually are. You never take anything for granted. You will be blessed with a confiding, dominant love in your life and will have a homelife and a career that will be mostly fulfilling.

DESTINY
Although you dislike appearing rude and go to great lengths to avoid offending others, you should not carry this too far. Your first obligation is to be true to yourself. If the advice offered is unacceptable to you, say so. Explain why, and your reasoning will convince any person that your stand is the correct one. Think of the future, as well as the present, when you are at work, and let that guide your interactions with your coworkers.

KARMIC LESSON
You are very exacting and careful in all that you do or undertake. You are neat in your personal appearance, and you like to see your home tidy and well-kept. You are very loyal and attentive in your friendships and affections. While you may like to travel, the gaudy, glamorous side of life does not appeal to you. You are fair and honest, and no one can accuse you of not being generous with your money when you have it. All forms of communications—podcasts, blogs, books, publishing, editing, and journaling—attract you. Your emotional nature is strong, and you are capable of deep and lasting affection. Your life will be one full of many interests and will be marked by a gradual but certain upward growth as you age gracefully.

SECRET
You are a lover of travel but are without the ability to adapt to change. Because of this, you might make a difficult passenger or guest.

AUGUST 27

How may a man obtain greatness? By fidelity, truth, and lofty thoughts.
—The Talmud

BORN ON THIS DAY

- **Lyndon B. Johnson**
  U.S. president
- **Tom Ford**
  fashion designer
- **C.S. Forester**
  author
- **Katherine Johnson**
  scientist
- **Cesar Millan**
  dog trainer

PERSONALITY
You have the capacity to see things as they are and to use your mental prowess to get ahead. You prefer the company of similar levelheaded, practical individuals. Spacey, unfocused people seem to get under your skin and cause you extreme annoyance. When you make a statement, you can back it up. You don't like people to try to impress you with a lot of lies or other products of their imaginations. This down-to-earth attitude that you have is a wonderful advantage in the world of business, and you could make a success of any endeavor. Even if you are an artist, you deal with people when you buy or sell, and your businesslike attitude will make a good impression and result in your making good deals. Learn to concentrate more when you have to deal with people you do not like and to apply yourself to one thing for long periods of time.

LIFE PATH
You have an instinctive judgment that is naturally accurate and seldom fails you. You are studious, serious-minded, and clever and possess an undercurrent of satirical humor that, while never intentionally severe, makes your friends careful never to have it directed against them. You must make an effort to show you are loving, kind, and fair. You will select a partner who will make you very happy even though they will be a very different type than you may have had in mind.

DESTINY
You will fulfill many of your dreams. Although your desire for recreation may seem incompatible with all your commitments and obligations, it would benefit you to find a way to do it all. Also, try to interest your business associates in your outside activities. Use your leisure moments to plan the next day's work schedule. You will find that both your social and occupational undertakings blend well. Keep out of your extended family's quarrels, and do not offer unsolicited advice, however sound it may be.

KARMIC LESSON
You are very active and can keep yourself on the go for as long as necessary. You have a good memory and grasp of complicated business situations. Truthful and straightforward, you have no use for fakes and silliness. You are a hard worker and stick closely to what must be done in business. There is every indication that you will be very successful and will accumulate a moderate fortune. You must learn to be lenient with others' shortcomings. Remember that experience is the only real teacher and that everyone must have a certain amount of this, no matter what sound advice they receive before they can succeed. You should learn to curtail your taste for rich food and drink; one day you may have a rude awakening, which will be hard for you to bear.

SECRET
You have a strong interest in writing. You could become a creative writer of merit if a block in you could be released.

FRIENDS & FAMILY

AUGUST 28

He is happiest, be he king or peasant, who finds peace in his home.
—Johann Wolfgang von Goethe

BORN ON THIS DAY

- **Johann Wolfgang von Goethe**
  poet
- **Shania Twain**
  singer
- **Jack Black**
  actor
- **David Fincher**
  filmmaker, director
- **Ai Weiwei**
  visual artist

FRIENDS & FAMILY

PERSONALITY

You seem to regulate your life according to a subtle philosophy that is a part of your inner nature. Experience has taught you a great deal, but you have adapted these lessons in such a way that they have evolved into a regular way of life. Your ethical and moral standards are very high, and you will not tolerate any act that does not live up to this code. For this reason, some people may think you act a bit superior, but it is better to have your own high opinion of yourself than the opinion of unthinking people. You have an interest in things psychic and mystical, which may only be latent in your makeup but which can easily be developed—and to your advantage. You sometimes react to situations as though you had an anxiety complex. This is due to your extreme sensitivity to the feelings of other people. Express your sympathy with less of a show of feeling and be more active in your daily routine to overcome this type of reaction.

LIFE PATH

You are orderly, systematic, and methodical, and you never act impulsively or let yourself be satisfied with a superficial view. You like to know how and why things are done, and while you do not accomplish things quickly, you are generally accurate. You will probably apply the same methodical methods to affairs of the heart.

DESTINY

Do not shun publicity. Your capabilities and achievements will draw deserved recognition, even if you acquire the reputation of being conceited because you have confidence in yourself. Some who are less confident will tend to be jealous. Your personality is one that naturally attracts others, and you should try to increase your level of charm as you make your talents apparent. Your multitasking activities will naturally grow as you expand your interests in the world. Short trips can be as informative as distant ones for you, because you are always learning.

KARMIC LESSON

You will be known as one of the originals of the world if you do not let fear stifle the gifts nature has given you. You are both artistic and musical and can appreciate these arts as few can. You can also write, as well as appreciate the works of others. You are also technical to a remarkable degree, and you have an excellent memory. A good judge of human nature, you know people's strengths and weaknesses and how to harness both to your advantage. Philosophical, you are interested in psychic and occult subjects, as they help give you power. You like to travel and are destined to journey a great deal in your lifetime, as you will do business in many locations. Your nature is amorous, and your passions are strong.

SECRET

You are a born strategist, able to outwit an opponent. You would make a good detective or a game designer.

AUGUST 29

Our deepest fear is not that we are inadequate. Our deepest fear is that we are powerful beyond measure.
—Marianne Williamson

BORN ON THIS DAY
- **Michael Jackson**
  singer
- **Ingrid Bergman**
  actor
- **Charlie Parker**
  jazz saxophonist
- **Dinah Washington**
  singer
- **Lea Michele**
  actor, singer

FRIENDS & FAMILY

PERSONALITY
You are the personification of the free spirit of entrepreneurship and enterprise. You are interested in gathering the material rewards of a life of creative effort, thought, and activity. Lack of freedom of motion makes you extremely unhappy; you must be up, busy, and always multitasking or else you get bored. You may often see things from the practical point of view; their functional elements are of the most importance to you, and their beauty or decorativeness comes second. Although you may go on a spending spree now and then, you are generally economical and know how to get a bargain and good value for what you spend. A strong selling ability will take you far in any profit-making project that you choose to enter. You are not aggressively domineering when you deal with people; you know how to get what you want by being diplomatic.

LIFE PATH
You derive the greatest pleasure from intellectual recreations—reading, interesting art shows, podcasts, antiques, history, and foreign TV and movies. You do not want to waste your time and energy on frivolous, lowbrow things. You like to associate with creative, intelligent people, but you form very few close friendships. You can, however, talk intelligently with anyone and everyone and be very entertaining when you choose to make the effort.

DESTINY
Social matters sometimes require more of your time and attention than you care to give them. As you get older, you will find increased enjoyment in meeting new people and establishing long-lasting relationships. You will use your income to your best advantage by careful planning. Indulging in extravagant gifts is unwise and not in your nature, but do not fight your inclination toward generosity and thoughtful gestures of affection when they come up.

KARMIC LESSON
You have a sarcastic sense of humor and see the fun where another would not. You like luxuries and know how to acquire them for very little. You cannot stand being poor and will make every effort to better yourself and rise out of your present conditions to those more expressive of your true self. You have a great deal of vitality and can do an extraordinary amount of work when you get excited about a job. If you are bored, you will find ways to procrastinate. You are a perfectionist, accurate, and painstaking. You have a nose for news and would make a good reporter. Be cautious in all that you begin in the month of May.

SECRET
You have a deep emotional nature but are reluctant to show your true feelings for fear of being judged. You would make a devoted partner, though rather critical and reserved.

AUGUST 30

That which is striking and beautiful is not always good; but that which is good is always beautiful.
—Ninon de L'Enclos

BORN ON THIS DAY

- **Mary Shelley**
  author
- **Cameron Diaz**
  actor
- **Paul Oakenfold**
  DJ, music producer
- **Andy Roddick**
  tennis player
- **Lewis Black**
  comedian, actor

FRIENDS & FAMILY

PERSONALITY

You are a rather moody person. When you are enthusiastic about something, you seem to bubble over, but when you lose your interest in anything, you just drop it as though you never cared at all. You are rather impersonal in your approach to life, as you are prone to regard things from an intellectual instead of an emotional point of view. Your mind and internal dialogue are very active. Your life of feeling resolves itself into impersonality or sentimentality rather than deep and moving emotions. You could be successful in dealing with the public, because you will not react to their wide variety of vibrations with fatigue but instead seem to be stimulated by them. A good sense of humor makes you livelier and more fun and is one of your outstanding traits. You see fun in situations that others miss out on, and you enjoy life's little jokes and quirks. You can build popularity on this trait alone because it is so strong in your character.

LIFE PATH

You are abrupt in speech, moody in temperament, intuitive in judgment, and fickle in love. You possess considerable originality and are apt to always do something unusual and unexpected. You are discreet and receive many confidences from people who tell you their deep, dark secrets. You are unselfish with your friends and strive to make your gatherings and home pleasant and interesting.

DESTINY

Your moods come from the fact that you have had doubts regarding the sincerity of a love interest based on an experience that was disappointing, and from gossip that was careless but without malicious intent. Even when you obtained the true facts of the matter, your suspicions did not disappear. Be careful not to go to the other extreme and trust people who are not worthy of your faith. Retaining your skeptical attitude will be wise. Your reasoning processes are logical, but make sure accurate information, and not rumors, is available to you. An individual of wide business experience will play a part in your future undertakings and lead you to the prosperity you seek.

KARMIC LESSON

You are a sort of person who takes life as it comes and seems easygoing but at the same time worries too much about small matters. You can be daring and speculative, ready to take a chance or rush into anything. You would make a successful investor and would have luck, as it is called, in all that you went in for. You are somewhat temperamental but seldom get really angry or irritable. You get lonely easily. You are kind, but you can be stern at times, if you want to be, though this is not your natural disposition. You are loyal and true in all your friendships and, overall, a very likable character.

SECRET

You have a capacity for detail and accuracy so great as to prove an annoyance to others; it is therefore a disadvantage. You would be most successful in independent ventures.

AUGUST 31

*People do not lack strength;
they lack will.*
—*Victor Hugo*

⊛ PERSONALITY
You possess a great many skills, and you have a special talent for being eloquent when you speak or write. Because of your power to handle words and messages with such skill, you could be a fine writer, public speaker, or teacher. You might also feel a call to work as a spiritual counselor, because the spiritual side of your nature is highly developed. In the practical world, this spirituality might be expressed in your working for social reforms that would better the present state of humanity. You should have a peaceful, contented homelife, yet you will travel much and make your mark in the world. You can find fun in the small and pleasant aspects of your experience.

⊛ LIFE PATH
You are forceful, energetic, and ambitious and endowed with much natural ability to manifest your goals. Your adaptability brings you success in almost any undertaking. You read remarkably quickly and assimilate readily. You are generally regarded as well informed and intellectual, and your judgment is respected. You can marry early in life if the opportunity presents itself.

⊛ DESTINY
You are always attracted to new scenes and pleasures. Listen to the progressive ideas of others with an open mind. However, you should not accept them without first subjecting them to careful trial and error testing. Some can be put into practice; some should be discarded. Do not let the past shackle you, but beware of unconventionality. Continue to avoid both radicalism and reactionary conservatism. Moderation in your diet, too, would be beneficial.

⊛ KARMIC LESSON
You have a positive attitude that is destined to help you succeed and to lead those in contact with you. You have excellent judgment and good common sense. You are sympathetic and understanding. You have a good business sense, and others are likely to go to you and ask your advice on certain questions, even about subjects that you would think they know more about than you. You are loving by nature and demonstrative in your affection toward others. You could have a very happy marriage, probably early on in life. Success is clearly marked out for you; if you do not attain it, it is your own fault. You have a good, original mind—cultivate it.

⊛ SECRET
You can be a little too formal in your dealings with others. Sometimes it's good for the soul to just be yourself and have fun.

BORN ON THIS DAY
★ **Richard Gere**
actor
★ **Itzhak Perlman**
violinist, conductor
★ **Frankie Robinson**
baseball player
★ **Debbie Gibson**
singer
★ **Van Morrison**
singer/songwriter

FRIENDS & FAMILY

SEPTEMBER 1

The wealth of the soul is the only true wealth.
—Lucian

⚀ PERSONALITY
Because you are ambitious and positive and know what you want, you have a great advantage in life. You see life clearly, and you see it with a holistic perspective. The pattern is of your own making, and you are determined that you will make it one that spells success, happiness, and real accomplishment. You are very precise in the way you think, talk, and act. No action of yours is ever impulsive, because you make all your plans in advance, and only some catastrophe in nature could prevent your carrying them out. Your very high standards sometimes prove very annoying to your associates who do not share them, and your ability to find fault may sometimes get you involved in a serious argument. However, you are right to defend your principles. You would make a very good agent, as you usually know what is good for people far better than they do themselves.

☯ LIFE PATH
You are magnanimous and direct. Your friends always know where you stand, and while you are sometimes brusque in your speech, there is never anything unkind intended. You possess a sentimental outlook and are excessively loyal to your loved ones. You are demonstrative and affectionate and will receive loyalty and love in return.

👁 DESTINY
Your home and clothes will always concern you. Time spent on them will not be wasted, for self-confidence is increased when your pride is activated. Your relaxed manner and even disposition will be a business asset. You look forward to special, planned evenings shared by close friends and business associates. Connections are made this way for you. Although several alternatives are usually possible, you make up your mind easily and decisively.

☯ KARMIC LESSON
You have great corporate ability and could undertake the management of an enterprise of large scale. You are determined, and you generally manage to push a project through until you succeed. You are a good friend and a fearsome enemy. You are at times inclined to be too serious and severe, so you should cultivate a greater sense of fun and humor. Yet you are always popular wherever you go, and your sincerity and forcefulness of character make you respected and liked. Often you are not understood by those around you, and you feel great things burning inside you that you cannot express. You have a good attitude, however, and know that all will come out right in the long run, as it usually does.

🔒 SECRET
You have a love of good food and fine cooking. You would make an excellent chef and could rise to a high position in that work.

BORN ON THIS DAY
- ★ Gloria Estefan
  singer
- ★ Zendaya
  actor, singer
- ★ Edgar Rice Burroughs
  author
- ★ Barry Gibb
  singer
- ★ Phil McGraw
  TV personality

FRIENDS & FAMILY

SEPTEMBER 2

Earnestness is the path of immortality, thoughtlessness, the path of death.
—Buddha

BORN ON THIS DAY
- **Keanu Reeves**
  actor
- **Lennox Lewis**
  boxer
- **Mark Harmon**
  actor
- **Selma Hayek**
  actor
- **Christa McAuliffe**
  teacher

FRIENDS & FAMILY

_____
_____
_____
_____
_____
_____
_____
_____

PERSONALITY
Although you do not care particularly to start new projects or learn new ways to do things, you are very quick to adapt yourself to any situation. For this reason, you are a perfect collaborator, partner, and coworker. You seem to get the drift of what is wanted in any proposal, and you fit in with superb adaptability. It appears you are the embodiment of the spirit of cooperation. Occasional moodiness and cycles of "the blues" or depression can take you over, and you should be more active at such times in your life. Instead of giving in to the mood, try to master it. You have the intellectual capacity to figure things out, so figure out what is bothering you, what you can do about it—and then go ahead.

LIFE PATH
A pleasing conversationalist, you can hide your moodiness and appear witty, bright, and amiable. You are generally well-liked and have friends in several distinct circles, because you are able to adapt yourself to varying environments. You are usually bubbling over with animation and energy, and things never lag or get boring when you are around.

DESTINY
When you are at your best, you radiate original thought and constructive action. Any misunderstanding you may have with someone you admire will be worked out satisfactorily, but unless you initiate the reconciliation, it will take years. Take the initiative in clearing up the difficulty instead of brooding. Volunteer your services to charities or civic organizations. The contribution you can make will be appreciated by coworkers and will be of benefit to those you help. Do not make decisions when you have seen only one side of the question.

KARMIC LESSON
Your funny stories about people you have known and situations you have encountered keep those around you laughing. You can see the funny side of everything, yet you can be very serious, and most of the time the stern events of daily tasks make you much more matter-of-fact than you could otherwise be. You have high ideals and aspirations, and you are determined to gratify them. There is no reason why you should not, for you have all the possibilities; they need only find the right manifestation. You can express yourself well and could make a good writer—only you have to have someone to write to of whom you are very fond, and then you will find that the words flow, and the messages almost write themselves, as if you were channeling.

SECRET
You are devoted to harmony and design in the home. You would make a good interior decorator.

SEPTEMBER 3

Poets utter great and wise things which they do not themselves understand.
—Plato

BORN ON THIS DAY
- **Charlie Sheen**, actor
- **Malcolm Gladwell**, author
- **Shaun White**, Olympic snowboarder
- **Irene Papas**, actor
- **DJ Envy**, DJ, radio personality

PERSONALITY
Because you have a cheerful disposition, a good sense of humor, and a pleasant outlook on life, you are very popular and considered "sexy" by more people than you know. People like you because you are friendly, not overcritical, and clever in conversation. You seem to arrive at a balance between the serious tasks of life and the leisure skills that you know is what everyone wants. You can enjoy yourself immensely at a party, but you can be perfectly happy alone, too, since you have learned the wonderful secret of how to be alone productively. Being current with the latest information gives you as much pleasure as talking about it, and a nice long walk will entertain you as much as the bantering atmosphere of a night out at a club. All in all, you lead a contented life, accepting its ups and downs as if you were playing a sport and doing your sincere best to make the most of what life has to offer.

LIFE PATH
You have mechanical ability and are methodical, careful, and patient. You are conservative in your judgment, observing, candid, and versatile. You have the gift of learning from the mistakes of others and will help others to avoid making their own. You do not form attachments easily and will probably not marry early in life. If you finally commit to a partner, your love will be deep, true, enduring, and strong.

DESTINY
Neither give nor ask great favors. You don't like to feel obligated. You will get many chances to show your self-reliance and courage. Do not be beguiled by a charming but lazy companion. Financial and social advancement will reward your serious self-application. Tasks should be completed as soon as possible, as you are the type to get bored before you finish. More interesting ones lie ahead, but do not start new undertakings when old ones are unfinished.

KARMIC LESSON
You are never happier than when you are communicating with or surrounded by friends. You live a great deal in an inner life that no one seems to penetrate or reach—save, perhaps, the one who you feel understands all. You can consume information at a great rate or browse the Internet for hours, researching your favorite subjects. You will have a good deal of commercial success if you learn to concentrate your forces instead of scattering them. You are destined to win a certain amount of fame and reputation in a subject that is now given little attention. Have a definite goal in life and determine to reach it. If you do, this success will ultimately be yours.

SECRET
You have an enjoyment of luxuries, and you would not mind acquiring them by being married to a person of wealth.

FRIENDS & FAMILY

SEPTEMBER 4

A weak mind is like a microscope, which magnifies trifling things, but cannot receive great ones.
—Lord Chesterfield

BORN ON THIS DAY

- ★ **Mark Ronson**
  DJ, music producer
- ★ **Mike Piazza**
  baseball player
- ★ **Damon Wayans**
  comedian, actor
- ★ **Earl Dibbles, Jr.**
  singer/songwriter
- ★ **Drew Pinsky**
  TV personality

FRIENDS & FAMILY

PERSONALITY

You are more serious in your outlook on life than most people. You try your best to better your position in life, get high-quality things for your loved ones, and eat well and exercise so you will not grow weaker as you grow older. You believe in regulating your existence by being on time in the performance of your duties, and you prefer to work on a schedule and a routine than to follow a haphazard career. People find you dependable and trustworthy. When you give your promise, it is understood that you will do everything in your power to keep it. You are rarely emotionally upset because you keep things on track through intelligent planning of what you want to accomplish. Most of the time, you are economical in the expenditure of your money, time, and energy. You really dislike waste and make every effort to avoid it, although you have a soft spot in your heart that makes you spoil those you consider your family.

LIFE PATH

You make your point by sheer force of will at times, and it can scare people when you do. Your mind is intense and that can make you not very patient when opposed or questioned. If success does not come immediately, inside you are inclined to quit in disgust. You are a true friend and a relentless enemy. People are not indifferent toward you. You will be liked or disliked.

DESTINY

Be courteous but not gullible when listening to the ideas of others. Couple your lively imagination with good judgment to evolve plans. Older friends will help you put them into action. Once you have made up your mind, do not change it. Perseverance will be necessary, but the reward is worth it.

KARMIC LESSON

You have a good head for mathematics and special relationships and would make a good engineer, architect, or game or graphic designer. You are interested in all forms of health and the body, especially in biology, though you do not have as much time as you would like for study. To succeed, you must know exactly what you want to do, as success is impossible if your mind is not clear on this point. Your natural ability and determination will then pull you through. Poised and self-assured, you are greatly influenced by your home environment, and if it is ugly or inharmonious, you can be unhappy and depressed in spirit. You are very affectionate to those you trust but can cut off friendships that no longer serve you when you have no time for them.

SECRET

You have friends in all walks of life. You would be successful in medicine, alternative healing, the military, or law enforcement.

SEPTEMBER 5

You can preach a better sermon with your life than with your lips.
—Oliver Goldsmith

BORN ON THIS DAY

★ **Freddie Mercury**
singer

★ **Beyoncé Knowles**
singer

★ **Jesse James**
outlaw, gang leader

★ **Raquel Welch**
model, actor

★ **Bob Newhart**
comedian, actor

PERSONALITY

The mercurial, playful, mischievous side of your nature shows itself so clearly that most people think of you as temperamental, moody, and somewhat undependable. In truth, this is the way you impress them because you believe, in your hours of relaxation, in having fun. If your fun happens at someone else's expense, you don't seem to mind. Of course, when you have a job to do, you are quite serious about it. But as you like to work in private, few people know the serious and sincere side of your makeup. If you want to have friends and influence people, you need to balance this humorous aspect of your character with the serious aspect so that you make a better impression. Your interests are in things that have a touch of the dramatic about them. You like to make an entrance, to attract attention, and, if possible, to keep the crowd laughing.

LIFE PATH

You are subject to moods and changes and need to cultivate a greater degree of self-confidence. You like socializing, excitement, and stirring things up, although you are capable of serious and deep thought when occasion demands it. You are impetuous, capricious, and vivacious and add life and brightness to any social gathering. You are endearing and lovable.

DESTINY

Remember that you are your own leader—"the master of your fate—the captain of your soul." If you accept this role and do not let someone else boss you around, there is no telling where you may be able to steer your craft. Many ports are open. The lights of romance glow in one; from another shines business opportunities and chances for substantial financial gains. Avoid getting pulled into scandals and gossip, for these are destructive currents that can wreck your boat.

KARMIC LESSON

You could succeed with a business idea if you entered into it by yourself and proved it to work gradually. Remember that most successful enterprises began in small ways, grew gradually, and then, when well established, grew by leaps and bounds. You are exacting and methodical and have a good memory for details. You are a hard worker and can carry on three or four different things at the same time, multitasking all the way. You are good at games. You love nature, and every summer finds you at the seashore or in the mountains. You are a savvy judge of human nature and are seldom deceived about a person's character. You are passionate in your love nature and should marry only the one who understands you thoroughly.

SECRET

You are mechanically versatile, with skills in photography. You are often more interested in amusement than in self-advancement.

FRIENDS & FAMILY

SEPTEMBER 6

Faith is the bird that feels the light and sings when the dawn is still dark.
—Rabindranath Tagore

BORN ON THIS DAY

- ★ **Macy Gray**
  singer
- ★ **Idris Elba**
  actor
- ★ **Jeff Foxworthy**
  comedian
- ★ **Rosie Perez**
  actor
- ★ **Foxy Brown**
  rapper

FRIENDS & FAMILY

PERSONALITY

You have a heart that is as big as you are. You want to make everybody happy, and your scope of interest is not limited to the people you know—it includes all people. It seems that you rarely do anything just for yourself, so unselfish are you, but are always planning gifts and surprises for friends and relatives, taking part in charity affairs, and working for committees and causes whose aim is the betterment of humankind. This is not surprising, as it is typical of those born on this day. You are practical in a business way and can organize well. You should be happy in your chosen role as benefactor. Invite business associates when planning formal as well as informal gatherings. You take the world as you find it, and it treats you well in return.

LIFE PATH

You are conservative, careful, plodding, conscientious, and faithful. You like to have things done well. You have a strong will, but despite it you are sometimes too easily led by others. You are caring, eager to please, and sympathetic. Your homelife is pleasant because you work hard to make it so.

DESTINY

Take advantage of opportunities to entertain in your home or where you feel at home, as it is a healing experience for your guests. You want to contribute your opinion in many discussions, so don't hold back by always letting others take over. What you have to say cannot be ignored, because you get to the core of a problem. Simple relaxation techniques can prove of benefit to you—when you just remember to do them, you recharge your batteries quickly.

KARMIC LESSON

You are inclined to be conventional in your tastes and have a resistance to many of the new ideas and new thoughts that so constantly fill our times: technological gadgets, social networking, fancy phones, and the metaverse. You believe in moving slowly. More tolerance should be cultivated for those of different viewpoints. You are fond of the sea and will probably make a great traveler on that account. Mountain climbing might be a recreation that especially appeals to you. You will doubtless bring whatever you undertake to a successful conclusion; for this reason, you will probably succeed in making money and investing well, and you should turn your energies in that direction even if you have to start small.

SECRET

Moderate success and satisfaction will be gained through doing that which your parents approved of.

SEPTEMBER 7

Listen to what you know instead of what you fear.
—Richard Bach

☻ PERSONALITY
You believe in making the best of everything in life. Because you are courageous and intelligent, you refuse to accept defeat on any level. When things seem complicated beyond straightening out, you calmly settle down to solving what's wrong—and you usually succeed. It takes real bravery to keep up the fight in the face of defeat; you act as though life is a field of battle from which you are bound to emerge victorious. You have a high degree of originality, which helps you in all areas. As a result, you can tackle problems in ways that many people are incapable of. Although you are not particularly interested in material wealth on a big scale, you are able to handle the financial department of your life efficiently. Occasional stubbornness shows itself in your makeup.

◉ LIFE PATH
You are self-reliant, authoritative, determined, and persevering. You have great focusing ability and spare no pains in accomplishing your desires. You like to read and stay up-to-the-minute on the news and those you care about. You are fond of travel or studying foreign cultures. Your aims are mainly high and noble, and you enjoy the respect and esteem of many who you know and a few you do not know yet.

⊙ DESTINY
Expectations will become realities because you are determined and work hard. Your serious attitude about life is a very valuable asset. You will always be glad that you can stick with a job until it is finished, even when it is a challenging one. However, you should take time off occasionally for recreation and pastimes that relax you. Take time to daydream. You will return to your tasks with renewed enthusiasm.

☯ KARMIC LESSON
You are serious but have a vivid imagination. You could be one of the world's futurist dreamers, who dreams great things and makes the dreams come true. You probably do not care about money to any great extent and are happy just to have what you need to get by. You are drawn to the stage, to drama, to movies, and to people in the theater. You are clever and gifted. You have great understanding and sympathy. You are very affectionate, and your passionate nature is strong. You should only marry someone whose tastes are similar to your own; any other marriage would be problematic. Remember your dreams; they have meaning. Do not, however, live too much in the subconscious world, as it is better for you to stay grounded and practical.

☗ SECRET
You have a strong will and an ability to carry out plans rather than just formulate them. You must use discernment when executing the orders of others.

BORN ON THIS DAY
- ★ **Queen Elizabeth I**
  Queen of England
- ★ **Gloria Gaynor**
  singer
- ★ **Buddy Holly**
  singer
- ★ **Easy-E**
  rapper
- ★ **Jacob Lawrence**
  painter

FRIENDS & FAMILY

SEPTEMBER 8

When it is a question of money, everybody is of the same religion.
—Voltaire

BORN ON THIS DAY
- **Bernie Sanders**
  politician
- **Antonín Dvořák**
  composer
- **Pink**
  singer
- **Peter Sellers**
  actor, comedian
- **Avicii**
  DJ, music producer

FRIENDS & FAMILY

_____
_____
_____
_____
_____
_____
_____
_____
_____

PERSONALITY
Since you have an innate talent for organizing, you generally take the lead in whatever project you associate yourself with. At home, you divide up the chores and errands to be done. In business, you arrange your schedule so that the most will be done with the minimum effort. In social life, you know how to be gracious without overextending yourself. You have a natural talent for the successful handling of finances, and you can—with equal ease—figure out the budget, arrange investments, and take care of your securities and savings, as well as those of your family and others. You have a fine sense of the value of things and therefore make an excellent fiduciary, notary, or agent. In the vocational world, you are suited to banking, corporative activities, administration, and institutional work.

LIFE PATH
Discriminating, shrewd, and observing, you are a careful student, a wise teacher, a deep thinker, and an interesting talker. You are artistic and musical and surprisingly positive. You enjoy being right and having your own way. You are loving, faithful and loyal, and devoted to your friends and family. You are not at all likely to fall in love at first sight, as you are very discriminating.

DESTINY
Your endeavors are benefited by your sense of duty and respect for established authority and tradition. Devote part of each day to play as well as to fulfilling obligations. Do not scorn dirty work, yours or that of another. The satisfaction of worthwhile accomplishments will be more lasting to you than memories of good times. Opportunities for self-improvement in your life will be enormous, and you will overcome much. Take advantage of teaching methods and habits that have worked for you. Do not harbor resentments or judge others too harshly.

KARMIC LESSON
You have a good head for figures and mathematics. You could utilize your special gifts to your advantage in business, as an accountant, or as an investor if you wished to. You have a good brain and are discriminating in your estimate of people, politics, and cultural affairs. You might make a good lawyer. You are spiritual but probably not orthodox in any way. You are exacting and precise in your dealings, and your word can always be trusted implicitly. This means that you always do your best to accomplish what you say you will. You are neat and orderly. You are doubtless popular among your friends. You possess a certain sexual attraction. Use it wisely.

SECRET
The cultivation of sympathy for others and greater self-confidence will make you a success.

SEPTEMBER 9

They think too little who talk too much.
—John Dryden

PERSONALITY
As you were born with a highly creative and vivid imagination, you can make your life a fascinating adventure. It should not take you long to discover your real interests, and you could begin to find acclaim at an early age, relatively speaking. You are blessed with a sense of sympathy for people that makes them feel the psychic sensitiveness of your emotions and a deep understanding of their situation. Because you have great strength of expression, all who come to know you will feel your empathetic powers. You can put yourself in other people's shoes, feel their feelings, and get their reactions. This adds up to a wealth of vicarious experience, which makes you wise beyond your years.

LIFE PATH
You are interested in philosophy and want to understand what the great thinkers have to say about life. You are inclined to be too hasty in your judgment and sometimes rush into helping someone without being able to see the potential outcomes clearly. You are magnetic and intuitive and capable of developing considerable psychic power. You are loving, kind, and sympathetic.

DESTINY
Doing, not dreaming, should be the keynote for you. Retain your ideals but translate them into deeds. Even when there are times you may not comprehend the invigorating power that stirs in you, make use of it. Begin working on the fulfillment of personal ambitions, and you will magnetize what you need. Regard the present as a stepping-stone to the future. As you jump from one activity or success to another, do not lose sight of your ultimate goal.

KARMIC LESSON
You have remarkably strong views and will become widely known through advocating for them. You are destined to have a varied and interesting life, experienced in many lands and under a variety of circumstances. The early part of your life will doubtless be very stimulating, and later you will settle down into a more practical routine. Fond of the fine arts, you have far more ability than most people realize, and you could accomplish amazing undertakings if the opportunities were given to you. Learn the value of time; do not acquire the fatal habit of putting off until tomorrow what can be done today. Keep moving, for upon your continual activity success depends. Learn how to keep a secret, yours and that of those who put their trust in you.

SECRET
You arouse love in others but are never carried away by your own emotions. You are an extraordinary worker and a loyal partner.

BORN ON THIS DAY
- **Leo Tolstoy**, author
- **Otis Redding**, singer
- **Adam Sandler**, comedian, actor
- **Michael Bublé**, singer
- **Michelle Williams**, actor

FRIENDS & FAMILY

SEPTEMBER 10

Look deep into nature, and then you will understand everything better.
—Albert Einstein

BORN ON THIS DAY
- **Karl Lagerfeld**
  fashion designer
- **Colin Firth**
  actor
- **Arnold Palmer**
  golfer
- **Ryan Phillippe**
  actor
- **Bill O'Reilly**
  political commentator

FRIENDS & FAMILY

PERSONALITY
Inventiveness and originality distinguish you. You enjoy tackling a problem, and you love finding a solution that would not have occurred to someone else. Your greatest aid is a sense of visualization. You can see things in your mind's eye, project yourself in your imagination, and as a result make wonderful and ingenious plans, inventions, and creations. You also possess the aggressiveness needed to put your ideas across or to sell them if they are commercially viable. This combination of practicality and vision gives you the latent opportunity to make your mark in the world despite all kinds of competition. Even in your home, you display this ability. You can set your intention, plan for your loved ones, save for your ideals and dreams, and make them actualities.

LIFE PATH
You are impulsive and emotional and guided by intuition rather than by outside influence. You are not overly communicative, and if you think anyone is trying to get information from you, you get very cryptic. You are ambitious and resourceful, fond of home and family, and capable of great love.

DESTINY
Matters associated with your feelings and affections may come first, before practical concerns. Seek and develop friendships with as much attention as you devote to business or home matters. Take time for the development of your artistic capabilities. You should find captivating interest in such fields as painting, literature, music, gardening, sculpting, and designing. Appreciation of art can be expressed in fixing up your home and helping others with theirs.

KARMIC LESSON
You are active and energetic, and you generally make your presence felt wherever you go. You are self-motivated and can accomplish a great deal in life simply by reason of the wonderful stamina and staying powers that you have. You are thoughtful and kind, solicitous of the welfare of others. Some unpleasant experiences will come into your life from time to time, but you will override them by sheer will and determination and be left all the stronger for the struggle. You see these challenges as life lessons. However, you will have some pleasant surprises, too, partly because of the kindness and consideration that you will receive from an unexpected source, which will be the means of your rising rapidly in the world, socially and financially.

SECRET
You have an eye always on the prize, and so you will go far. Do not, however, be swerved from relationship commitments by your goals.

SEPTEMBER 11

All human power is a compound of time and patience.
—Honoré de Balzac

BORN ON THIS DAY

★**D.H. Lawrence**
author

★**Harry Connick, Jr.**
singer, actor

★**Ludacris**
rapper, actor

★**Moby**
singer, DJ

★**Bashar al-Assad**
Syrian dictator

● PERSONALITY
Wherever a helping hand is needed, you seem to be in just the right place at the right time. Nor do you resent this seeming coincidence, for you feel that it is the right thing to help others as much as you can. In business, you build around you an aura of such goodwill that whether you are buying or selling, working for another or with others, you construct a spirit of cooperation that cannot be surpassed. There is a strong combination of traditionally feminine and masculine traits in your character. You can organize, plan, and execute ideas that work your will on the world. But you can also be receptive, nurturing, and supportive of the ideas of others. This gives you an advantage, as it doubles your understanding of human nature and makes you a well-balanced human being.

● LIFE PATH
You have a smart mind and sound judgment and are ruled by honest intentions. You are thorough and competent in your work, resourceful in your plans, and determined in their execution. You can be an indulgent parent, a staunch friend, and a loving partner.

● DESTINY
Cherished ambitions or valuable ideas will receive helpful impetus under the beneficent and original vibrations on your birthday. Take advantage of each opportunity to test your ideas but share only those thoughts that have merit. A strong desire for greater freedom may warrant the budgeting of your income. You can lose track of time, so using technology, time-saving devices, and schedules can enable you to do the things you have always been wanting to achieve.

● KARMIC LESSON
You have a brilliant all-around mind and are doubtless interested in a great variety of subjects. There is a strong spiritual hunger running through you that will assert itself in your exploring one belief system after another. You are practical and have eminent common sense. You are magnetic and are doubtless attractive to all you meet. You are shrewd in business matters, and you never get very far offtrack in your dealings with others. Your love nature is strongly developed, and you are never so happy as when you are surrounded by friends. You have talent for writing comedy; develop this.

● SECRET
You are inclined to be too idle and self-indulgent at times. You also enjoy having intimate relationships with many admirers.

FRIENDS & FAMILY

SEPTEMBER 12

Gratitude bestows reverence, allowing us to encounter everyday epiphanies.
—Sarah Ban Breathnach

BORN ON THIS DAY

- **Jesse Owens**
  Olympic track and field athlete
- **Jennifer Hudson**
  singer
- **Barry White**
  singer
- **Jeff Pulver**
  internet entrepreneur
- **Hans Zimmer**
  composer

FRIENDS & FAMILY

_____
_____
_____
_____
_____
_____
_____
_____
_____
_____

PERSONALITY

In business relations, a sharpness comes out in your recognition of values and in your astute criticisms that you usually keep to yourself. You are rather easygoing despite your critical acumen because you know from experience the foibles and weaknesses of human nature, and you are inclined to be tolerant of them. You are a quick study, to use a theatrical phrase, meaning that you pick up knowledge quickly and with ease. For this reason, you would do well in the field of journalism or teaching. You learn things fast, and you put your learning into short, clear phrases. This also enables you to succeed in bringing up children well. Versatility can be the making or breaking of your career. If you vacillate while choosing one talent in which to specialize, you will waste a lot of time. If you follow your natural bent for organizing, you will succeed.

LIFE PATH

You are orderly, methodical, thorough, and faithful. You possess a quiet, quaint humor that often wards off petulance and anger. If you do give way to your temper, everyone around knows it. You like pleasant surroundings and strive to have them in your home. You are quite demonstrative in your affections and expect the same in return.

DESTINY

Effective use of the talents you have long possessed can stand you in good stead, rather than always thinking you need to study, take more classes, and have the right degree. To promote these qualities, favorable publicity will help you gain the goals that are important to your ambitions. These objectives probably include financial security and a position of prestige. It is important that you do not let lethargy or obstacles slow you down. The dominant Mars rays are dominant in your birth date vibration and can help you overcome your inertia. Harness them.

KARMIC LESSON

You have all the natural power and the assertive qualities that are necessary for the execution of your ideas. You are a great talker—too much at times, perhaps—but always interesting. Original and inventive, you have the ability to say the right thing at the right time. You are witty and have a good sense of humor. You like excitement of all kinds and can thrive in a stimulating atmosphere. You are naturally quick tempered and inclined to fly off the handle for little things, yet you are sorry the next minute for what you have done or said—though it is often too late to undo the damage that has been wrought. You need to think clearly before doing this. Once you come to a definite decision, you seldom change your mind.

SECRET

You have a very different side of you that you conceal because you fear revealing it may upset others. You are secretive, even though you talk a lot.

SEPTEMBER 13

To meet wrong with endurance, and to overcome the present with a heart that looks beyond, are triumph.
—James Russell Lowell

BORN ON THIS DAY

★ **Mel Tormé**
singer

★ **Tyler Perry**
actor

★ **A.J. McCarron**
football player

★ **Judith Martin**
"Miss Manners" columnist

★ **Madhur Jaffrey**
food writer

PERSONALITY
It appears your greatest success comes to you in the face of your greatest adversities. When everything is going wrong, and all the odds seem to be stacked against you, you reinforce your moral courage and put up your biggest fight. This stamina and tenacity are bound to bring you success, for you are determined to allow no obstacle to stand in your path. This trait of character is a tremendous advantage to you, and it permits you to leave all your competitors far behind in the race for attainment. You have a very practical outlook on life. Although you have very high ideals, you also know that to achieve them takes hard work, sacrifice, and emotional resiliency, you are willing to do what it takes to attain your aspirations.

LIFE PATH
You are generally sturdy and robust and like to be outdoors. You like to excel, and you put all your energy into your work or your play. You are good-natured, considerate, and discreet and enjoy the confidence of your associates. You are lovable and sympathetic and know how to remain neutral when the situation calls for it.

DESTINY
The fires of enthusiasm and inspiration burn brightly within you because the Neptune rays are strong on your birth date. Do not let them get out of control. Budget your time and efforts, or you may find yourself undertaking more than you can accomplish or stand emotionally or physically. Keep your ideas concealed for the most part until you have made them realities through accomplishment. Always be careful about what you sign, or say, in public. Never volunteer information needlessly.

KARMIC LESSON
Much commercial success undoubtedly will be yours, though you must work for all you get. Yours will be no easy road to travel, but if you live up to your ideals and do the best you can, you will come through with flying colors. You will probably have many friends and be popular in wide circles. You can keep a secret. You do, however, have moods, which you cannot explain, even to yourself. You feel that you have great talents and abilities to do far more than you are called upon to do and you want this recognized. You are naturally quiet and retiring, but you must learn to come out of your shell, for the world does not understand a person who is too shy or self-effacing.

SECRET
You have a nervous temperament and have difficulty in finding relaxation after the day's work. If worry and upset can be successfully managed, you will have a successful life.

FRIENDS & FAMILY

SEPTEMBER 14

I say, follow your bliss and don't be afraid, and doors will open where you didn't know they were going to be.
—Joseph Campbell

BORN ON THIS DAY
- **Amy Winehouse**
  singer
- **Fiona Apple**
  singer
- **Dave Mustaine**
  singer
- **Nas**
  rapper, music producer
- **Sam Neill**
  actor

FRIENDS & FAMILY

PERSONALITY
A clever talker and communicator and an entertaining person, you have the mentality to make your mark on the world. Podcasting, blogs, videos, radio, lectures, workshops, and journaling appeal to you because of your pronounced love of ideas, words, and their magic. You can entrance an audience all by yourself when you wish. You are very fast in your thoughts and in your actions, and inactivity bores you to the extreme. Travel and adventure have a strong romantic appeal for you, and you respond to new places by learning how to be a local. You are very open-minded in your thinking but are a stickler for convention in the office and at home. You are inclined to be a little flirtatious and probably will not settle down until you have reached middle life.

LIFE PATH
Self-reliance, ambition, and modesty when called for are your most notable characteristics. You need to develop more discipline and aggressiveness. Many things that you could do, and that you know you could do, you do not attempt because of your fear of confrontation. You will love and be loved much, but it may be hard to settle on just one partner.

DESTINY
The idea of your future shines bright and inviting for you. The things that can be achieved in life are limited only by you. You are a positive person at heart. Any executive position, or a responsibility entrusted to you, will be handled with praiseworthy effectiveness. Prestige and subsequent financial gain could result. Although there are fluctuations in success during your life, at no time should you have cause for deep gloom or self-doubt.

KARMIC LESSON
You are one of those people who may end up spending a great part of their lives in thought and theory rather than action. In the business world, you are inclined to be a planner, a schemer, who might leave the carrying out of your ideas to others. You are very original and will doubtless be fascinated by inventions of all sorts. You can creatively improve a great many things. Attracted by philosophy and metaphysics, you would like to bury yourself in a great library and read there to your heart's content. You are not naturally committed in your affections, but you have a passionate nature and can be very loving if you could only step back and see these issues from the point of view of your partner.

SECRET
You possess tact and cleverness in commercial undertakings and a love of power. Success can be obtained through the Internet of Things.

SEPTEMBER 15

The act of forgiveness takes place in our own mind. It really has nothing to do with the other person.
—Louise Hay

BORN ON THIS DAY

★ **William Howard Taft**
U.S. president

★ **Prince Harry**
Duke of Sussex

★ **Agatha Christie**
author

★ **Oliver Stone**
filmmaker

★ **Dan Marino**
football player

PERSONALITY

Because you have a very strong sense of responsibility, you take on the duties of life as a solemn, almost religious obligation. What you really want as your highest ideal is solid, quiet comfort, harmonious family life, and spiritual contentment. You are a good friend to the people you like, and you are a good relative to those members of your family with whom you are intimately associated. Harmony is absolutely necessary in your surroundings, for you cannot concentrate on your work or your fun if there is noise, bad vibes, or even one belligerent person present. You do your best to keep everyone with whom you are associated uplifted, and you expect them to act the same way. Rather than have any argument or unpleasantness, you would prefer to remove yourself from the scene where it is taking place.

LIFE PATH

Honesty and frankness shine out in your disposition. You are energetic and determined, but your energy is often misapplied. You are bright, witty, entertaining, and, in general, a favorite friend. You are deeply loved by your family, by blood and extended, and will always receive great respect and appreciation from those close to you.

DESTINY

Many of your fondest hopes regarding your family may come to pass. Cosmic forces favor the development of your spiritual aspirations. Advice, in addition to the actual material assistance of friends, may help you through some tight spots. Be appreciative, but do not feel that you must spend more than you can afford in repaying favors. Helpfulness and loyalty show gratitude just as well as costly gifts do.

KARMIC LESSON

Your forceful personality will carry you through many adverse situations. Since you take responsibility seriously, you do not worry about petty issues. You distrust people with too much of a happy-go-lucky disposition. You will need all your powers of positive thinking and all your reserve forces for the work you must do in life. You are very interested in politics and can rise to a position of influence in that line. Your life should be one of action, one in which you go out and live and move among people, where you will be popular and influential. You are calm and shrewd when occasion demands and are quick to form judgments and conclusions, too. You would make an excellent detective, as you have all the necessary qualifications.

SECRET

You pay too much attention to imagined insults. You must cast off this defensiveness to achieve real success in life.

FRIENDS & FAMILY

SEPTEMBER 16

Where there is no hope, there can be no endeavor.
—Samuel Johnson

BORN ON THIS DAY
- **David Copperfield**
  magician
- **Henry Louis Gates, Jr.**
  historian, cultural critic
- **Nick Jonas**
  singer
- **Amy Poehler**
  comedian, actor
- **Marc Anthony**
  singer

FRIENDS & FAMILY

PERSONALITY
You are imbued with very lofty ideals. Among your outstanding aspirations is a desire to reform humanity so that this earth will be a better, less polluted place to dwell upon. You can hardly restrain your desire to change things around, and you are forceful in getting your way because you have such absolute faith in your being right. Many people criticize you for this attitude because they do not want the status quo or their own lives disturbed—even when it is for their own good. But you stick to your beliefs, and you usually accomplish what you set out to do. You enjoy all the books and other products of masterminds that deal with mystical subjects, occult philosophy, astrology, numerology, and so on. You have a well-developed psychic sense, and your hunches are often amazingly accurate.

LIFE PATH
Harmonious and pleasant surroundings, someone to love and to love you—you know these are the keys to happiness. Your tastes are decidedly organic, and fancy advertising does not sway you. You are demonstrative and impulsive, surprisingly jealous at times even though you are easy to please and unusually friendly. You should exercise care in the selection of your investments.

DESTINY
You do not need to remove your optimistic "rose-colored glasses." Enthusiasm and positivity will help you put over your ideas and set your plans into practice. The expansion of your activist endeavors could prove profitable financially as well as socially after midlife. Outdoor activity and new craft hobbies can make any minor disappointment or period of slow progress seem unimportant. Your financial position should improve steadily in your life.

KARMIC LESSON
You have very good taste and care only for the best of everything natural. You are an aristocrat by nature, and you feel that you are a little different from those around you; yet you are democratic, too, and kind and sympathetic to all with less than you have. You have a great sense of justice, are fond of animals, and love nature and the country. You are a good athlete or want to be. You are affectionate, emotional, and inclined to be a bit of a seducer. You cannot bear to be alone, always seeking the company of others. You are clever with your hands and can fix things when you are willing to take the time to do so. You are fond of studying new subjects.

SECRET
You have a magnetic power, which should bring the best results in a public career. Also, you have the gift of persuasion.

SEPTEMBER 17

The secret of achievement is to hold a picture of a successful outcome in the mind.
—Henry David Thoreau

BORN ON THIS DAY

★ **David Souter**
U.S. Supreme Court justice

★ **Warren E. Burger**
U.S. Supreme Court justice

★ **Baz Luhrmann**
filmmaker

★ **John Ritter**
actor

★ **Edgar Mitchell**
astronaut

PERSONALITY
You combine two qualities in your character that should take you far along the pathway to success, and they are your initiative and your imagination. It is often said of a successful businessperson that they have vision. That is a quality that you possess to a high degree. However, the vision without the practical ability to put it into a useful, functioning form is a mere dream. That is why you succeed where others fail: You have the practical point of view that is needed to make your vision or dream a reality. You have good financial sense, and you know how to get value for your dollar. You are not foolish or extravagant, but you demand—and get—value for value, whether you invest time, effort, or money.

LIFE PATH
You have an analytical mind and carefully examine both sides of a question before making a decision. You are painstaking, reliable and competent, and generally successful when you make up your mind to do a task or project. You love travel and good, inspiring writing and spend much time in intellectual pursuits. Your homelife will generally be bright, sunny, and happy because you invite that energy into your life.

DESTINY
You may find your whole outlook on life changed by a new app, rule, or gadget that helps you or your business trend toward a new level of success. Although financial advancement may be slow in your younger years, you will find that it is steady and will increase exponentially later. Plan expenditures and savings accordingly. You may take a long journey or make a big move that can have important and promising aftereffects on your career and social life.

KARMIC LESSON
You have a wide range of interests and are doubtless interested in technology and energy. You have a retentive memory and a fine power for making complex theories easy to grasp. You are a home lover and do not care so much for superficial socializing, as this means parting with the protective sanctuary of your beloved homelife. You are very magnanimous and fair in all dealings. You are quick with your perception, and you size up a situation quickly. You have a good deal of business ability and should visualize and affirm your intentions with a definite goal in view, which you can attain. You are a good manager and can usually find a method for getting things done if there is one to be had.

SECRET
You have an unusual balance of talents, all of which can be used to good advantage in the commercial field. You are of an acquisitive nature but a philanthropic spirit.

FRIENDS & FAMILY

September

SEPTEMBER 18

Good manners are made up of petty sacrifices.
—Ralph Waldo Emerson

BORN ON THIS DAY
- **James Gandolfini, Jr.**
  actor
- **Greta Garbo**
  actor
- **Lance Armstrong**
  bicycle racer
- **Aisha Tyler**
  actor, talk show host
- **Xzibit**
  rapper, actor

FRIENDS & FAMILY

_____
_____
_____
_____
_____
_____
_____
_____
_____

PERSONALITY
You are the visionary, the mystic, and the dreamer. Anything that offends your high ideals offends you, and you will not tolerate it. There are times when you despair and feel that the whole world is going nowhere because of the universal grasping for material things, and this depresses you. However, you try to live your life according to the high and noble spiritual aspirations that are so deeply a part of you, and that is the best that any person can do in a modern world of competition and overwhelming information. You have very good mental powers, and you approach a problem with directness and discernment. You have a devoted, fiery nature, and you need to feel love and affection to be happy. When the person you love fails to live up to your idea of true romance, you feel very much let down. It takes a long time for you to get over disappointments of the heart.

LIFE PATH
You are faithful and devoted to your business and home duties, even though they can annoy you greatly. You are sometimes self-effacing, yet other times impetuous and headstrong, but mainly tender, kindhearted, and loving. You are a good manager and know how to make the best of what you have. You form friendships readily and might easily fall in love at first sight.

DESTINY
You are good at puzzles and other mental games. You will involve yourself with cultural activities to contact your ancestors. You welcome a change of routine and like to be open to new ideas. Efficient planning can make your days seem more cheerful and satisfying and less boring. The effectiveness with which you write and speak can have a direct bearing on the advances you make. Stress the use of your knowledge and imagination to get ahead.

KARMIC LESSON
You are mostly optimistic, inclined to look upon the bright side. You dislike trouble, rudeness, waste, and noise, and when these things afflict you, you retire to a quiet room or your own thoughts and think about the meaning of life and your future. You indulge in daydreams and are far from satisfied with the way the world is and how too many people act. You feel that good manners have been lost. Learn that all possibilities lurk within you, and that you have only to exercise your reserve powers to achieve the success you long for. You are deeply contemplative, and you feel that the cares of the world rest upon your shoulders at times. Do not be too serious. Take life as it comes and develop a better sense of humor.

SECRET
You have an impulsive nature, and if you cannot indulge your impulse, you get moody. You must have constant praise and encouragement to be your best.

SEPTEMBER 19

To believe with certainty we must begin with doubting.
—*Stanislaus I*

BORN ON THIS DAY
- **Paulo Freire**
  author, philosopher
- **Jimmy Fallon**
  TV host
- **Jeremy Irons**
  actor
- **Trisha Yearwood**
  singer
- **Mario Batali**
  celebrity chef

PERSONALITY
You seem to be a veritable dynamo of energy, and even when you are sick or restricted in motion, you direct all your affairs and somehow manage everything connected with your home, business, and welfare. Yet, you do not offend people with your abilities because you put your ideas across gently, without being domineering or sarcastic, or unpleasant in any other way. One of the lessons you learned at an early age is that all good things flow from hard work, and that being lazy will get you nowhere. You have since put that policy to work whenever you have wanted anything, and you have found in truth that it does work. Because you are so willing to do so much, you also expect a lot from other people. Nothing distracts or annoys you as much as selfishness and laziness. You cannot tolerate those people in life who always take and never give.

LIFE PATH
Ambitious and energetic, you are a hard worker, and for those you love you would drive yourself to the verge of physical exhaustion. You are discreet, painstaking, accurate, and fastidious. You love sharing ideas and concepts and are an earnest and interesting conversationalist. You are loving and kindhearted to those you care about.

DESTINY
Your social relationships may seem unusually pleasant due to the predominant Venus vibrations on your birthday. Your sympathetic understanding and fostering of a romantic match could become a memorable event in a friend's life. To give satisfaction to your life after work, spend time in the search for beauty and in art appreciation. The development of one or more hobbies is an enjoyable means of increasing your circle of friends who have similar interests and abilities.

KARMIC LESSON
You have a good head for business and are farseeing in this direction. You should get into business for yourself, as you will never be successful or contented otherwise. You will travel a great deal. You are attractive to anyone looking for a committed partnership and you draw serious people to you in a remarkable manner. You are pleasure loving and are never so happy as when going out with friends or entertaining in your own home. You are fond of researching complex topics that affect you. You are musical and may sing well. The stage has a strange fascination for you, as you seek movement, excitement, and stimulation. You are self-reliant and do not care to take advice from others. You are a good organizer and can do this for others if they give you autonomy.

SECRET
You need to be correcting and advising others to feel confident. Yet, you are easily hurt when your advice is not followed.

FRIENDS & FAMILY

SEPTEMBER 20

*The mind is like a parachute—
it works only when it is open.*
—Anonymous

BORN ON THIS DAY

★ **George R.R. Martin**
author

★ **Sophia Loren**
actor

★ **Michelle Visage**
TV personality, singer

★ **Kristen Johnston**
actor

★ **Julian Draxler**
soccer player

FRIENDS & FAMILY

_____

_____

_____

_____

_____

_____

_____

_____

PERSONALITY

You like to be helpful, generally lending a hand when assistance of any kind is needed. You are full of surprises, even to the people who know you best. There is a quality in your makeup that just prompts you to do the unexpected, and nothing gives you more fun than to see the astonished faces of your friends when you pull one of your surprises out of your hat. The theory of negation was the secret of success of Oscar Wilde's literary work; he would take some popular phrase and just state the exact opposite. That is the same principle you use to get a laugh or some other desired reaction. Sometimes you shock people a little bit by answering their questions with frankness that they little expected, and you have thus discovered that the truth is a powerful sword indeed.

LIFE PATH

You possess a great deal of originality and are liable to do unexpected things, or if you do what is expected, it will be in an unusual way. You like to associate with unusual, interesting people and form your friendships among them. You will not be bossed around, but you are fond of personal attention, and one who understands your temperament can lead you.

DESTINY

Since your birthday falls on a Uranus-ruled day, unusual progress could be shown in the attainment of your goals and happiness. Ideas with which you played as a youngster may come onto the scene of your current activities to receive priority attention—what was old is new again. An unusual concept you have may bring financial gains, as well as increased public relations. Keep yourself up to mental par through playing games, which help with your nervous energy.

KARMIC LESSON

You have a naturally strong, resilient character, and you do not care much about the opinions of others. Once you think you are in the right, you will go ahead regardless of criticism. You like to make money, and you like the power that it brings. Early in life you should decide what you want to do, and then devote time and energy toward its accomplishment. You will never succeed if you scatter your forces, but do not force them all the time, and without intermission, on the person you are trying to convince. Do not wait for things to just turn up; instead, seek them out. They will not turn up, as a rule, but will wait for you to turn them up. You must move and hustle.

SECRET

You have a decided talent for writing, with just enough ambition to succeed. You possess a love of color and are aware of its power.

SEPTEMBER 21

When you have spoken the word, it reigns over you. When it is unspoken, you reign over it.
—Arabic proverb

BORN ON THIS DAY

★ **H.G. Wells**
author

★ **Stephen King**
author

★ **Billy Porter**
actor

★ **Bill Murray**
comedian, actor

★ **Cass Sunstein**
legal scholar, author

● PERSONALITY

You have a wonderful imagination, an orderly and scholarly mind, and the stamina to withstand many hard knocks that life gives you. Although you may have a longer period of formation of your mature character, you evolve at the top of the heap because in those formative years you do not stop yourself from experimenting. You sample every phase of life, every philosophy, every approach, and every recreation! As an intelligent skeptic, you believe nothing that is beyond your experience. Therefore, you experiment with life. What you find good and true, you retain in your storehouse of experience; what you find false and distasteful, you give up and discard.

● LIFE PATH

You have an indomitable spirit and refuse to acknowledge defeat, even though you've had many setbacks. You are intelligent, farsighted, and resourceful, possessing good problem-solving and decision-making abilities. You are affectionate, inspiring to your friends and family, and fond of belonging to groups of like-minded people. You have many friends and are dependable, staunch, and true to them.

● DESTINY

Stick to your job even though it may seem boring at times. Cash remuneration and other gains can be the reward for your hard work and courageous attitude in facing obstacles. For maximum success, when older, stay with the things you know well rather than venturing into untried fields. Effective use of the lessons you have learned through experience can open doors to satisfying progress, as you like to share coping methods, tips, and techniques that work.

● KARMIC LESSON

You are fond of reading and might be quite a connoisseur of ideas. You might write also, and if you do not do so, you should certainly cultivate your talent in that direction. Remember that the only way to learn to write is to write, and no matter if you tear up everything you write for a year, keep at it and eventually you will become a proficient author. You are fond of history and have a good and retentive memory. You have great powers of affection and could make someone infinitely happy. You are psychic and often have strange experiences and dreams that are symbolic and seem to foretell future events. You are self-reliant and believe in your own powers, which free you from many a trying position.

● SECRET

You have a generous nature that can be easily imposed upon under the guise of friendship.

FRIENDS & FAMILY

SEPTEMBER 22

Joy is what happens to us when we allow ourselves to recognize how good things really are.
—Marianne Williamson

BORN ON THIS DAY
- **Michael Faraday**
  scientist
- **Andrea Bocelli**
  singer
- **Scott Baio**
  actor
- **Doris Lessing**
  author
- **Godfrey Gao**
  fashion model

FRIENDS & FAMILY

PERSONALITY
According to astrology, you are what is called a "cusper." That means that you were born on a day when the Sun was moving from one sign of the zodiac into the next in its ever-changing apparent motion. For this reason, you share the traits of those born under the sign of Virgo and the sign of Libra. Your personality is a blend of both. You have a truly spiritual quality about you and are not necessarily attracted by the mere material or gaudy things in life. You can spend whole days sitting quietly by the side of a river or a lake, and you appreciate the small, beautiful things in life: flowers, birds, clouds, and a good meal. When you make a purchase, you never allow yourself to fall below a certain standard of excellence, as you are very discriminating. You are here to help others find a life of love, joy, and peace and the time and money to enjoy it.

LIFE PATH
You are imaginative and impulsive and somewhat of a dreamer. You formulate many plans that are never carried out and build many castles in the air. You are a bit of a procrastinator, as you are also a perfectionist. You need to cultivate more confidence, self-reliance, perseverance, and foresight. You are lovable, sweet-tempered, and attractive, a general favorite, and a much-sought-after friend.

DESTINY
Your life is filled with a variety of interesting potentialities. Work and play alike can afford opportunities for use of your talents, as well as provide creative pleasures. Although you have allowed many of your capabilities to lie dormant, a period of development comes after age thirty. Also, you may take part in, or be greatly affected by, a marriage in your family or among your circle of friends that opens you to a life-changing opportunity. Confidences of a personal nature will always be relayed to you, as people trust you with their secrets, but be careful to guard them well.

KARMIC LESSON
You are rather too wavering in your thoughts to achieve major success, as you are apt to stop yourself for fear of success. You must learn to concentrate, to focus your forces, and not to scatter them over so wide an area of interests. You must depend more upon yourself; you must have one goal, one ambition in life, and stick to it and keep pursuing it. You are inclined to think and criticize inwardly and not to be outspoken enough in your dealings with others. Cultivate greater frankness and openness of manner about your needs and desires. You are fond of the good things of this life, and nothing suits you better than to spend the day in the country, and then go to someplace good for dinner.

SECRET
You are too intense and critical for your own good. Balance your mental work with some interesting manual labor to relieve stress and worry.

SEPTEMBER 23

You must do the thing you think you cannot do.
—Eleanor Roosevelt

🎲 PERSONALITY
You have the analytical type of mind that loves to wrestle with deep and complex problems. As a student, you are very thorough and proficient, and you see in each lesson, or experiment, or example, an analogy to life itself, which makes you a wiser person. Of course, when your student days are over, you are still a student of life—and so this description of you still holds good. You have the power to get people to do as you say because what you say makes sense. You believe in the Law of Attraction. You are able to handle words well and are quite proficient at speaking and writing, especially in the field of journalism or blogging. However, technology, the metaverse, and photography also have an attraction for you, and you should get a lot out of pursuing these vocations as an amateur or professional.

🌀 LIFE PATH
You are observant, learn quickly, and are usually able to do what you have seen others do. You do not possess a great deal of originality, but you are careful, painstaking, and prudent. You are amiable, accommodating, and honest. You care a great deal about getting attention, although you will never complain if you do not receive as much as you would like.

👁 DESTINY
Adequate compensation for work done in the past may arrive unexpectedly. It can be both surprising and pleasant. Utilize your zeal to prove even greater accomplishments. If you have to work with someone who irritates you, concentrate on improving yourself rather than the other person. Your charm and popularity can usually work wonders because of the strong solar-ray influences of the Sun on your birthday. Your prestige may hit an all-time high after age thirty.

☯ KARMIC LESSON
Full of allure and personal magnetism, you are engaging and have a special charisma all your own. You are good company and doubtless very popular in your circle. You are fond of going out, and there can never be too many in the party to suit you. You are a bit of a flirt. You are capable of feeling and loving deeply and will doubtless ultimately settle down happily. Be very careful in your selection of a partner, for your whole future happiness will depend upon your discrimination. You have a good head for commerce and could be successful in business. You are capable of undertaking big ventures and have the self-assurance that is so necessary in large-scale projects.

🔒 SECRET
Reach your own decisions independently, and do not submit too often to the advice of others. Also, temper your desires with reasoning.

BORN ON THIS DAY
- ★ **Bruce Springsteen** — singer
- ★ **Julio Iglesias** — singer
- ★ **Ray Charles** — singer
- ★ **Ani DiFranco** — singer/songwriter
- ★ **Jermaine Dupri** — music producer, rapper

FRIENDS & FAMILY

SEPTEMBER 24

To cultivate kindness is a valuable part of the business of life.
—Samuel Johnson

BORN ON THIS DAY

★ **F. Scott Fitzgerald**
author

★ **Jim Henson**
puppeteer

★ **Lou Dobbs**
TV political commentator

★ **Phil Hartman**
comedian, actor

★ **Jessica Lucas**
actor

FRIENDS & FAMILY

PERSONALITY
You are distinguished by a very subtle sense of social consciousness. Because of your sensitivity, you are always aware of what is going on around you, and even of some things that are occurring at quite a distance from where you are. Your desire is to change things to some far better state, and to that end, you devote much of your energy. You have a deep feeling for what your friends are experiencing at all times, and you seem better able than they to put their emotions into words. Although you have a deep sympathy for your loved ones, you also have a somewhat strong desire to protect, to shield, and at the same time to manage them. You give your all to the happiness of those you love, yet you may succeed only in spoiling them. Occasional emotional outbursts depress you in the aftermath, and you should control your feelings to prevent your own embarrassment. Calming of thoughts through meditation should bring to you a more serene outlook on life.

LIFE PATH
You possess a great deal of natural ability to teach, and once you make up your mind, you can accomplish much. You need to cultivate more self-love. You are very sensitive and at times impulsive, and your conclusions reached by intuition are more reliable than those reached through reasoning. You like socializing and derive much of your pleasure from sources outside your home.

DESTINY
Do not let your feelings get upset by an increase of work or responsibilities. The result should be a challenge to your capabilities and should take you to the next level of success. Set an optimistic goal for business, social, and homelife, then proceed to live up to your schedule of planned activities. Gains will be in direct ratio to your efforts. Avoid letting impatience or grumpiness hold you back.

KARMIC LESSON
You are very straightforward and honest, and your word is always as good as your written promise. Learn the importance of habits, either good or bad, as they are hard to break, and they play a large part in life. You sometimes talk too much; you must learn to say little and do much. You are fond of children and should be around them often. You are impressionistic and open to external influences, which you must fight. Do not be afraid of speaking the truth, no matter what it costs. It may create a storm, but remember that a storm dispels clouds. Act upon your own judgment, yet do not repel the advice of others. Wise people receive instruction from all sources and decide themselves which they will act upon.

SECRET
You are shrewd in business and would be more capable of managing large enterprises than small concerns.

SEPTEMBER 25

The future belongs to those who believe in the beauty of their dreams.
—Eleanor Roosevelt

BORN ON THIS DAY
- **William Faulkner**
  author
- **Will Smith**
  actor
- **Michael Douglas**
  actor
- **Scotty Pippin**
  basketball player
- **bell hooks**
  author

◉ PERSONALITY
Although you are somewhat given to procrastination, you can work rapidly and efficiently when you make up your mind to do so. However, you usually need some stimulating person or circumstances to get you going at high speed. When you have such strong incentives as a satisfactory reward awaiting you, you can go ahead full speed on any task that is assigned to you. Your imagination is quite active, and you also have a deeply psychic intuition. You get hunches in the forms of quick flashes, and when you act on them, they generally turn out very well for you. You take life quite seriously, and you would like to specialize in psychology so that you could better understand the foibles and quirks of the human mind. You would be successful at healing of some sort, or any profession or vocation in which you could be of service to others.

◉ LIFE PATH
You are frank, outspoken, and honest, rather pliable, but on occasion very stubborn. You are fastidious, like beautiful and artistic surroundings, and devote much thought to making your home pleasant and attractive. You are very affectionate, quite demonstrative, and liable to fall in love at first sight.

◉ DESTINY
To say that you have acquired the magic touch may sound like an exaggeration, but you yourself will be impressed by the financial gains you can make from being true to your dream. The status of your business prestige or the magnitude of your dream can make a deep impression on everyone who knows you. Take time to expand and plan your ideas and to show your generosity to friends and family.

◉ KARMIC LESSON
Excitable, you sometimes lack balance between your intuitive and rational sides. You often listen too much to others and must learn to stand more firmly on your own two feet. You have great talents and ought to succeed in life, as it all lies within you and needs only to be encouraged. You take life as it comes, not thinking or planning ahead as much as you should. You must learn the value of money and should early cultivate the habit of saving, as later you will regret it if you do not. You have a complete inner life, which no one seems to be able to share with you. You are a good deal of a daydreamer and not as practical as others want you to be.

◉ SECRET
You have a desire to engage in philanthropy and may want to do this as a career. You are a lover of animals.

FRIENDS & FAMILY

SEPTEMBER 26

To be trusted is a greater compliment than to be loved.
—George MacDonald

BORN ON THIS DAY
- **Martin Heidegger**
  philosopher
- **George Gershwin**
  composer
- **Olivia Newton-John**
  singer, actor
- **Serena Williams**
  tennis player
- **Andrea Dworkin**
  feminist

FRIENDS & FAMILY

PERSONALITY
The ups and downs of your temperament are caused by an alternating current of goodwill and dominance in your makeup. At times, you cannot do enough for other people, especially the members of your family; at other times, it seems as though you had an imaginary whip in your hand and were trying to beat everyone around you into submission to your will. You can also be very impulsive, and on the spur of the moment you can make some terrifically generous gesture or some terrifically insulting remark. You are very sure of yourself, and as a result of your self-confidence, you have little or no use for people who cannot make up their minds. Acclaim for your personal achievements is your aim in life. You want to be noticed, and not for mere notoriety's sake, but for the sake of recognition of what you have achieved. Therefore, you work hard to do things better than others, and you push yourself forward so that fame and fortune may eventually be yours.

LIFE PATH
You have considerable talent for making an impression. You are energetic, ambitious, and positive, but sometimes obstinate. You will yield to love and persuasion, but you refuse to be dictated to. Your circle of friends is large, and your entertaining presence is always desired at any social function.

DESTINY
The Saturn rays of your birthday indicate opportunities to show your real work and gain the assistance or blessings of people who are in authority. Be purposeful and steadfast; you should have no reason to resent the time devoted to your responsibilities. Loyalty and fidelity can pay as rich a dividend as a cash investment, insofar as satisfaction to you. Ignore useless worry and concern over trivialities. Look ahead with faith and confidence, and you will be rewarded.

KARMIC LESSON
You are sincere, thorough, and businesslike. There is a powerful impetus working within you, urging you on to higher and nobler things. You are a person of faith, and all nature seems to show you the work of a master hand. You could write well, and you love every aspect of technology and entertainment that brings the world together. You enjoy travel but love your own home, and after you have seen a good deal of the world, you tire of it and come back home for rest and comfort. With a good deal of personal magnetism and charm, you are in love with loving. The world in turn finds you attractive, and you will spend more time than most satisfying your desires. You must be very careful that your attempt to have a good time is not misinterpreted as offensive.

SECRET
You are a born leader, and any other position will not bring as much success. Follow the calling, and you will rise to great heights.

SEPTEMBER 27

If you get up one more time than you fall, you will make it through.
—Chinese proverb

BORN ON THIS DAY

- **Gwyneth Paltrow**
  actor
- **Lil Wayne**
  rapper, music producer
- **Francesco Totti**
  soccer player
- **Avril Lavigne**
  singer
- **Wilford Brimley**
  actor

PERSONALITY

Generosity, flawless taste, and a certain impulsiveness characterize you. You enjoy seeing other people happy to such an extent that you might easily bankrupt yourself in satisfying your desire to bring joy to them. Your ideal in life is to have so much money that you could spread cheer everywhere; it might be said, figuratively speaking, that your chosen role in the drama of life is the part of the universal Santa Claus. The fears and doubts that so often assail human beings have a strange effect on you. Instead of fighting these mental demons with all your strength, you seem to withdraw from the field of combat. Your idea about keeping out of trouble is keeping away from it, and in this you may well be right. At any rate, you wish to lead a peaceful existence, although you go on an occasional spree that is far from quiet.

LIFE PATH

Small annoyances cause you more worry than they should. Cultivate buoyancy and cheerfulness, and meet the little troubles with the same spirit you show toward the large ones. You are kind, generous, and sympathetic; you will secure a loving and affectionate partner. You have an ardent nature, and love is your greatest quest.

DESTINY

Your versatility and mental alertness will be efficiently demonstrated so that many will take notice in your lifetime. Take advantage of all opportunities to speak in public or express your ideas in writing. You have the ability to speak and write effectively, even though you may not have practiced these talents. Either one of them may be the means of taking you far along the path to success or the fulfillment of your dearest desires.

KARMIC LESSON

You are optimistic and try always to look on the sunny side. You are interested in drama, and the glare of the footlights and the movies have a charm and a fascination for you that are not easily resisted, though you may channel this energy online. You have strong emotions and a temper, too, which is rather too easily aroused. Do not be so sensitive to the remarks and glances of others. You must learn to be franker in your dealings with others. You suffer much inwardly, often, when it would be quite easy to put straight the matter troubling you the most. Do not be too cheap in money matters; if only you hold in your mind the right attitude, it will come to you. Feel rich inside, and you will attract abundance to you.

SECRET

You have a natural understanding of legal matters. You are very active, and your career would not interfere with your personal life, as you are good at balancing.

FRIENDS & FAMILY

_____
_____
_____
_____
_____
_____
_____
_____
_____
_____
_____

SEPTEMBER 28

He is richest who is content with the least, for content is the wealth of nature.
—Socrates

BORN ON THIS DAY

- **Brigitte Bardot**
  actor, model
- **Janeane Garofalo**
  comedian, actor
- **Ben E. King**
  singer, music producer
- **Naomi Watts**
  actor
- **Jeezy**
  rapper

FRIENDS & FAMILY

PERSONALITY
Managerial work is your forte. There is no question of your executive ability, and you can run your home or assume duties of importance in a bank, corporation, real estate office, or public institution. Because you have a reputation for integrity and initiative as well as a controlled temper, you are always entrusted with duties that carry the requirement of a sense of responsibility. In your estimation, a broken pledge or promise is the worst of human weaknesses, and you would never allow yourself to lie or break your word. You prefer activities on the mental plane to those involving manual work, but you can lend a hand when one is needed at household jobs or making repairs. You are great at organizing and can lead a hike, steer a committee, or run a startup with equal enthusiasm and efficiency.

LIFE PATH
You are impulsive, emotional, and rather impatient. You like to get results quickly. You are versatile and original, quick to see a point, and shrewd in your judgment. You are humorous, whimsical, and vivacious. You do not believe in mixing business with pleasure but take your share of each in its proper place.

DESTINY
With Venus rays ruling your birth date, you often have cause to be optimistic and to make preparations for a serene but active life. Effort will not be dissipated in emotional disturbances, for the home scene will be harmonious, and happy friendships will prosper. Heartfelt desires can be gratified, and all in all your birth date can be quite fortunate.

KARMIC LESSON
Kind, sincere, and sympathetic, you would make a good therapist. You are intensely interested in your fellow beings and cannot bear to see them suffer or be downtrodden, as they often are in our great cities. You attract people to you by sheer force of personality. Psychic and impressionistic, you are subtle in your perceptions, penetrating deeply into the roots of things. Often you feel there is a burden weighing on your soul that is impossible to remove, as though the cares of the world were placed upon your shoulders. Try not to let this influence you. You can do a tremendous amount of work even if it is disagreeable, and you have the capacity to make yourself do things that are not natural or pleasant to you.

SECRET
You have a generous spirit, always ready to listen to the woes of others and to help, even in undeserving cases. You should guard against being conned.

SEPTEMBER 29

Live as if you were to die tomorrow. Learn as if you were to live forever.
—Mahatma Gandhi

BORN ON THIS DAY
- **Enrico Fermi**, physicist
- **Jerry Lee Lewis**, singer
- **Kevin Durant**, basketball player
- **Madeline Kahn**, actor, comedian
- **Andrew Dice Clay**, comedian

PERSONALITY
You are an expert at taking the blueprint made by someone else and converting it into a reality. Of course, this is a figurative way of saying that you are more interested in carrying out the concepts of another person than initiating plans, concepts, or ideas of your own. However, your job in life will be just as important as that of the architect or planner, because under your supervision, the structure dreamed by the other will take shape and form. You are quite a connoisseur of the arts, delighting in exhibitions of the latest art evolutions, as well as painting and sculpture, lectures, stage productions, and concerts. Things of historical significance appeal to you, and you enjoy visiting museums, landmarks, and antique shops. You also like to collect things and could be an efficient manager of a major collection. While friendly to the extreme, you deeply resent being used and can be as strong an opponent as you are a friend, if crossed.

LIFE PATH
You are bold and enterprising and possess a wonderfully strong will. Your dominant force carries you forward, and your associates look up to you as a mentor. You like to be amused, and you choose lively, vivacious people for your friends. You are affable and lovable and have great love for your family history.

DESTINY
Negative people are to be avoided. Take action and make significant strides toward your goal by working in a supportive group situation. Once you become freed from certain restraints of the past, at first you may feel a little bewildered. You will then experience a sense of relief and a new freedom. Trust your own judgment and rely on the decisions you make, but get feedback from your trusted advisers and counselors.

KARMIC LESSON
You are positive, self-assertive, and strong-willed. Be careful, however, not to mistake pigheadedness for determination. Learn to analyze yourself and make up your mind to eradicate any faults of character you believe you may possess. You desire money and the power that money brings. You have an almost military precision about things—in your business and in your family. You are calm and centered, and nothing stirs you up as it does some people. You have confidence in your own abilities, which is well justified. Partnership is the life suited to you.

SECRET
You are more interested in history than in modern life. You should indulge your talent for treasure hunting.

FRIENDS & FAMILY

SEPTEMBER 30

How wonderful it is that nobody need wait a single moment before starting to improve the world.
—Anne Frank

BORN ON THIS DAY

- **Truman Capote**
  author
- **Elie Wiesel**
  author, Holocaust survivor
- **Johnny Mathis**
  singer
- **T-Pain**
  rapper, music producer
- **Fran Drescher**
  actor

FRIENDS & FAMILY

PERSONALITY

Only the best in life is good enough for you. That is your slogan, and you refuse to bargain or compromise with anyone who offers you less. You are perfectly willing to work hard, actually to slave and sacrifice, if you see ahead of you a goal that is sparkling. But if you think your efforts will go to waste or bring mediocre compensation, you refuse to bother to make the deal. You enjoy having people around you, and you are generally the center of attraction because you have great wit and a gracious manner. Your friends come from every walk of life—not because you lack taste or discrimination but because you see good qualities in everyone and do not believe that social lines or economic status are what defines an individual. Legal work and teaching are fitting fields for you, although you have enough talent to succeed at anything you put your mind to.

LIFE PATH

You are intellectual, studious, sincere, and candid and have faith in your own abilities. You apply yourself with equal dedication to work and play, striving to excel in all you do. You do not confide secrets to others to any great extent but are yourself the recipient of many confidences. You are kind and considerate in your home, and you love to share what you have with your loved ones.

DESTINY

Make a dignified but graphic presentation of your ambitions and talents to attract the attention of those best qualified to assist you along the road to success. You have a magnetic personality, and you owe it to yourself not to hide your light under a bushel. If you find yourself in the spotlight, conduct yourself so that everyone realizes that this is where you belong.

KARMIC LESSON

You are fond of the good things of this life, being pleasure loving. You are capable of ascending to great heights but also capable of descending to the lowest of all depths. You must be very careful as to the guard you keep over your mood swings, for this is your nature. You are enthusiastic, impressionable, and subject to psychic impressions. You are dramatic, and performing is very alluring at all times. You are fortunate rather than wise in business, often rushing in where angels fear to tread, but generally come out all right. Learn self-mastery. It is the hardest of battles to win but the most rewarding.

SECRET

While you can conceive of big plans, you tend to worry over trifles. You derive peace and pleasure from homelife and spend a lot to make it beautiful.

OCTOBER 1

One conquers a bad habit more easily today than tomorrow.
—Confucius

BORN ON THIS DAY

★ **Jimmy Carter**
U.S. president

★ **William Rehnquist**
U.S. Supreme Court justice

★ **Julie Andrews**
singer, actor

★ **Mark McGwire**
baseball player

★ **Zach Galifianakis**
actor

FRIENDS & FAMILY

◉ PERSONALITY

You have been endowed with rather remarkable traits by a very special and unusual talent. Although it may not be until middle life that you discover your unique gift, it will be as though a door has suddenly opened when your big chance to acquire acclaim and do some special work in the world arrives. Your nature is very intense. You do everything with a strong will, driving yourself harder than any taskmaster could make you work. What you want to learn, you will expend untold energy to learn, and once you have mastered it, you will be tops in that field. While you are usually kindness itself, you can be very snarky to competitors. By training yourself to use your natural tact to get what you want, you will go further—and with less effort.

◉ LIFE PATH

You are amiable, magnetic, and faithful and have a positive disposition. You enjoy luxury but can adapt yourself to other conditions. You are idealistic and sensitive, kind and generous. You like music and art and get much enjoyment from both.

◉ DESTINY

Expand your activities into unexplored fields. You may discover a lot of latent talents and find yourself capable of handling new responsibilities. Do not worry about your ability to cope with the problems involved. Your accomplishments will be gratifying to you and your associates. Happiness will be by no means limited to the results of work or efforts toward financial advancement.

◉ KARMIC LESSON

Strongly intuitive and extremely psychic, you have a strong force of spirit and a very determined will. You are intensely interested in science, philosophy, and religious questions, particularly Eastern religions, which you want to investigate and then possibly join. Clearheaded and balanced, you carry out your plans and run your life largely by feeling and intuition. You will have many ups and downs and several reversals of fortune. But you keep a stiff upper lip and philosophical attitude, and when you have finally triumphed over many obstacles, no one will be able to say that you were ever a quitter. You are also intellectual, clever with ideas. You are affectionate and capable of deep love, but you do not make public displays of affection the way many do.

◉ SECRET

You could unravel complicated affairs but not reveal your findings for fear of offending. Reveal them sometimes.

OCTOBER 2

Habit, if not resisted, soon becomes necessity.
—Augustine of Hippo

☺ PERSONALITY

The innate integrity in your character is so strong that when you seem to be at your lowest ebb, your accomplishments will be valued and recognized. This refers to your validation not only in the monetary sense but also in the moral sense. For everyone who knows you would be glad to be of help to you, knowing full well that any favor done for you is bound to be repaid with compound interest. You know how to accept the unexpected changes of life, and you can go through the alternating cycles of prosperity and poverty, happiness and depression, with a deeply philosophical point of view. You know that everything but your own integrity is ephemeral, and so you pin your faith on the true spiritual and permanent values rather than the transient, material ones. Self-discipline makes your garden of good traits grow, and you evolve as a balanced, sensible, and tactful person.

◉ LIFE PATH

Sweet-tempered, kind, and loving, you are loved and admired and have many friends and few enemies. You like to learn and study spirituality. Your deepest interests are in teaching. You believe in giving pleasure and happiness; that is why your life is full. You are very devoted in your attachments, and no one could be more loyal and true to those they care about.

◉ DESTINY

Let the power of your personality dominate a number of distasteful situations in which you find yourself. When you translate your ideals into realities, you will be surprised by the influence that you can wield in matters of public as well as personal benefit. The completion of a number of big, long-term enterprises, which were begun more than ten years ago, will make the present and the future more inspiring and compelling.

☯ KARMIC LESSON

You are impulsive, inspirational, and fond of all the fine and subtle things of life. You are sensitive and take things to heart. You are extremely fond of all artistic pursuits. You are sincere and persevering. You are mastering the ancient wisdoms of this world and capable of giving good and sound advice, but you do not do so unless you are asked. You are sympathetic and interested in the lives of others. You are calm and serene; you have a certain dignity about you that seems natural and that few dare pierce. You have a good memory and seldom forget a name or a face. You are a good judge of human nature and can guess what lies behind a smiling exterior more quickly than anyone.

♟ SECRET

You will go far if you are able to curb your impatience for quick results. You are imperious and demand continuous attention.

BORN ON THIS DAY

★ **Mahatma Gandhi**
Indian revolutionary, political ethicist

★ **Nat Turner**
anti-slavery revolutionary

★ **Sting**
singer

★ **Annie Leibovitz**
photographer

★ **Brittany Howard**
singer/songwriter

FRIENDS & FAMILY

OCTOBER 3

Put all your eggs in one basket and then watch that basket.
—Andrew Carnegie

BORN ON THIS DAY

★ **Gore Vidal**
author, intellectual

★ **Gwen Stefani**
singer

★ **Al Sharpton**
civil rights activist

★ **Tessa Thompson**
actor

★ **Donna Karan**
fashion designer

FRIENDS & FAMILY

✦ PERSONALITY
You are somewhat reticent to show your emotions, for you believe that the true demonstration of feeling is in doing—not in just talking about it. Therefore, you may make great sacrifices for your family and friends, but you will do it in such a way that it seems that you are trying to hide your own good deeds. To a certain extent, you are what is called a lone wolf, for you prefer to work by yourself, to draw up your plans in solitude, and to enjoy solitary pleasures, such as reading, walking, and meditating. Figuratively speaking, you are a builder. You have strong ideas, and you possess an enormous amount of courage with which to carry them out. It is your belief that more can be accomplished by inner will than by sheer force, and you exercise your mind and talents to accomplish your high ideals in life.

✦ LIFE PATH
You are a great reader and a fluent talker. You have shrewd judgment and much ingenuity. You are not overly demonstrative in your love nor confiding in your friendships, although your love is fervent and your friends, many. You are dependable, trustworthy, faithful, and always discreet.

✦ DESTINY
You should appreciate much more the potentialities in your original ideas and follow through on your inspirations. "Do or do not. There is no try," from Yoda of *Star Wars*, might well be your motto. You need not ignore the invitation of changing scenes. New acquaintances and interests in metaphysics will be compatible with your fundamental goals in life. There is ample time to obtain a variety of profitable experiences.

✦ KARMIC LESSON
You are a very well-rounded person. You are a favorite of fortune in talents and personality. You have good business sense and are always capable of getting the money equivalent to the work you do. You are also musical and artistic, love fine design, read good books, are psychic and intuitive, and like socializing. You like to know about history and its lessons, are interested in people, and try to understand their trials and sorrows. You are a good listener. Think and analyze less, and act more. You have a clever brain, but there are many other people in the world who have clever brains also. You have great possibilities within you; live up to them and good karma will be yours.

✦ SECRET
You have a sense of harmony so great that it is willing to condone petty offenses in order to preserve it. You might be inclined to overpamper your children.

OCTOBER 4

The weak can never forgive. Forgiveness is the attribute of the strong.
—Mahatma Gandhi

BORN ON THIS DAY
- **Isaac Asimov**
  author
- **Anne Rice**
  author
- **Russell Simmons**
  music producer, entrepreneur
- **Charlton Heston**
  actor
- **Susan Sarandon**
  actor

PERSONALITY
You find friends and acquaintances from many walks of life. You excel as a conversationalist because you have a lively wit and a brilliant vocabulary. You can draw word pictures so vivid that you give your audience a sense of having the experiences you are describing. Your range of interests is so wide that you sometimes leave one activity, project, or job to start another before the one at hand is finished. This is a trait that common sense says you should abandon. Although you are inclined to moodiness, you keep your old friends because they understand that you are not petty or mean innately, even when you act that way. You create drama wherever you go, and you seem to thrive on applause. Life has much to offer you, and you have much to contribute.

LIFE PATH
You are persevering, painstaking, systematic, and farsighted, but you need more self-esteem. You are not afraid to assume responsibility and are generally successful in your undertakings. You need to be outdoors and engaging in athletics—this is good for your moods. You are sensitive to unpleasant people and surroundings.

DESTINY
Your wonderful assets of intelligence and problem solving will be capitalized on as you climb the ladder to success. You must learn to trust the workings of your own mind and nature more. You mistrust everything too much and are a bit too skeptical. A large measure of satisfied ambition is in store for you. You can undertake difficult projects and bring them to a successful conclusion.

KARMIC LESSON
You have good judgment and are interested in practical things. You are original and inventive. You have a good speaking voice and could excel in debate; you can detect inaccuracies. For this reason, you might make a first-rate lawyer or proofreader. You have a good intellect and might shine in an organization or club, becoming one of the top brass. You are quick-tempered, and this you must learn to curb. Pay less attention to the faults of commission and more to the faults of omission. Remember above all that charity begins at home, and if you wish to put any of your original ideas into operation, there is no place more suitable than your own home.

SECRET
A lover of excitement, crowds, and bright lights, you have a definite talent for advertising and the theater, but in a managerial capacity rather than as an actor or performer.

FRIENDS & FAMILY

OCTOBER 5

The doors we open and close each day decide the lives we live.
—Flora Whittemore

BORN ON THIS DAY
- **Neil deGrasse Tyson**
  physicist
- **Kate Winslet**
  actor
- **Grant Hill**
  basketball player
- **Michael Andretti**
  race car driver
- **Bernie Mac**
  actor, comedian

FRIENDS & FAMILY

PERSONALITY
Without seeming to be domineering or at all aggressive, you have a way about you that automatically puts you in charge of whatever is afoot. In business, at home, or at social gatherings, you take the lead with natural grace and charm, and you direct projects into mostly pleasant and sensible channels. This is all for the good, because you are a well-balanced person, motivated by fairness, consideration, and unselfishness. You know that there is a time for work and a time for play, and you establish equilibrium in your own life that would make a mighty fine example for anyone to follow. Your forte is personal service combined with good management. Because you possess this singular ability, you would make a successful supervisor or executive in any profession or vocation where the income is derived from sales or service.

LIFE PATH
You are impulsive and changeable, but underneath all this you have a very strong character, forceful and compelling. You have that personal touch that makes everyone like you, no matter what your relationship with people may be. You have many dear friends, and some will be lifelong in duration.

DESTINY
There is no necessity for you to change your opinions to suit the convenience of others. You should stand up for your own ideas. However, do this with courtesy while respecting individual differences in outlook. Your generosity and understanding in relation to family members will contribute to harmony, even though they sometimes get on your nerves.

KARMIC LESSON
You are a hard worker, inclined to overdo a good thing. You might be interested in politics, and you might make your mark there if you enter it locally. You are a true friend, but you speak your mind with brutal frankness at times. Remember that some people are preternaturally sensitive in this respect, and what you say can hurt. You lead an active, busy life and cannot understand those who spend their lives in lazy ways. You are eminently commonsensical. You are drawn to sexuality in a manner you do not understand; you do not know why this should be so, as it sometimes seems too uncontrolled. You may inherit a small sum of money or something valuable early in your life.

SECRET
Your work should be that of a consultant or coach, as you can readily see the one thing needed to make a venture or project take off.

OCTOBER 6

If you are irritated by every rub, how will your mirror be polished?
— Jalāl ad-Dīn Rumi

✦ PERSONALITY
You have a smart mind, generous qualities, strategic ability, innate courage, confidence in your work, and the ability to make up your mind with trigger-like speed. Such endowments cannot fail to see you through the most difficult situation that life may confront you with, and the best part of this is that you know it yourself. Even when things look darkest, you always manage to find the one ray of hope that lights up your optimism like a magic lamp. There are occasions when it seems inevitable that you will defer in order to play for time, but at the last minute your self-reliance comes to your aid. Your interests are more along intellectual lines than sports or other forms of social or group activities. By following the dictates of your intuition, you should arrive at the niche in life that you carve for yourself alone.

✦ LIFE PATH
You are energetic and competent, possessed of great mechanical and analytical ability. You never enter into a project half-heartedly, always putting forth your best efforts to do a project in the best possible manner. You enjoy the respect of those who work with you.

✦ DESTINY
Financial problems usually will be solved under the influence of the Jupiter rays of your birthday. You are lucky. But good fortune will not be confined to material gains. There are many interesting experiences awaiting you in the social and scholastic realms that can add to your enjoyment of life. Effort expended in any endeavor will be rewarded with satisfying accomplishment. You can expect private and public recognition of your capabilities.

✦ KARMIC LESSON
You are emotional, dramatic, and always interesting. You are witty and original. You shine within your social circle and are doubtless always a popular figure in it. You love social networking and all the technical savvy that goes with it. Communicating with people around the world fascinates you. You will never succeed in life unless you follow your natural bent. You must find out, early in life, what you can do best and stick to this through thick and thin. You are intensely curious, never satisfied until you have found out all there is to be known about a subject that interests you. You are intuitive, and you should follow your inner voice. You have good taste and judgment.

✦ SECRET
You have fine intuitive powers and instinctual intelligence but not enough aggressiveness, yielding to people who do not know as much as you do.

BORN ON THIS DAY
- **George Westinghouse**
  engineer, entrepreneur
- **Carole Lombard**
  actor
- **Elisabeth Shue**
  actor
- **Jazz Jennings**
  YouTube celebrity
- **Tony Dungy**
  football coach

FRIENDS & FAMILY

OCTOBER 7

I'm a great believer in luck, and I find the harder I work the more I have of it.
—Thomas Jefferson

BORN ON THIS DAY
- **Niels Bohr**
  physicist
- **Desmond Tutu**
  theologian
- **Simon Cowell**
  TV personality, music producer
- **Yo-Yo Ma**
  cellist
- **Elijah Muhammad**
  religious leader, black separatist

FRIENDS & FAMILY

PERSONALITY
You were born with the common touch. There is nothing detrimental meant by "common" here; it is, indeed, a compliment. Few people have this quality of universal human understanding, which you have, and those who have had it have done the most for the development of tolerance throughout the world. Because you have the sympathy and understanding to comprehend all people in all walks of life, you can do much to make them all happier. You promote goodwill in your family life, in your business dealings, and in the aid you render in humanitarian work on the practical plane.

LIFE PATH
Studious, intellectual, and very well informed, you are a good logical thinker and a lucid talker. You are scrupulously honest and very faithful, and you never say anything you do not mean. You chafe under restraint, a good virtue except when someone is testing your patience and loyalty.

DESTINY
You can surmount any obstacle that may arise with your practical approach to problem solving. Do not overemphasize petty annoyances. Chart your course with a view to making the most of each passing moment. Idleness will bring little pleasure, so use your free moments for study or the development of skills. There will be monetary rewards for both mental and manual labor. Keep emotional impulses in check, but learn to appreciate the special joys that each day will bring.

KARMIC LESSON
You never let an opportunity pass you by but grasp it by the tail, which is the only way opportunity can be caught. You are kind and sympathetic. You can state things clearly and simply and for this reason would make a good teacher. You will probably travel a great deal and see much of the world, as you are interested in other cultures. You must be careful to keep your word, no matter how insignificant that may appear to you. You will probably be successful financially—so much so, in fact, that others will fight over the money you will leave when you pass over. Much of this money will be made as the result of a chance remark, so keep your ears open.

SECRET
You are a forceful character, self-centered, and determined. You are impulsive and follow your own whims.

OCTOBER 8

An idea that is developed and put into action is more important than an idea that exists only as an idea.
—Edward de Bono

BORN ON THIS DAY
- **Matt Damon**
  actor
- **Bruno Mars**
  singer
- **Jesse Jackson**
  political activist
- **Chevy Chase**
  comedian, actor
- **Sigourney Weaver**
  actor

PERSONALITY
While the life of the imagination appeals to you more than a career of activity, business, or social contacts, there are so many demands made on your time that you cannot dream in a world of your own. Your intuitive understanding is so piercing and correct that people are always after you for advice, help, sympathy, and counseling. You extend this perceptive analytical ability beyond human relations and can see clearly the picture formed by nations in their dealings with one another and the effect that will be made by a podcast, blog, post, book, ad, or other invention or product. For this reason, you would be a wonderful cultural critic or a splendid political commentator. While this may sound very impersonal to you, you also have a deep interest in your own affairs, and the passion of your nature needs requited love for you to be truly happy.

LIFE PATH
No one will ever doubt whether you are a friend. Sincere, frank, and outspoken, you never disguise your true feelings. You are careful of details, thorough in your work, and clear on your position. You do not especially enjoy a busy social life, except in your own trusted circle, and there you are easygoing, friendly, and entertaining.

DESTINY
Periodically you may feel great surges of renewed mental and emotional inspiration. You have an avid interest in a variety of subjects and enough confidence to multitask and undertake a number of projects at one time. If this enthusiasm is put to proper use, you will make wonderful strides toward your goal. Channel your abilities into constructive work, and do not substitute restless activity for worthwhile undertakings.

KARMIC LESSON
You have great ability in certain specific directions, and this constitutes a veritable brilliance, in a way, since exceptional talent has been described as the infinite ability for taking pains. You are inclined to believe others too much; you must be careful that you are not deceived on an occasion when it may mean much to you. You have a strong imagination, which is capable of working wonders at times. You are a fast learner and moderate in most things. You notice everything that goes on around you, though you may not appear to. You possess a good head for business and much foresight. You are capable of doing much bigger and better things than you are called upon to do at present.

SECRET
You are very sensitive, especially to criticism, even when it is well-intentioned. You have high aspirations and like attention centered on you and your ideas.

FRIENDS & FAMILY

OCTOBER 9

One person with passion is better than forty people merely interested.
—E.M. Forster

BORN ON THIS DAY
- **Prince Edward**
  Duke of Kent
- **John Lennon**
  singer/songwriter
- **Guillermo del Toro**
  filmmaker
- **Tyler James Williams**
  rapper, actor
- **Bella Hadid**
  fashion model

FRIENDS & FAMILY

PERSONALITY
Your life will be filled with a variety of emotional and intellectual experiences. You have a very strong mental acuity, and eventually you will regulate the conduct of your career with such force that success is bound to come to you. However, along the path of life, you will have many ups and downs. The reason for this is that the vibration of your birthday is all-inclusive. There is great power to rule over the will of others, but there is also a mystical side that wars with this desire for dominance. Until you really know exactly what you want, you are liable to veer from one interest to another in a seemingly chartless sea. Only experience can teach you to see clearly, to define your aims, and to be direct in your approach to the highest aspirations in your life. A partner can help you with your direction.

LIFE PATH
You have careful, well-balanced judgment and confidence in your own will. You love parties and like to get dressed up and go out, provided it does not interfere with your business. Aesthetic and loving in your home, you will be fortunate in the selection of your partner and lucky with real estate.

DESTINY
The reestablishment of happy companionship with an old friend may result from an unexpected meeting or visit and affect your life greatly at some point. Also, you will have many occasions to be pleased by the trends of existing business events and relationships. Your social life will progress smoothly, and you are good at making interesting new acquaintances and developing these friendships. You are proud of the people you know, and this gives you great satisfaction.

KARMIC LESSON
You have a good sense of humor and take things very much as they come, without trying to control them too much. You are witty, caustic, and a little cynical, inclined to say cutting things about people. You yourself are quite a creature of moods. You are fond of fiction and humor of all sorts. You are a good mimic and have a good deal of talent in the direction of putting on a show. You enjoy entertaining people and should be able to perform. You are sometimes dreamy and impersonal and often have odd dreams, which are worth recording. Make a note of those that are particularly vivid and see whether something comes of them.

SECRET
You are of humble origins and will rise to high places through your natural charm, talent, grace, and tact.

OCTOBER 10

The joy of the mind is the measure of its strength.
—Ninon de L'Enclos

PERSONALITY

All that you experience is grist for your mill. You have a wonderful ability to retain things in your memory and can turn your experiences into fascinating anecdotes when you choose to be entertaining. Your hospitable nature has won you a large group of friends, and you, too, get pleasure from being the guest as well as the host. You have a rather intuitive understanding of people. Without deep analysis, you seem to strike the vital chord in a person's makeup, and you vibrate to it with kindliness and friendship. You need a lot of demonstrative affection to be happy, and you should surround yourself or connect with a large and loving community of like-minded people.

LIFE PATH

You are bright, witty, optimistic, and popular. The strength and capability that underlie your character are never in the foreground except in times of great stress, when you are capable of sharp and decisive action. A great home lover and gourmet, you are affectionate and demonstrative and expect the same in return.

DESTINY

Learn something from each new experience and each new person who comes into your life. You should make spectacular progress on the road to success by working with a small team. Freedom from former restraints will put you in a receptive mood to use each opportunity. This freedom comes from a breathing technique. Do not be afraid to try some of the new methods that occur to you. Much is to be gained by experimentation with yoga and Eastern ideas.

KARMIC LESSON

Persistent and determined in your efforts, you are even pigheaded at times. You have a great deal of charisma, and others respect you, though you may not be universally beloved. You might be interested in politics and current events. A newshound, you may be addicted to the Internet and social media. You are restless, a wanderer, and do not care for homelife as much as you do roving about the face of the Earth or online. It is hard for you to remain in any one place for long. You are doubtless fond of the water and would make a splendid swimmer. You are intuitional and would do well to follow these leads more fully. Kind and generous, you are resourceful, too, and know exactly what to do in an emergency.

SECRET

You are aggressive and ambitious in business, and a patron of the arts, when you can afford it. You should marry a partner of similar character traits for full happiness.

BORN ON THIS DAY

- **Harold Pinter**, playwright
- **Helen Hayes**, actor
- **Mya**, singer/songwriter
- **Brett Favre**, football player
- **Mario Lopez**, actor

FRIENDS & FAMILY

OCTOBER 11

Do not let your judges define you.
—Jules Feiffer

BORN ON THIS DAY

- **Eleanor Roosevelt**
  U.S. First Lady
- **Jerome Roberts**
  choreographer, director
- **MC Lyte**
  rapper, entrepreneur
- **Art Blakey**
  jazz drummer
- **Grigory Potemkin**
  Russian military leader

FRIENDS & FAMILY

PERSONALITY
You have a logical mind that approaches each problem and situation in life calmly. You always begin at the beginning and proceed, step by step, in what you are doing in a very methodical way until you have reached a logical conclusion. Your actions are as deliberate as your mental processes. Nothing can ever dim the common sense of your reasoning or your analysis of personality. Experience combined with intuition gives you deep insight into human affairs. Fortitude and determination drawn from your difficult childhood give strength to your character. You have such a wide variety of experiences that some of them are bound to be unpleasant. You may suffer setbacks that would seem tragic to someone with less stamina than you have. However, your strength is in your ability to make a comeback, no matter how imminent failure may seem.

LIFE PATH
You are prudent, thorough, and accurate. While your mind is not deeply probing, your intuition serves you well, and your judgment is seldom at fault. You are positive and assertive and like to take a prominent part in group activities. Unharmonious surroundings are exceedingly distasteful to you, as you have "been there, done that."

DESTINY
You will feel imbued with new courage and willingness to assume greater responsibilities as you get older. Opportunities will be numerous for you to demonstrate your talents and abilities between the ages of thirty and fifty. The counsel of those who are wiser and more experienced than you may be of considerable assistance in periods of stress. Be as willing to listen as you are to assert yourself.

KARMIC LESSON
You are conscientious and thorough, never giving up a project until it is well done. You are artistic and can be temperamental if your ideas are met with criticism. Thoughtful and contemplative, you ought to be able to write. You are a bit of a bohemian and love studio life. You should have a good fling at this early in life, as later you will grow more tired of it and want to settle down in a comfortable home of your own. If you had never tasted the joys of the artistic life, you would always be craving them.

SECRET
You have a high degree of perseverance, both in fixing things and in creative work. Animals seem to take to you, somehow knowing that you like them.

OCTOBER 12

Every noble work is at first impossible.
—Thomas Carlyle

⬥ PERSONALITY
Each person has his or her role in life, and not all the parts can be glamorous. Your part in the cosmic drama is that of the solid citizen, the helpmate, and the reliable go-to person in your social community. Everyone knows that you are a fine and dependable person and that when you give your word, it will not be broken no matter what sacrifice keeping it entails. Loyalty is one of your outstanding traits. Your employer, life partner, children, and relatives know your reliable and steadfast nature, and they trust you with their confidences, valuables, and love. You rarely give up or slow down on the job, no matter what type of chore or task you are performing. It seems as though a well of energy and faith is ever replenished within you, allowing you to go on relentlessly about the completion of your tasks.

⬥ LIFE PATH
You love deeply, work energetically, and play enthusiastically. In short, you are intense, putting your whole energy into whatever occupies your mind. You are proud, somewhat reserved, and careful of your associates, striving to attain high ideals.

⬥ DESTINY
You may experience conflicting loyalties and temporary periods of confusion in your family life—it's complicated. However, you usually will be able to determine what course of action is best for you to take. You should not lack the courage of your convictions when push comes to shove. Once you have made a well-considered decision, stick to it. Your practical reasoning will always stand you in good stead. Don't second-guess yourself.

⬥ KARMIC LESSON
Emotional and dramatic, you have a great deal of sensitivity—real caring, that is. There is a strikingly devoted vein running through your nature, which shows itself every now and then in your generosity of spirit. You feel things profoundly and are capable of a deep and lasting love. You do not carry your heart on your sleeve, for while you are capable of a few harmless flirtations you never let these affect you seriously. Fond of social media, podcasts, books, art, and a variety of other subjects, you are many-sided in your interests. You have a good head for business, and if you are wise and careful you should succeed in accumulating quite a bit of money during your lifetime—enough to obtain all you desire, as you are far from greedy.

⬥ SECRET
You are an adventurous, explorative type, building your plans carefully and biding your time before carrying them out. You are also interested in the paranormal.

BORN ON THIS DAY
- **Luciano Pavarotti** — singer
- **Hugh Jackman** — actor
- **Jane Krakowski** — actor, comedian
- **Dawn French** — actor, comedian
- **Aleister Crowley** — social critic, occultist

FRIENDS & FAMILY

OCTOBER 13

Most look up and admire the stars. A champion climbs a mountain and grabs one.
—Anonymous

BORN ON THIS DAY
- **Dwight D. Eisenhower**
  U.S. president
- **Margaret Thatcher**
  U.K. prime minister
- **Paul Simon**
  singer
- **Lenny Bruce**
  comedian
- **Alexandria Ocasio-Cortez**
  politician, activist

FRIENDS & FAMILY

PERSONALITY
Your natural glibness borders on, and may reach, exceptional vividness in conversation. At any rate, you never fail to keep the attention of anyone you are dealing with, meaning that you can put your all into any field of endeavor that you choose. As a parent, a student, an employee, or an employer, you have the essential qualities of attracting and retaining the interest of others, and while you have their interest, you can mold them at will. A lively curiosity in many things makes you a desirable and charming companion. You can get fun out of almost any situation because you see the bright and humorous side of things, and your good nature provokes laughter rather than sarcasm. Because you are well-liked for your outlook on life, many people of influence are willing to do favors for you, which advances your position. Take advantage of the glorious opportunities that life offers.

LIFE PATH
You possess the qualities of a mover and shaker. You grasp the salient points of a situation quickly, your judgment is good, and you can command attention and respect. You have a retentive memory and learn readily. Your nature demands strong love, and you are not averse to giving and receiving flattery. You like good manners.

DESTINY
Although you will have reason to be pleased with your accomplishments, do not become complacent. New fields to conquer will present themselves, and you should tackle them with enthusiasm. Take advantage of opportunities to relax so you can go back to your tasks fully renewed. Engage in worthwhile activities and allow your faith in the future to remain firm.

KARMIC LESSON
You think clearly and can express what you know in plain, simple language. You also have much patience. For these reasons, you are eminently fitted to become a teacher or instructor or to be in a position where you can impart information to others. You can adapt yourself to new situations and can fit in anywhere, doing the work you are given creditably and easily. You are deft with your hands and fingers; you are accurate and can remember a thing when you have seen or heard it once. Your memory is remarkable. You are interested in all new inventions and improvements, particularly those of a technological nature, such as photography. You are true and loyal and exceedingly good-natured and well-meaning in your disposition.

SECRET
You have a simple, unaffected nature, preferring a smooth, well-regulated life to the bizarre or the risky. You are the quintessential stay-at-home type.

OCTOBER 14

Everything has beauty, but not everyone sees it.
—Confucius

BORN ON THIS DAY
- **Usher**
  singer
- **Ralph Lauren**
  fashion designer
- **E.E. Cummings**
  poet
- **Hannah Arendt**
  political philosopher
- **Roger Moore**
  actor

PERSONALITY
You seem to have within you the secret of being a peacemaker. You work hard and sometimes even must fight for justice and to keep harmony. From the hidden depths of your inner being, you are able to transform experiences into illuminating and shining milestones in life. On the material plane, you express this selfsame quality in making the simplest things into creations of lasting loveliness. In your home, with a few deft touches, you can make everything seem bright and new. In your business, with a charming smile and tactful word, you can make things run smoothly. In your relations with other people—your family and friends—you are a natural arbiter to whom they turn for the good advice that you have to offer them. Many times, you will go out of your way to do someone a favor; you are a little too trusting in this respect.

LIFE PATH
You are positive, abrupt, and sometimes too quick in your actions. At times, you do things impulsively, believing they are for another person's own good, that serious consideration would preclude. You should, if possible, find a partner who will act as a balance for you.

DESTINY
Do not let timidity or fear of the opinions of family members keep you from taking advantage of any opportunity for advancement. However, if you decide to change your residence or job, explain patiently and in detail to people who are interested in how you arrived at your decision. The continued affection and help of your intimate associates are absolutely essential to your happiness now and in the future.

KARMIC LESSON
Practical, intelligent, and quick, you have fine perceptions. You are of a balanced nature, inclined to disregard those who are ultraradical or ultraconservative. You like the middle way. You can love deeply, but it will be more on a matter-of-fact basis, due to compatibility of temperament rather than because you are carried away by an excess of emotion. Your heart does run far away from your head. This does not mean that you are calculating in any way, only that you are matter-of-fact and have had enough experience with life to know what it means. You could make an excellent counselor or therapist. You help many and also will come in contact with many people who can and will help you.

SECRET
You are inclined to luxury and extravagance, devoting many of your ambitions to attracting those who interest you; usually you succeed.

FRIENDS & FAMILY

OCTOBER 15

Our doubts are traitors, and make us lose the good we oft might win, by fearing to attempt.
— William Shakespeare

BORN ON THIS DAY

★ **Friedrich Nietzsche**
philosopher, cultural critic

★ **Michel Foucault**
philosopher

★ **Emeril Lagasse**
celebrity chef

★ **Keyshia Cole**
singer

★ **Ginuwine**
singer/songwriter

FRIENDS & FAMILY

PERSONALITY

Because you never betray a trust, you are the confidant of many people. You are as careful a guardian of the secrets of others as you would be if they entrusted you with their jewels, money, or dearly beloved children. Your dependable traits make you a wise counselor, and your steady ways make you a wonderful example to those who would lead a sane and productive life. You have the roots of mysticism in your nature, and you show this by an interest in everything that is usually considered occult or spiritual. You could become a fine practitioner of the predictive arts if you concentrated on them. As it is, you have a well-developed intuition, which comes out in unusually accurate hunches of a prophetic nature. Your feelings are deep and subtle; you do not reveal them except to a special few.

LIFE PATH

You are very reserved and not in the least extroverted or overly enthusiastic. You are cautious and conservative and possess an ability for commercial ventures. You are fond of nature, read good books, and enjoy the company of gentle people. You have many friends, are loyal, and strive to make your home serene and attractive.

DESTINY

Your life will be packed with fulfilling experiences in social and economic endeavors. You will be able to accept a great challenge that will help many people. The moral support of your family in new endeavors and undertakings may add to your satisfaction, but it is not necessary for your success. In some situations you will get an additional thrill out of surprising those people who may have viewed your initial plans with a degree of skepticism.

KARMIC LESSON

You have very good common sense, good judgment, and a certain decision-making skill, which carries you through any undertaking. Yet the commercial life is not most suited to you. You are interested in a variety of other subjects, including metaphysical subjects, especially the unseen, paranormal, and supernatural. You are aesthetic and dislike anything connected with disharmony, fighting, or unpleasantness. You would make a good doctor or a healer, theoretically, but the practical side of those subjects does not appeal to you and would probably prevent you from entering the healing field. If you enter into business, you should have a partner who looks after all the practical details, which you are not suited for. In spite of this fact, however, you will probably do very well in life.

SECRET

You are ambitious for spiritual achievements rather than worldly prizes. You are scholarly and reserved but make temporary excursions into whirls of pleasure and excitement.

OCTOBER 16

If you would sleep soundly, take a clear conscience to bed with you.
—Benjamin Franklin

BORN ON THIS DAY
- **Oscar Wilde**
  poet
- **John Mayer**
  singer
- **Angela Lansbury**
  actor
- **Suzanne Somers**
  actor
- **Manute Bol**
  basketball player, activist

PERSONALITY
You acquit yourself in such a way that you win the acclaim of your fellow workers, family members, and friends. Sincerity is the keynote to your character, and you express it in everything you say and do. Although you are somewhat more serious than most people, you consider this an advantage. You dislike those who are forever superficial, frivolous, and seeking glamour and fun. Because you know that life is fleeting and composed of serious elements, you are somewhat inclined to criticize pleasure lovers and find yourself in their disfavor. However, you have no time to bother yourself with the comments of people you think are wasting their time. You accept the responsibilities of homelife with mature consideration. You are committed, willing to always do your part, and you sensibly expect the other members of your family and close friends to do the same.

LIFE PATH
Determined and somewhat calculating, you will not acknowledge defeat until you have exhausted all your resources. If you cannot force your way through an obstacle, you will go over or around it. You are a problem solver. You are patient, sympathetic, and generous, slow to anger and quick to forgive. You will live a grateful, contented life.

DESTINY
Tolerance will open the door to appreciation of other cultures, and you may be amazed by the enjoyment that is added to your life. Frustrations of your childhood may be forgotten, for you will have a clearer picture of your aims and new satisfaction in discharging your obligations to the best of your abilities as you get older. Self-discipline should play a part in the establishment and execution of your goals—practice tai chi or yoga.

KARMIC LESSON
You are a good communicator and a great lover of famous quotations. You are not always as lighthearted as you could be, mulling over the past too much at times; this is sometimes misunderstood by those around you, and hurt feelings may be felt. You must learn to stand up for your rights and value yourself more fully. You have considerable talents; value these at their proper worth. The world's estimate of you follows the estimate you place on yourself. Learn greater self-confidence. You are magnetic and caring and are doubtless captivating to those who are on your wavelength. Cultivate even greater frankness and straightforwardness.

SECRET
You are too willing to give your energy to projects that appeal to your emotions before you examine their merits. You must guard against this tendency in selecting a partner.

FRIENDS & FAMILY

OCTOBER 17

Our grand business in life is not to see what lies dimly in the distance but to do what lies clearly at hand.
—Thomas Carlyle

BORN ON THIS DAY

★ **Eminem**
rapper, singer

★ **Wyclef Jean**
singer

★ **Rita Hayworth**
actor

★ **Evel Knievel**
stunt performer

★ **Ziggy Marley**
singer, philanthropist

FRIENDS & FAMILY

PERSONALITY
Although you may appear to be an average person, pursuing the usual things in life, you are really imbued with a love of the artistic, the romantic, the beguiling, and the thrilling. Were you free to do so, you would probably roam the Earth in search of thrilling experiences, wandering from country to country, tasting the fruits of love and thrills, wherever your feet directed you. However, as life is made up of much more prosaic things for most people, you do your best to live a full and normal life in the circumstances in which fate has placed you, making every effort to rise in your chosen career path. In this way you make life an adventure even if the swashbuckling days of piracy and exploit are over.

LIFE PATH
You are competent and reliable and generally well satisfied with your work in life. You are apt to be extreme in your likes and dislikes and don't mind stating your opinion. You are bright and witty, good-natured, and affable, and your circle of friends means the world to you.

DESTINY
By modifying some of your ideas, you will increase your rate of progress in the attainment of your ambitions. Do not allow false pride to keep you from changing your opinions when you obtain new information. Keep an open outlook and do not neglect new subjects and pursuits in planning leisure-time activities. You might get bored easily. Allowing useless and unwarranted criticism to upset you will only stymie your plans.

KARMIC LESSON
You inherit great brainpower, above the ordinary, and you will not be doing justice to yourself unless you exert your brain faculties to their utmost limit. *Concentrate* must be your watchword. Yet, paradoxical as it may sound, your viewpoints and your outlook on affairs must be as broad as possible. Know a little of everything, but concentrate on one thing. At the same time, always plan a little ahead of time. Do this, and your life will be like a beautiful river, growing deeper and richer and fuller as the years go on. In fact, many persons take advantage of your good nature and impose upon your time and patience. Assert yourself, take the lead, and guide matters into better channels, as far as this lies in your power.

SECRET
You have a generous streak, which may make you appear to be a soft touch. Sometimes you are an extremist.

OCTOBER 18

There are people who have money and people who are rich.
—Coco Chanel

BORN ON THIS DAY
- **Zac Efron**
  actor, singer
- **Chuck Berry**
  singer
- **Ne-Yo**
  singer
- **Martina Navratilova**
  tennis player
- **Mike Ditka**
  football coach

PERSONALITY
You have remarkable powers of reasoning, and you can apply your logic and analytical abilities with courage and inspiration to every situation that you must face in life. Because you know that real independence can be attained only through economic independence, you devote much of your thought and energy to the devising of methods whereby you will eventually be your own master, completely devoid of dependency on the will or whim of anyone else. Because you have tenacity, fortitude, and stamina, you make a good analyst, particularly if you are placed in charge. Although you may run your home or office efficiently all day, you must get out and do something to break up the monotony when your day's work is done. Activity is absolutely necessary to your well-being.

LIFE PATH
You are determined and positive, sometimes stubborn, and sometimes impulsive. You are subject to mood swings but do not give in to them, as they do not last very long. Capable and energetic, you like to lead, to be in charge. You are demonstrative and very affectionate, and your nature demands faithfulness and consistency.

DESTINY
You will have more than one occasion during your life to recall the words of the poet Robert Louis Stevenson: "The world is so full of a number of things, I'm sure we should all be as happy as kings." Indeed, your life can be brimming over with interesting experiences, golden opportunities, and dedicated friendships. There will be special emphasis on beauty and all matters that tend toward increasing harmony.

KARMIC LESSON
You are the type who likes to flourish and grow; you need to be actively engaged. Your mind reaches out, looking to the future; trivial things and affairs do not interest you. You are always planning for the future, and if you are careful in your choice of associates, you could attain success of the best kind and should make a mark. Remember the little kindnesses that are yours to do in life. Do not forget the rights of others; respect their desires and wishes, so in later life you may have nothing to reproach yourself with. Believe in yourself, and others will soon come to your assistance in all your undertakings. Trust in "divine order," do your best to bring out the powers that are in you, and you will be startled at the results.

SECRET
You have real discernment and are attracted more by mental gifts and interesting personalities than by social position, fame, and money.

FRIENDS & FAMILY

OCTOBER 19

As one person you may not be able to change the whole world, but you can change the world of one person.
—Anonymous

BORN ON THIS DAY

★ **John Lithgow**
actor

★ **Jon Favreau**
actor

★ **John le Carré**
author

★ **Evander Holyfield**
boxer

★ **Trey Parker**
actor, animator

FRIENDS & FAMILY

◉ PERSONALITY

You have executive ability, the vision and power to plan big things, and the stamina to see through to the end the concepts that you initiate. Your gift for organizing is expressed in whatever you do, whether you have chosen a career as an artist or a businessperson. You are an ardent defender of civil rights, and you display this strong feeling in your participation in your immediate community as well as in national affairs. You are slow to anger and slow to forgive. Because you are essentially sensitive despite your strength, you dislike any kind of conduct that smacks of the offensive. The adventure of living is a reality to you, and you take what life offers with open hands. Once you pledge your loyalty, you are the staunchest of friends and lovers.

◉ LIFE PATH

You are sensitive and diffident and very considerate of others. It is your ambition to excel, and you would accomplish more if you were more assertive and aggressive. You are fond of beautiful and harmonious surroundings, love your home, and always strive to make it a nurturing, comfortable environment.

◉ DESTINY

At a certain point, a significant change in your economic status may turn the current of your thoughts and activities in new directions. It may scare you at first but will be of benefit in the long run. You will have more leisure time and discover fascinating ways to fill it. Former apprehensions will be supplanted by self-confidence and determination to make your original ideas count.

◉ KARMIC LESSON

You are forceful and original, and ideas fairly sizzle in your head—there are so many. A natural investigator, you have a keen eye for detail and would make a good reporter, investigator, or detective. You are probably interested in civil liberties, politics, and world affairs. Passionate about your beliefs, you have a great deal of personal magnetism and attract friends from all walks of life. You are affectionate, and you desire the input and company of young people all the time. Careful and shrewd in business affairs, you could make yourself a fortune, if you stick to business. You may see a great deal of the world in your travels, but the place that fascinates you most of all, in all probability, is Egypt, with its silent Sphinx and its timeless pyramids.

◉ SECRET

Underneath your smiling nature, there is real ability and strength of character. Try to be less distracted and more serious in your work.

OCTOBER 20

When everyone is against you, it means that you are absolutely wrong—or absolutely right.
—Albert Guinon

BORN ON THIS DAY
- **John Dewey**
  philosopher, educational reformer
- **Arthur Rimbaud**
  poet
- **Snoop Dog**
  rapper, media personality
- **Viggo Mortensen**
  actor
- **Mickey Mantle**
  baseball player

FRIENDS & FAMILY

PERSONALITY
If you have studied your own character, you are aware that your nature is composed of strangely opposing traits. For example, you have an infinite capacity for hard work, yet you love luxury, ease, and leisure. No one can concentrate more on a difficult task, yet no one can relax as completely when you are in the mood for a good time. You are either "on" or "off." Another strange combination of qualities in your makeup is your fondness for and attachment to your family, on the one hand, and your attraction to travel, adventure, and romance, on the other. Since you cannot be in two places at once, you try your best to compromise on your opposing wishes. No matter what your personal desires, you would never do anything to hurt a person you love. Your sense of duty is as strong as your sense of self-indulgence.

LIFE PATH
You are of a contented, comfort-loving disposition, but your love of ease does not interfere with your vigorous performance of duties. You are capable and reliable, looked up to by your associates. You are decidedly a homebody, yet your sense of adventure takes you on many trips, even if only from the comfort of your home. Your devotion to your family is very pronounced.

DESTINY
You should not hesitate to express yourself forcefully. Your aggressive enthusiasm can be easily aroused when you are fighting for what you believe in. A wide variety of interests can make your attention be diverted into many fascinating channels. Care should be taken, in fact, to avoid overdoing things. This is especially true where rest and calm emotions are needed.

KARMIC LESSON
You are strong-willed and do not like interference with your way of doing things. Courageous, you always have a smart way of handling a crisis or other trouble. You are a good logician and can argue well. You are also judgmental and observant and sometimes inclined to pick apart other people—a fault of which you should try to cure yourself. You are rather a plunger, jumping in to take many chances that another would shrink from. Yet you always win out, somehow, as luck seems to be in your favor. You are extremely fond of creative pursuits and like to attend venues that display art. You take on responsibility easily and could make a success of your life, if you live up to your best standards and ideals.

SECRET
You have a receptive and judicious mind, with a love of fair play in all fields. You would make a good judge or educator.

OCTOBER 21

Two persons cannot long be friends if they cannot forgive each other's little failings.
—Jean de La Bruyère

BORN ON THIS DAY

★ **Alfred Nobel**
chemist, inventor

★ **Kim Kardashian**
media personality, model

★ **Celia Cruz**
singer

★ **Carrie Fisher**
actor

★ **Ken Watanabe**
actor

FRIENDS & FAMILY

PERSONALITY
Pride of accomplishment makes you do everything with conscientious precision. You try to never let anyone down, because it is completely alien to your nature to do a thing in a slovenly or half-hearted fashion. You have an infinite capacity for taking pains, which is a defining characteristic of exceptional skill. You may not be a great original creative artist, but whatever task you undertake, you finish with the final touch that spells perfection. In your hours of leisure, you know how to relax and have a good time. You like engaging and interacting with people in real life or on social media, and you are a gracious host online or in your own home. When you go out publicly, you always make a nice impression because you are a good listener as well as an interesting talker.

LIFE PATH
A born motivator, you have an unusual ability to inspire. You can usually make others think that your way is best. In your social life, you plan many of the pleasant get-togethers, and you can make people feel at ease and appear to the best advantage. You are very loyal to your many dear friends.

DESTINY
Travel and serious study are indicated on your birthday. Explore your community and the neighboring vicinities—you need not go far to discover treasures and inspiration. If the opportunity to take a trip presents itself, avail yourself of it—you will have good luck on trips. Accept no statement without proof. If you have aspirations to write, take the time to satisfy them. Remember, however, that writing is a proposition that requires infinite patience, solitude, and immunity to discouragement and rejection.

KARMIC LESSON
You are witty and caustic and have great insight into human nature—its actions and motivations. You are entertaining and can keep a room full of people in uproarious laughter with your manner of storytelling. You are a good mimic and can point out funny little quirks of those around you. You have a sentimental nature, but it is not easily touched or got at, and few know of its existence. You always feel that you should be in other circumstances and surroundings than those that now encircle you. If you had the right stimulus and start in life, you could accomplish great things. You are generous in your praise and rarely say a hurtful word about another. Sound your own praises a little more.

SECRET
You have a particular fondness for animals and a compassion for human beings, no matter in what state of suffering.

OCTOBER 22

I am always doing that which I cannot do, in order that I may learn how to do it.
—Pablo Picasso

PERSONALITY
The concepts of your inventive mind can be translated into practical methods, crafty creations, or other profitable products. You have a gift for words that should enable you to be a writer or lecturer, while your other talents can find equally profitable outlets. You are inspired to seek fame and fortune, and you can do so if you make the effort to find out which of your latent abilities is strongest. Although you are occasionally given to moods of sadness or reflection, you should be able to overcome them by being active. As a matter of fact, you love motion and speed. The mercurial aspect of your nature may express itself in the manner in which you speak—quickly and with nimble wit—or in your love of exercise, or your desire to be on the go. However, you will always find an outlet for your energetic impulses in some inspired or interesting way.

LIFE PATH
You have a strong will, a quick mind, and shrewd judgment. You are a multitasker, capable of working under great stress. You are bright, witty, entertaining, and generally respected. You will receive the earnest, steadfast love of a partner, if you accept it, and will lead a productive life.

DESTINY
Beneficent rays light the way to success in love and business on your birthday, and you may find a way to combine them. You may be offered a leading post in a start-up enterprise or become active in a social or community project. Use your resourceful skills in planning and use your perceptive ability to set up a definite program of activities before bringing actual operations or instigating changes, as this business can grow big and wide.

KARMIC LESSON
You are energetic, enthusiastic, and full of vim and vigor. You are emotional and dramatic, prone to cry at times. You like city life and cannot stand the country for very long, but every summer you like to go away and like to be on the grass or in the sand and bask in the sun. You are capable and fill any position in which you are placed. Your passionate nature is very strong, and you can love deeply and fervently. Indeed, you must keep a close watch on yourself in this direction, or your heart will lead you into serious and complicated difficulties. You have a sharp sense of humor and always get a joke sooner than anyone else.

SECRET
You are a shrewd judge of affairs with a strong materialistic trend, which could lead to wide success in the business world.

BORN ON THIS DAY
- **Franz Liszt** — composer
- **Timothy Leary** — psychologist, psychedelic advocate
- **Catherine Deneuve** — actor
- **Doris Lessing** — author
- **Deepak Chopra** — alternative medicine advocate, author

FRIENDS & FAMILY

OCTOBER 23

Good taste is the flower of good sense.
—Achille Poincelot

BORN ON THIS DAY
- **Ryan Reynolds**
  actor
- **Pele**
  soccer player
- **"Weird Al" Yankovic**
  singer, musician
- **Johnny Carson**
  talk show host
- **Amandla Stenberg**
  actor, singer

FRIENDS & FAMILY

PERSONALITY
Life teaches you many lessons, and you in turn desire to teach these lessons to others. You have a naturally sympathetic nature, and you feel that if you can help others by the experiences you have gone through, it is your duty to pass this acquired wisdom on. You could be a good teacher in a school as well as in the school of life. You have a deep love for your family, and you are very generous where they are concerned. Everything that is artistic, historic, and cultural appeals to you. You have the ability to recognize the genuine in the midst of the second best and could be a good critic of all the arts. Music gives you many hours of pleasure. You want love for yourself, and you should lead a richly secure and bountiful life.

LIFE PATH
You are affable, kind, and affectionate. You are very gracious and self-contained, a fluent talker, and a great dispenser of information. You also possess considerable psychic ability. You are original in your ideas and clever in their execution. You may marry early in life and should select a partner who will encourage the development of all your talents.

DESTINY
You may look forward to harmony in the home and pleasurable activities with a diverse group of friends, some of whom will be lifelong companions. You may go into a business with a close friend. Your wildest dreams will be converted into practical plans for social and financial advancement. Emotional progress will keep pace with economic gains, and your life can be one of success and deep personal satisfaction.

KARMIC LESSON
Capable, original, and ingenious, you are fond of excitement and crave stimulation to an almost abnormal extent. Be careful that this craving does not master you or turn into an addiction. You are fond of the beautiful, and the poetic and aesthetic appeal to you. A great communicator, you always have something interesting to say. You have a good mind for systems and can see ahead as few can. You are alluring and are greatly admired for your compelling personality. You should be careful of investment gambles, as there are indications that you may meet with a setback sometime in midlife. If you are careful with your earnings and save a little for a rainy day, you will sail over financial ups and downs.

SECRET
You are an independent spirit, quietly but forcefully assertive, with a pronounced moneymaking ability when sufficiently interested.

OCTOBER 24

He is able who thinks he is able.
—Buddha

⚛ PERSONALITY

You are a very thorough and thoughtful student of many subjects; you do not limit your investigations to dry textbook matters or only looking things up on the Internet but expand your research to real people and life itself. Because you seem to have an affinity for distant things, you are always interested in and up to date on new forms of communication, which make real distances shrink in time and space. You are quite opinionated, and when you have decided that something is good, it remains so forever to your way of thinking. As the reverse also holds true, you are liable to lose friendships through the frank expression of your opinion. You believe the truth to be completely disarming, and you won't stoop to tell a white lie no matter how much embarrassment it might save. However, you are altruistic to a fault toward the people you love, and you are quite capable of spoiling them thoroughly.

◎ LIFE PATH

You are persevering and determined, and sometimes obstinate, although not disagreeable about it. You have a tenacity of purpose that often brings you success where a half-hearted endeavor would fail. You are a loyal friend and a bitter enemy, but you stay true to yourself, as that is your mantra.

⊙ DESTINY

If adventure beckons, be ready to follow. Seek new interests. You will find your adaptability very valuable, for there will always be many opportunities in your life to meet new people and participate in unusual activities. Although you may feel an urge to spend freely, and you like to shop, do not waste money on worthless objects or extravagant pleasures, only on timeless, long-lasting, well-made items.

☯ KARMIC LESSON

Ambitious and determined, you desire to get ahead in life and clearly want your success to be great. Far-seeing and shrewd, you have good discernment and can tell which way the wind blows. You are inclined to be moody when you are frustrated, but you must cover up this side of yourself, for the more you act the greater will be your success. There is a strong spiritual feeling running throughout your makeup, and this governs your actions, to a certain extent. On some things you are inclined to be fanatical and cannot bear to have your word doubted. You should learn to be a little more understanding, especially about money matters. You must continue to have faith in being the master of yourself, for this is the basis of all success.

⊛ SECRET

You possess remarkable powers of analysis and a wonderful ability to reason and to discover new truths within your family matters.

BORN ON THIS DAY

- **B.D. Wong**
  actor
- **Drake**
  rapper
- **Kevin Kline**
  actor
- **F. Murray Abraham**
  actor
- **PewDiePie**
  YouTube celebrity
- **Tony Walton**
  set and costume designer

FRIENDS & FAMILY

OCTOBER 25

Success comes in cans, failure in can'ts.
—Anonymous

BORN ON THIS DAY
- **Pablo Picasso**
  painter
- **Johann Strauss**
  composer
- **Katy Perry**
  singer
- **Ciara**
  singer
- **Jesper Vesterstrøm**
  windsurfer

FRIENDS & FAMILY

PERSONALITY
Intellectual curiosity is one of your outstanding traits. You are particularly interested in investigating fields of knowledge where little is known. You might be called an explorer of the mind and of uncharted subjects. In your work, you are very courageous, a pioneer. You are not daunted by others' opinions, and if you feel like trying a new way of doing something, you don't care how much anyone laughs at you. You may find yourself fighting a lone battle in trying to get people to think the way you do, but you have infinite patience, endurance, and stamina. You will likely be the victor in any contest because of your sheer staying power. You can head tours, organize businesses, run a website, manage a home, or lead an army. You can stifle your love life when ambition seems more important, and you can cast off the whole world when you think that love is more important.

LIFE PATH
You possess great nervous energy, like changes, and adapt to new situations when necessary. As your undertakings near completion, you are prone to lose interest in them, but you eventually finish. You have considerable pride and like to make as impressive an appearance as possible. You have a wicked sense of humor, you are an articulate talker, and you enjoy exploring ideas a great deal.

DESTINY
Sometimes you will find that compromise is expedient, but in most instances tenacity of purpose and resolute faith in your convictions will be a better policy to follow. You can be bold and daring without being reckless. Have confidence in yourself as well as in the integrity of those people with whom you are connected in the business world—you will be blessed to have trusted mentors and associates.

KARMIC LESSON
You are a hard worker and have somewhat of a photographic memory. Your thirst for knowledge is not easily quenched. You are not altogether suited to working for others and might eventually set up business for yourself. You love excitement of all kinds and cannot bear a humdrum life, which you may have to deal with, as not every day can be exciting. You feel that you are suited to and destined for greater things, and you are quite right, as you have a great deal of natural talent. Learn to place confidence in yourself and your own judgment, which is good. When you learn to trust your own powers, others will place you in a position of trust and greater financial responsibility. This will be the way you start to branch out.

SECRET
You are a born navigator. You dislike conventional surroundings and would be more at home on a boat or in a recreational vehicle.

OCTOBER 26

Great spirits have always encountered violent opposition from mediocre minds.
—Albert Einstein

BORN ON THIS DAY

★ **Hillary Clinton**
U.S. senator, U.S. First Lady

★ **Seth MacFarlane**
voice actor, comedian

★ **Mahalia Jackson**
gospel singer

★ **Amelia Clarke**
actor

★ **Jaclyn Smith**
actor, model

● PERSONALITY

You may be classified as a rebel because you accept nothing on faith. What you must be shown is proof—proof of claims that anyone makes to you, proof of any idea, opinion, or statement. Your skepticism makes you revolutionary or radical in your thinking. Only truth can impress you, and you must also be shown that the truth as it is presented to you is the whole picture. This attitude does not make you as harsh and judgmental as this may imply, because you are basically sympathetic to people, and you like them for what their good intentions are. You are helpful and tolerant of those in need, and you have a subtle understanding of human motives. You will really accept anyone as long as they refrain from lying, deception, or hypocrisy. Life will be a panorama of many chapters and vast experiences for you.

● LIFE PATH

You have considerable self-control and discipline. You are intellectual and scrutinizing, very amiable and even-tempered, and always fair, once you hear explanations. You are magnetic and have a great many friends and no real enemies. You have very few interests outside of your own business ventures.

● DESTINY

The animation with which you perform your daily tasks may attract the admiration and partnership of someone who is in a position to help you get ahead. Be appreciative of any assistance that is offered, and accept it, even though it is hard for you to accept help. Amiability will make you very popular. Your wry sense of humor will add a great deal to the enjoyment of all who share your social life.

● KARMIC LESSON

You are by nature a reformer and have strong convictions and beliefs about a variety of topics. You believe that a number of our social and political affairs need readjusting, and that it is your duty to readjust them. Yet you are not at all a fanatic but go about what you desire to accomplish in a businesslike and matter-of-fact way. You are a student, particularly fond of social science. You have a good head for figures and stocks. If you applied this practicality, you could be a successful investor or expert accountant. You are naturally timid and retiring, but you can be very strong-minded when you feel that your rights are being infringed. You are a natural home builder and are fond of children and pets.

● SECRET

You have an original mind with a disdain for the commonplace. Partnerships may be somewhat thwarted by your frank criticism and open disagreement—be aware.

FRIENDS & FAMILY

OCTOBER 27

The poorest way to face life is to face it with a sneer.
—Theodore Roosevelt

BORN ON THIS DAY
- **Theodore Roosevelt**
  U.S. president
- **Roy Lichtenstein**
  artist
- **John Cleese**
  actor
- **Sylvia Plath**
  poet, author
- **Roberto Benigni**
  actor

FRIENDS & FAMILY

PERSONALITY
Courage and initiative distinguish you, and these traits give you the opportunity to show the truest expression of your character. You do extremely well at evolving original ideas, concepts, and ways of doing things. In addition to this, you have the executive ability to put your ideas across in practical and profitable forms. As an analyst, you are ever on the alert and therefore get to the heart of the problem with no waste of time. Self-confidence about your business expertise gives you an air of assurance that takes you very far, even though you are less confident when it comes to love and relationships. You make a good impression because you look and act as though you always know what you're about, and people feel that a matter entrusted to your care will work out well.

LIFE PATH
Your emotional nature can be tempestuous and turbulent, even though you outwardly try to present yourself as cool and calm. You know how to regain control when you feel "off." Energetic and persistent, you need to be busy. Your nerves will not permit idleness. Your love is impulsive and demonstrative, and you require steadfast love in return, but you do not usually trust easily.

DESTINY
You can look for fulfilling experiences in the realm of business partnerships. If an unusual amount of money is expended on your behalf, be appreciative, but do not think that you must repay such generous favors in kind. The devotion to a cause, which you are capable of showing, will more than make up for material gifts and assistance. Favors you extend will be repaid, although, perhaps, not immediately.

KARMIC LESSON
You have great energy and determination and the ability to accomplish whatever you set out to manifest. You are very enthusiastic, strong-willed, and rather inclined to like the limelight. For all that, you are a very capable and competent person. When you enter business life, you will make an undoubted success, as you have all the necessary qualities and a remarkable power of organization and execution. You have much personal magnetism, and you often seem to hypnotize those in your immediate environment. You cannot bear restraint of any kind and should set up business for yourself early in life, if possible, as you will surely make it a success. You also can be temperamental, which you must learn to control.

SECRET
You like to parade your charm before large, appreciative audiences. You might naturally gravitate toward social media and video and have many creative ideas in those areas.

OCTOBER 28

Every action we take, everything we do, is either a victory or defeat in the struggle to become what we want to be.
—Ninon de L'Enclos

BORN ON THIS DAY

- **Bill Gates**
  business magnate, philanthropist
- **Charlie Daniels**
  singer/songwriter
- **Frank Ocean**
  rapper, songwriter
- **Joaquin Phoenix**
  actor
- **Caitlyn Jenner**
  media personality, Olympic decathlete

PERSONALITY
Because you have vision, the willingness to cooperate, and the stamina to see things through, you are the ideal collaborator, partner, and helpmate. All you need is the design for some new project, and you can see it in your mind's eye and carry it through until the actuality is successfully accomplished. You have a combination of qualities that coordinate excellently. Direction, practice, and technique mark your acts. You can also follow orders and carry out instructions to the letter. In addition to these traits, you have good money sense, know how to get value for what you spend, and know how to be compensated for work you do. This combination gives you a versatility that is an asset in any field of endeavor that you choose to enter. You prefer to go after what you want from life in a tactful way rather than in a pushy, blustering, or domineering fashion.

LIFE PATH
You are generous with your time and attention. You are fond of movies and shows, and they take a prominent part in your social life. You are trustworthy and dependable and receive many confidences, although you seldom make a confidante of others. You are loving yet aloof and will have a happy and blessed life.

DESTINY
A big change in occupation or residence may occur a few times in your life. Be ready to revise your plans at a moment's notice in line with unforeseen happenings. Your ability to adjust yourself to unexpected events will be of value. Do not be attached to places. Develop your talents in speaking and writing, for you may have a good opportunity to use either or both to social and business advantage.

KARMIC LESSON
Yours will probably be a very interesting life, filled with incidents of unusual occurrences. Some of these will be happy, others just the reverse. You must learn to judge human nature, for if you do not, and you place too much trust and faith in those around you, you might never accomplish what you desire with your dreams and goals. You must change this and become more free and independent before those opportunities can manifest for you. Then much good fortune will happen. You must learn not to chase bubbles, however, but learn the value of solid things and the realities of life. You must learn to assert yourself more fully and make your personality and powers more felt by those you hope will help you.

SECRET
Although your childhood may have been spent in adverse circumstances, you will overcome it and succeed through willpower and personality.

FRIENDS & FAMILY

OCTOBER 29

What we know here is very little, but what we are ignorant of is immense.
—Pierre-Simon Laplace

BORN ON THIS DAY
- **Fanny Brice**
  comedian
- **Bob Ross**
  painter, TV personality
- **Miguel Cotto**
  boxer
- **Gabrielle Union**
  actor
- **Richard Dreyfuss**
  actor

FRIENDS & FAMILY

PERSONALITY
A remarkably retentive memory gives you a great advantage over many people. You have what is called a photographic mind; that is, when you see a thing once, it becomes so fixed in your memory that you rarely forget it. You can recall the names of people you knew in the past and incidents that happened a long time ago. It may be that you forget things temporarily—recent things—but in fact they go to the storehouse of your mind. You could be a good reporter, chronicler, witness, and expert on testimony. Your sincerity adds validity to your observations. Sometimes you are so forthright in the expression of your thoughts and opinions that you anger friends or others, but you stick to your beliefs regardless of opposition. You like socializing, nevertheless, and you are happy in the company of smart, like-minded, interesting people.

LIFE PATH
You are great at handling details. Fairly competent in planning, you are better in executing others' plans. You are accurate, careful, and detailed, seldom taking a step without due consideration. You are inclined to worry over things that don't suit you. You are fond of wellness practices, love to be outdoors, and might take an avid interest in sports or fitness.

DESTINY
You can improve your talents by choosing activities that exercise them. Skills can be perfected even if they have been allowed to lie dormant for a long time. Take a good look at your personality and the things you most want out of life. Make your aims and your abilities coincide. Follow through with determination and self-discipline. Visualize and affirm.

KARMIC LESSON
Self-contained and dignified, you are cautious in most undertakings and inclined never to take a step until you feel the ground is secure under your feet. It would be unwise for you to speculate in any way, as one of your nature seldom has good luck in this direction. You are interested in humanity and are doubtless interested in social reforms. You are fond of psychology and healing therapies. You are a very intuitive and shrewd businessperson and could make a good deal of money. Your tendency to allow yourself to drift is one you must learn to overcome. Remember that if you drift, you drift with the tide, and this will land you in the ocean of mediocrity instead of lifting you to the higher place, where you belong.

SECRET
Your powerful gift of visualization combined with your explorative mind will lead you far.

OCTOBER 30

Old minds are like old horses—you must exercise them if you wish to keep them in working order.
—John Adams

⚇ PERSONALITY
You seek prominence because you are impelled to do so by the latent forces within you. One of the wisest policies you follow is keeping your plans to yourself until they are "ripe." You are somewhat secretive and don't believe in a lot of talk about what you are going to do; you do it and then spring it as a surprise. You are proud of your ethical standard, and you never break the codes of honor you believe in. Everyone respects you for your ethical modes of conduct, and you are completely dependable and trustworthy. You are very sensitive and feel things keenly. You have intellect and passion but not so much demonstrable affection. Cultivate the latter. You are capable of great things, but if you don't give and get love, you will often fall to great depths of moodiness.

◎ LIFE PATH
Independent, astute, and self-confident, you possess great manifesting ability. Intelligence is the ruling factor in your life, and you might marry young, but not without due consideration of the characteristics of your partner, as you can be picky, somewhat of a demanding perfectionist.

◉ DESTINY
You will not regret steps that you take toward reconciliation with someone who once played an important part in your life. Continued misunderstanding would be unfortunate and weigh on your shoulders. You may start a new endeavor of your own invention with success, but be cautious about revealing your plans prematurely. Poise and dignity will serve you well in work and in political or spiritual organizations and institutions.

☯ KARMIC LESSON
You are kind, gentle, and cordial in your relations with others. Be careful that you are not imposed upon for that reason. You have a love for exactness and could spend long hours at work in a laboratory, had you the time to do so. You have a good idea of your own opinion, and this is to a great extent justified, as you are cleverer than the majority in many ways, though not always wiser. You must learn to study human nature, above all your own, for you know yourself less than anybody in the world. You will doubtless have a certain amount of business success and are constantly inventing new ideas and schemes, which sometimes work out and sometimes don't.

◉ SECRET
Try to cultivate more sympathy and understanding for others. Your natural superiority makes you a little impatient with those around you.

BORN ON THIS DAY
- **John Adams**
  U.S. president
- **Henry Winkler**
  actor
- **Ivanka Trump**
  businesswoman, media personality
- **Nia Long**
  actor
- **Marcus Mariota**
  football player

FRIENDS & FAMILY

OCTOBER 31

The Lord gave us two ends— one to sit on and the other to think with. Success depends on which one we use the most.
—Ann Landers

BORN ON THIS DAY
- **Christopher Columbus**
  explorer
- **Peter Jackson**
  filmmaker
- **Zaha Hadid**
  architect
- **Gordon Parks**
  photographer
- **John Candy**
  comedian, actor

FRIENDS & FAMILY

___

PERSONALITY
You are impelled by natural curiosity to investigate a great many subjects, to become acquainted with a large number of people, and to dabble in many fields of art, culture, and education. You have a thirst for knowledge and probably spend many hours on the Internet, looking up facts, figures, and information. You do not stick to the study of any one topic for a long time because you lose interest after a while, and take up some new fad or fancy. However, this gives you a very wide range of knowledge, even if you don't use it to practical ends. It makes you a great conversationalist. But only by specializing in one area or field will you become prosperous or successful to the extent that you truly desire. You like social networking because it also appeals to your love of variety, change, and excitement. You must be active and on the go at all times.

LIFE PATH
You are kind, loving, and true, deeply sympathetic, intuitive, and very sensitive. You are modest and unassuming but shrewd and accurate in your judgment and very capable when you make up your mind to do something. You have many friends in very diverse places and areas of interest.

DESTINY
As you have the attributes for management, you need not hesitate in accepting a position in which you will be in full charge of much information, communications, and many activities. Personal magnetism, which you have in large measure, will ensure willing cooperation on the part of those people who work under your direction. Prominence and public honor are within the realm of possibility as a result of your efficient handling of obligations and duties.

KARMIC LESSON
You are very different from the being most people imagine you to be, and you are sometimes not true even to yourself. Your still waters run deep. This does not mean that you are in any way dishonest, but you will not admit certain faults and characteristics that you really possess but wish to ignore. You very often dislike the faults in others that you yourself possess. You must learn to see this clearly. You have a great deal of magnetism and can be very nice and charming when you have to be, especially if you want something or need to manipulate a situation. You are capable of being a leader in your circle should you care to exert yourself, since you certainly have the latent ability.

SECRET
You are skilled with your hands and have a vivid imagination. You can also be a competitive game player.

NOVEMBER 1

If we did all the things we are capable of doing, we would literally astound ourselves.
—Thomas Edison

BORN ON THIS DAY
★ **Lyle Lovett**
musician

★ **Hannah Höch**
artist

★ **Tim Cook**
CEO, Apple

★ **Larry Flynt**
publisher

★ **Penn Badgley**
actor

FRIENDS & FAMILY

PERSONALITY
Yours is a kaleidoscopic nature; you form patterns of conduct that are dazzling because there are so many sides and facets to your nature. While this makes for a very interesting, stimulating, and exciting life, it has its negative side, too. You may turn your attention to such a variety of things that you never master one. It is up to you, therefore, to devote yourself to some single interest in order to become a specialist in that field and reach the heights that are otherwise beyond your reach. A friendly disposition makes you well-liked, and you accept most people because you don't get too intimate with them but just share their happier moods and moments. Being tied down to anything or any individual goes somewhat against your grain.

LIFE PATH
An avid consumer of information and a ready conversationalist, you always appear to be upbeat. You are adaptable, quick-witted, able, and trustworthy. You are loving and lovable and fond of your home, and you like to entertain if you can have around you people whose minds are on the same wavelength as your own.

DESTINY
You can look to the past in setting up your program for the present and the future. Tradition is worthy of your respect, and the maintenance of a staunch reputation should be one of your most important aims. If it takes strenuous effort to accomplish some of the enterprises you start, do not be discouraged. You are observant and studious, careful in spending, and cautious in business affairs.

KARMIC LESSON
Yours is a very mixed character, hard to delineate, because it is so complex. You yourself do not understand it, at times. You are sometimes moody and impressionistic, subject to fits of brooding—not at all in conformity with the rest of your life. You are capable in business, fair and honorable. You are fond of travel, yet you love your home. You are fond of music on occasion, though you would be perfectly happy if you never heard another piece as long as you lived. You are exceedingly interested in the supernatural, and anything pertaining to it attracts and fascinates you—like a moth to a flame.

SECRET
You are exceedingly efficient when a course has been mapped out. You would make a good assistant to an executive who plans big things, so you could absorb all the methods.

NOVEMBER 2

Sometimes you have to get to know someone really well to realize you're really strangers.
—Mary Tyler Moore

BORN ON THIS DAY
- **Warren G. Harding**, U.S. president
- **Nelly**, singer, musician
- **K.D. Lang**, singer
- **David Schwimmer**, actor
- **Kendall Schmidt**, singer

PERSONALITY
Because you have an unusual talent for organizing and great stamina for hard work, you should reach the top of the ladder of success in your chosen occupation. It may be that you go along for many years, seemingly without reward. Then, suddenly, the opportunity you have been awaiting appears. You are prepared for it because during the years of waiting, you have been getting ready for success by study, experience, and preparation. So many people in your community, group, and family respect you for your ethical code of conduct, and you are deserving of this because you are capable, honest, dependable, and trustworthy. Everyone will have his or her hour; yours will come.

LIFE PATH
You are organized, forward-thinking, and ambitious, and your ideals are high. You are mostly very positive, and you will make an enemy rather than compromise your position. You are critical and severe in your judgment and would be relentless in the punishment of wrong. You will require a tactful and loving partner.

DESTINY
Your inspiration may better be directed toward the improvement of your present surroundings rather than turned to ideas of complete or sudden change. You can make your opinions count without forcing your ideas on other people. Do not waste time and effort on endeavors for which you are not emotionally or mentally suited. Keep calm, retain your enthusiasm, and keep your eyes fixed on your ultimate goal.

KARMIC LESSON
Inclined to be impatient, you could be seeing the faults of others while sometimes neglecting your own. You are very fond of harmony and order in every form and shape. You are very spontaneous, and at times you say just what you think. This may get you into hot water, yet on the whole you are admired for your candor and, again, laughed at for your simple and naive manner. You are fond of art and craftsmanship and ought to be able to create your own style well. The artistic life appeals to you, and you would like nothing better than to visit Paris for a year or so and study there. You are destined to travel a great deal, however, so this side of your nature will doubtless be satisfied at some point.

SECRET
You possess a talent for extemporaneous oratory, from stage or soapbox. You are a good, persuasive speaker and witty, too.

FRIENDS & FAMILY

NOVEMBER 3

The first great gift we can bestow on others is a good example.
—Thomas Morell

BORN ON THIS DAY

★ **John Barry**
composer

★ **Charles Bronson**
actor

★ **Kendall Jenner**
model, media personality

★ **Colin Kaepernick**
football player

★ **Anna Wintour**
editor-in-chief of *Vogue*

FRIENDS & FAMILY

● PERSONALITY
There is nothing in your nature that you try to keep from the world. You believe in free expression, and you say what you think to whomever you wish. You express your feelings in the same way, so that pride, resentment, and love all cross from you to the one who arouses the reaction. You love with all your heart when you do give your affection, and you are just as vehement in your dislikes. You know how to heighten the effect of anything you do by using the right word, wearing the right color, and choosing the right time. Because you are witty and clever in conversation and have magnetic appeal, you can cash in on your popularity by appearing on social media or in other places where the public can see you. Concentrate on establishing relationships with large groups, because your success is outlined in dealing with the masses.

● LIFE PATH
You can be abrupt, impulsive, and somewhat subject to moods. You will love with great strength and will demand the same love from your partner. You like a change of scene and can adapt yourself to almost any environment. You are generous with your time and take great pleasure in helping others or adding to their comfort.

● DESTINY
Diligence in work, enthusiasm in play, and consideration in relationships are important if you would make the most of your skills. Concentrate on activities for which you are especially equipped, for there are excellent chances for success. Esteem can mean as much to you as the accumulation of wealth, so do not worry if financial rewards seem a little slow in arriving.

● KARMIC LESSON
A free spirit, you are not easily ruffled by turbulent scenes. Sensitive and responsive, you have an expressive nature. You have a vivid imagination, and this is manifested in daydreams. You have a very gracious character, and your word is always to be depended upon. You must learn to not look ahead and invite trouble by anticipating it. Never cross bridges until you come to them. There will be time enough to take steps to prevent a catastrophe when it is really threatening. You are very affectionate and capable of giving much love, and you demand much in return. You ought to succeed in business, but not in the regular channels. You should initiate something entirely new and original, and this will be the basis of your future success.

● SECRET
There is an element of mystery in your self-confidence. You would make an efficient worker or caring parent and are not overly controlling.

NOVEMBER 4

The first and worst of all frauds is to cheat one's self. All sin is easy after that.
—Pearl Bailey

BORN ON THIS DAY
- **Matthew McConaughey**
  actor
- **Sean Combs**
  rapper, music executive
- **Kathy Griffin**
  comedian
- **Ralph Macchio**
  actor
- **Larry Holmes**
  boxer

PERSONALITY
There is an old aphorism that "hope springs eternal in the human heart." This may well be said of you, because you are optimistic, have a truly sanguine nature, and are full of the lust for life that only a courageous person has. Your enthusiasm and confidence stimulate your abilities so that you give an impressive performance no matter what you do. The capacity for concentration at your command makes it possible for you to penetrate the core of most every problem that you must solve. You have a deep sense of responsibility to your family, your employer, and your associates. As a matter of fact, you are sometimes too willing to do jobs that belong to someone else. As you are adaptable to new circumstances and situations, you are rarely upset. This placidity operates to make your youth last longer and gives you a wholesome outlook on life.

LIFE PATH
You are careful, painstaking and exacting, and very capable in the handling of details. You are looked up to as trustworthy and reliable, and you enjoy the confidence and esteem of your acquaintances. You are a great fan of children and devote much of your time to making your dwelling neat and attractive.

DESTINY
You can accurately estimate your resources and set up a program of spending that may be enjoyed with confidence. Do not deny yourself the things that will add to the beauty and comfort of your home. Economize on purchases of less-enduring value to make this possible. You may work with a pleasant colleague at a social festivity where you can derive tremendous satisfaction and plant seeds for a fruitful relationship.

KARMIC LESSON
Your emotional nature is strong, and you show this in your daily life. Inclined to be optimistic, you also are prone to take things hard when they are unfavorable. Yours is not an easy nature; you believe in the good, but your good cheer is not always reflected in your circumstances or the people close to you. You are always originating new schemes, but not many pan out. Yet there are many bright passages in your life, and if you look back, you will find that your disappointments have been few compared with those times you experienced genuine interest and pleasure. Logical in your thought, you can be almost too analytical for your own good. Bring your hidden self to the surface; let the daylight shine upon it, so that others may know you as you know yourself.

SECRET
You are one who will quietly rise to leadership in an emergency, possessing extraordinary powers, but might be happiest as a parent.

FRIENDS & FAMILY

NOVEMBER 5

For every bad there might be a worse, and when one breaks his leg let him be thankful it was not his neck.
—Joseph Hall

BORN ON THIS DAY
- **Robert Mapplethorpe**
  photographer
- **Roy Rogers**
  actor, singer
- **Sam Rockwell**
  actor
- **Tilda Swinton**
  actor
- **Vivien Leigh**
  actor

FRIENDS & FAMILY

PERSONALITY
You have very high ideals, to which you try to attract others besides yourself. Your mental concept of the universe is a place where everyone is spiritually connected and occupied in some interesting and creative activity. To try to establish this kind of world engages your interest, and you investigate economic theories, social reforms, and the various "isms" that have been proposed for the betterment of humankind. Once you decide that a philosophy or system or code is the right one, you become devoted to the dissemination of its ideas, one of its greatest champions. Your ability to use words well makes you a good press agent or propagandist. Sincerity is your strong point, and everyone respects you for the wholehearted, meaningful way you do things. There are no half measures in your way of living, and you use your intelligence to its full capacity.

LIFE PATH
You have shrewd intuitive judgment, good marketing ability, and considerable originality. You are enthusiastic and optimistic. Your love is demonstrative and your nature kind, sympathetic, and generous. Look forward to recognition and renown, because the qualities that distinguish you could eventually bring you these rewards.

DESTINY
Your actions should be based on ideals, not expediency. Be just, tolerant, and compassionate in your dealings with others. You will not regret generosity and help extended to one in need. Trust in your friends will add to your happiness. Invitations will always be plentiful. Indeed, the many pleasant memories of special gatherings will be a source of joy for a long time.

KARMIC LESSON
You have a very complex nature. Overall, you are bright and optimistic, but you also have some dark moods. You are clever, intellectual, and poetic, fond of books, art, and literature; there is little you do not take in and appreciate. You do not always live up to your ideals, however, and while you may present a smiling countenance to the world, you have a very protected, inward-turned side, which is more fully your true self. You can be both optimistic and cynical, but you distrust only when someone crosses your path. You have a good head for business and are capable of making money when others fail. Original and resourceful, you are interested in science, philosophy, and spiritual questions. You would make a good friend, but a bad enemy.

SECRET
Your chief difficulty lies in finding the work that will absorb you. Once you discover that, with your powers of concentration you will rise quickly.

NOVEMBER 6

I have lost my smile, but don't worry. The dandelion has it.
—Thich Nhat Hanh

⦿ PERSONALITY
The ability to concentrate on your work gives you a big advantage in the world of affairs. You dispatch e-mails, texts, phone calls, household tasks, paperwork, or chores with equal efficiency and speed. Because you are faithful to your job, you have a reputation for being trustworthy. This attitude ensures you steady employment and the approval of those with whom and for whom you work, no matter where it is. The trivia of daily routine do not get on your nerves because you have the ability to overlook petty things and annoyances. You enjoy championing a worthy cause, and your organizational ability makes you a great member of committees, events, and social functions. When aroused, you can be quite domineeringly aggressive. This is one way of getting what you want, but tactfulness will probably prove much more profitable. Develop your sense of diplomacy for best results.

⦿ LIFE PATH
You do not apply your energy and ability to the best advantage if left only to your own resources. You can accomplish much more when working under the supervision and direction of others. You need a partner who will spur your ambition and hold you up to your best. You are tender and true in your affection.

⦿ DESTINY
You should feel increased stability and strength of purpose as you mature. Financial and emotional security will be augmented, so do not be afraid to start a new venture, which you are capable of successfully and profitably carrying through with the help of a partner. You also will benefit others through aggressive and purposeful action. Occupational matters take on new luster after age forty; plan far in advance.

⦿ KARMIC LESSON
You have a very well-rounded nature. On the one hand, you are eminently businesslike; on the other hand, you are artistic, with all the qualities and qualifications of the artist. This is a rare combination, and you are fortunate to possess it. You are emotional and very considerate in your affections. You care for your own home more than many others with your temperament care for theirs. You will have a large circle of friends and acquaintances, and you will be admired by them. You are inclined to assert yourself in the matter of expressing your opinions, and some who are insecure may find this a little hard to take. One day, someone is going to walk into your life and make you realize why it never worked out with anyone else.

⦿ SECRET
You have a love of painting and sculpture, great deftness with your fingers, and artistic feeling. You are profoundly emotional with the ones you love.

BORN ON THIS DAY
- **Sally Field** — actor
- **Ethan Hawke** — actor
- **Gerald Epstein** — psychiatrist
- **Aaron Hernandez** — football player, convicted murderer
- **Walter Johnson** — baseball player

FRIENDS & FAMILY

NOVEMBER 7

The people who are crazy enough to think they can change the world are the ones who do.
—Jack Kerouac

BORN ON THIS DAY

- **Albert Camus**
  philosopher
- **Marie Curie**
  scientist
- **Joni Mitchell**
  singer/songwriter
- **David Guetta**
  DJ, music producer
- **Billy Graham**
  televangelist

FRIENDS & FAMILY

PERSONALITY

Discriminating taste makes you somewhat aloof, for you do not wish to soil yourself or your reputation by having traffic of any kind with people or things you consider mediocre. However, when you choose someone for a friend, you please them very much, for everyone is aware of your acumen. You like to investigate the secret forces of nature, the hidden motives behind actions, and the mystical aspects of life. Your ability to penetrate the core of truth qualifies you to be a good detective, a perspicacious research worker, or a fine psychologist. Travel by water has a romantic lure for you, for the call of the sea is in your blood. Passion rules you to a great extent.

LIFE PATH

You are sometimes quick-tempered and nervous and jump at conclusions hastily. You should restrain your impetuous nature, for your judgment is good and your conclusions are generally accurate when you take the time to view a situation from all sides. You can at times have a rollicking, jovial disposition and are popular and well-liked by your acquaintances. Your love is liable to be tempestuous at times.

DESTINY

Calmness is a quality upon which you may have to concentrate. Your life is so rich in opportunities and novel experiences that you are likely to overwork. Capability alone cannot be the deciding factor when it comes to participation in activities because there are too many things that you can do well. Choose with an eye to your stamina and the possibility of doing the most with the least draining effort expended.

KARMIC LESSON

Clever, literary, and of an inquiring turn of mind, you are strongly attracted to the occult and the supernatural and would like to dedicate time to the investigation of these subjects. You are sometimes inclined to trust too much and are apt to be imposed upon. You have a great deal of determination; you follow a trail to its bitter end. You have a roving disposition and will doubtless travel in many lands. You want money, yet you do not always take the necessary steps to get it. Somehow you are not practical enough; in any case, it seems to elude you, no matter how hard you try to obtain it. You must learn to save, for one thing, as the little sums are the important ones. Be more practical.

SECRET

You have a benevolent nature, are eager to befriend those in need, and derive much comfort from your ability to do so.

NOVEMBER 8

Anything I cannot transform into something marvelous, I let go.
—Anaïs Nin

BORN ON THIS DAY
- **Bram Stoker**
  author
- **Gordon Ramsay**
  celebrity chef, TV personality
- **Alfre Woodard**
  actor, producer
- **Bonnie Raitt**
  singer
- **Courtney Thorne-Smith**
  actor

FRIENDS & FAMILY

PERSONALITY
Initiating big projects is the most interesting pursuit you can find. When you are not busily engaged in starting clubs, businesses, events, or even romances, you are ill at ease. Soon you chomp at the bit and get into action again. Many of the ideas you have are concerned with the public welfare. Community projects form a large part of your interests. Housing, education, and cultural developments are matters of real concern to you, so you would do well at serving on committees to establish schools, libraries, museums, and so on. Since you are good at organizing, you should succeed in undertakings of this nature. Homelife is attractive to you, but only mildly so, for your real interests are on the outside. You are inclined to take people casually but can make a very good impression when you want to extend yourself.

LIFE PATH
You are determined, discreet and conservative, fastidious in your tastes, and emotional in your quests. You like to be surrounded by beautiful things and enjoy comfort and ease. You are resourceful and shrewd, and few people can place you at a disadvantage. You have a very deep nature, which few can appreciate or understand.

DESTINY
Benign Venus rays influence your birthday and do away with disharmony. Let your conscience guide you in any contemplated change in relationship with friends or members of the family. Sometimes it is wiser to concede on small matters than to make an unpleasant issue of them. Give credit where it is due, and always be tactful. You may experience pleasant results in combining business and social relationships.

KARMIC LESSON
You have great ability, and this needs only cultivation to make you a shining light in your community if not in far larger circles. You are intuitive, scientific, and fond of occult and metaphysical subjects. Yet you are not credulous; on the contrary, you approach these subjects from a severely skeptical point of view. You are intellectual, and your attitude of gratitude is strongly developed, but on the whole you are not overly affectionate. You live more in your head than in your heart—but this is only right for you. You have very wide interests, delving into a variety of different subjects. You have a great deal of natural genius for organization; you are open-minded and fearless and should be respected. On the whole, you are a well-rounded character.

SECRET
Your life is one that welcomes adversity as a challenge to its powers, seeking to conquer for its own satisfaction, rather than for rewards. You are not the domestic type.

NOVEMBER 9

There is but one virtue—the eternal sacrifice of self.
—George Sand

BORN ON THIS DAY
- **Muhammad Iqbal**
  poet, philosopher
- **Hedy Lamarr**
  actor
- **Carl Sagan**
  astronomer, TV personality
- **Nick Lachey**
  singer, actor
- **Lou Ferrigno**
  actor, bodybuilder

FRIENDS & FAMILY

PERSONALITY
Mental agility distinguishes your thought processes. You have a great wit and a lively sense of humor. The form of expression is rather dry, and it takes another quick-witted person to appreciate your remarks. You are very helpful and enjoy cooperative projects. When the neighbors get together on a community activity, you like to participate with all your heart, and you feel the same way about family, school, and social affairs. A strong sense of duty directs the conduct of your personal life. You never do a wrong willfully, and you extend every effort to prevent others from wrongdoing. Much of your life is taken up with reveries and dreams of establishing a personal Utopia for you and your loved ones.

LIFE PATH
You are persistent and determined and will never acknowledge defeat. You seldom take anyone into your confidence; you like to work out your own plans in your own way. Your homelife will be tranquil and happy, and you will receive love from a special someone who is whole-souled and deep. You will have many friends, and you are loyal and faithful to all trusts.

DESTINY
The Uranus rays on your birthday may help you attract someone who can be of definite assistance to you in starting a project that has long held fascination and promise for you. These same rays also will help you to free yourself from restraints that have encumbered your progress in the past. Do what you can to advance the welfare of younger people. A fond hope in regard to one of them, in whom you are personally interested, can be realized.

KARMIC LESSON
You are a person of action along with being a big dreamer. You have a great deal of tact and diplomacy, though you would not ordinarily be suspected of having it. You desire the good things of this life, taking and appreciating everything as it comes, without worrying too much. Frank, direct, and straightforward, you have a good sense of humor, though you do not always fully cultivate your intellect as much as you should. You are fleeting in your affections and will have a good many love affairs in your life until you meet The One. You will have commercial success if you learn how to reinvest the money you make. You must be careful not to dissipate your energies in unwise living, or you will suffer for it later in life.

SECRET
You are motivated by a desire to see good prevail over evil. You have a sense of justice too high for average human beings.

NOVEMBER 10

We have to continually be jumping off cliffs and developing our wings on the way down.
—Kurt Vonnegut

BORN ON THIS DAY

- **Martin Luther**
  theologian, religious leader
- **Richard Burton**
  actor
- **Eve**
  rapper
- **Tracy Morgan**
  comedian, actor
- **Brittany Murphy**
  actor

PERSONALITY
You have a lot of talent, which may take one or more forms of artistic expression. Many geniuses have been born on this day, testifying to its powerful vibrations. Your social instincts are strong, and you love having a good time with a crowd of friendly folks. Because you have such pronounced gregarious impulses, everybody finds you charming and delightful. You sometimes tend to fritter your time away, but when it's time to be serious, you can settle down and concentrate. You are sometimes inclined to be obstinate and will not take the advice of others as much as you should. Try to weigh everything that is said, from all sides, and then make up your mind as to what you want to do. Most likely, you will find greater happiness after middle life than in early youth.

LIFE PATH
You like to lead and will never fill a secondary place if you can possibly forge your way to the front. You are philanthropic and take a great deal of interest in social and public affairs. You should select as a partner one who will be in sympathy with your broad-minded interests. You love travel and like to read and study and collect high-minded books.

DESTINY
The persistence and fortitude you have shown in the face of past discouragements may be rewarded. The results of your study and work are likely to inspire pride in the hearts of your associates and deep satisfaction in your own. Enjoy agreeable companions and exciting recreations. August is favorable for travel.

KARMIC LESSON
Yours is a life survived against adverse circumstances. Yet the indications are that you will come through with flying colors; it all depends on you. You are sensitive and intuitive. You have strong convictions, for which you are always ready to do battle. Your beliefs are deeply rooted in your nature. You are very fond of acquiring knowledge, are sympathetic and kind, and can keep a secret. You are strong-minded but are often too easily led by what others say on some questions. Learn to think for yourself; your mind is as good as theirs—use it. Learn to find yourself early in life; formulate clearly your own goal, and then determine that nothing will prevent your attaining it. Realize the powers within yourself, and success will be yours.

SECRET
You have a forceful, strong-willed personality, and would go far in businesses involving international affairs.

FRIENDS & FAMILY

NOVEMBER 11

Those who dream by day are cognizant of many things which escape those who dream only at night.
—Edgar Allan Poe

BORN ON THIS DAY

- **Fyodor Dostoevsky**
  author
- **Leonardo DiCaprio**
  actor
- **Kurt Vonnegut**
  author
- **George S. Patton**
  WWII military hero
- **Stanley Tucci**
  actor

FRIENDS & FAMILY

PERSONALITY
There is great power at your command because your birthday is marked by tremendously potent vibrations. In astrology and numerology, this date has always been one on which important events took place and that has endowed upon its children unusual and vital potency. You have ideas that are intellectually brilliant, and you have the stamina, staying power, and determination to see that your ideas are established and kept in practice. Thus, when you decide upon a course of conduct, you do so with such a strong will that nothing can make you change your ways. And when you wish to impose your will upon another, you do so with just as much force as you exercise on yourself. You are helpful and inspiring, and your life should be full and rich.

LIFE PATH
You are shrewd, determined, and combative. You always stand up for what you consider your rights, and you will never be brushed aside without a vigorous protest. You do not like to be driven, but for love you will do much. You are generally centered and grounded and have many close friendships with kindred spirits.

DESTINY
While your gaze will be fixed on the future, a past acquaintance is likely to be of assistance in getting you started on a new project. There may be some conflict between your desire to enjoy a calm, serene life, on the one hand, and follow an active, progressive life, on the other. Your ability to balance these two tendencies can be one of your outstanding accomplishments.

KARMIC LESSON
You have a great deal of aptitude, but you do not always use your natural powers as you should. You are inclined to be a perfectionist—but when a subject truly interests you, then you are energetic and driven. You have brilliant ideas, but you need help to carry them out. Learn to be an actor as well as a dreamer. The only way to succeed is to try. You have excellent judgment in business affairs but cannot always be bothered to attend to details. Once you start on a project, you are quite focused. You are happy and good-natured, always ready to laugh and joke. You could learn to concentrate more; passing events easily distract you. Yet you are a very diligent person and have a good deal of power and talent. You have a winning way that is most attractive.

SECRET
You are attracted by enterprises that involve novelty and daring, and through your ingenuity, you will win rewards. Do not restrain your generous impulses.

NOVEMBER 12

All you need is love.
—John Lennon

⬢ PERSONALITY
You like to have a lot of fun, be on the go all the time, and make yourself the center of whatever activity and excitement is going on. Because you have a good vocabulary and a quick wit, you can be very sharp about what you say. To avoid hurting others, you must really control your tongue because you can be a bitterly sarcastic person when you feel like lashing out at someone. Travel appeals to you mightily. You like to go to new, strange, and romantic places. The call of adventure is strong, and, circumstances allowing, you would certainly be the first to answer it. You have ability as an actor, influencer, spokesperson, mimic, announcer, master of ceremonies, or any vocation that puts you in the spotlight. You work well with large groups. Although flirtatious in the extreme, you eventually settle down.

⬢ LIFE PATH
You have a retentive memory and a good mind for details. You are amiable, magnetic, intuitive, and a general favorite with your friends. Your presence is always desired at social gatherings. You are fond of travel and like to read along these lines. Your homelife will be interesting, harmonious, and happy.

⬢ DESTINY
Your enthusiasm and intelligent handling of difficult situations will result in personal gain. Business and social affairs will flourish. If you are obliged to take a test of any kind, you can come out with flying colors. Your record may be the basis for promotion. Have no qualms about your ability to take care of managerial responsibilities or to make a success of directing the activities of others.

⬢ KARMIC LESSON
A keen observer, you are imaginative, fond of travel, entertaining, and witty. You are intuitive and immensely interested in all that pertains to the supernatural. You may be subject to psychic impressions yourself, but you are more likely an investigator in these realms. You are clever in a variety of ways, but your chief gift is your ability to read human nature and penetrate the motives and desires of others. You are sympathetic, however, in this, and others often come to you for aid and assistance. Do not undertake new enterprises, if possible, during the summer; wintertime is most favorable for any venture. Be careful in your choice of associates; do not make friends too easily. Cultivate firmness of character and place a greater estimate upon your own abilities.

⬢ SECRET
You possess a fluency of language and ease in writing. Some literary pursuit should be your career, perhaps advertising.

BORN ON THIS DAY
- **Grace Kelly** actor, Princess of Monaco
- **Ryan Gosling** actor
- **Neil Young** singer
- **Nadia Comăneci** Olympic gymnast
- **Sammy Sosa** baseball player

FRIENDS & FAMILY

NOVEMBER 13

The Master doesn't take sides; she welcomes both saints and sinners.
—Tao Te Ching

BORN ON THIS DAY

- **Robert Louis Stevenson**
  author, poet
- **Whoopi Goldberg**
  actor
- **Jimmy Kimmel**
  comedian, talk show host
- **Chris Noth**
  actor
- **Steven Zahn**
  actor

FRIENDS & FAMILY

PERSONALITY
You have an important sense of responsibility, and you like to do things in a restrained way. In all things, you listen to, and heed, the dictates of your conscience, and you try your best to avoid hurting anyone. Temper your remarks with goodwill to avoid friction. Although your main interests are in your home and family affairs, it is likely that business takes you away quite often. You have dignity, grace, and natural charm. Because of these qualities, you attract many friends in all stations and walks of life. You are fond of the country and outdoor life, and the city does not have the same attraction for you that it does for many. You should have a bright future waiting for you, and will doubtless attain it, if you live up to the best that is in you.

LIFE PATH
You are frank, candid, and outspoken. You like changes of scene and environment, but you do not fret and worry if your desires are not instantly gratified. You read a great deal, you are a good talker, and you are entertaining. Your homelife will be enjoyable, and you might marry early.

DESTINY
The ties that bind you to your home and family will be strengthened by your realization of the importance of a big real estate transaction. Many outside pleasures may lose their appeal, and you will find that you will get more and more pleasure out of entertaining in your own home and planning family and neighborhood events, parties, and picnics. Chances for service in your community also will bring happy experiences.

KARMIC LESSON
You have a fine nature—frank, open, and true. The martial spirit about you is very appealing to those who are attracted to you. You are adventurous, and you will doubtless travel a great deal, particularly in out-of-the-way places in odd corners of the world. You cannot stand hypocrisy in anyone, and often you are led to say things to people because of this, which makes them adversaries. Do not try to reform the world all at once. Take it as it comes; it is a pretty good place. Above all, cultivate a saving sense of humor. You have a vivid imagination and can build castles in the air all day with the greatest of pleasure. Yet you are no idle dreamer; you are intensely practical and lead an active, productive life.

SECRET
You have the power to attain the desirable things in life. You have mannerisms that are direct to the point of bluntness.

NOVEMBER 14

Better keep yourself clean and bright; you are the window through which you must see the world.
—George Bernard Shaw

BORN ON THIS DAY
- **Prince Charles**
  Prince of Wales
- **Claude Monet**
  painter
- **Astrid Lindgren**
  author
- **Joseph Simmons**
  rapper, music producer
- **Yanni**
  musician

PERSONALITY
Within you are latent talents that should find expression in the arts. You have a subtle understanding of the creative faculty, and you can bring out your own talents if you will seek to develop them by training, concentration, study, and hard work. There may be a strong urge toward the field of songwriting or musical composition within you, and you may express it in classical or modern form. You could also be a good performer, and in this sense, you would not be limited to music. You could develop into a performer, play an instrument, and even be a good salesperson—which is a kind of acting or performance, too. You are interested in the field of psychic research and mysticism. You could well develop this interest and become a profound researcher of such subjects. Be sure that you do not waste the talent that has been so lavishly bestowed on you.

LIFE PATH
Hasty in your judgment, you can sometimes lose your temper easily, although you do not give in to violent fits of passion. You do not harbor resentment and are always sorry the moment you speak hastily. You like children, but you do not want them to bother you for too long. You have powers of encouragement and can easily motivate, influence, and lead others.

DESTINY
Among your blessings may be much advancement in your career and extensions of your circle of friends. Your financial foundation may be made firmer by the acquisition of some valuable property. If you have any outstanding debts, make every attempt to clear them up. Include some touches of bright colors when you add to your wardrobe in order to express the good cheer and optimism of your character in a graphic manner.

KARMIC LESSON
You are imaginative and have an appreciative understanding of the lives and motives of others, which is attained by few. You have a balanced disposition but must not be pushed too far, or you are liable to turn, and then your attackers must look out. You are kind and sympathetic and particularly fond of animals. You are interested in the strange and the supernatural, and anything odd or out-of-the-way attracts and fascinates you. You have a good nose for news and should make a very good reporter or detective. You also have good business sense, though it would be better for you to have a partner, in all probability. You are affectionate and would make an excellent partner and an indulgent, though fussy parent.

SECRET
You are a natural leader of social activities. In business, you lean toward the dissemination of art products that tend to make life more beautiful.

FRIENDS & FAMILY

NOVEMBER 15

Conscience warns us as a friend before it punishes as a judge.
—Stanislaus I

BORN ON THIS DAY
- **Georgia O'Keeffe**
  artist
- **Edward Asner**
  actor
- **Petula Clark**
  singer, actor
- **Jimmy Choo**
  fashion designer
- **Jeffree Star**
  YouTube celebrity, makeup artist

FRIENDS & FAMILY

PERSONALITY
The gregarious instinct, assisted by good money sense, makes you a clever manipulator of situations and people. You see opportunities where others fail to do so, and, as a result, you have a special talent for making your way in the world. People may think you are lucky, but your success is actually due to your perspicacity. You are no mere opportunist, however, because you have high ideals, and you are willing to sacrifice profit for your ideas. Versatility enables you to participate in many different types of activity. Your greatest talent lies in the handling of financial affairs, and you can balance the household budget and handle business affairs with equal ease and shrewdness. In your spare time, you like to write poetry or thoughts on social media or amusing texts and e-mails to your friends. You enjoy parties and have a good time because you are good-humored.

LIFE PATH
You are original, of an inventive turn of mind, patient and attentive to detail, and quite persevering. You are practical and matter-of-fact and have very little depression in your makeup. You are grounded, self-contained, proud, fond of interaction, and generally popular. You have a love of being out-of-doors.

DESTINY
Important decisions should be made without outside interference—keep your own counsel. First decide the cause of action you think best to take; then consult with members of your family. Accuracy is essential in all your dealings if you want to save yourself time and money. Professional and personal loyalties are stimulated under the beneficent Saturn rays of your birthday.

KARMIC LESSON
You have a good deal of initiative, which needs only more cultivation. You are probably interested in political questions and ought to be able to rise to a position of prominence in that field or a related field. You are ingenious, original, and inventive. You are rather deliberate in manner, but a great deal of thought lies behind your actions, and when you say anything, it is worth listening to and is heard with respect. You must form the habit, early in life, of never waiting for opportunities to come to you but rather going after them and making them for yourself. You are affectionate, and your love nature needs expansion and an opportunity to express itself. Marry, but use wisdom and discretion in your choice.

SECRET
You have a jovial and sympathetic nature and are disposed to some degree of self-indulgence with its risks and indiscretion. A wise marriage would prove to be a good anchor.

NOVEMBER 16

Forgiveness is the fragrance that the violet sheds on the heel that has crushed it.
—Mark Twain

BORN ON THIS DAY
- **Pete Davidson**
  comedian, actor
- **Maggie Gyllenhaal**
  actor
- **Amar'e Stoudemire**
  basketball coach
- **Martha Plimpton**
  actor, singer
- **Nonito Donaire**
  boxer

PERSONALITY
A subtle understanding of human nature makes you a tolerant and sympathetic person. You would never willfully hurt anyone, and you hate to see anyone else indulge their temper in meanness. There is a strange or unique healing power innate to your makeup that draws people in trouble to you. From you they expect, and usually receive, the consolation they are seeking for their problems, whether mental, spiritual, or physical. You can see the point of view of other people, and that is what gives you the understanding that distinguishes you. Your humor is dry, and you get quite a lot of fun out of life because you see it as a great adventure. Although you take your duties seriously, you see the lighter side of existence, and this gives you a balance that puts life's mishaps in their proper perspective.

LIFE PATH
You have an authentic, spiritual nature. A pleasant, soothing talker, you are reasonable, capable and discerning, and quite convincing. You are quite open-minded in your views but never spend any time in investigating fields that do not tie into your goals. Your temperament in love is strong and true, and you will receive strong commitment in return.

DESTINY
Be careful not to let your enthusiasm arouse the animosity of those who favor slower and surer methods of operation. Keep your impetuosity under control and be patient in explaining the reasons for your opinions and courses of action. An increase in luxuries for your home is possible without denial of necessities if you plan in advance. You can find yourself enriched emotionally as well as inspirationally by helping others.

KARMIC LESSON
You are interested in social questions and in trends and topics of the day. Your grounded presence and copious personal power will procure for you a wide range of friends. Do not scatter your forces. Determine what you want early in life and let nothing deter you from obtaining what you desire. Choose your friends carefully, selecting those who can benefit you, or from whom you can learn something of value. You could be successful in business, but not until you have broken away from old traditions and gotten set up in business for yourself. Cultivate greater frankness and cordiality. You have more than the usual talents, but you don't always make the most of them. Develop your latent powers more, and success will come to you.

SECRET
You possess a romantic nature, with the charm and appeal to attract romance. You have splendid taste.

FRIENDS & FAMILY

NOVEMBER 17

Poverty wants some, luxury many, avarice all things.
—Abraham Cowley

BORN ON THIS DAY
- **Martin Scorsese**
  filmmaker
- **RuPaul**
  drag queen
- **Rock Hudson**
  actor
- **Lorne Michaels**
  producer
- **Isamu Noguchi**
  artist, landscape architect

FRIENDS & FAMILY

PERSONALITY
Because you like to analyze events and people, you have developed your technique of probing to the point where you get to the core of the truth of things with startling speed. You have a gentle sense of humor and do not take yourself too seriously. This gives you a rational outlook on life, so that you accept what it brings you without having meltdowns over its misfortunes and without becoming too elated over its lucky breaks. You have a lot of initiative and can promulgate brilliant plans for your own success and the careers of your loved ones. Managing money matters is one of your strong points, and you should be able to plan your security with confidence. To be active at all times is necessary for your peace of mind, for you fret when you are unable to get around. Systems and business management are two good fields of endeavor for your type of mind.

LIFE PATH
A careful manager and a shrewd manipulator, you have fine judgment. You are always practical in your notions and will never embark upon an enterprise unless you can be reasonably sure of the outcome. You are affectionate, tender, and thoroughly reliable. Your friends always know where you stand, and they rely upon you for anything within reason.

DESTINY
Your sense of elation, which you will probably notice more after age thirty, is due to the power of Venus, ruler of your birth date. Turn your original ideas and creative work into money. You will find laughter an excellent antidote for irritations, which may, of course, arise in personal relationships. Your upbeat attitude will be communicated to others and much unpleasantness averted, as a result.

KARMIC LESSON
You have a great deal of ability that you sometimes fail to use, or you use only a small fraction of it. You can work hard when you want to, but you don't always like work very much, unless you find it interesting, and then you can undertake any amount. You can be too easily led and influenced by those around you; cultivate a greater stamina of your own, to counterbalance these influences. You are fond of all the good things of this life. You have a loving nature and give much in your expressive conversation, often without getting its equivalent in return. You are inclined to get irritated or impatient if you don't see immediate results. Your head is all right; cultivate your heart more.

SECRET
Your life will be a bit unfocused until your ideal partner is discovered. Then will begin an era of business success and domestic happiness.

NOVEMBER 18

It is only with the heart that one can see rightly; what is essential is invisible to the eye.
—Antoine de Saint-Exupéry

BORN ON THIS DAY
- **Owen Wilson**
  actor
- **Chloë Sevigny**
  actor
- **Mike Epps**
  comedian, actor
- **Kirk Hammett**
  guitarist
- **Christian Siriano**
  fashion designer

PERSONALITY
Your happiest times are those spent in outdoor activities. Sports, gardening, hikes, picnics, swimming, and such pastimes have a strong appeal to you, and you indulge yourself in them as much as you can. You respond to nature with all your heart, and it seems that nature in turn reveals all its secrets to you. You have a rather poetic character, even if you have never written a line of verse. You understand things from the poet's gentle, tolerant, and idealistic point of view. Your friends care for you deeply, think of you, and do what they can to show you that they like you. All things mystical attract you, and you have a strong psychic sense. Your intuition tells you what the right thing is and what to say and do at the appropriate times. Because you have these traits, you should be able to navigate a natural and peaceful life.

LIFE PATH
You are accurate in your perceptions, just and conscientious, bright, breezy, and entertaining. You do not act quickly, but you are steady and reliable and may be counted upon to accomplish what you undertake. You are creative and have high ideals and refined tastes.

DESTINY
Enthusiasm, ambition, and skill will be in plentiful supply in your life. Do not let your remarkable zest be confined to personal matters. Your community needs your talents to promote the welfare of others. Give as freely of your time as you can to organizations interested in the improvement of social conditions. You may gain a position of esteem as a result of your contributions. You can expect satisfying accomplishments.

KARMIC LESSON
You have innate wisdom about people and situations. Quick, intuitive, and brilliant, you are a good deal of a genius. You will travel much and have many friends wherever you go. You are cultured and artistic—gifted, in fact, in a number of ways. You will make a business success, owing to your application and to the fact that you can turn your ability in any channel you may choose. You are inventive and might be quite an inventor. You are loving and affectionate, and your love of nature is striking. Your head and heart are in almost perfect sympathy; in fact, you are a very evenly balanced nature, one capable of accomplishing great things in life. The powers are within you. Use them.

SECRET
Yours is a powerful and independent nature; you rely on your own counsel and always stand alone as a free spirit.

FRIENDS & FAMILY

NOVEMBER 19

The fountain of beauty is the heart, and every generous thought illustrates the walls of your chamber.
—Francis Quarles

BORN ON THIS DAY

- **James A. Garfield**
  U.S. president
- **Adam Driver**
  actor
- **Meg Ryan**
  actor
- **Calvin Klein**
  fashion designer
- **Jack Dorsey**
  cofounder of Twitter

FRIENDS & FAMILY

PERSONALITY
Public life appeals to you, and you work for recognition of your talents with all your strength. You are not the type to bury your light under a bushel, regardless of your forte. You could be successful in television, podcasting, radio, or politics, but whatever you choose, it must have some connection with the public. Groups of people seem to fall under your sway, and you employ your magnetism and charm to promote yourself and your cause. In family life, you are a gentle and diplomatic guide. It may take you a long time to put your mark upon the world or to gain the acclaim or recognition that you desire. However, it's in your destiny to be at the head of an organization, no matter how long or arduously you must work for your aim. Your love life is important to you but could become submerged under career matters.

LIFE PATH
Your life runs smoothly and is orderly. You are cheerful, contented, truthful, and affectionate. You have a slight vein of selfishness, which comes to the surface when your personal comfort is threatened. But you are a very agreeable companion, and you have many cherished friendships.

DESTINY
Although you will not waver in devotion to your high standards, you will find yourself able to adjust to new situations. Courage will characterize your attitude toward new duties. Your determination and perseverance will be rewarded. Maintain your credit rating by meeting financial obligations promptly.

KARMIC LESSON
You have a variety of talents that seem, at times, in strange contradiction to one another and make your life a paradox even to yourself. You have business ability, yet you should have a partner, if possible, who attends to the money end of the business, as they probably would be more suited to this than you are. You are sociable, and people enjoy your sharing and your company very much, and for that reason you can be popular. The beautiful and the sublime in nature fascinate you, and you love the grand and the colossal. You are rather too open and trusting, and this may lead to disappointments at times, but probably everything will turn out to your advantage in the end.

SECRET
The ocean appeals to you, and you are carried away in awe at the wonder of it. You are drawn to all that is mysterious and deep in nature.

NOVEMBER 20

Happiness radiates like the fragrance from a flower and draws all good things toward you.
—Maharishi Mahesh Yogi

BORN ON THIS DAY
- **Joe Biden** — U.S. president
- **Bo Derek** — model, actor
- **Joel McHale** — actor, comedian
- **Joe Walsh** — singer
- **Sean Young** — actor

PERSONALITY
You are sensitive. This seemingly plain fact is stated simply because it is the vital clue to your character. There seems to be a well of feeling within you that is demanding expression of some kind. With luck and determination, your talent or sentiment, or whatever is basic there, will find some form of fine expression. However, you may continue for years without being able to bring out the depth of your inner being. What you need for happiness, self-expression, and the true joy of living is another person who loves you deeply, who will fight hard battles for you and thus enable you to find the support, trust, help, and strength that will bring out the best in you. In everyday life, you follow the routine requirements, for you can work hard. Your ideals must win out, however, and they will.

LIFE PATH
You are not argumentative, although you hold very definite opinions. You never make a pretense of liking people who do not interest you, as you are honest to a fault. You are cautious and self-contained, and never violate a trust. You are thoughtful, dependable, and reliable, possessed of much dormant ability that will emerge over time.

DESTINY
Although environmental and real estate restrictions will decrease after age forty, it is up to you to remove the psychological barriers for expansion. Do not be too sensitive about your plans but take others into your confidence even before you attempt to put your original ideas into operation. Seek evidence to support your personal views, for, though you may count on your intuitions, others are apt to demand more concrete substantiation.

KARMIC LESSON
You have much to be thankful for, as your natural gifts are great and need only to be cultivated to make you greater. You perhaps lack self-confidence at times, but this will vanish as you gain experience. You are independent in thought and action—more so in the former than in the latter, and you should develop the active side of yourself a little more. You are reliable and like doing a task right away. Procrastination is not your problem. You know how to keep a secret, which is one of the most valuable possessions in the world, and you have no use for scandal or gossip or those who delight in it. You are strong and true in your affections but must guard against being too easily hurt.

SECRET
Your greatest satisfaction will come by artistic pursuits, either as a profession or as a hobby. You are essentially a homebody and love your routine.

FRIENDS & FAMILY

NOVEMBER 21

The truth is always exciting. Speak it, then. Life is dull without it.
—Pearl S. Buck

BORN ON THIS DAY

- ★ **Goldie Hawn**
  actor
- ★ **Michael Strahan**
  football player, TV personality
- ★ **Ken Watanabe**
  actor
- ★ **Björk**
  singer
- ★ **Ken Griffey, Jr.**
  baseball player

FRIENDS & FAMILY

_____

_____

_____

_____

_____

_____

_____

_____

PERSONALITY
You have a scientific type of mind. Your ability to do research work and investigate new fields is very pronounced. In private life, this trait is expressed in the form of intellectual curiosity. You want to know all about everything. Your favorite question is "Why?" This gives you an interest in writing, science, art, and history. The negative side or expression of this trait is idle curiosity, which can lead you into gossiping ways and much wasting of time. Never allow this negative expression to sway your impulses. You have strong powers of expression and should do well with speaking and writing. You may do these things professionally or as a talented amateur. Participate in social networking and in community affairs, for you have the ability to be helpful and inspirational in organizing and promoting projects.

LIFE PATH
Prompt, reliable, and competent, you are a great communicator, a freethinker, and a knowledgeable conversationalist. You are somewhat sensitive and proportionately careful of the feelings and opinions of others. You love your home and strive to make it bright, cheerful, and harmonious. You are quite fond of children and may work with them in some capacity.

DESTINY
You will always become enthusiastically interested in new people and activities. You can win respect or an award for the capable way you handle an executive position in a club, group, or organization. This may lead to similar assignments professionally. Obstacles will not seem formidable to you, for your clear-cut thinking and intuition will show you how to remove them from your path.

KARMIC LESSON
You are inclined to be a little too caring in all your dealings and should learn to be more easygoing. Your other greatest failing is faultfinding, which you must suppress. Apart from these two faults, you have a genuinely good character, at times one that could hardly be improved upon. You have exceptional powers as a storyteller. Your ability in this direction would amuse your friends and a wider audience should you decide to develop it. You are clever and could earn more degrees if you put the requisite amount of work into your studies. You are not a natural clown, but on the contrary have a natural dignity, which has a charm of its own. You have many gifts and should use them wisely and not squander them.

SECRET
Conflicting emotions wage continual warfare in your being. Take your own advice and let yourself be guided by your highest ideals.

NOVEMBER 22

All brave men love; for he only is brave who has affections to fight for.
—Nathaniel Hawthorne

BORN ON THIS DAY
- **George Eliot**
  author
- **Terry Gilliam**
  actor, filmmaker
- **Scarlett Johansson**
  actor
- **Dora Maar**
  artist, poet
- **Steve Van Zandt**
  singer/songwriter

PERSONALITY
You were born on the cusp between two signs, and therefore you share the traits of both Scorpio and Sagittarius. In a sense, you have a dual personality. That is, you show to the world the more practical traits of your character, but you have a deep emotional sensitivity that you rarely reveal except to your closest and most intimate friends. You have a reflective mind and a keen vision into the lives and motives of others. This birth date brings to its children many talents in the visual arts. You should endeavor to express the particular gifts with which you have been endowed. By planning your career with all the wisdom at your command, you should carve a highly successful, satisfying niche for yourself in life. You are active and have great power for detailed work.

LIFE PATH
You are inclined to think it is incumbent upon you to correct all the wrongs you see, and you cause yourself much needless worry. You are serious-minded and studious, fond of high-minded matters, careful of appearances, and generally cautious and vigilant. Your love is deep-seated.

DESTINY
Cooperation rather than competition will be the keynote of your life. Compassion will be coupled with efficiency to make your philanthropic contributions of great value. Remember that sympathy and sincerity are important in personal relationships as well as in organized humanitarian enterprises. Your persuasive manner can sell your opinions to people in the business as well as the social worlds.

KARMIC LESSON
You have great natural willpower; you are a naturally sensible person and like all the best that this life has to offer. You have a taste for vintage collecting and history, but your life is probably too busy and practical for you to become obsessed this way. The talent is there, nonetheless. You are generally kind to others and like to hear nice things said about you. You are a hard worker and feel that you could make good in any position. You are a bit temperamental, but the next minute your naturally big heart comes to the rescue, and you are just as ready to forgive everything and make friends again. At all costs, you must learn to curb the tendency to put off until tomorrow what should be done today.

SECRET
You have an intense nature, carrying both friendship and enmity to the extreme.

FRIENDS & FAMILY

NOVEMBER 23

To pity distress is but human; to relieve it is Godlike.
—Horace Mann

BORN ON THIS DAY
- **Franklin Pierce**
  U.S. president
- **Tom Joyner**
  radio host
- **José Clemente Orozco**
  caricaturist
- **Miley Cyrus**
  singer
- **Nicole "Snooki" Polizzi**
  reality TV star

FRIENDS & FAMILY

PERSONALITY
Devotion and loyalty are such mainsprings of your being that you have a remarkable reputation for commitment to people, causes, and even memories. You are impelled to deeds of charity and consideration because you have a deep sense of obligation to all your fellow human beings. Although you are devoted to your loved ones, you really have such a big heart that you consider the whole human race to be your family, and you can't do enough to allay suffering and ameliorate the condition of the unfortunate. Occasionally, you go off the deep end, and you splurge by taking a trip, treating yourself to some extravagant luxury, or indulging in an emotional spree. Soon, however, you snap back to your normal self and once more become the reliable person that everyone knows and loves.

LIFE PATH
You are forceful and adventuresome, at times to the verge of recklessness, but very affirmative in your manner. When you know something to be true, it is next to impossible to deter you. Some of your friends accuse you of stubbornness. You are fair and exacting. Your love is rugged and vigorous.

DESTINY
The prospects for achievement in your life are bright. Use your influence over others to further causes that will bring general benefits. You are well equipped to deal with the public and should devote part of your time to unselfish projects. As far as your personal life is concerned, you are receiving an abundance of cosmic blessings, and you may expect significant advances financially, intellectually, and socially.

KARMIC LESSON
You have a strong nature and a firm, military type of mind; discipline and decisiveness attract you. You are naturally masterful, and this trait leads you at times to be too dogmatic and intolerant of the views of others. You are blunt and straightforward in your manner of speech. You have no fear of anything, but you are a great lover of discipline and like to see it maintained everywhere. Cultivate the gentler side of your nature, learn to be a little less unbending, and your opinions would be more accepted. Do not keep criticizing and tearing down—build up and motivate, instead. Remember that the destroyer adds nothing to the world, but the positive teacher does—and you are that teacher.

SECRET
You are gifted with wisdom and a viewpoint on most matters different from the ordinary. Cultivate the affectionate side of your character more.

NOVEMBER 24

It is by going down into the abyss that we recover the treasures of life. Where you stumble, there lies your treasure.
—Joseph Campbell

BORN ON THIS DAY
★ **Zachary Taylor**
U.S. president

★ **Henri de Toulouse-Lautrec**
painter

★ **William F. Buckley, Jr.**
author, political commentator

★ **Sarah Hyland**
actor

★ **Scott Joplin**
composer, "King of Ragtime"

◉ PERSONALITY
You are a mighty champion of equality, a real knight in armor fighting for right. You cannot bear the sight of cruelty to the weak or injustice to the defenseless. Because you possess this high ideal, you gather many followers or adherents to your cause. You are naturally admired on the stand you take, and people take your side with much pride in what you are doing. As a natural executive, you like taking the lead, and sometimes you seem to be pretty aggressive about getting your way. Even though you may be right, you must realize that others resent being ordered around or having their wills bent to yours. For this reason, you should learn how to use your wit, tact, and diplomacy to get your ideas across. Once you have achieved this aim, you should rapidly rise to the top of the ladder of success.

◉ LIFE PATH
You have great poise and abundant self-confidence. You are ambitious and idealistic, but you are sometimes lacking in perseverance and tenacity for taking care of details and often fall just short of attaining your goal.

◉ DESTINY
You will demonstrate your good judgment and ability many times during your life. Opportunities for self-improvement will be available, and you should grasp them. Do not go off the deep end for every suggestion, but give thoughtful consideration to advice that is offered. Be trustworthy about private confidences made to you and careful about giving your own.

◉ KARMIC LESSON
Your character should be, overall, virtuous, but you have certain weaknesses that must be guarded against. You are a little prone to jealousy, which is due to the fact that you sometimes do not think your own work and efforts are sufficiently appreciated. This makes you at times sulking and sensitive, but after you realize how small this all is, then you are all right again. You are not naturally demonstrative with your affections by nature and do not fall in love easily. You have intellect and passion, without overt tenderness. For this reason, the heartfelt side of you should be cultivated more. You must learn that only love begets love, and that it will never be given to you unless you are more loving yourself.

◉ SECRET
You are rather guarded in money matters and prone to be conservative in all investments. You can be generous and charitable when convinced the object is worthy.

FRIENDS & FAMILY

NOVEMBER 25

Only when the last tree has died, and the last river been poisoned, and the last fish been caught will we realize we cannot eat money.
—Cree American Indian proverb

BORN ON THIS DAY
- **Joe DiMaggio**
  baseball player
- **Percy Sledge**
  singer
- **Donovan McNabb**
  football player
- **Christina Applegate**
  actor
- **Joel Kinnaman**
  actor

FRIENDS & FAMILY

PERSONALITY
You have the instincts of a true humanitarian. Were you able to do so, you would put a halt to all suffering. There are times when you are so moved by the sight of the needs of others that you sacrifice things you could use yourself. This is an admirable trait; however, do not go so far that you will have to lean on anyone else for help. You have a lot of psychic power and intuition, which you may depend upon for guidance. This perceptive power gives you an advantage, as you can tell what people are thinking, what they plan to do, and what motives make them act as they do. You should be successful in any field where personal service is the basis of the business. Love is all-important to you, but you could seem to be more concerned with loving the world than loving an individual.

LIFE PATH
You are diligent and unassuming and very capable. You possess good executive ability, think logically, act with good judgment, and try to hold your emotions under control. You seldom become overly dramatic or enthusiastic, even though you have strong feelings. You are fond of art and music, like to travel, and are quite adaptable to different situations. You love your home and nest above all else.

DESTINY
Your daily routine will always include interesting activities and companionship. You may be singled out for an innovative job, which will give you the chance to exercise your tact and efficiency. Diplomacy and mental alertness will inspire the cooperation of associates so that success can be accomplished with less effort on your part than you thought.

KARMIC LESSON
You are naturally an independent thinker and arrive at what you consider conclusively proved opinions. For this reason, you are somewhat intolerant of opposing views and ideas of others. You are a champion of free thought and free action, yet you are often intolerant of views expressed by others that do not coincide with yours. You mostly keep these judgments to yourself, as you are learning to suppress this instinct. You are practical and worldly, but there is an unusual mystical vein to your thought and life that you hardly know what to make of yourself. You are suited to being at the head of things and make your best successes in life when you have a free hand to run things as you think they should be run.

SECRET
It is difficult for you to be subordinate, even when others are in authority. There could be friction in your business and domestic affairs if you don't get your way.

NOVEMBER 26

Common sense is the knack of seeing things as they are and doing things as they ought to be done.
—C.E. Stowe

⬥ PERSONALITY
To you, life is a great adventure, and you are a seeker on the pathways to excitement, romance, and success. Because you find it sport to take a chance, you are ever ready to start new projects, to begin travels, and to broaden your horizons of experience on every level. You love nothing more than a suggestion for some daring venture or project, and regardless of the time or place, you are on the spot urging everyone else on and taking a strong lead yourself. However, you rarely get into any serious trouble over your daring deeds because you are clever (or naive!); your mind works so fast that you see trouble when it's ahead, and you know well how to prevent catastrophes. By devoting some of that spirit to serious accomplishments, you can go very far in life.

⬥ LIFE PATH
Genuine and faithful, you are capable of great self-sacrifice. You are unique and fanciful, a general favorite in your circle of acquaintances, and dearly loved by many in your family. You have a personality that draws people to you, and there is little that your friends would not do for you.

⬥ DESTINY
While you may love to go out, travel, and be on the move, your home will remain your favorite scene for friendly gatherings. From discussions in your own home, you will derive pleasure as well as profitable information, which may later be of practical value. Your natural resourcefulness will prove useful in any job you undertake, and your genial disposition will be a wonderful asset in all social interactions and activities.

⬥ KARMIC LESSON
You are marked by a very strong will, which often brings you through difficult situations by its sheer force and power. Being of this nature, you cannot understand the attitude of those who are less strong and daring than yourself; you should cultivate an attitude of tolerance and understanding. You would be a good organizer of large affairs and events, both online and in real life. In contrast, your interest in human potential is very great, so that you might be an author, writing essays or articles of the self-help type that deal with the lessons of life. You are energetic and love work for its own sake. Your natural power and endurance are very great, and you should make the most of them while at the same time not wearing yourself out.

⬥ SECRET
You are quirky and candid to the point of being misunderstood. But you are respected for your scrupulous honesty and fairness.

BORN ON THIS DAY
- **Saint Francis of Assisi** religious leader, mystic
- **Charles Schulz** cartoonist
- **Tina Turner** singer
- **DJ Khaled** DJ, music producer
- **Hilma af Klint** artist

FRIENDS & FAMILY

NOVEMBER 27

To forgive is to set a prisoner free and discover that the prisoner was you.
—Lewis B. Smedes

BORN ON THIS DAY

- **Jimi Hendrix**
  singer, guitarist
- **Bruce Lee**
  actor, martial artist
- **Bill Nye, the science guy**
  scientist and TV personality
- **Robin Givens**
  actor, model
- **Jil Sander**
  fashion designer

FRIENDS & FAMILY

PERSONALITY

Regardless of the duties or tasks that you assume, you are bound to make a success of the form of activity that you indulge in or follow as your life's work. You are especially capable of making adjustments of every nature. For that reason, you can establish equity in all kinds of relationships and situations. For example, you might succeed as a clerk who makes adjustments for a retail store or an insurance company. At the same time, you might be an excellent therapist or counselor in vocational or marital affairs. Moreover, your advice would be excellent and useful whether you gave it professionally or as an amateur advising a friend. Keep up the good work, as you become a more decent, gracious person with every kind deed.

LIFE PATH

You are original and aggressive and have the ability to guide, be it in an association or a business. Humorous and affable, you are an omnivorous reader, a careful student, and a lucid thinker. You love to excel, putting the same vigor into an athletic game that you put into your most serious undertaking.

DESTINY

The role of onlooker will not suit you. Offer, rather than accept, advice. You may be able to help a close friend solve a perplexing problem, and your friend, in turn, will recommend you for a better position. Mental pursuits particularly will claim your attention, and your greatest triumph will probably result from developing an original idea. Do everything you can to promote the cause of individual freedom, for this will bring you lasting satisfaction.

KARMIC LESSON

Your expressive abilities need only development and encouragement to bring about their successful emergence. Your character is an odd combination that loves the world and yet does not. Half the time you are right in the swing of a social whirl and big events, and the other half you do not care for these at all, becoming almost a spiritual ascetic. You are not as lavish in your praise of others as you should be. You like to be at the head of things and run them to suit yourself. You feel that if you could do this, all would be well. You have a great idea of duty and honor and are unflinching in your devotion to them. You should, perhaps, cultivate a greater sense of tolerance.

SECRET

You have boundless energy and exuberance. You are a lover of intense physical and mental activity, doing one for a livelihood and the other for recreation.

NOVEMBER 28

Our deeds determine us, as much as we determine our deeds.
—George Eliot

BORN ON THIS DAY
- **William Blake**
  poet
- **Jon Stewart**
  comedian, political commentator
- **Randy Newman**
  songwriter
- **Berry Gordy**
  music executive, film producer
- **Judd Nelson**
  actor

PERSONALITY
Clarity of vision and accuracy of perception make you a good judge of people, places, and things. You have an uncanny power to pierce right through the veil of covering that conceals the inner core of things and get to the potent and astounding truth. You could be a fine professional critic because you see the outstanding quality and the outstanding fault at once, while your inner eye is busy probing for the rest of the analysis of the subject or person under discussion. You are a good student, no matter what subject you undertake to master. However, you also are rather impatient. If anything takes too long, you lose interest in it, and you chomp at the bit—eager to get on with the next thing. Take care not to extend this ennui to people, or you may lose the friends you love.

LIFE PATH
You are trustworthy, kind, loving, and true, but, with all of your gentler traits, you are at times domineering. You are independent and sometimes secretive. You have a great deal of confidence in your own ability. Maybe you will marry early in life.

DESTINY
You will stick to the tried-and-true methods of doing things in your business despite pressure from associates to try untested ways. You have the perseverance and determination required for success. Although one enterprise may require considerable time and effort, you will have the satisfaction of knowing that your triumphs will be enduring. You will receive assistance from people who admire you and your courageous stand.

KARMIC LESSON
You are straightforward and upright in most all that you do, and you like the best quality in everything. You like the best clothes, which must be of good cut and taste. You are fond of jewelry, but this, too, must be of the best, and you do not at all care for that fake, imitation stuff that many other people delight in. You always give full and just returns for all you receive and expect the same in return. You are a little inclined to exaggerate at times, but this is not excessive. You have an intense love of nature. It seems to you often that you can never find anyone who can completely gratify your longings.

SECRET
You are aggressive in business, especially in the salesmanship and promotion field. You have a nature sympathetic to the arts and delight in beautiful surroundings.

FRIENDS & FAMILY

NOVEMBER 29

Talking and eloquence are not the same. To speak and to speak well are two things.
—Ben Jonson

BORN ON THIS DAY

★ **C.S. Lewis**
author

★ **Chadwick Boseman**
actor

★ **Don Cheadle**
actor

★ **Jackie Stallone**
astronomer, dancer

★ **Anna Faris**
actor

FRIENDS & FAMILY

PERSONALITY

The world is composed of serious and constructive people and of those who have entered this life to play. Fortunately, you are so constituted that you enjoy your duties, so that it is no great difficulty to play the serious role in which you have been cast for this performance of life. You avoid the conflicts that most people find so perplexing by going on with your job from day to day, accepting your chores with perseverance, and enjoying the simple pleasures that life offers to you. This is a sane, rational, and balanced way of looking at things, and it will lead to your continued peace of mind and satisfaction in living. You are fond of your family, and you think more of homelife than of running around in a mad social whirl. Domestic happiness and harmony are promised to you by a kind destiny.

LIFE PATH

You have stamina and are full of energy. You would rather do things yourself than stand around and direct others. You are shrewd and capable and have good intuitive judgment. You are fond of the outdoors, enjoy handmade things, and take an active interest in many matters outside of your regular routine. You are loving and sympathetic to those who deserve it.

DESTINY

Your mental resourcefulness will stand you in good stead. Logical conclusions and practical decisions can have far-reaching effects. Put nothing ahead of personal integrity. If this involves conceding some points in disagreements or subjugating your own desires on occasion, do so willingly; the results will be gratifying.

KARMIC LESSON

Your distinguishing trait, according to your birth date, is your patient disposition. However, you can be irritated at times when dealing with stupidity but as ready to pacify the next moment. You may harbor slight grudges against people—a habit that represents the worst side of your nature and that you must eradicate at all costs. You are basically full of goodwill and good humor and are active and energetic. You are fairly thorough but dislike detail work, which you feel is more suited for others. Although free and easy, you are not a natural hippie and, at times, just the reverse. You love intensely and scatter your affections over a great many. Maybe you are of an apparently quiet nature, but wait until the brakes are off, and see the result!

SECRET

You are able to think in systematic terms and are a good planner. You are very desirous of taking a supportive part in all that you undertake.

NOVEMBER 30

There are two times in a man's life when he should not speculate: when he can't afford it, and when he can.
—Mark Twain

BORN ON THIS DAY

★ **Winston Churchill**
Prime Minister of the U.K.

★ **Mark Twain**
author, humorist

★ **Ridley Scott**
filmmaker

★ **David Mamet**
playwright

★ **Mandy Patinkin**
actor, singer

◉ PERSONALITY

You get a lot of fun out of action. To be on the go, causing excitement, and being in the midst of it is dessert and drink to you. There is always a lot of fun when you are around because you're full of humorous suggestions, clever remarks, and practical jokes. However, even your humor is good-natured, and you just like to laugh. Your mischief is appealing for this reason and makes people like you. You are good at talking yourself into almost any situation that you wish to create. Because you can command attention, people take you at your own value, which is high indeed—and with good reason. Always think well of yourself, demand the respect that you give to others, and maintain your respectful place in the thoughts of your colleagues.

◉ LIFE PATH

Positive, excitable, and impulsive, you possess ready wit, a sharp intellect, and sound judgment. You are thorough and reliable in most all you do and enjoy the utmost confidence of your friends. You should marry, and your homelife will be rewarding.

◉ DESTINY

Your leadership ability is innate and may be an important factor in your chance to assume a position of increased authority in the future. Your knowledge of when to refrain from giving orders is equally important. By using it, you will not arouse antagonism or envy even though you are in a superior position. In fact, you will undoubtedly gain in popularity and receive invitations and compliments attesting to your prestige.

◉ KARMIC LESSON

You have an active mind; you learn quickly and easily, and remember what you read and what was said. You are inclined to worry too much, however, and while doing so, you have a tendency to make some of those around you worry also. This you must learn to overcome. You have strong ideas about things, and you invariably believe you are in the right. As a matter of fact, you generally are, but you don't like to have the opposite proved to you. You make it a point to know thoroughly any business into which you enter, and this absorbs a large part of your time. You have plenty of self-confidence. At the same time, you are not arrogant. You must concentrate more than you do and develop your mind even more.

◉ SECRET

You are naturally suited to public life and would fill any position, no matter how responsible, with great credit to yourself.

FRIENDS & FAMILY

DECEMBER 1

Tomorrow is a mystery. Today is a gift. That is why it is called the present.
—Eleanor Roosevelt

BORN ON THIS DAY
- **Woody Allen**
  filmmaker
- **Bette Midler**
  singer, actor
- **Richard Pryor**
  comedian, actor
- **Sarah Silverman**
  comedian, actor
- **DeSean Jackson**
  football player

PERSONALITY
With your careful expression, studied phraseology, and immaculate appearance, you give the impression of being extremely ethical and subtle about your attitude toward life. You are not really giving anyone a false impression, either, by the precision with which you express yourself, because you have a disciplined mind and an efficient way. Accuracy is as natural to you as slovenliness is to so many people. Socially, you prefer to be at the top of the heap. You can easily take the lead in any situation. In business, you are known for your conscientious ways and dependability. You also have your lighter side, can get a joke, and can make one. This makes life a pretty well-balanced proposition for you, and you should enjoy it. When it comes to the words you choose, whether in your mind or among friends, let them be about what you like and love—what you care about and cherish.

LIFE PATH
You are self-confident, forceful, and determined, somewhat picky, but full of fun. You have a well-balanced, discriminating mind and much leadership ability, and people generally follow your good example. You are lovable and affectionate but not a phony. You are always looking for an opportunity to add to the happiness of your loved ones.

DESTINY
You display originality in thought. Although you can produce good work when you are free to follow your own dictates, be sure to consider the opinions of others, too. You may have an unusual opportunity to contribute to an international endeavor that will aid many. Financial problems can always be solved with your hunches. New friends may introduce you to interesting social activities, which will stimulate your daily routines and help you to develop enhanced wellness habits.

KARMIC LESSON
Quiet and reserved, you do not like anyone else to interfere with your affairs. Even if you make an error, you like to take the responsibility for it. You love power and do not like to see others have positions over you; you feel you should have this power yourself. You are a great believer in allowing everyone to shape his or her own life, free from interference. Giving advice is as unpalatable to you as receiving it. Oddly, you have a tendency to believe in the unseen and mysterious. You use this when necessary, but you do not allow this to interfere with your life or business. You are affectionate by nature, and you love to be loved. You have ambition and determination; don't let these good qualities go unused.

SECRET
You have a ready wit and upbeat spirit and are devoted to lifting others out of sadness. You are more interested in making people happy than in accumulating money.

FRIENDS & FAMILY

DECEMBER 2

Strive not to be a success, but rather to be of value.
—Albert Einstein

BORN ON THIS DAY

- **Georges Seurat**
  painter
- **Britney Spears**
  singer
- **Lucy Liu**
  actor
- **Aaron Rodgers**
  football player
- **Frederic Tuten**
  author

FRIENDS & FAMILY

_____
_____
_____
_____
_____
_____
_____
_____

PERSONALITY

While others more serious than you are hard at work, you are liable to be playing—and to be having a great time at it, too. You can do your work rapidly and efficiently, so that you are able to indulge in more leisure than others. Since you prefer to play, there is no reason you shouldn't once you have completed your chores for the day or the occasion. It would not be wise to indulge your taste for excitement too much, because there is usually a high price to pay for such lavish experience. However, a little adventure is not liable to be harmful. You have innovative ideas, especially regarding school, education, and community affairs. These you contribute willingly, and you lend a helping hand where one is needed. As a salesperson, marketer, writer, or communicator, you are bound to succeed, as your natural talent will push you to the forefront.

LIFE PATH

Persistent in a relaxed sort of way, you are actuated by high ideals and uncompromised values—you are against any wrongdoing. You are sociable and enjoy entertaining; you love music and art, like to read, and strive to improve yourself. You are sometimes impractical and sometimes allow your emotions to get the best of you. You are loving, helpful, and upbeat most of the time.

DESTINY

A subordinate position can be the stepping-stone to one of authority. Do not work in spurts and starts but try to maintain an even level of productivity. Keep enough cash in reserve so that no one will suffer if retrenchment becomes necessary. Consider the respect of your associates every bit as important as public applause, if not more so. Affection is preferable to praise. Live up to everything that is expected of you.

KARMIC LESSON

You are naturally brave and love excitement of all kinds. It seems to bring out the best that is in you. You are not suited to live in the country, as the quietness does not seem to agree with you. You love the bustle and excitement of city life, which seems to stimulate you into greater actions and thoughts. All that you accomplish in life you will have to do yourself, as no one will ever help you materially, much as you hope so at times. You are ingenious and might be an inventor. You have talents beyond the average. Try to discipline yourself, and a great future should be yours.

SECRET

Your nature is given to peering into the future, and you are something of a prophet. You are sure of yourself on most occasions.

DECEMBER 3

It is much easier to suppress a first desire than to satisfy those that follow.
—François de La Rochefoucauld

BORN ON THIS DAY
- **Joseph Conrad**, author
- **David Villa**, soccer player
- **Ozzy Osbourne**, singer
- **Benny Hinn**, televangelist
- **Julianne Moore**, actor

PERSONALITY
For the most part, you take life as it comes. Having observed that continuous complaining does not do as much good as making an effort toward better things, you don't waste your time on whining. Since this is a sensible and efficient way to figure things out, you are likely to have less to complain about than other people. People find you soothing and helpful in your attitude because you don't get overexcited but act rationally to adjust the situation or right the wrong. The only time you get overwrought is when people fail to understand what you are driving at. Because you are clear in what you say and express yourself well, you expect to be understood and obeyed when you act in a position of authority. It distracts you to be misunderstood, to have delays take place, or to be disappointed. Then you can put on a pretty good show of displeasure.

LIFE PATH
You can be impatient and hasty in your judgment, and you sometimes make sudden and unexpected changes. You are idealistic and plan many things, which you tire of and drop before completion. You have a strong will, a bright mind, and great adaptability. You are humane, noble, and charitable, and you hold your friends close, in a strong grasp.

DESTINY
The cooperative spirit that you have shown in the past will be influential in the success you attain in the future. Your ideals are admirable and can serve you well in everything that claims your attention. They also can win you the sincere praise of most everyone who knows you. Do not substitute dreams for action.

KARMIC LESSON
Born on this day, you are self-possessed and reserved, you usually follow your own line of action and thought, and you are not overly influenced by others to any great extent. You are very fair in all your dealings with others and have a love for what you think is justice and a hatred of what you consider injustice. You are usually quick at perceiving and sizing up a person, and, if you have once seen through someone, you have no further use for that individual. You have a good sense of humor but are more the type who appreciates fun in others rather than originating the fun yourself.

SECRET
You have a studious mind and are interested in penetrating the depths of many subjects. You would do well in a career of science or research.

FRIENDS & FAMILY

DECEMBER 4

Doubt is the incentive to truth, and inquiry leads the way.
—Hosea Ballou

BORN ON THIS DAY
★ **Thomas Carlyle**
cultural critic

★ **Jay-Z**
rapper, music executive

★ **Marisa Tomei**
actor

★ **Tyra Banks**
model, TV personality

★ **Ferry Corsten**
DJ, music producer

FRIENDS & FAMILY

☻ PERSONALITY
You have been truly blessed, for you possess idealism, imagination, and intuition. This trinity of traits will bring you whatever your heart desires, for it is such a powerful combination. It also makes you very well-liked, because your desires will always be altruistic, and your expression will be unselfish. You can easily see what others are driving at, and you are accommodating to the extreme. You are almost a perfect relative because you're so kind to your family. Life is sure to hold a considerable number of pleasant surprises for you. Partnership, mutual understanding, and compatibility in love are essential to your happiness. Although you are a hard worker and an independent thinker, you feel that nothing is worthwhile unless shared with the ones you love.

☻ LIFE PATH
You are shrewd, capable, persevering, and energetic. You have great confidence in your own ability, and not without cause. You like to be in charge and are quite able to be. You are well-liked by many who know you, but you form very few intimate friendships. You are loving in your homelife and good-natured most of the time, unless you get overtired.

☻ DESTINY
Your capable leadership will be displayed on many occasions during your life. You will gratefully accept new duties and handle them with enthusiasm and competence. Your determination to succeed will always help you to better your living standards. Take proper care of all your possessions and be sure to keep important papers in a safe place.

☻ KARMIC LESSON
Born on this day, you should excel in business ability, as you have the natural talent and are by nature shrewd and sharp, almost too much so at times. You should live in the country, as you are a great lover of nature and of all animals. You are inclined to worry too much about your own affairs and about things that might happen but that never do. You must stop this in order to make a success of life. Put the past behind you and determine to live only in the present and the future. Your love nature is strongly developed, and you might marry fairly young. Yours will not be a monotonous life.

☻ SECRET
You possess a rare musical talent for performing and playing an instrument. You respond to music and are of a romantic nature.

DECEMBER 5

Forgive your enemies, but never forget their names.
—John F. Kennedy

BORN ON THIS DAY
- **Martin Van Buren** — U.S. president
- **Walt Disney** — entrepreneur, animator
- **Margaret Cho** — comedian
- **LeGarrette Blount** — football player
- **Eddie the Eagle** — Olympic ski jumper

PERSONALITY
You may have a fiery temperament—it requires a lot of patience and willingness on your part to overcome this trait and to learn, probably at a great expense, the lesson that you can't be a firebrand without burning something in your path. Your impatience comes from the fact that you believe your way of doing things is quicker, better, and smarter than the way anyone else does things. A little tact will get you more than you think. Take the time and energy that things of true worth really require, and you'll be much more at ease. You are blessed with a strong personal vision that informs everything you do. Your dreams and intentions are particularly captivating, and your challenge is to stay motivated and true to your ideals without being intimidated by the judgments of others.

LIFE PATH
You are sincere and scrupulously honest and have a somewhat dramatic disposition that, even though you are fiery, wins you special friends and makes you the center of attention. You love outdoor life. You are proud and careful of your appearance, and you like to dress well. You should marry but not take the step blindly.

DESTINY
Let the discouragements of the past be forgotten. The possibilities of the present and promise of the future are the things that deserve your undivided attention. Association with people who are interested in your advancement will prove advantageous, both professionally and socially. As a student, you may be inspired to take up the study of a new subject that will eventually become your focused passion. Go into it with an open mind, discarding former prejudices, as they should be.

KARMIC LESSON
You can be impulsive and turbulent, liabilities you must overcome by practice and habit. You will then find many more friends and greater peace of mind. You are often misunderstood by others, but this is largely your own fault, for you say things you do not really mean, you regret them the moment after you have said them, but you are too proud to retract your words. Do not be anxious about your future, as you tend to be. Work along steadily at the business at hand and be confident that something much better will turn up in the near future if you will only work faithfully and attend to the job at hand. Your dedicated passion and enthusiasm can be channeled into extraordinary manifestations.

SECRET
You are considered a dreamer by your friends but have unusual insight into material and spiritual problems.

FRIENDS & FAMILY

DECEMBER 6

What if life itself were the sweetheart?
—Willa Cather

BORN ON THIS DAY
- **Ira Gershwin**
  composer
- **Randy Rhoads**
  guitarist
- **Judd Apatow**
  comedian, filmmaker
- **Kenneth Copeland**
  televangelist
- **Tony Lazzeri**
  baseball player

FRIENDS & FAMILY

_____
_____
_____
_____
_____
_____
_____
_____

PERSONALITY
You are somewhat paradoxical in your conduct because your mind seems to go two ways at once. Crowds seem to bore you, yet you are impatient and restless when you are alone. You dislike vulgarity, noise, and mobs, yet you seem to get involved in parties, events, and meetings. You become the one who is the advice lord among the group. Essentially, your difficulty may be in finding the proper level of socializing for your mental stimulation, boundaries, and talents. You should really decide as early in life as you can what you want to do and what you want to be. Then you must make every effort and every sacrifice required to get that wish. Mostly, you are searching for peace and understanding. Nothing less than pure self-expression will ever make you happy, so aim for the highest. That way alone will bring you the achievement, contentment, and happiness you desire.

LIFE PATH
You are original, careful, cautious, accurate, and faithful. You have great willpower, and it is very difficult to move you once your mind is made up. You are a loyal friend and will sacrifice much in friendship's name. You love travel. In your home, you demand obedience, but through love rather than force.

DESTINY
Patience with associates will be rewarded. After age thirty-three, your imaginative ideas will be given a better opportunity for expression than in the past. Do not hesitate to be frank when asked for your honest opinion on controversial matters. However, do not criticize or volunteer unsolicited advice. Limit your interests so that each one receives a proper amount of attention.

KARMIC LESSON
Born on this day, you are, above all, cautious in all you undertake. You like to have what you do for others appreciated, and you are generally willing to help others, but you want them to be willing to help you in return. You believe in tit for tat. You are of a strong, opinionated nature, as a rule, and if you say no, you mean it and stick to it. You probably have an undeveloped talent, as an actor or maker, if you are of the more emotional type. If you are inclined to the more intellectual fields, you could make a great success there, for you have an infinite capacity for taking pains and doing any amount of work to achieve a desired end.

SECRET
You have a love of travel and visiting new places. You are more ambitious than loyal and always seek to better your situation.

DECEMBER 7

One enemy is too many, and a hundred friends are too few.
—Italian proverb

✦ PERSONALITY
This date of birth endows special artistic talents, and you should seek out these innate capabilities in yourself so that you may express them successfully. You also have a great deal of initiative and can be a social and business success. Your nature is placid, and you possess a great deal of sympathy and caring for other people. Always helpful and tolerant, you are liked for these tender, nurturing qualities. Every requirement for being a truly fine human being exists in your makeup; it is your duty to express this Higher Self. You are very creative and could do well as a designer if you had the necessary application for it. You are affectionate and demonstrative. A keen sense of humor and an incisive wit make you noticed on social media or at social gatherings, and you receive many followers and invitations as a result.

✦ LIFE PATH
You have shrewd, intuitive judgment, an intelligent mind, and a storehouse of energy. You get great enjoyment out of overcoming difficulties and in consummating your plans. You can be led but not driven. You are demonstrative in your affection, devoted to your friends and family, and generally kind, affable, and cheerful.

✦ DESTINY
You will often be sympathetic and sensitive to the problems of your close associates. Many of them will confide in you and seek your opinion. Although you may be helpful, do not permit yourself to be imposed upon. You will turn a great deal of attention to your home and add to its comfort and beauty by several large, expensive purchases, upgrades, and renovations.

✦ KARMIC LESSON
You are naturally bright and quick thinking, are strongly intuitive, and at times seem to be almost psychic. You are inclined to think great thoughts, to hitch your wagon to a star, but this is all right in your case, for, if you live up to the best that is in you, you cannot aim too high and can achieve anything along certain lines of endeavor. Your natural sincerity and honesty would prevent you from entering any business that was not strictly honorable and aboveboard. Thus, owing to your intuitive or psychic ability, you might be tempted, at times, to enter that profession and become a professional clairvoyant, but you may feel that you could not do this.

✦ SECRET
Your nature is given to accumulating wealth, and you take pride in your possessions. You would be well suited to real estate ventures.

BORN ON THIS DAY
- **Willa Cather**
  author
- **Noam Chomsky**
  linguist, social critic
- **Larry Bird**
  basketball player
- **Sara Bareilles**
  singer/songwriter, actor
- **Eli Wallach**
  actor

FRIENDS & FAMILY

DECEMBER 8

There is no genius in life like the genius of energy and industry.
—Donald G. Mitchell

BORN ON THIS DAY

★ **Jim Morrison**
singer

★ **Nicki Minaj**
singer

★ **Bill Bryson**
author

★ **David Carradine**
actor

★ **Sinéad O'Connor**
singer

FRIENDS & FAMILY

_____

_____

_____

_____

_____

_____

_____

_____

PERSONALITY

There are powerful vibratory emanations on the date on which you were born. Innate within you is the power to become a leader, a thinker of deep philosophical potency, and a dreamer of Utopian ideals. To express the thoughts and impulses that surge through your nature requires stamina and courage. You possess these qualities, also, and must make your way in life because of the nobility of the aspirations that motivate you. Your sincerity, talent, and perseverance will always be recognized and appreciated, even from a young age. You may win awards. You have the ability to succeed in affairs where money matters a great deal because you have good economic sense. You know how to get your money's worth, and you are good at handling the financial affairs of others, too. You work best in groups or in a large corporation.

LIFE PATH

You are fond of sports and travel. You read a great deal, and your taste is for information of the more serious type. You are a convincing talker, bright and entertaining, and you are seldom left out of any debate at a social affair. You love with strength and ardor, and you will receive love as strong, in return.

DESTINY

You will regard some of the ideas of business associates with skepticism, as your own vision has greater reach. However, it will be best if you sometimes go along with them at first. Eventually you will be given the chance to air your own ideas and carry them out. Take advantage of opportunities to participate in outdoor events that provide a pleasant diversion from work and could recharge your batteries. Occupational progress will be linked to effort shown, not luck.

KARMIC LESSON

You are a student, either of human nature or humanity or of history and its lessons. The two are closely allied, but one is a little more practical than the other, and it all depends upon your turn of mind. You have a good memory, which helps you greatly in what you do. Should you enter the lecture field, you could doubtless be a pleasant personality on the rostrum and would make a good motivational speaker or coach. You see into the heart of matters and personalities quickly, and for that reason anyone who attempts to bluff or fool you has little chance. You are probably emotional and long for romantic, adoring love, which you feel you could return fully if it were given to you.

SECRET

You have a personality that wins confidence easily and delights in partnerships. You have a tendency to spread spiritual truths.

DECEMBER 9

Until you've lost your reputation, you never realize what a burden it was.
—Margaret Mitchell

BORN ON THIS DAY
- **John Milton**, author
- **Judi Dench**, actor
- **Kirk Douglas**, actor
- **Donny Osmond**, singer
- **John Malkovich**, actor

PERSONALITY
If you could have your way, you would convert the world to a philosophy of peace, tolerance, and compassion for all humankind. You are convinced that only when all people have economic security, health care, education, and the freedom to express their greatest talents and gifts will there be universal goodwill. Of course, such an ideal is very difficult to bring into reality, but it is your nature to work, wish, and pray for such a millennium. In your own way, you do what you can to bring about the miracles and status that you aspire to. In your relations with others, you are absolutely ethical. In dealing with your family, you are kind, humane, and tolerant. The seriousness of your outlook does not mar your having a good time. You still enjoy your fun, and you can be the life of the party when you are in the right mood.

LIFE PATH
You can sometimes be melancholy and do not always look on the bright side. Your intuitive insight often saves you and your friends from bad luck and disaster. You are versatile, judicious, desirous of information, quick of action, and very sensitive. You work to make your home more beautiful, and you are loving and considerate in it.

DESTINY
Prospects will be brighter for you after age thirty-five. Opportunities you have long been seeking will present themselves then. Keep your purposes steady and your efforts on an even keel. If someone tries to sell you a bill of goods sight unseen, demand the chance to examine what is offered from every angle. Several spur-of-the-moment decisions may be wise ones, but do not take action without careful consideration of all factors involved, along with the advice of a trusted counselor.

KARMIC LESSON
Practical and energetic, you should excel in business if you desire to enter it. You have firmness of character and a vivid imagination; you hold it in check so that it does not run away with you, though, and so it is helpful rather than harmful. You possess an affectionate nature, strong and tender, but are not ardent or overbearing. Your head generally rules your heart. You are inclined to be gloomy at times, and when such spells are on, you foresee difficulty in everything. Learn that most such fears are groundless, that all the trouble comes from your worrying, and that all you must do to overcome such tendencies is to determine to change your attitude and develop the right stress-reduction techniques for your special nature.

SECRET
You are proud and sensitive at the same time; you desire a life of the highest principles, and you have the resilience to come back from disappointments.

FRIENDS & FAMILY

December 10

For some must follow, and some command, Though all are made of clay!
—Henry Wadsworth Longfellow

BORN ON THIS DAY
- ★ **Emily Dickinson**
  poet
- ★ **Kenneth Branagh**
  actor, filmmaker
- ★ **Bobby Flay**
  celebrity chef
- ★ **Gonzalo Higuaín**
  soccer player
- ★ **Raven-Symoné**
  actor

FRIENDS & FAMILY

PERSONALITY
You have an exceedingly practical point of view. Your standard of judgment is the functional or useful value of ideas, articles, or whatever else is under consideration. This makes you seem somewhat cynical, but you prefer a reputation for speaking your truth and showing good sense and discretion rather than one for being an easy mark. However, your sense of humor saves you from being too coldly analytical, for even when you see the uselessness of some things in life, you know they can at least provide a laugh. No one can change your mind once you have it made up, and no one can direct or deter your way of thinking. You may be willful at times because you believe that you are right, and you will insist on getting your own way. Mistakes caused by your stubbornness may cost you at times, but it is human to err. With age, you will feel a lot more comfortable with yourself and your accomplishments.

LIFE PATH
You are rather excitable, energetic, and capable while, at the same time, careful and cautious. You possess a remarkable executive talent, and you are positive, honest, and earnest. Your mind is judicial, sensible, and discriminating. You are kind and affectionate to those you truly care for.

DESTINY
The ideal setup for you is a place where you can think and do the creative work at hand. Do not hesitate to make practical use of your inspirations. Although an enthusiasm may not be constant, you will be amazed by the amount of work you can accomplish when your ambitions are at a peak level. Plan quiet pleasures and opportunities for meditation when you find yourself weary of too much activity. A one-sided routine would not be satisfactory to you.

KARMIC LESSON
You have very decided intuitive faculties, which you should cultivate, develop, and learn to trust more. When these promptings come to you, you are inclined to set them aside, as you emphasize the practical—a habit that makes these powers gradually become weaker, until they may leave you altogether. Then, perhaps someday, you will wish you had them, and they will be gone forever. Intuitions of this character are generally right. Your serious bent of mind should suit you to take up serious subjects. This is later in life, however, and it may be that you must have an overdose of things of this world first—before you become tired of them. You have a good sense of humor, and you like entertaining a crowd, which you can do well.

SECRET
You are aggressive, impatient, and full of initiative. You succeed best where permitted to work alone.

DECEMBER 11

Our greatest glory is not in never falling, but in rising every time we fall.
—Confucius

BORN ON THIS DAY
- **Brenda Lee**
  singer
- **Rita Moreno**
  dancer, actor
- **Mos Def**
  rapper, singer/songwriter
- **Mo'Nique**
  comedian, actor
- **Teri Garr**
  actor, comedian

PERSONALITY
Because you have an innate knowledge of what people like and what they want, you can succeed in dealing with the public. In any capacity in which you have contact with large numbers of persons, you are bound to reach the heights of success. It is as though you had a feeling for the pulse of public taste, and therefore know what will sell, become a trend, and be popular. For this reason, you should choose a profession such as buying, publicity, marketing, manufacturing, and the like. Although you may never originate any fad or fancy, you have the remarkable knack of foreseeing and popularizing any fad you take up. You are able to tune in to color, fashion, and popular taste and culture. In your romantic outlook, you are somewhat conventional. Home and family represent the happiest of moments for you because you have a nurturing nature and love children and the peace and calm of home.

LIFE PATH
Inclined to be hasty in speech and impulsive in some decisions, you are always sorry if a rash word wounds another's feelings. You are a good communicator and a great reader, bright, witty, and vivacious. You love fine clothes and decor and luxurious surroundings and are very sensitive to an unpleasant, messy environment. You are demonstrative and devoted in your love.

DESTINY
The decisions you make during your twenties will be important ones. Do not be hurried and reckless when a long-range effect will result. Be determined, persevering, and self-confident in your undertakings. You will find that there are occasions when your ability to help others is more satisfying than the thrill of being in a superior position.

KARMIC LESSON
You probably have good business judgment and are rather careful with your money—as you have plans and goals that you invest in. You save to spend on the finer items you desire that inspire and harmonize your life. It is rare to find anyone born on this day who lacks money; they are never completely out of that useful commodity, even if they never get superrich. You are inclined to worry over things a little too much, and you should learn that worry never prevented anything bad from happening but oftentimes prevents you from accomplishing some good. Listen to the advice of others but make up your mind independently before you act.

SECRET
You are fastidious, given to extreme care in outward appearances, and may be very judgmental of the appearances of others.

FRIENDS & FAMILY

DECEMBER 12

The intellect of the wise is like glass; it admits the light of heaven and reflects it.
—Augustus W. Hare

BORN ON THIS DAY
- **Edvard Munch**
  painter
- **Frank Sinatra**
  singer
- **Dionne Warwick**
  singer
- **Mayim Bialik**
  actor
- **Jennifer Connelly**
  actor

FRIENDS & FAMILY

_____
_____
_____
_____
_____
_____
_____
_____
_____

PERSONALITY
You see humanity as a group of individuals, not masses of similar people or races. For this reason, you take the trouble to try to understand every person of your acquaintance as having unique tastes, individuality, and particular rights and privileges. Naturally you will be well-liked for this wide and considerate attitude, and you, in turn, will be treated with respect and affection. Because of your deep understanding of diversity, which evolves from your way of life, you could be a great writer. You should practice this art and learn its tricks to gain acclaim and readership and profit from it, through avenues such as social media, a column, a blog, or a website. As you mature, life will become ever more meaningful. Love will seem even more beautiful as you grow older, you will have much gratitude for what you have, and each day will unfold some charming, special secret to you.

LIFE PATH
You are sympathetic, kind, helpful, and generous. Proud and self-confident, you are capable of accomplishing most of the things you attempt in this life. You are truthful, honest, direct, and loving, and you show much persistence and persuasive abilities. You seldom worry about anything that is petty and are a comfortable and wise sort of person to have around.

DESTINY
Influential business connections will be strengthened, and your circle of friends enlarged as you mature. Be careful that you do not make an enemy through a misunderstanding over real estate. Try to understand the other person's point of view on any controversial issue and be patient and exacting in making your beliefs clear. Plan for enjoyable holidays and short trips with relatives and neighbors—this will be a source of relaxation and escape for you.

KARMIC LESSON
You could have a good knowledge of politics, in which you are interested, and should possess intuition and insightful judgment and opinions of government and problems of the world. You are interested in all affairs of laws and regulations, and your political ambition could even be to be sent abroad as a representative to some foreign country. You are kind and thoughtful and take an interest in the affairs of others. You have big ideas on most things—on occasion too large, and they could at some point lead you into financial difficulties, because you overstep your limits. You can be calm and collected, especially in times of jeopardy. On the whole, you are a very thoughtful and likable person.

SECRET
You possess a rare ingenuity for completing the inventions or plans conceived by others. Your mind can grasp things readily but should never be put to questionable uses.

DECEMBER 13

Experience is a jewel, and it had need be so, for it is often purchased at an infinite rate.
—William Shakespeare

BORN ON THIS DAY

- **Taylor Swift**
  singer/songwriter
- **Ben Bernanke**
  economist
- **Jamie Foxx**
  actor, singer, comedian
- **NeNe Leakes**
  TV personality
- **Steve Buscemi**
  actor

PERSONALITY
You need never fear that having been born on the thirteenth of the month implies any of the traditional ill fortune associated with this number by superstition. There is, at any rate, no disadvantage in the world that willpower cannot overcome, and you possess that quality to a high degree. Your nature is generally placid, and you have a soothing effect on others, too. You are a healer of sorts, a wonderful help in the sick room, and a boon to all those who are troubled, anxious, distressed, or ill at ease. Life seems to have taught you patience, a great virtue indeed. You are capable of hard work when it is necessary, and you also know the right time to relax, recalibrate, and gather fresh forces. Because you are fair and just in the way you think, you are like a magnet, and people like and trust you.

LIFE PATH
You are bold, venturesome, and fearless, and you decide and act quickly and impulsively. You have many friends and will always help them in any way possible. You enjoy the responsibility and esteem of your circle, and your views and judgment are respected and sought after. You could be a counselor or therapist.

DESTINY
After age forty, good fortune will be showered on you in the form of increased opportunities and the accomplishment of long-standing endeavors. Midlife will be a pulsating period for creative work and maximum profit. You could make a record in some competitive activity that will be part of your recreational program. Additions to your wardrobe will result from a stimulated interest in your personal appearance that may be related to your profession or required by your job.

KARMIC LESSON
You are poetic at times, though not all the time. You are naturally a bit serious, would make a good coach or group leader, and have a deep interest in all those practical problems that affect human life. If you tried, you could probably write good poetry or essays, but to be properly inspired for this you need a quiet life in the country, with nature all around you. You are certainly fond of studying and learning and would make a fine teacher or instructor for the young. You have an instinctive bent toward the occult and the mysterious and might be seriously interested in ancient magic and in the discoveries related to ancient Egypt, the pyramids, and the like. Yours may be considered a very balanced temperament.

SECRET
You are spirited, but you tire quickly of a given task, seeking change. You are inclined to be flirtatious.

FRIENDS & FAMILY

DECEMBER 14

People seldom improve when they have no model but themselves to copy after.
—Oliver Goldsmith

BORN ON THIS DAY
- **Tyco Brahe**
  astronomer
- **John Mearsheimer**
  international relations scholar
- **Vanessa Hudgens**
  singer, actor
- **Patty Duke**
  actor
- **Michael Owen**
  soccer player

FRIENDS & FAMILY

PERSONALITY
Abundant energy and effort seem to distinguish everything you do. There is strong willpower in your makeup and the stamina to carry out your ideas and projects with efficiency. You are great at managing things, be they your household affairs, a business, or a profession. Executive ability makes it easier for you to give orders than to take them. You should always aim to get into the managerial branch of every undertaking that attracts your interest and attention. As you have a knack for handling money successfully, you probably will never want for the material things in life. By exercising economy and wisdom in the earlier part of your life, you should be able to enjoy an old age of peace and security. You have a strong love nature and will doubtless be partnered very happily.

LIFE PATH
You are positive and aggressive and sometimes domineering. A good schmoozer, you are serious-minded and studious but liable to make a joke or be sarcastic and critical at times. Your mind is logical, and you hold firmly to your deductions. You also have a little vanity in your makeup. You enjoy being around bright, witty, and intellectual people.

DESTINY
Additional cash may periodically come to you in the shape of a bonus or gifts. Use it to improve your home environment or for the purchase of articles that will bring lasting pleasure to the entire family. Brush up your memory by glancing through a book that you read in the past. This knowledge may be synchronistic and of great practical value to you. Avoid arousing enmity by practicing self-control in your emotional reactions.

KARMIC LESSON
Clever, willful, and determined, you generally get your way about most things. At the same time, you are tender with regard to the feelings of others, and this often prevents you from doing things that you otherwise might be tempted to do. While you are interested in your business, you also like home comforts—good food, soothing colors, and beloved pets. If you travel anywhere, you try to make the place as cheerful and homelike as possible, no matter how short a time you are staying. You probably have a great interest in, not to say curiosity about, all secret societies and long to know the hidden details of mystical organizations. You could make a good detective and probably have great talents in that direction.

SECRET
You have a high-strung and nervous temperament and are quick to judge and equally quick to regret. If this is curbed, you will succeed in your chosen profession.

DECEMBER 15

He that is good for making excuses is seldom good for anything else.
—Benjamin Franklin

BORN ON THIS DAY
- **Gustave Eiffel**
  civil engineer
- **William Orbit**
  musician, music producer
- **Tim Conway**
  actor, comedian
- **Helen Slater**
  actor, singer/songwriter
- **Don Johnson**
  actor

PERSONALITY
Artistic talent abounds in your makeup, and you should make every effort to explore and find which of the arts you can best use to express yourself. If you have not discovered this innate power in your nature, you should try the various branches of the arts, take an aptitude test or classes that will bring out the best that is in you, or consult with a career counselor. Many brilliant artists, designers, and writers in history are an encouraging inspiration to you. You want to do good works in your life because your instincts are wholly humanitarian. Every effort you make is aimed at making someone or some group a little happier. This noble aspiration brings its own reward: the happiness and joy you feel at conceiving, producing, constructing, creating, and sharing.

LIFE PATH
You are quiet and unobtrusive and accomplish a great deal without making a noise about it. You are winsome, bright and lovable, fond of recreation if it does not interfere with anything important, and very fond of travel. You learn readily, have a very retentive memory, and are able to impart difficult information clearly to others in an accessible way.

DESTINY
Quick, out-of-the-blue, impulsive action will often characterize your undertakings. Sudden decisions may prove wise ones because of your mental alertness. The correct answers will come to you without effort, as you are very intuitive. You will be able to see the connection between different experiences, and profit because of them. A charming manner will always help you to put your ideas across.

KARMIC LESSON
You are probably a great reader, love books of all kinds, and in fact become at times a veritable bookworm. You also enjoy social networking, as you can still be reclusive but touch a lot of people. You have a good memory, which enables you to retain all you have read and historical and important dates as well. You have an admirable knowledge of many subjects and can impart what you know in clear, simple language, so that others can understand it. You could be suited to a job as a teacher, a guide, or a historian. You are not naturally emotional, but you like to see others happy. At times you are too self-deprecating and must learn to see that you are human and forgive yourself and others.

SECRET
You have an artistic nature, loving beauty, esoteric knowledge, and adornment more than success.

FRIENDS & FAMILY

DECEMBER 16

All that we see or seem
Is but a dream within a dream.
—Edgar Allan Poe

BORN ON THIS DAY

- **Ludwig van Beethoven**
  composer
- **Wassily Kandinsky**
  painter
- **Jane Austen**
  author
- **Margaret Mead**
  cultural anthropologist
- **Benny Andersson**
  singer/songwriter

FRIENDS & FAMILY

◉ PERSONALITY

No one could ever say that you are a simple person or easy to understand, because your personality is complex, deep, and mystical. You seem to have a very subtle understanding of the workings of the human mind, and this X-ray eye of yours can bring you much misunderstanding. People do not like to be the open books they are to you. They may feel that you can see deeply inside of them and know their secrets, and they may feel judged by you. Thus, you must conceal much of what you learn and sense about them if you do not wish to arouse their ire or jealousy. Others born on this day have possessed your comprehensive powers and have chosen to express themselves and reveal their insights in writing or communications, a very lucrative outlet for them. Life can be your oyster if you wish to make it so.

◉ LIFE PATH

You have a spiritual and idealistic nature, an active mind, and much tact. You are honest, straightforward, and frank, true and faithful to those you love, and capable of making boundaries where needed. You are fond of cultural events, like to be amused and entertained, and enjoy social media for sharing creative inspirations. You should have a balanced and harmonious homelife.

◉ DESTINY

As you move into becoming yourself more fully, give thought to the values that are most precious to you. You can enjoy popularity and obtain it easily if you practice the social graces you have acquired. Put your artistic talents to work in your home or in the planning of your wardrobe. Let your appreciation of the beautiful be expressed by attendance at concerts, the theater, and art displays.

◉ KARMIC LESSON

Born on this day, you have a distinct interest in things mystical, and the spiritual side of all these questions will probably attract you most. You have a congenial, happy nature and would doubtless make a good companion. You are sometimes impatient, inclined to push forward too fast when once you have undertaken a job or task. You are a trifle pugnacious and inclined to fight for truth and justice whenever the opportunity presents itself. You are used to defending your beliefs. You have great self-reliance, but this you should cultivate and rely upon, since it is important that you learn to depend solely upon yourself and not upon the advice or material help of others.

◉ SECRET

You have a methodical and, at the same time, an intuitive mind with a special gift for investments and other financial ventures.

DECEMBER 17

There is nothing more truly artistic than to love people.
—Vincent van Gogh

⊙ PERSONALITY
You have wonderful powers of expression and can make yourself one of humankind's spokespeople if you develop the natural latent abilities in your makeup. Because you have an affinity for the beauty of nature, you enjoy being outdoors, playing sports, and admiring the scenes so lavishly painted by sunsets, rainbows, and gardens. In conversation, you are a master of the right word, and this enhances not only your powers of expression but also your diplomacy and tact. You seek to improve by your criticisms, not to hurt, and therefore your opinions are highly valued. When anyone needs help, you are a willing assistant. Because of your cooperative spirit, you are often entrusted with carrying out complex and important tasks. In social life, you can be witty and amusing, delightful company. A balance of fun and work would make you feel fulfilled.

⊙ LIFE PATH
You are imaginative, at times impractical, fickle, and quirky. You need alone time to be contemplative and to process the day's events. You need constant, trusted love and devotion and are moody without it. You are essentially of a positive disposition, and you manage to secure a reasonable amount of comfort. You have a few lifelong, intimate friends who are also creative.

⊙ DESTINY
You can expect to secure achievements in fields of endeavor that you have loved since you were a child. A comparative stranger may be of considerable assistance to you. In turn, you will find yourself in a position to give a helping hand to others. Act with the same independence as you speak and think, but be careful not to infringe on anyone else's rights. Be tactful, but do not sacrifice your natural candor.

⊙ KARMIC LESSON
You have a good deal of self-confidence and belief in your own ability to do things, which will take you far. You are inclined to undertake big enterprises, but be realistic about what you can really accomplish. You do not care for detail work or the small things of life but "strike high" and hope for the best. You are quiet and dignified, even cold to those who do not know you well enough to break through this reserve. You are sometimes inclined to force things, instead of letting them take their natural course, but remember that this is not always wise. Remember that love is a thing that cannot be forced, but must grow naturally, and that "those who pick the buds forfeit the flower."

⊙ SECRET
You have a tendency to accomplish things in haste, but your motivation and enthusiasm is a natural resource.

BORN ON THIS DAY
- **Pope Francis** — leader of the Catholic Church
- **Wes Studi** — actor
- **Bill Pullman** — actor
- **Chris Matthews** — political commentator
- **Sarah Paulson** — actor

FRIENDS & FAMILY

DECEMBER 18

We often pretend to fear what we really despise, and more often despise what we really fear.
—Charles Caleb Colton

BORN ON THIS DAY

★ **Joseph Stalin**
Soviet political leader

★ **Christina Aguilera**
singer

★ **Brad Pitt**
actor

★ **Steven Spielberg**
film director

★ **Billie Eilish**
singer

FRIENDS & FAMILY

_____
_____
_____
_____
_____
_____
_____
_____

PERSONALITY

The serious side of your nature is rather neatly balanced by a fine gregarious instinct and the ability to enjoy yourself at the appropriate times. There is a deep spiritual side to your nature that makes you grateful, tolerant, and understanding. You have compassion for the weaknesses and shortcomings of others, and you try to be as helpful as you can on the proper occasions. You temper justice with mercy, and your opinions are sought because you are known to be so fair in your judgment and so generous with your assistance when you are able. Many people look to you for advice, and you do your best to be of help to them. Your love life is all-inclusive: body, mind, and soul. But you could never love any one individual as much as you love all people, for to you the whole human race is your family.

LIFE PATH

You have a powerful will, and you are liable to brush opposition aside, sometimes without regard for others' opinions, though not always consciously. You are self-confident and aggressive, and if you do not secure your share, it will be because it is impossible to attain. You have a fine control over your emotions, and it is difficult for others to know your true feelings.

DESTINY

You will introduce an efficient system into many of your undertakings. This will often result in your having more free time for pleasant recreations. You may meet problems that will call for audacity as well as intelligence. You are capable of both and may well win public attention or an award by the use of your skillful combination of mental dexterity and a daring spirit.

KARMIC LESSON

Naturally guarded, you are disinclined to communicate secrets to others. You keep your affairs to yourself. You are private, but you are a good friend when once you get to know a person. But you want to know people very thoroughly first—you do not jump into friendships quickly. You are naturally honest and fair in your dealings with others. You are interested in studies and theories of the mind and have good natural scientific tendencies, which you should cultivate. You are rather too easily influenced by your parents' judgments and should become as independent in action as you are in thought. You are naturally attractive sexually and sometimes attract people who you are not attracted to. Develop the best traits of yourself, and you would make a fine partner.

SECRET

You are a symbol of discretion and carefulness, curiously allied to a love of combat and rivalry in business.

DECEMBER 19

There are only two mistakes one can make along the road to truth: not going all the way, and not starting.
—Anonymous

BORN ON THIS DAY

- **Jake Gyllenhaal**
  actor
- **Édith Piaf**
  singer
- **Bill Hader**
  actor
- **Alexis Sánchez**
  soccer player
- **Tyson Beckford**
  model, actor

PERSONALITY
Having a brilliant sense of taste, you are able to appreciate good quality, to notice subtle differences, to distinguish right from wrong, good taste from bad, and ethics from sins. This allows you to lead a good life, to avoid the sufferings of conscience and consequences, and to feel that you are improving your material and spiritual welfare. Carried to the extremes, such as criticizing others, this way of life would lead to unpleasantness, but you have too much common sense to try to impose your way of life on those who seek the wider but more dangerous path. You are rather a purist, preferring the classic, traditional ways of doing things over newfangled fads and untried methods. The past and history bring out the reverence you feel is their due, and as long as you model your life after those leaders and creatives who have made their lives productive ones, you can never go astray.

LIFE PATH
You are ambitious and capable and will meet with a reasonable degree of success. Thrifty and economical, you make the most of your possessions. You are a creative thinker, always making decisions that serve your higher good, and give a great deal of attention to making your home and yourself more attractive. You are loving, helpful, and affable and have many talented, gifted friends.

DESTINY
As you get older, you will be able to give more time to your original ideas and thoughts. Friends will be interested and helpful when you discuss your ideas. You can help promote movements that will benefit you and others. Do not concentrate your attention solely on ways to earn money. Find happiness and contentment in reading, writing, traveling, studying, and planning ways and means to help the younger generations to get ahead.

KARMIC LESSON
You are above all naturally artistic and know how to make any place in which you live attractive. You are very fond of flowers and like to have them in any room in which you are living. You have an instinct for color and can help guide others to choose the colors that best suit them and their environment. You love music and, indeed, all forms or expressions of art. You have ingenuity and originality and should make a good inventor if you turn your interests in that direction. You have lots of ideas and need only to learn that in order to be successful, a life must be carefully steered along its course; if you do this, anything you wish for will be yours.

SECRET
You have a clever and cunning nature, capable of asserting yourself over others by persuasion or fascination.

FRIENDS & FAMILY

DECEMBER 20

*My religion is very simple.
My religion is kindness.*
—Dalai Lama

BORN ON THIS DAY

- **Uri Geller**
  magician, psychic
- **Jonah Hill**
  actor, comedian, filmmaker
- **David Wright**
  baseball player
- **JoJo**
  singer, actor
- **Billy Bragg**
  leftist singer/songwriter

FRIENDS & FAMILY

PERSONALITY

If you ever suffer from a sense of insecurity, the feeling is owing to your desire for fame and glamour. Only discouragement along the lines of your chosen work can get you down, for you are very ambitious and motivated, you work hard and plan ahead, and you feel that only the acclaim of your group, your community, or the public will reward you for the high aspirations you possess. Fickleness is one of the traits in your nature that you must learn to fight against. You soon become bored with the things you are doing, and you change your job, studies, and friends too often to attain your life's ambition. You must learn to stick to a single purpose until you have achieved it. Then, make another goal and focus on it until you reach it; you will go to a higher level, spiritually and mentally, each time you have had a success.

LIFE PATH

You are a spiritual seeker and are truthful, understanding, and committed to personal growth. You are precise in your work, usually punctual in keeping appointments, and fastidious in your dress. You are a homebody at times and seek comfort in your tastes, although you have many interests outside of your home. You are very affectionate but not outwardly demonstrative.

DESTINY

New projects will always demand your attention. Although you are a good follower, you may expect opportunities that will prove you to be extremely capable. Almost instantaneous success will attend the inauguration of new projects that have to do with fashion or adornment. Put your enthusiasm into everything you do, for it is through constant exercise that your talents will be developed. Personal magnetism will help you to retain the prestige and popularity that you gain.

KARMIC LESSON

Full of contradictions, yours is a temperament that is often hard to understand. You do not always understand yourself or your actions; hence, you can hardly expect others to understand you. You are sensitive, though you do not like this to be noted, and you often cover it up with drama or bluntness, which unintentionally hurts others. This is one of the paradoxes of your nature and often gives people a very different impression of you than you really are; yet you somehow can't change what you do. You should cultivate greater calmness and stop the hurry and worry—especially about things that you believe will happen but never do. You must learn to express and nurture your inner spiritual world, and you will find much more that is real in the outer world.

SECRET

You are dependent upon the love and approval of your friends and therefore must be careful in your selections.

DECEMBER 21

Waste of time is the most costly and most extravagant of all expenses.
—Theophrastus

BORN ON THIS DAY

- **Nostradamus**
  astrologer, seer
- **Frank Zappa**
  musician
- **Samuel L. Jackson**
  actor
- **Carl Wilson**
  singer/songwriter
- **Florence Griffith Joyner**
  Olympic sprinter

PERSONALITY
Diplomacy is your strong point. You have a natural talent or knack for getting quarrelsome factions together and making them agree on essential points. This quality comes in for a good deal of play both in family life and at your place of work. Because others recognize your ability as an arbitrator, you are frequently called upon to settle arguments. In leading your own life, you attempt to get your way by smoothing the path for accomplishment rather than by forcing your will upon others. In the end, this gets you much further than aggressiveness would, so you should be well-off. In general, you make a good first impression, and you make friends because you know how to make this impression last. You prefer quiet amusements to noisy ones and enjoy supporting talent as a true follower of the cultural movements in your locale.

LIFE PATH
You are intensely optimistic, and your plans generally succeed. You have original ideas and are determined, shrewd, and persevering. You have many good friends and very few enemies. You are classic in your tastes, fond of children, demonstrative in your love, and generally bright and cheerful.

DESTINY
Your magnanimity and kindliness will always win friends. You may have to rely on your own judgment in a very controversial matter involving your family. Your counsel may be the means of getting a discouraged member of your family started on a new path. Your income may be increased over time, permitting greater expenditures. Be careful, however, to guard the possessions that you already have.

KARMIC LESSON
Originality is one of your strong points, both of thought and of action. You are always having new ideas, new schemes. You like to please people and dislike hurting their feelings. You form your own estimate about things and are not influenced much by others' opinions. You are loving, but your heart never runs away with your head. You are to be trusted in all that you undertake and are naturally thorough and detail oriented. You have an instinctive leaning toward the mystical and occult but are sometimes inclined to be too credulous. Do not believe so much in signs and omens, as you can be overly superstitious. Determine to master fate instead of letting it master you. Your character is good, but you should cultivate more force and power.

SECRET
You are fully devoted to helping a special someone, although you desire neither credit nor recognition for doing so.

FRIENDS & FAMILY

DECEMBER 22

There are those who give with joy, and that joy is their reward.
—Kahlil Gibran

BORN ON THIS DAY
- ★ **Giacomo Puccini**
  composer
- ★ **Jean-Michel Basquiat**
  artist
- ★ **Ralph Fiennes**
  actor
- ★ **Meghan Trainor**
  singer
- ★ **Mia Tyler**
  actor, socialite

FRIENDS & FAMILY

PERSONALITY
Your birthday falls on the cusp between two signs, Sagittarius and Capricorn. You enjoy music, and this art is one in which you might succeed as a musician, DJ, radio host, or critic. As you have creative talent, you should not neglect investigating this latent ability in your makeup. Given to having your own way, you can develop the negative side of this aspect of your nature. However, the wiser thing to do is to insinuate your will upon others by showing them that you are right and that you seek to establish your way of doing things because it is a better way—not merely your way. Affection is very necessary to your happiness, and you should marry someone who is quite demonstrative and ardent. This person will be very supportive of your talent and will be your biggest fan.

LIFE PATH
You are generous, spontaneous, enthusiastic, and affectionate and would never intentionally hurt another's feelings. You need to get out and socialize; you have a pronounced streak of humor in your makeup. You are vivacious and energetic, independent and authoritative. You probably will be very fulfilled in your family life.

DESTINY
The period of your late twenties will be one of expansion if you organize your time and talents so that there will be no lost opportunity. You may come into prominence in your forties through work that you have done in the past and for which you may not have received full credit. Your philosophy of life may be put to a test in your workplace, but continued devotion to your ideals will prove that your convictions are sound and your standards worthy.

KARMIC LESSON
Oversensitive to slights and injuries from others, you are apt to take offense too easily. Learn to pay attention to other things; do not worry, and keep busy, for, remember, "the devil finds some mischief for idle hands to do." Persevere, try to work on yourself to eliminate phobias and unfounded fears from your makeup, and determine to conquer, singlehandedly, if need be, the obstacles that confront you. You live an intense life and do not sleep enough; you are inclined to keep late hours. Sleep is very important—remember that you cannot afford to do without it. You do not care much for traveling and would rather be in your own cozy, warm home. Cultivate self-reliance, for "confidence in self breeds confidence in others."

SECRET
Money and position are the goals dearest to you, and with your capacity for hard work, you should achieve them.

DECEMBER 23

As human beings, our greatness lies not so much in being able to remake the world... as in being able to remake ourselves.
—Mahatma Gandhi

BORN ON THIS DAY

★ **Joseph Smith**
Mormon religious leader

★ **Eddie Vedder**
singer/songwriter

★ **Harry Shearer**
comedian, voice actor

★ **Chet Baker**
jazz trumpeter

★ **Carol Ann Duffy**
poet, playwright

PERSONALITY

Wherever the ability to organize is needed, you stand the best possible chance to get the assignment. You have a marked talent for getting people together, for explaining to them the exact requirements of a job, and for getting them to cooperate so that the project proceeds efficiently to its eventual success. Whether your area of activity is the home or a farm, office, or factory, you put your abilities to work so that the product is worthy. You guard your reputation and good name by acting diplomatically and by exercising your intelligence. You are wiser than to try to force your will on others. In many ways you are a pioneer, investigating new fields of thought and trying out new methods. Tradition is important to you only as long as its ways are useful. By applying yourself to financial management and the field of investment, even on a small scale, you can build your security.

LIFE PATH

You have sharp insight and good planning ability, and your tactics and strategies seldom fail. You are generous in your judgment and always willing to lend a helping hand. You are alert, cautious, and self-possessed. You have many friends, although none is accepted as a friend until they have proven their value and trustworthiness. You will not fall in love at first sight.

DESTINY

You will tend to devote your attention to improving conditions where you are rather than looking around for new fields of endeavor. When the right opportunity comes your way, you will recognize it. In the meantime, simply apply yourself diligently to your present duties and obligations. If you accept your present cycle as a period of preparation for bigger things to come, you will be ready for promotion and honor when they materialize.

KARMIC LESSON

You have good ability in a commercial way and should make a success of whatever business ventures you undertake. You are at times overmodest, as well as loving, kind, and generous, but these good qualities are carried to an extreme in your case. You have a vivid imagination, which is inclined to run away with you at times. You have a habit of building castles in the air, but you should not practice this too much, as it is harmful to the mind if not balanced by grounded, practical steps. You are generous; you despise anything underhanded or mean. You are not much given to words, but what you do say is to the point, and you think out problems clearly before passing judgment. You possess distinct abilities with a camera.

SECRET

You possess a sagacious mind with an ability to organize, especially large enterprises.

FRIENDS & FAMILY

_____

_____

_____

_____

_____

_____

_____

_____

_____

_____

DECEMBER 24

Faith is the pencil of the soul that pictures heavenly things.
—Thomas Burbridge

BORN ON THIS DAY

- **Howard Hughes**
  business magnate, engineer
- **Ava Gardner**
  actor
- **Ricky Martin**
  singer
- **Ryan Seacrest**
  media personality
- **Kate Spade**
  fashion designer

FRIENDS & FAMILY

PERSONALITY

Although you are a severe taskmaster, you are also full of compassion, and your thoughts are basically for the good of other people. Your strictness is not the result of the nature of a martinet but of your observation that some people learn only from costly experience, and you would teach them by command rather than by suffering. Your high ideals make you beloved by older people more than by younger ones, for they are difficult for the youth that is carefree to comprehend. Once you have instilled your way of thought into your associates, you are sure to receive their accolades. No one can gather a group of adherents of greater loyalty than you. By choosing your friends for their free spiritedness, and by sticking to your inspired tasks in life, you will achieve the goal that is your highest aim.

LIFE PATH

You are bold, courageous, and energetic, have an intuitive nature, and possess considerable but possibly latent talent. You love with a concentration that is whole-souled but resent with great bitterness any interference with your individuality. Practice self-restraint and do not let your passions get beyond your control. It is a gift well worth having.

DESTINY

You may feel undecided about where lies the best opportunity for you to attain happiness. In your thirties, you will have a clearer picture of your ambitions and potentialities than you had before. This self-knowledge will help you to express your personality in dynamic fashion as you mature and to make rapid strides toward success once you become focused.

KARMIC LESSON

You are naturally bright and clever, marked by common sense, which you are apt to make too little of, as it is capable of bringing you real distinction in the world, if only you would cultivate it more. You dislike creeds of any kind, especially those that restrict character. You are of a naturally independent spirit and should not be under the sway or orders of others. It is best for you to be an entrepreneur and to run your own small business. You have a great interest in and sympathy for human welfare. You see the good in most people and are optimistic most of the time. Learn to take yourself more seriously; it will be better for you.

SECRET

You have a talent for construction work, with an interest in crafts, scrapbooking, and miniature works of art.

December 25

Do unto others as you would have them do unto you.
—Jesus Christ

BORN ON THIS DAY
- **Isaac Newton**
  mathematician, physicist
- **Mao Zedong**
  Chinese communist revolutionary
- **Humphrey Bogart**
  actor
- **Annie Lennox**
  singer
- **Armin van Buuren**
  DJ

PERSONALITY
In the development of your life, you will take your place as a leader in a specific area of your expertise. Of course, this applies to you regardless of your occupation, for leadership is a quality that knows no boundaries. You seem to bring out the quality of loyalty in others that you possess to such a high degree yourself. Because of this, you can take an active part in politics, community affairs, educational work, and social networking. Foresight is another ability or trait that you are fortunate to have at your command, for it enables you to see events not only ahead of their occurrence but with such precision that you can prevent foolish moves and encourage wise ones. It is indeed an honor to have been born on this historic date, and you have every quality within you to live up to that honor.

LIFE PATH
You are just, conscientious, methodical, and discreet. You love studying reports and informative journalism and are an intelligent and fluent talker. You assimilate what you read and gather information by observation. You are true and loyal to your friends and devoted to the ones you love.

DESTINY
Do not waste what you have saved in extravagant purchases. Use your talents to create something of lasting value. You will be successful in persuading others to see your views. Travel and successful romance are reflected in your cosmic mirror of the future. Be ready to appreciate these experiences. Make your daily routine as systematic as possible.

KARMIC LESSON
You have many latent qualities of the highest order, which you need only to develop in order to win success. You are emotional, are a naturally strong character, possess a wide range of interests, take a great interest in the love affairs of others, and are often getting into them yourself. In love with love, you like to read romantic novels, watch romantic movies, and even check out dating sites and relationship experts. You are most happy when following your own line of work and inspirations that come to you out of the blue, which are often very good. You are naturally mercurial, and your moods can swing within hours and days. You should learn to cultivate a calm, judicious manner by meditating, doing yoga, or taking long walks.

SECRET
You are a spiritual soul, with a desire to spread faith among those you meet.

FRIENDS & FAMILY

DECEMBER 26

We make our fortunes, and we call them fate.
—Benjamin Disraeli

BORN ON THIS DAY
- **Phil Spector**
  music producer, songwriter
- **Jared Leto**
  actor, musician
- **David Sedaris**
  author, humorist
- **Kit Harrington**
  actor
- **Jade Thirlwall**
  singer

FRIENDS & FAMILY

___

PERSONALITY
While you may not be considered a genius, you have such remarkable talent for concentrating on what you are doing that you will achieve as much as any genius at the same task. Once your interest is aroused, you are able to work long and hard at a problem, a job, or any project with such stamina that you literally astound those who are watching you. It would seem that you can cast out all distractions and just force your energies into the channels that will get the job in hand done in record time. Your best bet in your efforts to get ahead in the world is to listen to the dictates of your own conscience. You don't need the advice of other people. Follow your own inclinations, and you are bound to get what you want from life. This advice goes for your romantic inclinations as well as for your business career.

LIFE PATH
You will have better success if you rely more upon your own judgment than upon the advice of others. You have analytical and diagnostic ability; you also like to play and have fun and are generally considered to be good company. You are farsighted, reasoned, and aspiring, a devoted partner, and a great homebody.

DESTINY
The scope of your daily activities will be considerably widened after age forty-four. Put your ideas on paper and spend time later enlarging and perfecting them. Combining high ideals with hard work will take you far on the road to success. Do not judge new acquaintances too quickly, nor put impediments in the path of anyone's progress. Freedom is a precious concept to you, and you may engage in many heated discussions about governmental matters.

KARMIC LESSON
You are naturally resourceful and ingenious and a good observer of psychology and human nature. You are interested in things unseen and mysterious, and it is probable that you are particularly interested in either astrology or some other related metaphysical belief system. Often you feel so out of your element, without just knowing why; you feel, so to say, "like a fish out of water," but you cannot put it into words. This is probably due to your family environment while growing up, which perhaps was not well suited to you. You should change your attitude, if possible, and let go of past hurts, but also remember that ours is the power to mold and change the environment to suit ourselves. Try it and determine that you will.

SECRET
You have a strong sense of economy and scrutinize every expenditure.

DECEMBER 27

If you want the rainbow, you've got to put up with the rain.
—Dolly Parton

BORN ON THIS DAY
- **Johannes Kepler**
  astronomer
- **Marlene Dietrich**
  actor
- **Chyna**
  wrestler, TV personality
- **Carson Palmer**
  football player
- **Timothée Chalamet**
  actor

PERSONALITY
Fame can be yours if you seek it through the expression of the talents bestowed on you. Those born today have talent in the field of drama and theater as well as singing, movie, television, or video work. Any form of communication between you and other people will bring you acclaim if you learn your trade and then stick to it. You should seek vocational guidance early in life, as you may have some difficulty in finding your level of expression. You have a tendency to scatter your abilities in too many directions. If you feel that you are in the wrong field of endeavor, by all means seek expert advice that will bring out your proper talents. You are lively, talkative, interesting, and admired. Make the most of the gifts that have been granted you.

LIFE PATH
You are accurate, calm, considerate, tolerant, and optimistic. You are ambitious, persevering, and determined, and no ordinary reversal will discourage you. You love your unique family of friends above everything. You are very affectionate and demonstrative and very fond of children, whom you may work with.

DESTINY
If you follow an organized procedure in everything you do, the results in saving time will make possible participation in a variety of new activities, as you are interested in many subjects. Among these may be hobbies, games, and other means of recreation. Mental and emotional well-being will follow. Take an interest in current events. Allow time to read, research, and think. Your example may impress others, especially the younger generation.

KARMIC LESSON
You are one of those whom it is often hard to understand, but once understood, you will rightly be valued at your just estimate. You often feel that you are not appreciated, that the world does not see your real worth. There may be some truth to this; at the same time, you must remember that our natural vanity makes all of us sometimes think more of ourselves than we deserve. Try to look at yourself from an outsider's point of view. You have a good many fine qualities, but they need expression. You have a good mind, a good memory, and a grasp of the facts, which should make you successful at most everything you set out to accomplish.

SECRET
You have an interest in historical matters, with an emphasis on art and collections from the past.

FRIENDS & FAMILY

DECEMBER 28

The greatest griefs are those we cause ourselves.
—Sophocles

BORN ON THIS DAY
- **Woodrow Wilson**
  U.S. president
- **Denzel Washington**
  actor
- **John Legend**
  singer
- **Maggie Smith**
  actor
- **Seth Meyers**
  comedian, talk show host

FRIENDS & FAMILY

___

PERSONALITY
As an idealist, you would like to see a world in which the Golden Rule is the Universal Law—"Do unto others as you would have them do unto you." To the extent that your talents, vision, and intuition permit you, you devote your efforts to such an end. Even if you are restricted by family life, you make every effort to make your home a charming place where all the inhabitants are comfortable and cared for. If your social or business status permits a wider scope of activity, you are sure to do more, the more people you come in contact with. For this reason, you should make a strong effort to lead a life that will allow you to associate with groups, such as in your neighborhood, in your community, and on social media. You have a lot of mental energy, and you can concentrate on a job with great willpower.

LIFE PATH
You are diplomatic, shrewd, energetic and bold, and very affable and obliging. You make friends easily and are generally well-liked. You are frank, open, and aboveboard and would never stoop to a mean trick to make a point. You are nurturing, kind, and patient in your home and strive to make it attractive, efficient, and pleasant.

DESTINY
Your nebulous thoughts can be molded into tangible achievements. Pursue your plans with confidence. Intellectual growth will accompany practical accomplishments. A chance meeting with someone who is considered eccentric may give you an opportunity to study human nature and thus add to your knowledge of psychology, a subject in which you can be deeply interested. Take advantage of the opportunities that will be offered you.

KARMIC LESSON
You have a sharp, probing mind, with an interest in detail, which should suit you to some of the sciences requiring great skill and a knowledge of facts, such as chemistry or electrical engineering. You are very inquisitive by nature, and even as a child were always trying to solve the riddle of the universe and the mystery of being. You are suited to undertaking large enterprises, and small jobs may not interest you as much. You are open and aboveboard in all that you do and think, and if you wish to do a certain thing, you do it regardless of the consequences. Cultivate forgiveness, gentleness, and the power of affirmation.

SECRET
You are extremely cautious when it comes to intimate relationships and reluctant to trust anyone. This limits possibilities for lasting love.

DECEMBER 29

Duty is a power that rises with us in the morning, and goes to rest with us at night.
—William E. Gladstone

BORN ON THIS DAY
- ★ **Andrew Johnson**
  U.S. president
- ★ **Mary Tyler Moore**
  actor
- ★ **Jon Voight**
  actor
- ★ **Marianne Faithfull**
  singer, actor
- ★ **Ted Danson**
  actor

PERSONALITY
You look at life from the point of view of competitive sports. You know that the most you can get out of anything is a return of the effort you put into it, so you play the game fairly. Because you expect no more than you give, and you feel that giving your best is only right, you are repaid for your efforts and actions with courtesy, respect, and consideration. You enjoy the pleasures of social life, and a good party with good friends truly warms your heart. At home, you like to be surrounded by material comforts, family, and pets. Noise and bustle do not seem to disturb you much, for you love conversation, music, and the sounds of a good time. You are a wonderful host and great as a master of ceremonies, amateur actor or influencer, and public speaker. There is a lot of fun in store for you, so make the most of it.

LIFE PATH
You possess indomitable courage, and you are resourceful and original. You are very competent in the handling of details and possess considerable managerial ability. You love good books, art, video, and photography and are a good entertainer. Your homelife will probably be pleasant and harmonious, and your love will be strong and inviting.

DESTINY
You may assume new responsibilities and climb the ladder of success. Although you will not seek the limelight, your efforts will not go unappreciated or unrecognized. Learn to accept praise with the same grace that you have always shown in taking criticism. Never lose sight of the desire for self-improvement and the lofty aim of helping others to get ahead in the world.

KARMIC LESSON
Your liberal approach to thought and freedom of speech causes you to be looked upon in certain quarters as a threat, one many people may wish to avoid. But this does not influence you, as you regard such people as insecure and narrow-minded. Your enthusiastic, outgoing manner and natural honesty will overcome all obstacles in time and win many friends for you who formerly regarded you with a suspicious eye. You are one of those people who give love generously and so often find it hard to concentrate your affections on one person. You make many friends, and keep those you have made.

SECRET
Though you are outwardly jovial, you are intensely active mentally and carry out your plans with great persistence.

FRIENDS & FAMILY

DECEMBER 30

It is better to remain silent at the risk of being thought a fool, than to talk and remove all doubt of it.
—Maurice Switzer

BORN ON THIS DAY
- **Rudyard Kipling**
  author, journalist
- **Tiger Woods**
  golfer
- **Patti Smith**
  singer/songwriter
- **Tracey Ullman**
  comedian, actor
- **LeBron James**
  basketball player

FRIENDS & FAMILY

PERSONALITY
You have a strong sense of duty, and you lead your family, participate in community affairs, and in all ways show your pride and involvement in the politics, causes, and charities you believe in. No one could ever say that you were lax in the performance of your functions as a citizen, for you sacrifice time and pleasure to do the greatest good for the greatest number, your real idea of democracy in action. You have a keen eye for observation. When you take a trip, you can describe in the greatest detail all that you have seen. That quality would make you a good photographer or a good videographer. But the important point is that your creative eye can see the special characteristic features, so that you are able to bring out, in words or in a picture, what is really distinguishing and typical. You could also do well as a teacher, gallerist, lecturer, or writer.

LIFE PATH
You are studious, intellectual, cautious, and discreet and have a quick, discerning mind. You are politically correct, fair, considerate, shrewd, and honest. You love travel and are fond of outdoor life and sport. You love with honor and are fond of your friends and family, although you also take great interest in community affairs.

DESTINY
You would like to always be active. Be sure you take enough time from pressing engagements and duties to relax properly. Most of your undertakings will be satisfyingly successful. Do not lose faith in your ideas just because they are criticized—this is an important lesson to learn. However, do not turn a deaf ear to constructive advice offered by trusted friends and close relatives.

KARMIC LESSON
You are friendly and well-liked but lack a certain candor, although you mean to be a perfectly sincere human being. You are inclined to be somewhat narrow in your views on spirituality, and in politics, particularly, you are not always as open-minded as you could be. By nature, you are suited for a political profession, but the pressure of modern civilized life has rather put that idea out of your head. You are ambitious but not quite egocentric enough to pursue a career in that competitive spotlight. You should cultivate this more, make more of yourself, not in thought but by building up your physical self, and cultivate a greater integrity and unaffected manner.

SECRET
You are a natural leader in the commercial field, basing progress on sure, well-strategized foundations.

DECEMBER 31

If we could see the miracle of a single flower clearly, our whole life would change.
—Buddha

⬢ PERSONALITY

There is nothing obvious in your personality. Although people may think that they know you really well, all that they know is the surface that you care to show them. In that sense, you are a consummate actor, for you can "kid" people into thinking that they have you down pat, whereas they know only one or two of the facets of your complex personality. You are not much of a talker, but you show what you think by your actions. You are very dependable once you commit to a task. When you find a real friend, you are as loyal as anyone can be. However, if anyone is mean to you, you never forgive or forget it. Because you are sensitive and truthful, you make few friends, but they are very choice ones. Always depend upon your own judgment in order to get the furthest in this life.

⬢ LIFE PATH

You are mesmerized by creativity—you devour those subjects that fascinate and intrigue you. Thorough and observant, you have many interests and are bright and charming while also somewhat mysterious. You might fall in love at first sight, for in affairs of the heart you are impulsive and emotional. You need a great deal of love and devotion to make you feel secure.

⬢ DESTINY

Your life can be filled with enterprise and profit. You will meet someone from the past whose companionship may offer you pleasure and perhaps financial assistance. Place honesty with yourself before all other values, and you will attract others with similarly high standards. Happy romance, prosperity, and likely chances to travel are among the many reasons for your maintaining an optimistic outlook toward the future.

⬢ KARMIC LESSON

You have diverse abilities spread out in several directions. You are intelligent and have an intuitively wise judgment in most things. You are generous and sparing of the feelings of others. You are always ready to concede the rights of others and the validity of the other person's point of view. Loving and affectionate, you require devotion and committed love in return. You are honest and reliable. You should be fortunate, from all indications; you could be quite successful, and after having several ups and downs along the way, you will make enough income to give you a comfortable living and enable you to do what you want. You have a pleasant personality and can make a success of your life, if you live up to the best that lies within you.

⬢ SECRET

You have a great interest in scientific affairs, archaeology, and space exploration, especially new discoveries.

BORN ON THIS DAY

- **Henri Matisse**
  artist
- **Donna Summer**
  singer/songwriter
- **Anthony Hopkins**
  actor
- **Diane von Furstenberg**
  fashion designer
- **Gabby Douglas**
  Olympic gymnast

FRIENDS & FAMILY

ABOUT THE AUTHORS

When artist Amy Zerner met author Monte Farber, an enchanted relationship was formed. They are a best-selling husband and wife team whose expertise and inspiring approach to oracular wisdom is highly sought after. Since 1988, they have shared their distinctive brand of life mastery and artistic excellence through their unique, award-winning works, which have sold nearly three million copies and have been published in eighteen languages.

Based on intuition-building techniques and their original interpretations of astrology, tarot, alchemy, metaphysics, and creativity, these useful and beautifully designed systems are accessible to a mainstream audience. Zerner and Farber have been featured in such media outlets as *Forbes*, the *Observer*, the *New York Times*, *Oprah*, *Well+Good*, *Vogue*, *News 12 Long Island*, *MindBodyGreen*, *FabFitFun*, *Bustle*, and *Refinery29*, as well as on many TV, radio, and podcast shows.

Their best-selling titles include *The Enchanted Tarot*, *Karma Cards*, *The Psychic Circle*, *The Enchanted Spellboard*, *Little Reminders: Law of Attraction*, *Mindful Astrology*, *Astrology for Wellness*, *The Creativity Oracle*, *The Wild Goddess Oracle*, *Enchanted Worlds: The Visionary Collages & Art Couture of Amy Zerner*, *The Art of Affirmations*, and *The Intuition Oracle*. Their website is www.theenchantedworld.com.